W9-BQX-301

BRITAIN
TRAVELBOOK ™

THIRD EDITION

AAA

President & CEO: Robert Darbelnet
Executive Vice President, Publishing &
    Administration: Rick Rinner
Managing Director, Travel Information: Bob
    Hopkins

Director, Product Development: Bill Wood
Director, Sales & Marketing: John Coerper
Director, Purchasing & Corporate Services:
    Becky Barrett
Director, Business Development: Gary Sisco
Director, Tourism Information Development
    (TID): Michael Petrone
Director, Travel Information: Jeff
    Zimmerman
Director, Publishing Operations: Susan Sears
Director, GIS/Cartography: Jan Coyne
Director, Publishing/GIS Systems &
    Development: Ramin Kalhor

Managing Editor, Product Development:
    Margaret Cavanaugh
Development Editor: Sharon Kudlowitz

AAA Travel Store & e-store Manager: Sharon
    Edwards

Marketing Manager: Bart Peluso
Manager, Product Support: Linda Indolfi
Manager, Electronic Media Design: Mike
    McCrary

Published by AAA Publishing, 1000 AAA
Drive, Heathrow, Florida 32746

Text © AAA Publishing 2002, 2006
All rights reserved

Maps © Automobile Association
Developments Limited 2001, 2002, 2005

Ordnance Survey® This product includes
mapping data licensed
from Ordnance Survey® with the permission
of the Controller of Her Majesty's
Stationery Office.
© Crown copyright 2005. All rights
reserved. Licence number 399221.

Traffic signs © Crown copyright.
Reproduced with the permission of the
Controller of Her Majesty's Stationery
Office.

No part of this book may be reproduced in
any form or by any electronic or mechanical
means, including information storage and
retrieval devices or systems, without prior
written permission from the publisher,
except that brief passages may be quoted
for reviews.

The contents of this book are believed to be
correct at the time of printing. The
publishers are not responsible for changes
that occur after publication.

The *AAA Britain TravelBook* was created and
produced for AAA Publishing by
Automobile Association Developments
Limited, Fanum House, Basing View,
Basingstoke, Hampshire, RG21 4EA,
England.

Written by Christopher Somerville
Managing Editor: Sheila Hawkins
Third edition verified by Colin Follett
Page make-up by Keenes

Cover photos
Main cover photo: England
© Steve Vidler/eStock Photo
Spine: England
© Medioimages/Imagestate

ISBN-13: 978-1-59508 095-0
ISBN-10: 1-59508 095-3

Cataloging-in-Publication Data is on file
with the Library of Congress.

Color separations by Leo Reprographic
Ltd., Hong Kong
Printed in Dubai by Oriental Press

A02491

Cottages in Castle Combe, Wiltshire

FOREWORD

Welcome to the AAA Britain TravelBook!

If you're planning a vacation to Britain, this book will help you discover the real heart of this fascinating country. We've selected not only the great cities, but a range of smaller towns and stunning countryside that will give a true taste of Britain's diversified regions. You'll experience historic city centers filled with world-class sights and museums, wonderful landscapes, and some of Europe's most beguiling small towns and villages. Discover the many glories of London, the capital of Britain and one of the great cities of the world, delight in the historic cathedral cities of York and Canterbury, and retrace the steps of the great playwright William Shakespeare in his hometown of Stratford-upon-Avon. You'll find what lies behind the national pride in Edinburgh, Scotland's premier city, and in Cardiff, the civic capital of Wales, while the elegant towns of Cheltenham, Stamford and Harrogate offer a pleasant contrast to big-city bustle.

Britain is a country steeped in history, dotted with castles and grand country houses. Wherever you go – and you will never have far to travel – you also will experience intriguing new aspects of the land and its people. Leave any preconceptions behind and let this book be your guide, whether along the well-trodden tourist trails or off the beaten track.

Dip into the AAA Britain TravelBook to get your initial taste from the informative text and evocative photographs, then use it for more solid planning. There's plenty of practical information to smooth your way, from tips on getting around to suggestions on where to stay. We've included maps to help you find your way, suggestions for eating, drinking and shopping, and descriptions of what to see. The insider advice offered by our specialist author will help you get the most out of Britain, one of Europe's most enchanting countries.

BRITAIN TRAVELBOOK™

CONTENTS

Introduction to
Britain

*"Historic, easy-going
and stunningly beautiful;
a patchwork of green fields and
craggy hills, bustling
cosmopolitan cities and sleepy
rural villages – Britain in all
her endless variety awaits
you."*

Opposite: Ambleside in the Lake District

Introduction to Britain

BRITAIN

The image of Britain in the eyes of the world is a contradictory one. Here is a little ragged-edged cluster of islands, stuck out in the sea off the shoulder of Europe, which until recently wielded more power and influence than any other country on earth. These islands are some of the most densely populated in the world, yet they are famous for their tranquil green ruralism, the sense of space and leisure that they maintain. Their people are proverbially polite, yet notoriously pugnacious. They are well known to be reserved and insular, yet they have spread their culture enthusiastically around the globe. They are said to be philistine to the core, yet have given rise to artistic giants as diverse as Shakespeare, Wordsworth, the Beatles and the Brontës. And the British are famous for being tongue-tied in social situations, yet have had their language accepted as the *lingua franca* of the world.

A Historic Land

History has dealt a full deck to Britain, scattering aces across the land in the form of prehistoric stone monuments and Iron Age hill forts, historic castles and great country houses, medieval market towns and Georgian spa resorts. Here you can follow the life stories of names as illustrious as Queen Elizabeth I, Sir Winston Churchill, Jane Austen and Charles Darwin, through the houses and landscapes where they were born and lived, worked and died. You may choose to plunge into London, one of the world's greatest cities, for a rich diet of pomp, pageantry, culture and fun. You can visit Windsor Castle to savor the heady scent of a thousand years of monarchy. You could photograph the scarlet-coated Beefeaters at the Tower of London, listen to a kilted bagpiper on the ramparts of Edinburgh Castle, muse among the dreaming spires of Oxford University or stroll through Stratford-upon-Avon, from the house where William Shakespeare was born to the church where he was buried.

An Explorable Country

Such potent symbols of Britain are unquestionably "must-see" attractions. The mellow images of pageantry and history that they conjure up are what

Britain Explained

The name "Britain" (or "Great Britain") refers to the countries of England, Scotland and Wales located on the main island of Britain. To include Northern Ireland, the correct name is the "United Kingdom." The United Kingdom is the official unified entity, governed by the central parliament in London and (nominally) by Queen Elizabeth II.

However, political boundaries are becoming increasingly blurred and Scotland and Wales – historically uneasy with what they saw as an English parliament (and Queen) in London – now have their own national assemblies and a degree of autonomy. However, the legacy of London remains, and when the British talk about "this country," they usually mean Britain.

whets most people's appetite to visit Britain. And they are so seductive that it is easy to spend a couple of weeks here and never lift your nose from the well-worn tourist trail. But Britain is far more than a museum of ancient buildings and quaint costumes. Packed within its shores is an enormous variety of landscapes – a green and brown patchwork quilt, smooth and soft here, lumpy and rough there. In Britain marshes blend with cornfields, chalk downs with mighty cliffs and oak woods with mountains, all within a scrap of land that you could drive across between breakfast and dinner. There are more quiet villages, small woods, inviting footpaths and friendly pubs

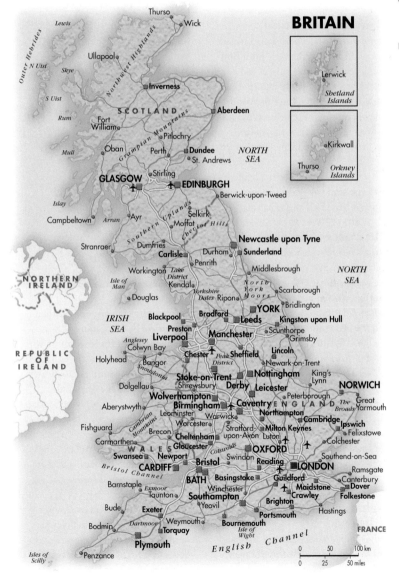

Introduction to Britain

tucked away down country lanes than there are along the main roads and highways, and more memorable views hiding just over the horizon than you'll see from the window of a tour bus. Above all Britain is an explorable country, a place where the traveling can be far more fun than the arriving. So slow down, and give yourself the time to be taken by surprise.

Don't Rush the British

Don't rush Britain, and don't rush the British. A typical Brit (or "John Bull") might seem all buttoned-up and defensive on first acquaintance. But those who approach the British quietly have their reward as the reserve cracks away to reveal some of the oddest, warmest and most distinctive characters on Earth. Bring a sense of the ridiculous and a taste for ironic understatement with you, and you'll like and understand Mr. and Mrs. Bull all the better.

The Bones of Britain

Britain lies off the northwest corner of Europe, with her ragged coat collar – the weatherbeaten islands of the Scottish coast – turned to the wild North Atlantic. These westerly winds, and the ocean waves they drive in from the open Atlantic, have cut the western coast of Scotland into dramatic clefts.

It is the underlying volcanic rocks of these most northerly and westerly regions – the Scottish islands and Highlands, the Lake District mountains, Snowdonia in northwest Wales, Dartmoor and the Cornish peninsula in the southwest – that form the highest and craggiest country in Britain.

Light Limestone, Dark Gritstone

Other high country areas in Scotland and Wales were formed by younger rocks, heaved several miles high during underground convulsions and then worn down by frost, rain and winds into a muddle of fractured rocks with suitably slithery names: slates, shales, schists. Moving south and eastward, you leave behind the great red sandstone cliffs of southwest Scotland and the Cumbrian coast to skim across the limestone of the Pennine hills and dales. To the south lie rolling moors bedded on gritstone, dark and dour when weathered and oxidized, clear and sparkly when newly cut or cleaned. These northern mountains, moors and dales – the wettest region of a country blessed with a generous allowance of rain – make wonderful walking country, and so does the

The Seven Sisters chalk cliffs dip into the English Channel on the south coast in East Sussex

snaking band of speckly oolitic limestone that comes next in our southeasterly journey. The oolitic hill ranges are "wolds" – the Lincolnshire Wolds, the Cotswolds – and their towns, villages, farmsteads and field walls are constructed from stone that can vary from silver to a rich honey color. The city of Bath is the queen of the oolite, with gracious streets, avenues, and crescents of houses and buildings made of the golden stone.

Chalk Cliffs and Downs
The county of Dorset along England's southern coast is also the westernmost outpost of the great blanket of chalk that covers the southeastern corner of Britain. Up to 1,800 feet thick, this smooth white wedge of lime is entirely made up of the shells of microscopic sea creatures. Beech woods, herb-rich downlands (many now cultivated) and high white cliffs are the features of the chalk downs, rolling with a beautiful elasticity from the counties of Dorset through Wiltshire, Hampshire and East and West Sussex into Kent.

A Bleak Beauty
Easternmost of all – and driest, being sheltered from Britain's prevailing westerly winds – are the flat lands of gravel and silt washed down by melting

Ice Age glaciers into what is now the Thames estuary and the bulging rump of East Anglia. This level countryside, so rich in churches built from flint, produces wonderful wheat and vegetables. The salt marshes and pebbly shores where southeast England meets the North Sea have a bleak beauty all their own. Wildfowl congregate in huge numbers here, along the best bird-watching coast in Britain.

Pioneers

Ten thousand years ago, as the great ice sheets of the last Ice Age steadily retreated northward, the hunter-gatherer pioneers of the current phase of British civilization arrived across

Ordnance Survey Maps

The Ordnance Survey (OS), based in the south coast city of Southampton, is a national institution of which the British are rightly proud. Drivers, bikers, hikers and lovers of landscape and the open air acknowledge the superior quality of the maps produced by the OS.

Handiest for finding your way around small sections of Britain, and appreciating what you see while you do so, are the crimson-covered, 1:50,000-scale Landrangers, which cover the entire country in a series of 204 maps. For countryside rambling and more serious hiking, try the yellow-covered Outdoor Leisure series covering popular recreation areas, or the orange-covered Explorer series of local leisure maps. Footpaths and other public off-road rights of way are marked with red dots or dashes on the Landranger maps, green on Outdoor Leisure and Explorer maps. You can buy OS maps at tourist offices and many bookstores.

land bridges from the Continent. Forests fell to stone tools as the newcomers began to clear the land. More foreign immigrants arrived as the millennia went by – late Stone Age farmers from the Mediterranean, bronze workers from Spain and the Low Countries (present-day Belgium, Luxembourg and The Netherlands), iron-smelting Celts from France. Each contributed new skills to the community, and fresh genes to the pool. They raised stone monuments and tombs, worked gold, worshiped the sun and the trees, and sowed and reaped the land.

This was the state of things when the Romans invaded in AD 43.

The dreaming spires of Oxford have inspired students and travelers alike

Effective Romans

For nearly 400 years Britain was the northernmost piece in the jigsaw of the Roman Empire. The impact of the Romans on the country was profound. These practical-minded overlords put in place a serviceable legal system. They organized agriculture effectively, built sumptuous country houses and public buildings, and laid down a network of long-distance roads that were the envy of the empire. They mined, smelted, crafted, ditched and drained. Britain would never again be so efficiently managed and governed.

But the Roman Empire rotted from within and crumbled in the face of barbarian attacks. By AD 420 the last of the Romans were gone, and the Dark Ages rolled in to cover their traces.

Saxons and Danes

Fair-haired Saxons arrived around AD 450 from the Low Countries of continental Europe, bringing with them hugely improved farming techniques. They plowed the land with ox teams and settled the river valleys with villages, managing their affairs through decision making by discussion in council rather than by decree.

Saxon civilization was rocked when Danish raiding parties began to arrive on the east coast around the

The mighty West Gate at Canterbury that forms part of the old city walls, beside the River Stour

end of the eighth century. But King Alfred rallied the Saxons and defeated the Danes at Edington in AD 878. Uneasy compromise and adjustment followed, although stability and unification of the country would not really be established until long after the Norman invasion of 1066.

The Norman Conquerors

The energetic and self-confident Normans snuffed out resistance in northern and eastern Britain. In 1086 King William I ordered the compilation of the definitive Domesday Book to record exactly what his new possession was worth. The Normans made sure they maximized their investment (and stayed on top of it) by means of the feudal system, which guaranteed the Norman nobleman a place at the top of the pile and humble peasants a subsistence-level existence in his shadow.

The feudal system softened and then faded out after the disastrous depopulation caused by the Black Death plague of 1348-49. Prosperity in the later Middle Ages of the 15th century came through wool exporting, but the medieval era also saw Britain lose all its land held in France.

In 1455 the aristocratic warlords of the houses of Lancaster and York led

political tensions, set simmering by the rejection of Roman Catholicism during the Reformation, boiled over in the bitter Civil War of 1642-46. The Stuart king Charles I was executed in 1649, and 11 years of quasi-republican "Commonwealth" followed – mostly under the stern eye of the Puritan leader Oliver Cromwell – until Charles II returned from exile in 1660 to restore the monarchy.

Georgian Flowering, Victorian Pomp

There was another cultural flowering during the 18th and early 19th centuries under four successive King Georges – particularly in philosophical thought and in the wonderful uncluttered squares and crescents, town houses and grand Palladian country houses of Georgian architecture. The Industrial Revolution got under way, and Britain went to the top of the world tree of enterprise and innovation. Waterpower was harnessed, then steam. The French/Corsican dictator Napoleon Bonaparte, conqueror of most of Europe, was engaged and defeated by 1815, which pushed national confidence sky-high.

During the reign of Queen Victoria (1837-1901) things seemed to get better and better, with Britain dominating the world manufacturing scene and ruling a vast overseas empire. Yet there were cracks in the edifice. Britain had lost its biggest colony, North America, in the 1775-83 War of Independence.

At home, rich landowners dispossessed the rural population. The manufacturing towns became a byword for hellish conditions, crowded, unhealthy and miserably ugly. Mineral extraction scarred the landscape. Poverty and inequality underpinned the pomp of late Victorian Britain.

their peasant followers into the bloody civil strife of the Wars of the Roses.

Golden Age, Civil War

The Tudors formed a short dynasty from 1485 to 1603. The five rulers – in particular Henry VII, Henry VIII and Elizabeth I – presided over a golden age for Britain, an exciting century of exploration and discovery, national confidence and pride, embodied in such figures as Sir Francis Drake and Sir Walter Raleigh. A remarkable artistic flowering culminated in the genius of William Shakespeare.

But the country suffered during the 17th century when religious and

Loss and Gain

The two cataclysmic World Wars of the 20th century cost Britain dearly, both in dead (2 million) and in global influence. By the turn of the third millennium the greatest empire the world had ever seen was dismantled, and Britain seemed to have shrunk to a diffident shadow of its former proud self. Yet a largely harmonious multiethnic society has been forged, the fragile countryside and wildlife are both vigilantly protected, and a reputation for tolerance and fairness is intact – not inconsiderable achievements to celebrate as the country faces the new age.

Britain today is a multicultural society – one of the most profound and conspicuous changes in these islands since World War II. Alongside the influence of the modern media, and now the Internet, in broadening perspectives and opening eyes, this ethnic diversity has made the British a far less insular and narrow-minded people. The old sense of superiority, of being a cut above "Johnny Foreigner," is gone. This liberating effect can be seen in a hodgepodge of international influences on British cuisine, on the pop music that dominates the charts, on people's dress, speech and manners, on the way they react to strangers and to each other, and on the schooling and leisure pursuits of their children.

Class Caricature

The British are no longer (if they ever were) the condescending, tight-lipped puritans of familiar stereotype. They are black, white, straight, gay, conventional, off-the-wall: a thoroughly mixed bunch with – on the whole – a relaxed and easygoing attitude toward each other. The class system is still alive and living inside most British heads, but more in caricature than actuality nowadays. It surfaces from time to time – when there is a proposal to ban foxhunting, or to abolish the House of Lords, for example, or when one of the tabloid newspapers sends a photographer to mock the moneyed spectators parading in their finery at Henley Regatta or

The Pilgrim Fathers

The first of Britain's shaky attempts to settle North America was Sir Walter Raleigh's foundation of a colony in 1584 in Virginia. It heralded a trickle of migration through the 17th century, mostly by religious dissenters in flight from Catholic or Protestant intolerance. First and best known of these pioneers were the Pilgrim Fathers. Led by William Brewster and William Bradford, they had first tried to emigrate from the Lincolnshire river port of Boston in 1607, but were captured and jailed for their pains. The following year, however, they did get away.

In 1620 the little group of dissenting families sailed from Holland to Britain, intending to use the old country as a stepping-stone to the new. In two tiny ships, the *Mayflower* and the *Speedwell*, they departed from the south coast port of Southampton on August 15, 1620. A storm in the English Channel forced them into Dartmouth for emergency patching up. The leaky little *Speedwell* proved beyond repair, so the Pilgrim Fathers were all crammed into the *Mayflower* when they finally set out from Plymouth on September 6, 1620. Just over 100 passengers and crew under the command of Captain Christopher Jones of Harwich sailed across the Atlantic and found a new world in New England.

Canterbury: Mother cathedral of the Church of England

Royal Ascot. But the British themselves treat class as a joke these days.

Young People's Party Place

Where a social divide does show is in the increasingly divergent lifestyles of old and young. For young people, especially those in the cities, Britain has become a 24-hour party place over the last couple of decades. Its clubbing scene is famous throughout Europe. The centers of big provincial cities such as Bristol, Manchester, Leeds and Newcastle, which would have been deserted after midnight only a few years ago, now come to life in the wee hours. Young Brits drink cappuccino at sidewalk tables or stroll, beer bottle to lips, through lively gay enclaves. They are far less concerned than their parents were about settling down early to a steady job and a sensible family life – partly because, in common with most of the developed world these days, the steady job-for-life is becoming a rare species.

North and South

Many parts of Britain are facing a new start in the new millennium, forced on them by the collapse of industries – coal mining, steelmaking, shipbuilding, textile manufacturing, heavy engineering – on which their prosperity and ways of life were founded. Most heavily industrialized regions are in the northern part of the country, and the industrial decline and high unemployment that plagued them late in the 20th century have helped to reinforce the idea of a "north–south divide." There certainly are strong regional differences, very noticeable as you travel through Britain. Accent and

The view of Brighton beach from Brighton Pier, on the south coast

dialect tend to be more marked the farther away from London you go, speech becomes plainer and more direct, and each region is more proudly championed by its natives.

Softer Left, Harder Right?

It used to be the case that rural political allegiances tended to the right and urban industrial ones to the left, a distinction reflected in the gulf between the policies of the Conservative (right) and Labour (left) parties. But since its May 1997 election, and subsequent 2005 re-election into government, the Labour party has maintained its "New Labour" title and followed its leader, Prime Minister Tony Blair, into a middle-ground leftism that has confounded its political opponents. It remains to be seen whether the Conservatives will revert to the abrasive right-wing certainties characteristic of their formidable former leader, Margaret Thatcher. None of the political parties has been able to embrace the issue of engaging fully with the European Union, of which Britain has been a member since 1973,

and neither have the British people. These islanders seem as reluctant as ever to abandon their beloved oddities and idiosyncratic national institutions – the pint, the mile, the pound sterling, the left-side driving – symbols of independence and a certain "bloody-mindedness."

Breakup of Britain

However, these national institutions may soon lack a nation to symbolize. The political union between Scotland, England and Wales has suddenly slackened after centuries of tight bonding. Scotland now has its own parliament, with considerable power; Wales has a national assembly with somewhat less power. The mood of independence in both countries is stronger than at any time in the 300-year history of the union. Northern Ireland, too, is struggling more or less painfully toward establishing an independent political executive. Whether this fragmenting of the national conglomeration that was once proud to call itself Great Britain will be a strengthening or

The Royal Shakespeare Theatre on the banks of the River Avon at Stratford-upon-Avon

enfeebling development remains to be seen.

So, too, does the future of the monarchy under which these islands have lived more or less willingly for a thousand years. The royal family, an unassailable icon since Victorian times, has come under sharp criticism in recent years – partly through a series of self-inflicted indignities, partly due to obsessive interest on the part of a salacious media, and partly a reflection of the changing identity and allegiances of Britons themselves.

Britain has always considered itself a land of tradition and stability. Now it stands on the threshold of great changes. All in all, there has never been a more interesting time to pay a visit to this grand old dame who is discovering a new spring in her step.

Music, Mystery and the Muse

Writing for the printed page and for the theater is far and away the most significant field of British contribution to the world of the arts, and here the past casts a long shadow. William Shakespeare still bestrides the theater like a god, selling out performances not only at the Royal Shakespeare Theatre in Stratford-upon-Avon and the brilliant replica of his Globe Theatre on London's South Bank, but at provincial theaters across the country. He is still the man to catch when you visit Britain. Poetry has similarly been dominated by William Wordsworth, although both the late poet laureate, Ted Hughes, and the brilliant Irish Nobel Prize winner Seamus Heaney have succeeded in turning the contemporary spotlight on this neglected art form. As for novelists, who would not pale in the mighty 19th-century shadows of Jane Austen, the Brontë sisters, Charles Dickens and Thomas Hardy?

Modern writers keeping the flag flying include the dark and subtle Ian McEwan, the frank and explicit Jeannette Winterson and the lighter but quintessentially English Joanna Trollope – all well worth seeking out.

No one seems quite sure what art is any more. Is it the readily appreciated paintings of David Hockney or the bulgy, enigmatic sculptures of Henry Moore? The crumpled and soiled

Introduction to Britain

An ancient footpath is marked by an antique sign at Grindleford in the Peak District National Park

unmade bed displayed by Tracey Emin or the body fluids of Gilbert and George? Or perhaps Damien Hirst's sliced cow in formaldehyde? If the function of modern art is to get people talking and keep them at it, then contemporary British artists are doing their job brilliantly.

Heritage Pass

The Great British Heritage Pass offers unlimited free entry (except The Tower of London, half price) to almost 600 historic houses, castles and gardens, including almost all the major sites listed in this book. The pass is valid for 4 consecutive days (£28), 7 days (£39), 15 days (£52) or 30 days (£70) – prices for 2005. You can buy a pass in advance through VisitBritain in New York (see page 276), or in Britain at tourist offices located at points of entry or selected towns and cities.

You are on more solid ground with the musical arts. The sumptuous refurbishment of the Royal Opera House in Covent Garden has given London an opera and ballet venue to rival any in the world. The Beatles are still the yardstick by which all rock bands are judged, and the club scene has its own eternally dividing and specialized groupings and sub-groupings.

Eating and Drinking

A multicultural society has revolutionized British cuisine, and in the big cities you can sample the very best of literally hundreds of different national cuisines, from Afghan to Zambian. Country pubs with any pretensions offer blackboard menus of up to 50 dishes. The best of British fare – fresh fish, game and beef, together with their traditional trimmings – is hard to beat, as long as it's top quality.

Wines and spirits from every corner of the world can be sampled. And the

The great British pub is the place to relax and sample local ales and traditional fare

famous British pint of beer – pulled from a hand-pump or straight out of a barrel, and drunk slowly – has subtleties of flavor that can spoil you for all those sad, chilled, pasteurized, fizzy concoctions passing for beer elsewhere.

Quintessentially British

To see English culture and the English at their most characteristic, drop in on a church fete in summer or attend one of the eccentric village festivals, such as the Hare Pie Scramble and Bottle Kicking at Hallaton, Leicestershire on Easter Monday. Catch the Scots at their nationalistic and cheery best on Hogmanay (New Year's Eve – but not New Year's Day, a national day of mourning in Scotland!), or on Burns Night, January 25, when they celebrate their national poet, Robert Burns. For the Welsh it should be St. David's Day, March 1, in some small country church or village school, or the Royal National Eisteddfod, the Welsh language pride and musical joy, the first week of August.

As for the *English* – try the Notting Hill Carnival in London during the last weekend in August, a crowded and noisy celebration with fantastic costumes and ear-splitting music, based on Caribbean tradition but now infused with Asian and Latin American strands.

TIMELINE

AD 43	Romans invade and conquer Britain.
AD 407	Roman legions withdraw from Britain.
AD 450	Saxons and others begin waves of invasion and settlement from the Low Countries.
AD 563	St. Columba begins spreading Christianity in Britain.
AD 878	King Alfred of Wessex defeats invading Danes at Battle of Edington.
1066	Normans invade and conquer Britain.
1215	Barons force King John to sign Magna Carta, Britain's first bill of civil liberties and political rights.
1348–49	Black Death plague wipes out a third of Britain's population.
1381	Peasant's Revolt is put down with savagery; feudal system crumbles.
1485	Tudor dynasty (1485-1603) begins, a Golden Age for Britain.
1534–40	Henry VIII breaks with Rome and founds the Church of England.
1642–46	Civil War is fought between King Charles I and Parliament.
1649	King Charles I is executed; Commonwealth (Republic) of England initiated; Oliver Cromwell governs from 1653.
1660	Charles II is restored to the throne.
1707	Act of Union between England and Scotland is enacted.
1746	Scot rebels under Bonnie Prince Charlie defeated at Battle of Culloden; collapse of the clan system and way of life follows.
1769	James Watt patents the first efficient steam engine, beginning the Industrial Revolution.

EFFECTS OF WORLD WAR II

The British have only recently begun to put World War II and its long-term effects on their society into perspective. This war saw many of Britain's cities badly damaged and 58,000 civilians killed by bombs. The devastation of important industrial cities and ports is graphically recorded in their museums. Five million volunteers from the British Empire joined 6 million Britons in the Allied services; the experiences of these "colonials" provided a great impetus toward postwar independence movements that saw the empire disappear. Weakness, introspection and exhaustion after the war caused Britain to lose its place among the most prosperous and influential of the world's nations.

With 275,000 British servicemen and women dead, the war also had a profound effect at the personal level.

Moated and magnificent, Leeds Castle in Kent, which dates from Norman times

1783	American independence is achieved.
1815	Twenty-five years of war with France ends with Napoleon Bonaparte's defeat at the Battle of Waterloo.
1837	Queen Victoria ascends the throne for her 64-year reign.
1851	The Great Exhibition reflects Imperial Britain's 19th-century pride and prosperity.
1914–18	A million British die during World War I.
1939–45	World War II (see sidebar).
1947	India achieves independence, beginning the dissolution of the British Empire.
1952	Elizabeth II becomes queen at the age of 25 on the death of her father, George VI.
1969	Start of "The Troubles" in Northern Ireland, which will continue for 30 years.
1973	Britain joins the European Community.
2002	The Queen Mother dies at age 101; celebrations for Queen Elizabeth's Golden Jubilee.

Introduction to Britain

SURVIVAL GUIDE

- Don't forget to pack your raingear, a portable umbrella and some sensible walking shoes – it rains quite a lot in Britain.
- If you enter Central London by car during the week you will incur a daily congestion charge of £8, which must be paid by 10 p.m. if not prepaid. For additional information phone 0845 900 1234; www.cclondon.com. For most other big cities in the U.K. use the anti-congestion "park and ride" plans; you leave your car in a parking lot on the outskirts, and frequent buses (every 10 to 15 minutes) take you into the center.
- Many of the famous scarlet telephone boxes were replaced during the 1990s by smaller plastic booths – cheaper to maintain but shoddier, and much harder to spot.

- In spite of recent scandals involving corruption and racism, the British police are still among the world's friendliest and most helpful.
- Baked potatoes and other take-away (to go) foods have become immensely popular, but probably the best fast-food bet is still good old fish and chips – cheap and delicious.
- How to buy a drink in a pub: Walk to the bar, order your drink and pay for it when you receive it. No one tips the bar staff, but if you are feeling particularly friendly the offer of a drink is often welcome.
- Famous tourist attractions such as William Shakespeare's birthplace at Stratford-upon-Avon, the Crown Jewels in the Tower of London or the ancient monument of Stonehenge on Salisbury Plain can

Ducks complete the tranquil scene in an Essex village

become unpleasantly crowded on summer weekends – particularly on public holidays. It's wise to visit as early in the day as you can, before the crowds gather.

- In high-end restaurants and hotels you may feel more comfortable in a suit and tie or a nice dress and heels. But usually the British are relaxed about dress codes when eating out. Jeans and sneakers, however, are generally frowned upon except in a fast-food joint.

- It has become acceptable to greet female acquaintances with a kiss on the cheek, provided that you know them well enough. Between men a handshake is still the usual mode of greeting.

- Don't stick to the main roads and highways. Buy a book of road maps (available at all big service stations) or better yet, an Ordnance Survey Landranger map for your area (see page 12), and take time traveling the side roads and country lanes. Don't worry about becoming lost: Britain is a small country full of people to ask.

Daffodils in their spring glory in Devon woodland

- Consider taking a boat trip to one of the islands just off the coast of Scotland (page 248) or Northumberland (page 206). You'll see more seabirds and wildflowers than you could dream of and have the pleasure of being entirely out of the everyday world for a few hours.

- Beggars – many damaged by drugs or drink – have become a feature of most English towns and cities. Only extremely rarely will they make a nuisance of themselves, but sooner or later you will have to decide on your policy. To give or not to give? That's up to you, but it is worth remembering that many of these unfortunates are very young and vulnerable, and many are homeless.

- Walking in the country: Britain boasts the world's most extensive and well-maintained network of legal rights-of-way for walkers. Don't be afraid to try out the footpaths. You can go it independently with the right map, or take one of the thousands of short circular hikes for which there are easy-to-follow leaflet guides – just ask at the nearest tourist office.

- Be aware that Scottish and Welsh people do not like to be referred to as "English."

- Some of the more famous cathedrals now ask for standard donations from visitors – generally £3 to £5. A determined visitor can get in without paying, but without such donations no diocese can maintain these wonderful buildings in the condition in which everyone likes to see them.

SOUTHEAST ENGLAND

"THE beautiful cathedral cities of Canterbury and Winchester; pretty villages in pastoral settings; and one of the world's great capitals – vibrant and historic London..."

Opposite: Beachy Head in East Sussex, the highest cliff along the south coast

SOUTHEAST ENGLAND

Southeastern Britain is the country's most populous region, and the richest in per capita income. Its beautiful landscapes, founded on chalk and greensand, are the most threatened by building development, and the most jealously championed by well-heeled local residents. In London it boasts one of the best-known, liveliest and most historic national capitals in the world. The main roads and railroad lines are notoriously congested, thanks to a very high proportion of London commuters. More horses are ridden in this countryside than anywhere else, more gin-and-tonics drunk, more personal bodyguards employed. It is the driest and sunniest region in Britain. Southerners seem, to those from less well-favored regions, to have things soft and easy.

Billowing Chalk

It is the chalk and greensand that give the southeast its gentle elasticity of shape. Gilbert White, the great 18th-century English naturalist, wondered whether the chalk downs might not in ancient times have been quickened by some singular moisture, as bread dough is quickened by yeast, and thus bulged skyward like fungi out of the level plains. It's an attractive idea;

the chalk downs do have a dip and roll to them, as they undulate from Kent through Surrey and Sussex into Hampshire, which makes them look as if they are in just-suspended motion. Beech woods known as hangers grow well on the chalky ridges of the North Downs below London, and farther west are wide tracts of heathland, sandy wildernesses dark with heather and pine trees, exuding an atmosphere of lonely mystery. Farther west, the greensand and gravel flatten into the classic shallow valleys of southern Hampshire, where trout-filled rivers hurry over gravel and flint beds, teeming with healthy green waterweed.

Southeastern Landscapes

The coastline of the southeast starts in industrial confusion and muddle along

Southeast England

the flat south shore of the Thames Estuary as it straggles seaward out of London. At the easternmost tip of Kent it rises to form the bulbous nose of the North Foreland. Here fine chalk cliffs run south and west into the narrows around Dover and Folkestone, where the English Channel meets the North Sea. Then come the strange flat grazing lands of Romney Marsh, reclaimed centuries ago from the sea, and the even stranger landscape of pebbly Dungeness, the arrowhead-shaped spit of land that forms the largest shingle beach in the world.

Farther west along the Channel coast the chalk reappears, rising to Beachy Head and the magnificent Seven Sisters cliffs, before declining again into the built-up holiday coast of Sussex, with its beautiful sand and shingle

beaches and the wide inlet of Chichester harbor. Still farther west, a charmless mess of docks and development has a little jewel in its center: Portsmouth Historic Dockyard, where Admiral Nelson's famous flagship HMS *Victory* is superbly maintained.

Historic Region

Historic sites lie thick in this corner of Britain, so close to London and to the Continental seaports. Kent, with its Channel ferries and sub-Channel rail tunnel, is the gateway into Britain from Europe for non-air travelers. The county is full of the castles and fine houses of noble and influential figures of the past. It also boasts the lovely medieval city and cathedral of Canterbury, whose archbishop is the Church of England's supreme

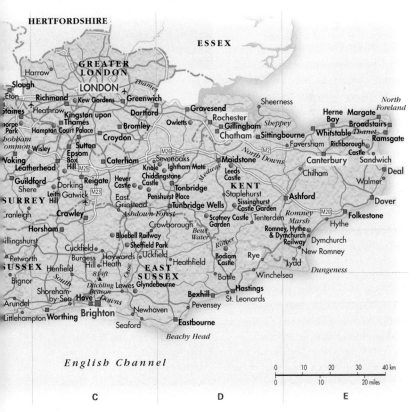

Southeast England

clergyman. The Chatham Historic Dockyard and the harbors at Dover and Folkestone have sustained Britain's seafarers through the centuries.

Tame and Wild

The counties of Surrey and Berkshire have a rich, opulent feel to them, with some of England's prettiest villages tucked away in the well-wooded folds of the North Downs. This is commuter country, which accounts for the carefully manicured and slightly unreal atmosphere of some of these gorgeous places. It also is the site of the monarch's out-of-town residence – mighty Windsor Castle, near the River Thames west of London. The river scenery here is glorious, celebrated in Kenneth Grahame's *The Wind in the Willows* and Jerome K. Jerome's *Three Men in a Boat*, and in the strange and haunting paintings of Sir Stanley Spencer. If you want a taste of something lonely and wild, however, all you need to do is walk across the dark heathery wastes of Chobham Common, on the Surrey-Berkshire border. "A vast tract of land given up to barrenness," wrote Daniel Defoe in the 1720s, "horrid and frightful to look upon, not only good for little, but good for nothing." Today it is a nature reserve for foxes, deer, butterflies, hawks and rare plants.

Resorts and Romans

Sussex has the beautiful, billowing South Downs, villages of flint and brick, and a coast dedicated to seaside pleasures, where the queen of the resorts is undoubtedly "old Ocean's Bauble, glittering Brighton." Chichester is a beautiful small cathedral town at the feet of the downs. Superb mosaic pavements have been unearthed in the ruins of Roman buildings at Fishbourne, on Chichester harbor, and

Brighton's Royal Pavilion, in the south coast resort

at Bignor, up in the downs northeast of the city.

Walk, Fish, Read

You can stride the South Downs Way along the crest of the downs for over 100 miles, from Eastbourne in East Sussex west to Winchester in Hampshire. Don't forget to pack your fly-fishing rod, for Hampshire's clear, gravel-bedded rivers of Meon and Test are among the best in the world for trout fishing. Pack your Jane Austen, too, so that after you have visited her house in Chawton and her memorial in Winchester Cathedral you can walk the beech woods and downland paths in company with Mr. Darcy, Elinor Dashwood, Miss Elizabeth Bennet and the rest of the Austen gang.

The head of Venus depicted on a floor mosaic in a Roman villa at Bignor

Southeast England

LONDON

London, the capital of Britain, is one of the great cities of the world.

Westminster Abbey, Big Ben, Buckingham Palace, St. Paul's Cathedral, the Tower of London: The city boasts dozens of famous showpieces. But London is more than a collection of historic buildings, essential viewing though these are. Taking in a show in the West End of town, shopping in the grand stores of Knightsbridge, dining out in a range of restaurants that span the culinary globe, strolling in Kensington Gardens or on the riverside walkways along the Thames – it's no wonder so many visitors who come to explore Britain

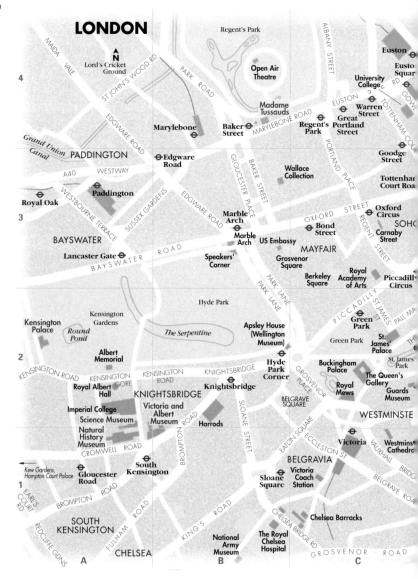

LONDON

Regent's Park

MAIDA VALE

Lord's Cricket Ground

ST JOHN'S WOOD RD

PARK ROAD

ALBANY STREET

Open Air Theatre

Euston

Eusto Squar

University College

EUSTON RD

Madame Tussauds

MARYLEBONE ROAD

Regent's Park

Warren Street

Great Portland Street

TOTTENHAM COU

GOW

EDGWARE ROAD

Marylebone

Baker Street

Goodge Street

Grand Union Canal

PADDINGTON

Edgware Road

WESTWAY

A40

GLOUCESTER PLACE

BAKER STREET

PORTLAND PLACE

Wallace Collection

Tottenhar Court Roa

WESTBOURNE TERRACE

Paddington

Royal Oak

SUSSEX GARDENS

EDGWARE ROAD

Marble Arch

OXFORD STREET

Bond Street

Oxford Circus

SOHO

REGENT STREET

Carnaby Street

BAYSWATER

Lancaster Gate

BAYSWATER ROAD

Marble Arch

US Embassy

Speakers' Corner

Grosvenor Square

MAYFAIR

PARK LANE

Berkeley Square

Royal Academy of Arts

Piccadill Circus

ST JAMES'S

PALL MA

Hyde Park

PICCADILLY

Kensington Palace

Kensington Gardens

Round Pond

The Serpentine

Apsley House (Wellington Museum)

Green Park

Green Park

St. James' Palace

St James' Park

TH

Kensington

KENSINGTON ROAD

KENSINGTON ROAD

Albert Memorial

KENSINGTON ROAD

KNIGHTSBRIDGE

Hyde Park Corner

GROSVENOR PLACE

Buckingham Palace

The Queen's Gallery

KENSINGTON GORE

Royal Albert Hall

Knightsbridge

Royal Mews

Guards Museum

Imperial College

KNIGHTSBRIDGE

BELGRAVE SQUARE

WESTMINSTE

Science Museum

Victoria and Albert Museum

BROMPTON ROAD

Harrods

SLOANE STREET

EATON SQUARE

ECCLESTON ST

Victoria

Westmins Cathedr

Natural History Museum

CROMWELL ROAD

BELGRAVIA

VAUXHALL BRIDG

Kew Gardens, Hampton Court Palace

Gloucester Road

BROMPTON ROAD

South Kensington

Sloane Square

Victoria Coach Station

BELGRAVE ROAD

EARL'S COURT

REDCLIFFE GDNS

BROMPTON ROAD

OLD BROMPTON ROAD

FULHAM ROAD

KING'S ROAD

CHELSEA BRIDGE RD

Chelsea Barracks

SOUTH KENSINGTON

National Army Museum

The Royal Chelsea Hospital

GROSVENOR ROAD

CHELSEA

A   B   C

4

3

2

1

never get any further than London. Special rate cards, available from tourist information centers, offer discounts to a whole range of these attractions.

A Sharp Bunch

Londoners are a mixed lot, becoming more culturally and racially mixed with every passing decade. You'll find London a safe and pleasant place to explore, and

Londoners themselves a witty and eclectic bunch of people. Of course there are one or two bad apples in the basket, and one or two neighborhoods (far from the central locations visitors generally frequent) where an outsider might feel uncomfortable. But London poses no threat to the visitor, provided you follow the common-sense rules about not carrying valuables where a pickpocket

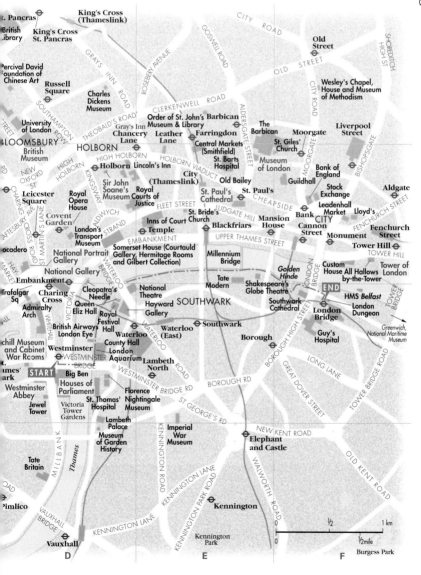

Southeast England

can spot them, and not walking or traveling on public transportation alone late at night.

The London "Clock"

Orienting yourself in the city is not too difficult. Almost everything in central London that a visitor would want to see is north of the River Thames, and this area can be pictured as a clockface with Trafalgar Square at the center. Trafalgar Square itself contains the National Gallery, the National Portrait Gallery, Nelson's Column and enough pigeons to spoil your Sunday suit.

At 12 o'clock north from Trafalgar Square is the West End and its theaters and Leicester Square and its movie theaters; elegant Bloomsbury and the British Museum lie beyond. At 1 o'clock you will find Covent Garden and the Royal Opera House. At 2 o'clock are the city's financial quarter and St. Paul's Cathedral, with the Barbican Centre and the Museum of London a little to the north.

From 3 o'clock to 5 o'clock is the River Thames. The north Embankment runs east toward the Tower of London, while the south bank is lined with attractions that include the British Airways London Eye (a Ferris wheel with glass-enclosed seats), Royal Festival Hall, the Tate Modern art gallery and the replica Shakespeare's Globe Theatre.

At 6 o'clock are Westminster Abbey, Big Ben and the Houses of Parliament. At 7 o'clock it's the Cabinet War Rooms on the edge of St. James's Park. At 8 o'clock comes Buckingham Palace, with the upper-crust districts of

---

ESSENTIAL INFORMATION

TOURIST INFORMATION
• Britain and London Visitor Centre, 1 Regent Street, Piccadilly Circus, SW1 (personal callers only)
• Visit London ☎ 08701 566366 (call within the UK only); www.visitlondon.com

URBAN TRANSPORTATION
The London Underground (subway) trains operate Mon.–Sat. 5:30 a.m.–midnight, Sun. 7:30 a.m.–11:30 p.m. and serve central London stations every 5–10 minutes. Lines are color coded and maps are displayed in all stations. Tickets can be purchased at ticket booths or machines in station entrance halls. The symbol of the subway is a red circle crossed by a blue horizontal line and is marked on the London city map. London's distinctive red buses serve the city and suburbs from early morning to around midnight with night buses (midnight–4:30 a.m.) on most major routes. Tickets can be purchased on board from the driver or an attendant. For information about the subway or buses, contact London Travel Information ☎ 020 7222 1234 (24hrs). London's cabs are metered and

are available for passengers when the yellow light is on. They can be flagged down in the street or ordered by calling ☎ 020 7286 0286 or 020 7272 0272.

AIRPORT INFORMATION
London is served by two main airports: Heathrow, 15 miles west of the city (☎ 08700 000123), and Gatwick, 30 miles south (☎ 08700 002468). Services below operate daily from around 6 a.m.–midnight (outside these times service will be less frequent). From Heathrow, the Heathrow Express train goes to London's Paddington Station every 15 minutes (journey time 15–25 minutes). The subway's Piccadilly line departs to central London every 5–10 minutes (journey time about 1 hour). There also are buses to London's Victoria Coach Station which depart every half hour (journey time about 1 hour, 30 minutes). Taxis are expensive but available 24 hours from the Arrivals area. From Gatwick, Gatwick Express and South Eastern Trains go to London's Victoria Station every 15 minutes (journey time about 30 minutes). There are Thameslink trains to London Bridge Station every 15 minutes (journey time 30 minutes).

CLIMATE – Average highs and lows

JAN.	FEB.	MAR.	APR.	MAY	JUN.	JUL.	AUG.	SEP.	OCT.	NOV.	DEC.
6°C	6°C	10°C	13°C	16°C	20°C	21°C	21°C	18°C	14°C	10°C	7°C
43°F	43°F	50°F	55°F	61°F	68°F	70°F	70°F	64°F	57°F	50°F	45°F
2°C	2°C	3°C	5°C	8°C	11°C	13°C	13°C	11°C	7°C	5°C	3°C
36°F	36°F	37°F	41°F	46°F	52°F	55°F	55°F	52°F	45°F	41°F	37°F

Knightsbridge and Kensington a little farther out. Here you will find Harrods department store and three splendid museums: Victoria and Albert, Science, and Natural History.

At 9 o'clock lie the parks – Green Park, Hyde Park and then Kensington Gardens with Kensington Palace. Also here is the exclusive Mayfair district. Finally, Oxford Street brings you from 10 o'clock back to 12, with Madame Tussauds waxworks, the Auditorium and Regent's Park beyond.

Getting around in London is simple, provided you don't try and drive this congested city. Public transportation consists of the generally efficient underground subway system, known universally as the "Tube." London's red buses offer frequent service, and the famed black taxicabs are everywhere. Bear in mind that cab drivers will turn up their noses if you do not add 10 percent of the fare as a tip.

From Breakfast to Dinner

The cuisines of the world meet and mingle in London, and some of the most exciting cooking stems from this creative infusion of different cultures. You could start at your hotel with a full English breakfast (bacon, eggs and all the trimmings), have lunch at one of the really smart restaurants such as the Ivy in trendy Covent Garden, take afternoon tea at the Savoy, and dine at any one of the hundreds of brasseries.

Of course you would need to work up an appropriate appetite – and what better way than shopping? Harrods is a realm unto itself. Fortnum and Mason has all you need in the food and drink line. Harvey Nichols and the boutiques of Knightsbridge keep ladies in classic or up-to-the-second fashion style; gentlemen should seek out Gieves and Hawkes on Savile Row and Bates the Hatter on Jermyn Street for their

Pubs and cafés spill out onto the streets

apparel requirements. Silverware and jewelry? Try Bond Street and elsewhere in Mayfair. Cheaper and maybe more cheerful shopping flourishes in the ragbag atmosphere of the street markets in Camden (Thursday to Sunday) and Petticoat Lane (Monday to Saturday), while Charing Cross Road is lined with bookstores of every description.

Plays and Pubs

What to do in the evening? Those organized enough to book seats well in advance can enjoy world-class opera and ballet at the Royal Opera House in Covent Garden. Shakespeare fans will revel in the rambunctious atmosphere at the open-air Shakespeare's Globe Theatre on the South Bank of the Thames. There also are dozens of plays and shows in the West End around Shaftesbury Avenue. Concerts at Royal Festival Hall and the Royal Albert Hall are worth checking on. Or you could just walk into one of the thousands of London pubs and sit chatting over a pint of beer.

Pageantry: A Horse Guard on parade

LONDON SIGHTS

Key to symbols

🖪 map coordinates refer to the London map on pages 32–33; sights below are highlighted in yellow on the map.

✉ address or location ☎ telephone number

⊙ opening times 🍴 restaurant or café on site or nearby ⊜ nearest subway ⊠ river boat

🍸 admission charge: $$$ more than £6, $$ £2–£6, $ less than £2 ℹ information

BRITISH MUSEUM

The British Museum, founded around the private collection of royal physician Sir Hans Sloane (1660–1753), has grown over 250 years to become one of the world's premier museums, with a collection of over 7 million items. The British Library has moved from the museum to a new home at St. Pancras, but the famous cylindrical Reading Room, (where Karl Marx, Mahatma Gandhi and George Bernard Shaw all studied under the huge dome) remains.

There are more than 2 miles of galleries, far too much for any visitor to cover. The best approach is to select a few must-see items from the museum plan at the information desk, and then to enjoy whatever crosses your path as you seek them out. Among the treasures are the controversial Elgin Marbles, a group of

5th-century BC sculptures brought from the Parthenon in Athens to London in 1801 (the Greek government is still trying to have them returned); the famous Rosetta Stone, carved with hieroglyphic, demotic and Greek script that proved the key to understanding Eygptian hieroglyphics; the Sutton Hoo Treasure, a hoard of gold and bronze items from Saxon times; and the exquisite Portland Vase, a masterpiece of Roman glassware. The Great Court, added in 2000, has increased the museum's space by 50 percent. A massive glass roof spans the central courtyard, making it the largest covered square in Europe.

🖪 D3 ✉ Great Russell Street, WC1 ☎ 020 7323 8000 ⊙ Daily 10–5:30 (also Thu.–Fri. 5:30–8:30); Great Court: Sun.–Wed. 9–6, Thu.–Sat. 9 a.m.–11 p.m. 🍴 Restaurant and cafés ⊜ Tottenham Court Road, Holborn, Russell Square 🍸 Free (charge for special exhibitions) ℹ Guided tours $$–$$$

Café society in the Central Market at Covent Garden

CHURCHILL MUSEUM AND CABINET WAR ROOMS

The Cabinet War Rooms were constructed as a subterranean command center in 1939 in the expectation that London would be bombed flat. Walking around with an audio guide, you peer into the bleak rooms from which Winston Churchill and Britain's other wartime leaders conducted the war. Memorabilia include maps, communication devices and scramblers, huge radio sets, and Churchill's bedroom, with ashtray for the famous cigar. A series of recently discovered rooms contains the Churchill Museum, which opened in 2005.

✠ D2 ✉ Clive Steps, King Charles Street, SW1 ☎ 020 7930 6961 🕐 Daily 9:30–6. Last admission at 5 🍴 Café 🚇 Westminster, St. James's Park ✋ $$$

COVENT GARDEN

Covent Garden's Royal Opera House is Britain's finest venue for opera and ballet. The centerpiece is the Floral Hall, a sunny Victorian cast-iron and glass shed where flowers were sold during Covent Garden's heyday as a working market. You can stroll around the hall by day, taking in the atmosphere that audiences enjoy at night, and there are exhibitions and backstage guided tours. You also can attend one of the free lunchtime concerts or other events before strolling across the piazza to the Central Market building for lunch while being entertained by street performers.

Royal Opera House ✠ D3 ✉ Off Bow Street, Covent Garden, WC2 ☎ Tours: 020 7304 4000 🕐 Tours: Mon.–Sat. at 10:30 and 2:30 (duration 75–90 minutes) 🍴 Restaurants and cafés 🚇 Covent Garden ✋ Tours: $$$

Big Ben and the Houses of Parliament silhouetted against the night sky

HOUSES OF PARLIAMENT

The finest view of the Houses of Parliament, and the clock tower that houses the great bell known as Big Ben, is from across the Thames on the South Bank; best of all, from the British Airways London Eye that operates there (see page 40). Close up, from Parliament Square, you see the work of architects Augustus Pugin and Sir Charles Barry, replacing the original building which survived Guy Fawkes' Gunpowder Plot of November 5, 1605, but burned down in 1834.

Inside, the Houses of Parliament are a labyrinthine maze. When the Houses are in session, you can ascend to the Strangers' Gallery and view the proceedings below in the chamber of the House of Commons. Prime Minister's Question Time, Wednesday from noon until 12:30 p.m., when members of the Opposition get to challenge the Prime Minister, makes for interesting viewing. In the scarlet and gold somnolence of the House of Lords, manners are better and the tone quieter.

Another must is a look into ancient Westminster Hall, a thousand years old, under a wonderful medieval timber roof.
🚩 D2 ✉ Parliament Square (St. Stephen's Entrance), Westminster, SW1 ☎ 020 7219 4272 🕐 Mon.–Wed. 2:30–10:30 or later, Thu. 11:30–7:30, Fri. 9:30–3 (but not every Fri.); when parliament is in recess hours vary, and tours are given. Call for details 🚇 Westminster

🚢 Westminster Millennium Pier 🎟 Free; tours $$$
ℹ Entrance is first-come-first-served, unless you apply to the U.S. Embassy in London several weeks in advance for an appointment

KENSINGTON PALACE

These days Kensington Palace is inextricably associated with Diana, Princess of Wales, who lived here until her death in 1997. Visiting the palace at the west end of Kensington Gardens, you may see wreaths of flowers at the gates, tokens of respect from those who continue to admire the princess.

Kensington Palace, built in 1605, was the principal royal London residence from 1689 until King George III's move to Buckingham Palace in the 1760s. Parts of the building are still maintained as royal apartments; the remainder, open to the public, contains 18th-century state rooms with notable murals and painted ceilings, and an exhibition of court dress since 1760 that includes some Diana-related exhibits.

Outside is a charming sunken garden, and nearby an 18th-century orangery with decorations by master carver Grinling Gibbons, where you can take tea.
🚩 A2 ✉ Kensington Gardens, W8 ☎ 08707 515176 🕐 Daily 10–6, mid-Mar. to mid-Oct.; 10–5, rest of year. Last admission 1 hour before closing 🍴 Restaurant 🚇 Queensway, High Street Kensington, Bayswater 🎟 $$$

MADAME TUSSAUDS

This is one of London's top tourist attractions – beware long lines! Madame Tussauds offers a bizarre collection of waxwork dummies, ranging from brilliant likenesses to inexplicable aberrations. The business was started in 1835 by Madame Tussaud herself, an *emigrée* Frenchwoman who had arrived in London 30 years before with a case full of wax death masks she had molded from the faces of executed victims of the French Revolution.

Some of the originals are on display, along with thousands more recently made. It's fun to visit "Blush" and have your picture taken hobnobbing with the stars, and to try and spot the wax stooges placed in lifelike poses to fool the unwary. Visitors need a morbid curiosity to enjoy the horribly gory Chamber of Horrors or the Live Chamber where effigies of serial killers are confronted.

Alternatively, the Auditorium offers an excellent voyage of the imagination through space and the stars, from an outsize model of the earth to laser shows, interactive displays on space, and the exciting Journey to Infinity show projected on a domed roof.

🚼 B4 ✉ Marylebone Road, NW1 ☎ 08704 003000 🕐 Madame Tussauds: Mon.–Fri. 9:30–5:30, Sat.–Sun. 9–6 (extended hours during school holidays). Auditorium: Mon.–Fri. 12:30–5:30, Sat.–Sun. (also Mon.–Fri. during school holidays) 10:30–6 🍴 Café 🚇 Baker Street 🎟 $$$; Live Chamber extra $$

MUSEUM OF LONDON

This is one of London's most enjoyable museums, taking you on a chronological stroll through the history of the city from earliest prehistory to the present day. It could be a dry-as-dust history lesson, but it isn't.

Highlights include Roman marbles and wall paintings salvaged nearby, jewelry and leatherwear from Shakespeare's London, a grim mock-up of a cell in the notorious Newgate prison, and Victorian shop fronts and interiors. You can hear Samuel Pepys' account of the Great Fire of 1666 while watching the city burn (in miniature), relive the miseries of the Blitz bombings of 1940–41, and groove through swinging London of the 1960s. Fab, man!

🚼 E3 ✉ 150 London Wall, EC2 ☎ 08704 443852 🕐 Mon.–Sat. 10–5:50, Sun. noon–5:50. Last admission 20 minutes before closing 🍴 Café 🚇 St. Paul's, Barbican, Moorgate 🎟 Free

Wax effigies of The Beatles entertain visitors to Madame Tussaud's

Big Ben and the Houses of Parliament

WALK: THE SOUTH BANK OF THE THAMES

Refer to route marked on city map on page 33

This short walk along the South Bank of the River Thames, designated the Millennium Mile, offers you a great variety of attractions, river views all the way, and stunning vistas across the Thames to the skyline of central London. A brisk walk takes half an hour, but you will probably want to devote at least half a day to enjoy the experience as well as a selection of the attractions. The paving throughout is suitable for citified footwear.

Start from Westminster tube station.

Emerging from the station, you are confronted by the full majestic height of Big Ben clock tower, with the Houses of Parliament beyond. *Turn left and cross Westminster Bridge.* Pause midway over the bridge to admire the parliamentary buildings. Britain's most illustrious poet stopped here, too, to admire the view on a still morning in 1802. "Earth hath not anything to show more fair," wrote William Wordsworth, recalling the "ships, towers, domes, theatres and temples" he saw that day, "all bright and glittering in the smokeless air." *Turn left along the south bank of the river.* You will pass below the giant 450-foot bicycle wheel shape of the British Airways London Eye. A ride in one of its gleaming glass pods will give you a unique view of London's famous landmarks and the surrounding countryside. Dwarfed in its shadow is County

Hall, where the marine and freshwater creatures of the London Aquarium gape and flicker in their tanks.

Follow the river wall path past strings of rusty barges, smart cruise boats and the stocky little launches of the river police as they fuss up and down the Thames. Pass under Waterloo Bridge, where there are secondhand book stalls, then under Blackfriars Bridge. Note the gaudy cast-iron company badge of the London, Chatham and Dover Railway, known to Victorian travelers as the "Smash 'em and Turnover" because of its frequent accidents (Charles Dickens was almost killed in one of them).

Next on your right is the huge, dark bulk of Bankside Power Station. It opened in 1963 and lasted fewer than 30 years. Now it has taken a glorious new lease on life as the Tate Modern, featuring 20th-century works by Andy Warhol, Henry Moore, Pablo Picasso and others of the older guard, as well as those by up-to-the-minute artists. The original Tate Gallery, west of here on the riverside at Millbank, has been reinvented as Tate Britain, exhibiting the world's greatest collection of British art.

Stretching across the Thames outside Tate Modern is the Millennium Bridge, opened in 2000. This is the first pedestrian crossing to be built over the Thames in more than a century.

In the shadow of Tate Modern, on the east side, stands a dignified little pair of 17th-century houses, Cardinal's Wharf. Here, as the plaque on the wall tells you, Sir Christopher Wren lived while he was supervising the building of St. Paul's Cathedral after the disastrous Great Fire of London in 1666. If so (and there is certainly an excellent view of St. Paul's across the river from here), Wren chose a racy area, because Bankside was then London's red-light district. Here stood the Globe Theatre, partly owned and made famous by William Shakespeare – and it stands once more, beautifully reconstructed and putting on plays in authentic Elizabethan open-air style.

Beyond the Globe, duck into the Anchor Bankside pub for a pint of beer and a bite to eat; then continue along narrow, dark Clink Street (the epitome of Dickensian London) past the Clink Prison, once the grimmest of jails and now a museum chronicling incarceration and roisterous misdeeds.

Inside the Globe – a replica of the open-air theater as it was in Shakespeare's day

Farther along lie the *Golden Hinde*, a replica of Sir Francis Drake's famed vessel, and lovely Southwark Cathedral, both worth a visit before you climb the steps to London Bridge tube station and your return train.

British Airways London Eye ✚ D2 ✉ Jubilee Gardens ☎ 08705 000600 🕐 Daily 9:30 a.m.–10 p.m., Jul.–Aug.; 9:30–9 May–Jun. and in Sep.; 9:30–8 rest of year (call for maintenance closure) 🚇 Waterloo, Embankment 🎟 $$$ – tickets available in advance

London Aquarium ✚ D2 ✉ County Hall, Riverside Building, Westminster Bridge Road ☎ 020 7967 8000 🕐 Daily 10–6. Last admission 1 hour before closing 🍴 Café 🚇 Waterloo, Westminster 🎟 $$$

Tate Modern ✚ E3 ✉ Bankside ☎ 020 7887 8000 or 020 7887 8008 (24hrs) 🕐 Sun.–Thu. 10–6, Fri.– Sat. 10–10. Last admission 45 minutes before closing 🍴 Cafés 🚇 Blackfriars, Southwark 🎟 Free, except special exhibitions/events

Shakespeare's Globe Theatre ✚ E3 ✉ 21 New Globe Walk, Bankside ☎ 020 7902 1500 🕐 Exhibition and theater tour: daily 9–5, May–Sep.; 10–5, rest of year 🍴 Restaurant and Café 🚇 London Bridge, Cannon Street, Blackfriars 🎟 $$$

Southwark Cathedral ✚ F2 ✉ Montague Close ☎ 020 7367 6700 🕐 Daily 8–6. Visitor Center and exhibition Mon.–Sat. 10–6, Sun 11–5. Last admission 45 minutes before closing 🚇 London Bridge 🎟 Free, donation recommended

People, pigeons, fountains and statues fill Trafalgar Square in front of the National Gallery

NATIONAL GALLERY

Britain's premier art gallery faces the lions, fountains and Nelson's Column in Trafalgar Square. It tells the story of painting in Europe from pre-Renaissance times to the turn of the 20th century. There is an embarrassment of riches here, so take a few minutes to familiarize yourself with the layout and to pick a few special treats from the catalogue.

Particular treasures in the Sainsbury Wing (1260–1510) include Leonardo da Vinci's cartoon of *The Virgin and Child with St. John the Baptist and St. Anne*, Botticelli's *Venus and Mars*, and a beautiful unfinished *Nativity* by Piero della Francesca. The West Wing (1510–1600) contains several Titians, a moody *Agony in the Garden of Gethsemane* by El Greco, and Michelangelo's *Entombment of Christ*. In the North Wing (1600–1700) you will find glorious fleshy Rembrandts and a sexy post-coital *Samson and Delilah* by Rubens.

Most fully stuffed with masterpieces, though, is the East Wing (1700–1900).

Here is the flower of England's Golden Age of landscape painting – including John Constable's great East Anglian scenes filled with water, trees and light, and J.M.W. Turner's increasingly wild and impressionistic seascapes and movement paintings. There also is a superb collection of French Impressionists, from Degas dancers to Monet (*Bathers at La Grenouillère*), Renoir (*Umbrellas*), Gauguin (*Fao Theihe*) and van Gogh (*Wheatfield with Cypresses* and the vivid *Sunflowers*).

✚ D3 ✉ Trafalgar Square, WC2 ☎ 020 7747 2885 🕐 Daily 10–6 (also Wed. 6–9 p.m.) 🍽 Restaurant and café 🚇 Charing Cross, Leicester Square 🎟 Free (charge for special exhibitions); audio tour free, donation suggested

NATIONAL PORTRAIT GALLERY

The best-known British men and women from the Middle Ages onward are depicted here: ascetic (composer Frederick Delius), powerful (Margaret Thatcher, Queen Elizabeth I), soulful (poets

The dinosaurs are a favorite attraction in the Natural History Museum

The Life Galleries are a fine blend of traditional but fascinating glass-case gazing and interactive exhibitions based on a variety of themes inspired by nature. Pride of place here goes to those perennial favorites with all young visitors – the dinosaurs, viewed from every possible angle thanks to the walkway layout.

➕ A1 ✉ Cromwell Road, SW7 ☎ 020 7942 5000
🕐 Mon.–Sat. 10–5:50, Sun. 11–5:50. Last admission 20 minutes before closing 🍴 Restaurant and cafés
🚇 South Kensington 🎫 Free (charge for special exhibitions)

SCIENCE MUSEUM

The Science Museum adjoins the Natural History Museum and was opened, like its sister museum, to satisfy the public thirst for knowledge created by London's Great Exhibition of 1851. This it still achieves in endearingly piecemeal style through exhibitions covering nearly 50 topics. They range from space exploration to the earliest attempts at flight, from steam engines to microchips, from advanced nuclear physics to children's puzzles. Don't miss the Wellcome Wing with its IMAX cinema or the display of bygone surgical and dental equipment that makes you cringe with relief that medical science has moved on.

➕ A2 ✉ Exhibition Road, SW7 ☎ 08708 704868
🕐 Daily 10–6 🍴 Cafés 🚇 South Kensington
🎫 Free. IMAX cinema $$$. Motion-ride simulators $$

William Cowper and William Wordsworth), suffering (AIDS-reduced film director Derek Jarman) and confident (Victorian engineer Isambard Kingdom Brunel), among others.

➕ D2–D3 ✉ St. Martin's Place, WC2 ☎ 020 7306 0055 or 020 7312 2463 (recorded information)
🕐 Daily 10–6 (also Thu.–Fri. 6–9 p.m.). Last admission 10 minutes before closing 🍴 Restaurant and café 🚇 Charing Cross, Leicester Square
🎫 Free (charge for special exhibitions)

NATURAL HISTORY MUSEUM

The Natural History Museum is one of the world's leading museums of natural history. Housed in a fine 19th-century Victorian building (the modern walkways inside allow you to appreciate all the hitherto obscured architectural and decorative details), the museum is currently divided into two sections, the Earth Galleries and the Life Galleries.

The high-tech Earth Galleries in "The Power Within" feature an escalator ride through the center of the earth to witness volcanic eruptions and earthquakes.

Buckingham Palace looks over ornamental gardens at the head of The Mall

LONDON'S PARKS

London is proud of its parks, a wide network of open green spaces well provided with trees and water features. Here locals and visitors can escape traffic noise and crowded pavements to stroll, laze, flirt, run, go boating or fly a kite.

Nearest to Trafalgar Square is St. James's Park (Tube: St. James's Park), London's oldest park. These green wooded acres were used as a royal deer-hunting forest in the time of King Henry VIII. Across the park on a January day in 1649 walked King Charles I, on his way to execution in Whitehall. The land was opened to the public by Charles II and it quickly became a favorite resort of Londoners. Architect John Nash landscaped it, complete with lake, around 1828, when he was redesigning Buckingham Palace for King George IV. Looking west from the elegant bridge across the waist of the lake is a fine view of the palace.

Just north of Buckingham Palace, and separated from St. James's Park by The Mall, a broad, straight avenue, is Green Park (Tube: Green Park), rich in beautiful trees and a more informal open space than its manicured neighbor. The gallant and hot-tempered young bloods of 18th-century London fought their duels here. During World War II the park was plowed up and turned over to vegetable production, but all traces of such rough treatment have long since vanished.

Walking west from Green Park, the next open space you come to is Hyde Park (Tube: Hyde Park Corner) and its twin sister Kensington Gardens (Tube: Lancaster Gate). Together they preserve 600 acres of quiet green ground on the flank of London's most exclusive districts, Mayfair, Kensington and Knightsbridge. Hyde Park was part of the lands belonging to Westminster Abbey, which were confiscated by King Henry VIII in the 1530s at the time of the Reformation. It was King James I who opened the land to the public. The bridle path along the south side, known as Rotten Row, soon became a hangout for duelists, highwaymen and prostitutes.

A band in St. James's Park performs a relaxing escape from the metropolitan bustle

Around the turn of the 18th century lamps were installed to deter the worst criminals; the prostitutes retaliated by taking to the saddle and displaying their charms for hire on horseback during the day. There's no such excitement these days, but plenty of enjoyment is still available at Speaker's Corner in Hyde Park's northeast corner, where anyone with a cause can climb on a soapbox and state their case at length – often to wisecracking crowds. It's fun, too, to boat on the curved lake called The Serpentine, created in Georgian times by damming the Westbourne River.

Kensington Gardens, the more westerly of these twin parks, once formed the grounds of Kensington Palace (see page 38). Queen Victoria gifted the land to the nation in 1841. Model boats set sail on Round Pond; there is a beautiful Flower Walk, and acres of open grassland for kite-flying and ball games. Also in Kensington Gardens is George Frampton's celebrated 1912 statue of Peter Pan, an object of pilgrimage for children of all ages.

Holland Park, a 10-minute walk west of Kensington Gardens (Tube: Holland Park), is small and well-wooded. Holland House was destroyed by bombs during World War II, and this pleasant little park with its café and open-air theater was opened in 1952 on what remained of the grounds.

A 15-minute walk north of Hyde Park is central London's other great green space, Regent's Park (Tube: Regent's Park or Baker Street). This elegant park was laid out in the early 19th century by John Nash, landscaper of St. James's Park, at the behest of George, Prince of Wales. At that time the self-indulgent "Prinny" – later to become King George IV – was acting as a proxy monarch, owing to his father's mental incapacity. He wanted something nice to look at when he drove out from his house in St. James's: hence the superb Nash-designed terraces that flank the park. London Zoo is in the park's northern corner, with its animals housed in some interesting architectural features. There also is a boating lake, and an open-air theater where you can enjoy alfresco performances in summer.

Soaring arches lead the eye to the vast space beneath the main dome of St. Paul's Cathedral

ST. PAUL'S CATHEDRAL

Sir Christopher Wren's great baroque church (built 1675–1710) rose like a phoenix from the ashes of the 1666 Great Fire of London to become the symbol of the city, an image reinforced when it miraculously survived ferocious bombing during the 1940-41 Blitz.

The central dome is 364 feet high and 157 feet across; the summit lantern alone weighs 850 tons. Heavy statistics, and the whole church carries a bulky, solid atmosphere. In the crypt, national heroes are buried: Admiral Horatio Nelson (1805), the Duke of Wellington (1852) and Florence Nightingale (1910).

Climb to the Whispering Gallery inside the dome – sounds carry around the curve of the wall to someone listening on the opposite side. It was from here in 1981 that TV cameras took shots of the wedding of Prince Charles and Lady Diana Spencer. Climb to the Stone Gallery and then ascend the iron staircase for a view of London from 350 feet up.

E3 ✉ St. Paul's Churchyard, EC4 ☎ 020 7246 8348 🕐 Mon.–Sat. 8:30–5. Last admission 1 hour before closing 🍴 Restaurant and café 🚇 St. Paul's 💷 $$ 🛈 Guided tours at 11, 11:30, 1:30 and 2 ($$). Audio tours ($$)

SIR JOHN SOANE'S MUSEUM

Three modest-looking, though elegant, terrace homes on the north edge of Lincoln's Inn Fields contain London's oddest museum, unknown to most visitors but a genuine delight. One of the world's great private collections, it was put together by Sir John Soane (1753–1837), architect of the Bank of England. The exhibits range from the sarcophagus of an Egyptian pharaoh to Roman marbles and urns, Italian busts, and paintings by such artists as Canaletto, Piranesi, J.M.W. Turner and Joshua Reynolds, along with William Hogarth's complete sequences *The Election* and *A Rake's Progress*.

D3 ✉ 13 Lincoln's Inn Fields, WC2 ☎ 020 7405 2107 🕐 Tue.–Sat. 10–5 (also 6–9 p.m. first Tue. of every month) 🚇 Holborn 💷 Free; donations recommended 🛈 Guided tours ($$) on Saturdays – tickets available from 2 p.m. for tour at 2:30

Centuries of bloody history are locked up in The Tower

TOWER OF LONDON

The Tower of London is one of London's premier attractions, drawing 3 million visitors a year. They come to see the Yeoman Warders – better known as Beefeaters – in their red uniforms and white Elizabethan neck ruffs, to admire the resident ravens (if the birds ever leave, The Tower will fall), and to thrill to tales of torture, murder and beheadings.

On Tower Hill hundreds found guilty of treason died in public under the axe; a privileged handful (including King Henry VIII's second and fifth wives, Anne Boleyn and Catherine Howard) were beheaded in private on Tower Green. You will see the spot on a guided tour, as well as the Bloody Tower, where in 1483 the young heir to the throne, Prince Edward, and his younger brother, Prince Richard, were killed – probably smothered with pillows – on the orders of their uncle Richard, Duke of Gloucester, who was crowned King Richard III shortly afterwards. Overlooking the Thames is St. Thomas' Tower; those accused of treachery were brought here

A Beefeater in traditional costume

through its arched and barred gateway, known as Traitor's Gate, to be incarcerated. At the Jewel House you can line up to see the Crown Jewels – a fabulous monarchical treasure of gold, crowns, orbs and scepters.

✚ F3 ✉ Tower Hill, EC3 ☎ 08707 508080; 08707 566060 (recorded information) 🕐 Tue.–Sat. 9–6, Sun.–Mon. 10–6, Mar.–Oct.; Tue.–Sat. 9–5, Sun.–Mon. 10–5, rest of year. Last admission 1 hour before closing 🍴 Restaurant and café 🚇 Tower Hill; DLR Tower Gateway ⛴ Tower Millennium Pier from Westminster Millennium and Embankment Piers 💰 $$$

Westminster Abbey: Gothic setting for coronations and state weddings and funerals

VICTORIA AND ALBERT MUSEUM

The V & A, founded after the 1851 Great Exhibition to inspire the British with examples of artistic achievement, extends through 7 miles of galleries. Here are life-size plaster casts of famous sculpture, from Michelangelo's "David" to the door of Santiago de Compostela's cathedral; Raphael cartoons for his Sistine Chapel paintings; Islamic and Japanese treasures; and English painting, silverware and 18th-century furniture. After visiting the Frank Lloyd Wright Gallery you can relax in a Victorian Arts and Crafts tearoom.

✚ A1, A2, B1, B2 ✉ Cromwell Road, SW7 ☎ 020 7942 2000 or 08704 420808 (24-hour recorded information) 🕐 Daily 10–5:45 (also Wed. and last Fri. of the month 5:45–10) 🍴 Restaurant and cafés Ⓜ South Kensington 🎟 Free (charge for special exhibitions)

WESTMINSTER ABBEY

Westminster Abbey is the meeting place of the nation's religious, political and monarchical life. This superb Gothic church has seen every coronation but two of the 38 since William the Conqueror's on December 25, 1066. Here you will find the tombs and memorials of monarchs, poets such as Alfred, Lord Tennyson, writers like Charles Dickens and Henry James, and politicians such as Sir Winston Churchill.

✚ D2 ✉ Broad Sanctuary, SW1 ☎ 020 7654 4900 🕐 Mon.–Fri. 9:30–4:45 (also Wed. 4:45–7), Sat. 9:30–2:45, late Mar.–late Oct.; Mon.–Fri. 9:30–4:45 (also Wed. 4:45–6), Sat. 9:30–2:45, rest of year. Last admission 1 hour before closing. Cloisters: daily 8–6. Abbey Museum, Pyx Chamber and Chapter House: daily 10:30–4 Ⓜ Westminster, St. James's Park ⛴ Westminster Millennium Pier 🎟 Abbey: $$$ Cloisters, Abbey Museum, Pyx Chamber and Chapter House: Free

The formal gardens of Hampton Court enhance the Tudor palace of King Henry VIII

THAMES CRUISES: GREENWICH, KEW AND HAMPTON COURT

River cruises make a great day out, and London has a couple of classics along the Thames in each direction.

Downriver, a boat ride of about an hour from Westminster Millennium Pier will take you to Greenwich, scene of one of London's finest waterfront vistas. Get your camera out on the boat – the best views are from the river. The Royal Naval College flanks the National Maritime Museum (begun by Inigo Jones as a house for King James I's wife, Anne of Denmark) and is a splendid ensemble of domes and pillars. Alongside the National Maritime Museum is the splendid Queen's House, England's first classical Palladian building and the architectural ancestor of Washington D.C.'s White House. Nearby rear the masts and rigging of the famous Victorian tea clipper *Cutty Sark*, dwarfing the tiny yacht *Gipsy Moth IV*, in which Sir Francis Chichester made the first solo circumnavigation of the world in 1966-67. Inland rises the hill of Greenwich Park, where in the yard of the Royal Observatory you can straddle the famed Meridian Line.

Upriver from Westminster Millennium Pier, it is a three hour round-trip journey along the Thames to some of London's most beautiful riverside scenery on the western outskirts of the city. At Kew you'll find the Royal Botanic Gardens, featuring two giant Victorian conservatories. Farther upriver, in superb gardens with their own maze, sprawls the mighty Hampton Court Palace, the grandest Tudor building in Britain. King Henry VIII embellished it for his beloved (but soon executed) second wife, Anne Boleyn.

Greenwich ✚ F2 **Thames River Services**
✉ Westminster Millennium Pier, Victoria Embankment ☎ 020 7930 4097 ⏱ Sailings daily 10–5 (every 30 minutes), Apr.–Oct.; 10:40–4:20 (every 40 minutes), rest of year 👆 $$$

Kew, Hampton Court ✚ A1 **Westminster Passenger Service Association (Upriver)**
✉ Westminster Millennium Pier, Victoria Embankment ☎ 020 7930 2062 or 020 7930 4721 (recorded information) ⏱ Sailings daily at 10:30, 11:15, noon and 2, early Apr.–late Sep.; at 10:30, 11 and noon, late Sep.–late Oct. 👆 $$$

REGIONAL SIGHTS

Key to symbols

⊞ map coordinates refer to the Southeast England map on pages 28–29; sights below are highlighted in yellow on the map.
⊠ address or location   ☎ telephone number
🕐 opening times   🍴 restaurant or café on site or nearby   🍽 admission charge: $$$ more than £6, $$ £2–£6, $ less than £2   ℹ information

BRIGHTON

Raffish and roguish Brighton is still the No. 1 seaside resort on England's south coast. Here, an hour from London, you find everything close to the heart of the seaside: plenty of pebble beach, the glitzy attractions of Brighton Pier, swimming and a lively town atmosphere. You can shop for souvenirs and antiques in The Lanes (the cramped old fishing quarter), or walk through the transparent tunnel at the Brighton Sea Life Centre near Brighton Pier and marvel at the sea creatures around and above you. To the east are the crescents and terraces of Kemp Town, the finest Regency architecture ever created.

It was the Prince Regent, George Prince of Wales, whose patronage at the turn of the 19th century changed Brighton from a humble fishing village into "old Ocean's bauble," and his monstrously extravagant Royal Pavilion stands in overblown splendor in the town center. Oriental onion domes and minarets grace the exterior; inside are ornamental dragons, tree-shaped chandeliers and much that is amazing and entertaining.

Oriental magic: Brighton's ornate Royal Pavilion

⊞ C1
Tourist information ⊠ 10 Bartholomew Square
☎ 09067 112255 (there is a charge of 50p per minute for this call); www.visitbrighton.com
Royal Pavilion ⊠ Pavilion Parade ☎ 01273 290900
🕐 Daily 9:30–5:45, Apr.–Sep.; 10–5:15, rest of year.
Last admission 45 minutes before closing 🍴 Café
🍽 $$ (tour $ extra) ℹ Guided tours at 11:30 and 2:30
Brighton Sea Life Centre ⊠ Marine Parade
☎ 01273 604234 🕐 Daily 10–6, mid-Feb. through Dec. 31; 10–5, rest of year. Last admission 1 hour before closing 🍽 $–$$

The South Downs

This billowing ridge of chalk downland forms the spine of Sussex and extends west into Hampshire. The valleys hide such charming flint and brick villages as South Harting, Bury and Alfriston. "On the Downs the mind becomes more aerial," wrote naturalist W.H. Hudson in 1900. "Standing on one great green hill and looking across vast intervening hollows to other round heights and hills beyond and far away, I can almost realise the sensation of being other than I am – that in a little while I shall lift great heron-like wings and fly..."

Today you can enjoy such aerial sensations by tramping the South Downs Way, a well-marked National Trail that runs 106 miles west from Eastbourne to Winchester.

Opposite: Modern-day pilgrims outside Christchurch Gate, which leads to Canterbury Cathedral

Canterbury Cathedral – a place of pilgrimage through the centuries

CANTERBURY

Canterbury was a famous place long before Geoffrey Chaucer set his merry band of travelers storytelling in *The Canterbury Tales* as they rode on a pilgrimage from London. St. Augustine based himself here after his arrival on the Kentish coast to convert Britons to Christianity in AD 597, and by the time of Thomas à Becket's martyrdom in

December 1170 Canterbury had become the country's major religious center.

It was the murder of Archbishop Becket in his own cathedral, however, that catapulted Canterbury to the top of the list of pilgrimage destinations. Much remains of the medieval city that grew up catering to the millions of penitents who came each year to pray at the saint's shrine. The centerpiece of Canterbury is the cathedral, where any visit to the city should start. The church in which Becket was killed was a Norman building, and some of it still stands incorporated in the cathedral that emerged over centuries from periods of rebuilding, stimulated by Canterbury's success as a pilgrimage destination.

The first place everyone wants to see is The Martyrdom, a commemorative slab in the northwest transept marking the spot where four knights cut Becket down on what they thought were the orders of King Henry II. The question of whether church or king should wield ultimate authority had caused an angry division between Henry and his erstwhile friend, but the king probably did not expect to be taken literally when he gave vent to the notorious outburst: "Of all the cowards who eat my bread, are there none to rid me of this turbulent priest?" Henry came humbly to Canterbury to be scourged in expiation of the murder; within three years Becket had been canonized as a saint, and the flood of pilgrimages began.

Becket's spirit pervades this great church, mother cathedral of the Church of England. The martyr's golden shrine in Trinity Chapel at the east end, an object of wonder to pilgrims all through the Middle Ages, was destroyed during the Reformation in 1538; now the Altar of Sword Point stands on the spot. The knees of penitents during the four centuries of medieval pilgrimage wore hollows in the stone steps; their shadows flicker in the light of candles still kept burning in the chapel. Among the scenes depicted in Canterbury Cathedral's renowned display of stained glass are images of pilgrimages and portrayals of miraculous healing performed by the saint. Don't miss the beautiful fan vaulting in the Lady Chapel and the Chapter House, and be sure to descend into the Norman-era crypt to see the 12th-century wall paintings and the lively faces and foliage carved on the columns.

You can stroll around the medieval center of Canterbury city in an hour. Good portions of the old city walls still stand, along with one of the original 14th-century gates. Streets like Mercery Lane are lined with attractive houses, some half-timbered and crouching with

age, with glimpses over their red-tiled roofs of the four rocket pinnacles on the cathedral's central Bell Harry Tower.

A couple of exhibitions worth visiting are the excellent Museum of Canterbury, housed in the 900-year-old Poor Priests' Hospital on Stour Street, and the smell-and-sound-enhanced tableaux recounting five of Chaucer's tales at The Canterbury Tales, in the former St. Margaret's Church.

✚ E2

Tourist information ✉ 12–13 Sun Street, Buttermarket ☎ 01227 378100; www.canterbury.co.uk

Cathedral ✉ 11 The Precincts ☎ 01227 762862 🕐 Mon.–Sat. 9–6:30, Sun. 12:30–2:30 and 4:30–5:30,

The Canterbury Tales exhibition is ever popular

mid-Feb to late Oct.; Mon.–Sat. 9–5, Sun. 12:30–2:30 and 4:30–5:30, rest of year 🅿 $$

Museum of Canterbury ✉ Stour Street ☎ 01227 475202 🕐 Mon.–Sat. 10:30–5, Sun. 1:30–5, Jun.–Sep.; Mon.–Sat. 10:30–5, rest of year. Last admission 1 hour before closing 🅿 $$ ℹ Guided tours

The Canterbury Tales ✉ St. Margaret's Church, St. Margaret's Street ☎ 01227 479227 🕐 Daily 9–5, Jul.–Aug.; 10–5, Mar.–Jun. and Sep.–Oct.; 10–4:30, rest of year 🍴 Café 🅿 $$$

Southeast England

Southeast England

A cannon at Deal Castle to deter French invaders

CHATHAM, THE HISTORIC DOCKYARD

The naval base at Chatham, on the River Medway in north Kent, was founded by King Henry VIII. With its sheltered dockyard and easy access to the Thames estuary and the open sea, it became a mainstay of Britain's naval strength. The dockyards closed in 1984 and then took a new lease on life as The Historic Dockyard, Chatham. Here are historic ships, gigantic timber-roofed shipbuilding sheds, a ropery, sawmills that produced sailing ship timbers, a museum of shipbuilding, displays of knotting and other nautical crafts, and one of the world's best collections of old ships' figureheads. In the "Wooden Walls" gallery you can experience the hardships of an 18th-century dockyards apprentice.

French prisoners of war had a forced hand in carrying out extensions to grim Fort Amherst just upriver, during the Napoleonic Wars of the early 19th century. You can take a guided tour through the spooky labyrinth of tunnels.

✚ D3

Dockyard ✉ Dock Road, Chatham ☎ 01634 823800 or 01634 823807 (recorded information) ⏰ Daily 10–6 (or dusk if earlier), mid-Feb. through Oct. 31 💷 $$$
Fort Amherst ✉ Dock Road, Chatham ☎ 01634 847747 ⏰ Daily 10:30–5, Aug. and school holidays (last admission at 4); Sat.–Sun. 10:30–5, mid-Feb. to late Jul. and in Sep.; Sat.–Sun. 10–4, in Nov. Last entry at 2, mid-Feb through Easter and in Nov. 💷 $$
🚹 Guided tours at 11:15 and 2:30, Easter–Sep. 30

CHICHESTER

Brighton (see page 51) may be the flashiest town in Sussex, but Chichester, 30 miles west, is the county's true heart, an elegant small Georgian city at the feet of the South Downs with a notable cathedral at its core. The slim spire of Chichester Cathedral, 277 feet tall, is a landmark for many miles around. The nave is tall, too, giving the whole building an uplifting atmosphere. The furnishings range from medieval (12th-century stone sculpture in the choir, including Lazarus being raised from the dead) to modern (a John Piper tapestry, large paintings by Graham Sutherland, beautiful Marc Chagall stained glass); all seem somehow to achieve harmony.

If you want to see how a well-to-do Sussex wine merchant lived in the Georgian era, take a look at Pallant House on North Pallant Street, just off East Street. For a glimpse of how similarly affluent people lived 1,500 years ago, Fishbourne Roman Palace, just 2 miles west of Chichester, will get your imagination going. Here are superb mosaic floors, bathrooms and an original heating system, all beautifully displayed after this early Roman villa was excavated in the 1960s.

Ancient buildings evoke a medieval skyline at Sandwich, one of the Cinque Ports

⊞ B1
Tourist information ✉ 29A South Street ☎ 01243 775888; www.visitchichester.org
Chichester Cathedral ✉ West Street ☎ 01243 782595 🕐 Daily 7:15–7, Easter–Sep. 30; 7:15–6, rest of year 🍽 Restaurant 🖐 Donation ($) suggested 🚹 Guided tours at 11:15 and 2:30, Easter–Sep. 30
Pallant House Gallery ✉ 9 North Pallant Street ☎ 01243 774557 🕐 Closed for refurbishment 🍽 Restaurant 🖐 $$ 🚹 Guided tours
Fishbourne Roman Palace ⊞ B1 ✉ Salthill Road, Fishbourne ☎ 01243 785859 🕐 Daily 10–6, in Aug.; daily 10–5, Mar.–Jul. and Sep.–Oct.; daily 10–4, in Feb and Nov. 1 to mid-Dec.; Sat.–Sun. 10–4, rest of year 🖐 $$ 🚹 Guided tours twice daily Sat.–Sun. and during school holidays

DEAL

With the French coast only 30 miles away, the little town of Deal became prosperous during the 18th century as much through smuggling as fishing. These days Deal makes a charming place to stroll through or along its pebbly beach. On the seafront stands Deal Castle, built by King Henry VIII against the threat of French invasion, designed in the shape of a Tudor rose.

Deal's sister town of Sandwich was medieval England's foremost port before the harbor silted up. This is another delightful town to explore, with its ancient town walls, crooked old alleyways and timber-framed merchants' houses.
⊞ E2
Tourist information ✉ Landmark Centre, High Street ☎ 01304 369576; www.whitecliffscountry.org.uk
Sandwich ⊞ E2
Tourist information ✉ Guildhall ☎ 01304 613565; www.whitecliffscountry.org.uk 🕐 Open Apr.–Sep. only

Blodwit and Fledwit

Medieval Sandwich was one of the Cinque Ports; the others were Hastings, Dover, Romney and Hythe. In return for defending the coast, the five towns were granted exemption from certain taxes and rights over fishing and wrecks. These privileges had resonant titles such as blodwit and fledwit, sac and sol, infangentheof and outfangentheof, pillory, mundbryce and tumbril.

The Old High Street at Folkestone

DOVER

Dover is the chief cross-Channel ferry port on this stretch of the south coast, but its real claim to fame and interest for the visitor resides in its Norman castle, which stands high on cliffs honeycombed and burrowed into tunnels by French prisoners during the Napoleonic Wars. Dover Castle – known in medieval times as the "Key to England," because whoever held it controlled entry to the country – is one of the most interesting in England to explore, with its still-standing Roman lighthouse, restored Saxon Church of St. Mary-in-Castro, and keep with walls 20 feet thick.

The castle saw dramatic action during both world wars. During World War I it was the base from which anti-submarine strategies were carried out, and in World War II it was the headquarters from which the evacuation of the retreating British army from Dunkirk was co-ordinated. This was an extraordinary venture during which 338,226 men were brought home in a ramshackle flotilla consisting of every conceivable kind of vessel pressed or volunteered into service.

Hellfire Corner, so named because it endured intense wartime bombardment, is a section of cliff tunnels refurbished to give a vivid idea of conditions in an emergency hospital and in the co-ordinating nerve center. The cliffs themselves, ramparts of solid chalk hundreds of feet high, are famous as the White Cliffs of Dover. The Dover Museum and Bronze Age Boat Gallery traces the development of the town and port and has a Bronze Age-era boat, said to be the world's oldest seagoing vessel.

A footpath runs west for 7 miles along the edge of the cliffs, a breezy walk that brings you to the Channel Tunnel rail entrance near the old Victorian resort and port town of Folkestone.

✚ E2

Tourist information ✉ Old Town Gaol, Biggin Street ☎ 01304 205108; www.whitecliffscountry.org.uk
Dover Castle ✉ Castle Hill ☎ 01304 211067
🕐 Daily 9:30–6:30, Jul.–Aug.; daily 10–6, Apr.–Jun. and in Sep.; daily 10–4, Feb.–Mar.; Thu.–Mon. 10–4, rest of year 🍴 Restaurants 🎫 $$$
Dover Museum and Bronze Age Boat Gallery
✉ Market Square ☎ 01304 201066 🕐 Mon.–Sat. 10–5:30, Sun. 2–5:30, Apr.–Sep.; Mon.–Sat. 10–5:30, rest of year 🎫 $$
Folkestone ✚ E2
Tourist information ✉ Harbour Street ☎ 01303 258594; www.kents-garden-coast.co.uk

THE NEW FOREST

The 150 square miles of the New Forest, on the Hampshire/Dorset border form the oldest royal hunting forest in the country. Poachers of the king's deer in olden days could expect no mercy; even to disturb the animals carried a penalty of blinding, while to kill one meant death. It was not only poachers who died in the New Forest: King William Rufus, son of William the Conqueror, had his reign cut short by an arrow while hunting here in August 1100.

Do not rush through the New Forest. This ancient patchwork of woodland, farms, wetlands and heaths looks, and works, as the countryside used to before the mechanization of farming. Everyone loves the free-roaming New Forest ponies, and there are fallow deer, butterflies, foxes, birds and wildflowers to delight any amateur naturalist.

At Beaulieu (pronounced "Bew-ly"), in the southeast corner of the forest, is the splendid car collection at the National Motor Museum. Here you can see over 250 vintage vehicles, from gleaming Rolls-Royces to monsters that have broken the world land speed record. Down at the mouth of the Beaulieu River is the charming small village of Buckler's Hard, with a remarkably wide main street. Oak timber from the New Forest was stacked in the street to season, in the days of the Napoleonic Wars 200 years ago when Buckler's Hard was an important shipbuilding center. The village's excellent Maritime Museum tells the tale.

🔒 A1

Tourist Information ✉ New Street, Lymington, Hampshire ☎ 01590 689000; www.thenewforest.co.uk

New Forest Museum ✉ Main Car Park, High Street, Lyndhurst, Hampshire ☎ 023 8028 3444 🕐 Daily 10–5 (also 5–6, in Aug.) 🖐 $$

National Motor Museum 🔒 A1 ✉ Beaulieu, Brockenhurst, Hampshire ☎ 01590 612345 🕐 Daily 10–6, May–Oct.; 10–5, rest of year 🍴 Café 🖐 $$$

Maritime Museum 🔒 A1 ✉ Buckler's Hard, Beaulieu, Hampshire ☎ 01590 616203 🕐 Daily 10:30–5, Easter–Sep. 30; 11–4, rest of year. Last entry 40 minutes before closing 🍴 Restaurant 🖐 $$

Southeast England

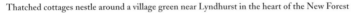

Thatched cottages nestle around a village green near Lyndhurst in the heart of the New Forest

Romantic Hever Castle, which holds memories of two of King Henry VIII's six wives

DRIVE: GREAT HOUSES AND CASTLES OF KENT

Distance: 90 miles

This drive from Tunbridge Wells passes eight of the fine castles and houses for which Kent is famous. It would take two days if you visited all of them.

From Tunbridge Wells proceed north on A26; at B2176 turn left, passing through Bidborough to Penshurst.

Here you will find one of Britain's oldest country houses, Penshurst Place, built in 1341 for a well-to-do merchant, Sir John de Pulteney. The vast Baron's Hall under its splendid wooden roof still exists. Constructed at a time when architecture was based on religious buildings, the original window frames and doorways seem more ecclesiastical than secular. Sir Philip Sidney, ideal of all that was manly and courtly in Elizabethan England, was born here in 1554.

Continue north on B2176. Turn left onto B2027 past the Penshurst railroad station, then left again after 1 mile.

Chiddingstone Castle is a 17th-century country house retaining plenty of its original fixtures and fittings, with others added in 1805 when the house was turned into a mock-Gothic castle.

Continue on the local road for 3 miles to Hever Castle.

Moated and handsome, Hever Castle is set in wide grounds. King Henry VIII dallied with the youthful Anne Boleyn here, and later gave Hever Castle to his fourth wife, Anne of Cleves. Essentially a Tudor house, it was splendidly refurbished early in the 20th century when American newspaper magnate William Waldorf Astor bought it on a whim.

Continue 2 miles eastward, pass through the village of Leigh and go under A21. Immediately turn left, proceed 1 mile, turn left again on B245 (which becomes A225) to the outskirts of Sevenoaks.

Turn right into the extensive grounds of Knole, one of Britain's finest country houses. Begun in 1456 by Archbishop Thomas Bourchier, it was altered by King Henry VIII and remodeled in 1603 in the Jacobean style it exhibits today. Inside, the plasterwork, furniture, great hall and staircase are all surviving Jacobean features. The Sackville family owned Knole since Tudor times; Vita Sackville-West (see Sissinghurst opposite) was born here.

From Sevenoaks proceed east on A25, then south at Ightham Common on local roads through Ivy Hatch to Ightham Mote.

The moated medieval manor house of Ightham Mote, cloaked in woodland, is a beauty. The picturesque half-timbered building dates from the 14th century.

Backtrack to A25 and join M26/M20 at Wrotham Heath. Proceed east 10 miles to A20 beyond Maidstone.

Leeds Castle lies just off the road. Described by some as the most beautiful castle in England, a Norman foundation improved on by subsequent generations rises like a fairy-tale castle from a lake. The 500-acre grounds were landscaped by Capability Brown.

B2163 and A274 take you south to Headcorn. Turn left and proceed on local roads through Frittenden to Sissinghurst.

At Sissinghurst, Vita Sackville-West and her husband, Sir Harold Nicolson – founding members of the intellectual London-based Bloomsbury Group – created a garden in the 1930s around the ruin of a Tudor castle. In the gate tower stands the printing press off which Virginia Woolf ran the first few copies of T.S. Eliot's *The Waste Land* in 1922.

A262 leads west to Goudhurst. Just southwest near Lamberhurst is Scotney Castle.

Scotney Castle is a 14th-century island fortress in picturesque ruin amid wonderful grounds that were landscaped in the 19th century.

A21 and then A264 return you to Tunbridge Wells.

Penshurst Place ✉ Penshurst, Tonbridge ☎ 01892 870307 🕐 House: daily noon–4, early Mar.–late Oct. Grounds: daily 10:30–6, late Mar.–late Oct.; Sat.–Sun. 10:30–6, early Mar.–late Mar. 🍴 Café 🏠 House and grounds $$$; grounds only $$

Chiddingstone Castle ✉ Edenbridge ☎ 01892 870347 🕐 Thu. 2–5, Sun. 11:30–5, Jun.–Sep. 🍴 Café 🏠 $$

Hever Castle ✉ Hever, Edenbridge ☎ 01732 865224 🕐 Daily 11–6 (house opens at noon), Apr.–Oct.; 11–4 (house opens at noon), in Mar. and Nov. 🍴 Restaurants 🏠 $$$

Knole ✉ Sevenoaks ☎ 01732 462100 🕐 House: Wed.–Sun. noon–4, late Mar.–late Oct. Garden: Wed. 11–4, late Mar.–late Oct. Deer park: daily dawn–dusk 🍴 Café 🏠 House $$$; Garden $$; Deer park free

Ightham Mote ✉ Ivy Hatch, Sevenoaks ☎ 01732 810378 🕐 Wed.–Fri. and Sun.–Mon. 10–5:30 (house opens at 10:30), Mar.1 –late Oct. Estate: daily dawn–dusk 🍴 Restaurant 🏠 $$$; Estate free

Leeds Castle ✉ Maidstone ☎ 01622 765400 🕐 Daily 10–5:30, Mar.–Oct.; 10–3:30, rest of year 🍴 Restaurants 🏠 $$$

Sissinghurst Castle Garden ✉ Sissinghurst ☎ 01508 710700 🕐 Mon.–Tue. and Fri. 11–6:30 (or dusk if earlier), Sat.–Sun. 10–6:30 (or dusk if earlier), late Mar.–late Oct. Woodland and lake walks: daily dawn–dusk 🍴 Restaurant 🏠 $$$

Scotney Castle Garden and Estate ✉ Lamberhurst, Tunbridge Wells ☎ 01892 891081 🕐 Garden: Wed.–Sun. 11–6, late Mar.–early Nov.; Sat.–Sun. 11–6, early Mar. to mid-Mar. Castle: Wed.–Sun. 11–6, May 1–late Sep. Estate: daily dawn–dusk 🏠 $$; Estate free

Horatio Nelson's flagship, HMS *Victory*

PORTSMOUTH

"Pompey," as generations of naval men have nicknamed Portsmouth, has been the home port of the British Royal Navy for hundreds of years. Because of this, much of the city was bombed flat during World War II. However, its naval spirit is fittingly preserved around the waterfront and its historic atmosphere at Portsmouth Historic Dockyard.

The docks themselves are of the size and complexity of a town. There you will find miles of Victorian and Georgian naval architecture – storehouses, offices, barracks, chapels, houses – a Royal Naval Museum, and some classic veteran ships. Queen of the docks is HMS *Victory*, the battleship in which Lord Nelson flew his flag and in whose cockpit he died of wounds at the moment of victory during the Battle of Trafalgar on October 21, 1805. The *Victory* is a popular attraction, so there may be a long wait before your guided tour. Nearby is the Tudor battleship *Mary Rose*, sunk on her maiden voyage in 1545 and raised from Portsmouth Harbor with dazzling technical skill in 1982. The displays include the military and everyday objects that sank with her and were preserved in the harbor mud. The world's first iron-hulled armored battleship, HMS *Warrior* (1860) is also docked here.

In the D-Day Museum at Southsea, a few minutes' drive away, you can admire the amazing Overlord Embroidery, a tapestry 272 feet long, which depicts the epic events of the Allied landings in Normandy in June 1944.

⊞ B1
Tourist information ⊠ The Hard and Clarence Esplanade, Southsea ☎ 02392 826722; www.portsmouthand.co.uk
Portsmouth Historic Dockyard ⊠ Entry through Victory Gate (corner of Queen Street and The Hard) ☎ 02392 861512 🕐 Daily 10–5:30, Apr.–Oct.; 10–5, rest of year 🍴 Restaurant and cafés 🎟 Free entrance to site. Museum $$; $$$ for each ship, *Mary Rose*, HMS *Warrior* and HMS *Victory*
D-Day Museum ⊞ B1 ⊠ Clarence Esplanade, Southsea ☎ 02392 827261 🕐 Daily 10–5:30, Apr.–Oct.; 10–5, rest of year. Last admission 30 minutes before closing 🎟 $$

The timber-framed Mermaid Inn at Rye

ROCHESTER AND CHARLES DICKENS

Rochester stands on the River Medway at the heart of the countryside immortalized in the novels of Charles Dickens – most notably in *Great Expectations*. The city's Norman cathedral has a beautiful west doorway; in the choir are stalls and a wall painting 800 years old. Rochester Castle also is Norman, and has a giant keep.

Dickens knew Rochester well as a boy, and settled at nearby Gads Hill from 1856 until his death in 1870. *Great Expectations* sites around town include the wood-framed building on High Street, which Dickens used as the shop of self-important Uncle Pumblechook, and Restoration House on Crow Lane, which became the cobwebbed mausoleum of Satis House, Miss Havisham's abode. Close to High Street, this is a fine example of a city mansion and is beautifully furnished and decorated.

Northwest of Rochester, St. Mary's Church at Higham is the marsh church where Pip first met the convict Magwitch. In the village of Chalk, a pretty white wood-slatted cottage on the A225 road is Joe Gargery's forge, where Pip lived as a boy. At Cobham, the Dickens connections are Pickwickian. At the Leather Bottle Inn Mr. Pickwick dissuaded Mr. Tupman from suicide.

D3

Tourist information ✉ 95 High Street ☎ 01634 843666; www.medway.gov.uk/tourism

Rochester Castle ✉ The Esplanade ☎ 01634 402276 ⏰ Daily 10–6, Apr.–Sep.; 10–4, rest of year ♿ \$\$

RYE

The charming town of Rye, for centuries the haunt of smugglers, huddles on a hilltop on the East Sussex/Kent border. Streets are crooked, cobbled and steep; houses are whitewashed, red-tiled and hung with flower baskets. A view over Rye can be enjoyed from St. Mary's Church tower.

American novelist Henry James settled at Lamb House on West Street in 1898; he lived here until his death in 1916.

D2

Tourist information ✉ Strand Quay ☎ 01797 226696; www.rye.uk.co

Lamb House ✉ West Street ☎ 01372 453401 ⏰ Wed. and Sat. 2–6, early Apr.–early Nov.; closed rest of year ♿ \$\$

St. Mary's Church ✉ Church Square ☎ 01797 222430 ⏰ Daily 9–7, Jun.–Aug.; 9–6:30, in May and Sep.; 9–6, in Apr. and Oct.; 9–5, in Mar. and Nov.; 9–4:30, in Feb.; 9–4, rest of year ♿ Free (tower \$\$)

Above: The 13th-century Round Table that hangs in the Great Hall at Winchester

Right: Massive Winchester Cathedral stands at the heart of the historic city

WINCHESTER

Winchester, the capital of the Saxon kingdom of Wessex before the Norman Conquest, is a delightful and historic cathedral city set among meadows along the River Itchen in central Hampshire. Winchester Cathedral is the longest medieval building in the world (556 feet), and one of the most impressive. Memorials include those to Jane Austen; to King Alfred's old teacher, St. Swithun; and to King William Rufus, son of William the Conqueror. Rufus was shot dead by his companion's arrow while out hunting in the New Forest – the arrowhead itself was found within his remains inside his tomb in Victorian times. There are some beautiful early 14th-century misericords (wood carvings on the underside of tip-up seats) in the choir, fine stained-glass windows and a notable library of medieval books.

In the Great Hall on Castle Avenue, the only surviving part of Winchester Castle, hangs the famous 13th-century Round Table. Romantics insist this is the very one magically created by the wizard Merlin for King Arthur, in order to avoid squabbles over seating precedence among the knights at Camelot.

Walk through the meadows along the riverbank to the 12th-century Hospital of St. Cross and knock at the Porter's Lodge to receive the traditional "wayfarer's dole" of ale and bread. Or stop for a drink or a bite to eat at the Wykeham Arms on Kingsgate Street, a gem of an inn (see page 259).

Eighteen miles northeast of Winchester, just off the A31, lies the little village of Chawton, where Jane Austen lived during her most prolific years from 1809 until her death in 1817.

You can visit her plain, square redbrick house, now a museum, and see the rooms where she wrote some of her best-loved novels, including as *Mansfield Park, Emma* and *Persuasion*.

➕ A2

Tourist information ✉ Guildhall, Broadway ☎ 01962 840500; www.visitwinchester.gov.uk

Cathedral ✉ The Close ☎ 01962 857200 🕐 Daily 8:30–6, except during services. Visitor Center daily 9:30–5 🍴 Cathedral Refectory 💷 $$ donation requested

Great Hall ✉ Castle Avenue ☎ 01962 846476 🕐 Daily 10–5 💷 Free

Hospital of St. Cross ✉ St. Cross Road ☎ 01962 851375 🕐 Mon.–Sat. 9:30–5, Apr.–Oct.; 9:30–4:30, rest of year 🍴 Café in summer 💷 $$

Jane Austen's House ✉ Chawton, near Alton ☎ 01420 83262 🕐 Daily 11–4, Mar.–Nov.; Sat.–Sun. 11–4, rest of year 💷 $$

Dedicated Diver

Built on water meadows, the mighty cathedral in Winchester has an uneasy relationship with the water table. Between 1906 and 1911, diver Bill Walker worked beneath the cathedral in darkness and cold water in order to prevent the rotting Norman timber foundations from sinking into the mud, inserting some 1 million bricks and sacks of concrete under the collapsing east end of the church.

A statue of Walker stands in the crypt, in the company of St. Swithun and William of Wykeham.

Windsor Castle dominates the scene above the Thames

WINDSOR

Windsor and royalty – they go together like ham and eggs. This town beside the Thames west of London and its castle have been the monarch's out-of-town residence for almost a thousand years. If the Royal Standard is flying from the flagpole, the monarch is in residence.

The town itself is an attractive place for a stroll, but it is the castle that draws visitors. Its distinctive Round Tower, originally of wood, was rebuilt in stone along with the rest of the castle in the mid-12th century and forms the eye-catching focus of an ensemble laid out in two wards, or great walled enclosures. Many rooms have been extensively restored after a disastrous fire in 1992.

The Upper Ward contains the State Apartments, full of opulent furnishings and art treasures. Here you can view Queen Mary's Dolls' House, designed at a scale of 1:12 by master architect Sir Edwin Lutyens in 1923. The water runs, the electric lights work, even the books and pictures are genuine miniatures. In the Lower Ward is the glorious Tudor masterpiece of St. George's Chapel, where 10 monarchs lie buried – among them the decapitated King Charles I and the much-married King Henry VIII.

South of the castle stretches Windsor Great Park, 5,000 acres of beautifully tended and thickly wooded parkland crisscrossed with footpaths open to the public. Walking here among ancient trees and across wide grassland spaces is a pleasure. North of Windsor across the Thames is the village of Eton, home of Britain's most exclusive and prestigious private school, Eton College. The school was founded in 1440, and has since accrued a roll call of distinguished former pupils, including 18 prime ministers and countless other luminaries of public, commercial and military life. Its pupils wear a distinctive uniform of top hat and tails on public occasions. There is a museum dedicated to the school, and a Gothic chapel with fine frescoes, beautifully restored and dating from the late 15th century.

🚌 B3

Tourist information ✉ 24 High Street ☎ 01753 743900; www.windsor.gov.uk

Windsor Castle ✉ Castle Hill ☎ 01753 831118 🕐 Daily 9:45–5:15, Mar.–Oct.; 9:45–4:15, rest of year. Last admission 1 hour, 15 minutes before closing. Opening times subject to change at short notice 💳 $$$ ℹ️ Chapel closed on Sun., except for services

Eton College ✉ Eton High Street ☎ 01753 671177 🕐 Daily 10:30–4:30, late Mar. to mid-Apr. and early Jul.–early Sep.; 2–4:30, mid-Apr. to early Jul. and early Sep.–early Oct. 💳 $$

ALONG THE PILGRIM'S WAY

The Pilgrim's Way along the heights of the North Downs was followed by millions of penitent (and not so penitent) travelers riding or tramping to the tomb of St. Thomas à Becket at Canterbury (see page 52).

The pilgrims – Geoffrey Chaucer's *Canterbury Tales* yarn-spinners among them – traveled this way for the best part of four centuries, coming northeast from Winchester to bypass London along the high chalk downs of Surrey before sloping off into Kent toward Canterbury. The route they followed was far older than the cult of the martyred saint, however. For thousands of years this old road was used as a thoroughfare connecting the great Stone and Bronze Age centers on Salisbury Plain to the Kentish coast and its short sea connections to the Continent.

Today a National Trail, the 141-mile North Downs Way footpath, keeps company with the Pilgrim's Way for much of its length along the downs south of London. In some places it is damp and chalky; in others it is floored with clay or earth. The modern North Downs Way path runs through beautiful woodland, pastoral hillsides and fields, generally keeping to the crest of the ridge and offering spectacular views. The original route tends to be lower: Ancient travelers preferred to journey above the dangers of the valley floor but below the skyline, where their silhouettes would give them away. Huge yews, juniper and holly trees lie along its course. With its fairly gentle undulations, the North Downs Way provides dozens of opportunities for invigorating walks.

Some of the small villages around the Pilgrim's Way in Surrey are particularly attractive. Shere, 6 miles east of Guildford along the A25 Dorking Road, has charming 16th- and 17th-century village houses overhanging the streets, a Tudor pub and the really exceptional Norman parish church of St. James. The central tower is early Norman, as is the south

A walker passes the parish church in Shere

doorway, and the oaken door it holds is 800 years old. Some of the stained glass dates back to the 14th century and features symbols of the Four Evangelists. There are some fine late medieval memorial brasses and a display of early 19th-century woodwind instruments, used in church orchestras of that era. Also on view is a beautiful little bronze statuette of the Virgin and Baby Jesus, only the height of a thumb – probably an icon mislaid by some Canterbury-bound penitent on the Pilgrim's Way, which runs along the downs above the village.

From here it is a very fine 7-mile walk eastward to Box Hill, an escarpment owned by the National Trust with a wonderful view to the south. You can return to Shere by train.

Footpaths and bridleways are clearly marked on the Ordnance Survey maps covering this region (see page 12), and by using these you can devise your own journeys.

North Downs Way, A User's Guide, and *North Downs Way*, a booklet describing self-guiding walks along the trail, are both available from bookstores and tourist information centers.

THE WEST COUNTRY

"THROW away your watch and your worries as you travel the rural roads and beautiful holiday coasts of the West Country, Britain's greenest and mellowest region. "

Opposite: Bronze Age stones on Bodmin Moor, with an abandoned Cornish tin mine on the skyline

The West Country

THE WEST COUNTRY

To the British, these are mind's-eye images of the West Country: dairy cattle grazing in sloping green fields, a glass of strong cider on a hot day, thatched cottages clustered around churches of golden stone, seaside vacations on a coast of rocky coves and sandy beaches. The southwestern corner of Britain forms a long peninsula like an outstretched leg, its toe tip dipping into the Atlantic at Land's End in westernmost Cornwall. Plentiful rainfall gives the countryside of the interior a lush appearance, smooth and green. The coast, on the other hand, is famous for its ruggedness and for the wild danger of the seas that have carved it. It is a superb vacation coast, with a handful of big resorts and hundreds of smaller villages and hamlets. Visitors come in their millions during the summer months. But in the less crowded spring and fall you can see the small coast villages at their best, while lovers of furious seas and storms can get all the thrills they want on the cliffs and headlands of the West Country in winter.

Farmers and Fishermen

Fishing and farming are this intensely rural region's mainstays, together with tourism. West Country people have a well-earned reputation for being easy-going and mild-mannered, with little use for bureaucracy and a lot of time for conversation and bucolic leg-pulling. They are not always in such good humor when their village centers and local services are overrun with busloads of tourists – "grockles" or "emmets," as they call them – on holiday weekends. Since any visitor to the West Country is bound to spend a lot of time exploring, strolling or driving around the glorious countryside, the observance of such common courtesies as shutting field gates behind you when out walking, or negotiating the narrow, high-banked lanes at appropriate speeds, is always appreciated.

County of Antiquities

Five counties make up the West Country – Wiltshire, Somerset, Dorset, Devon and Cornwall. Wiltshire, in the northeastern part of the region, is founded on chalk. At the heart of this county lies the great grassland of Salisbury Plain, much of it untouched by modern intensive farming methods and thus providing a haven for wildlife. In southern Wiltshire is the handsome small city of Salisbury; its famous 404-foot cathedral spire is the tallest in Britain.

Prehistoric antiquities are scattered thickly around and across Salisbury Plain; most celebrated among them are the double stone circle enclosing Avebury village, the man-made hill of Silbury, and Britain's best-known stone monument, the enigmatic structure of Stonehenge.

From Mendip to the Moors

Of the West Country's five counties, Somerset has the greatest variety of landscape. The soft golden limestone of the Cotswold Hills rolls south to meet the harder grey limestone of the Mendip Hills. Here lies the beautiful and popular city of Bath, rightly admired for its matchless Georgian architecture. Much of central Somerset is a low-lying tableland known as the Levels, with the legend-encrusted knoll of Glastonbury Tor rising from the

The West Country

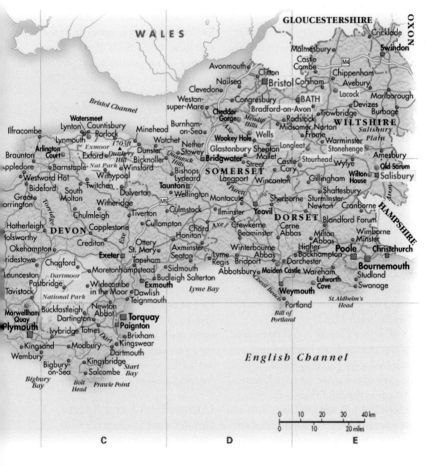

Thomas Hardy: Literary hero of Dorset

surrounding flat country. The muddy tidal waters of the wide Severn Estuary wash its western flank.

Farther west, Somerset rises into the moorland hills of Quantock and Exmoor, while to the south it rolls into Dorset on a tide of deep gold stone, known as "hamstone" after Ham Hill, where it is quarried.

Thomas Hardy's Wessex

The chalk makes its final flourish in the southern half of Dorset, producing fine billowing downs. The limestone here is a hard but easily worked white rock called "freestone," forming some spectacular cliffs. It provided stone for the rebuilding of London through the centuries, which has resulted in some harshly scarred land.

The Dorset beaches and coves west of Bournemouth are beautiful, and there are some stunning fishing villages to explore and pause for refreshment, including East and West Lulworth, which lead to Lulworth Cove. This area of coast is thick with fossils, although visitors are discouraged from removing

them. The chalk pokes through the green fields here and there – notably on the hillside above Cerne Abbas, where a rampantly phallic giant (his knobby club is not the only weapon he raises) lies as clearly outlined as when he was cut out of the turf 2,000 or more years ago (see page 87).

Dorset's literary hero is Thomas Hardy; you can visit the cottage where he was born, the house in which he lived the last 43 years of his life, the churchyard where his heart is buried and scenes from all his great Wessex novels – from *Under The Greenwood Tree* to *The Mayor of Casterbridge*.

Easygoing Devon

Dorset's westerly neighbor is Devon, often thought of as the "softest" of the five West Country counties. It is true that these rolling fields of red earth are clothed in rich grassland, and produce champion thick cream, beef and milk. It's also true that the "combes," or valleys, of mid-Devon, west Exmoor and the South Hams are wonderful places for easy, sheltered idling.

But Devon has a wild enough coastline, and plenty of harsh drama in the dark granite moorland of Dartmoor, with its mists and moody weather. This is a historic seafaring county, with the famous ports of Dartmouth and Plymouth, and full-of-character fishing towns such as Brixham and Appledore. Sailing in small boats is extremely popular. Picturesque coast settlements like Combe Martin and Clovelly in the north and Sidmouth and Salcombe in the south have become holiday havens, but there also are plenty of out-of-the-way places where tourists don't throng.

Cornwall – A Land Apart

Granite-boned Cornwall, Britain's southwesternmost county, really is a land

Fishing boats in the natural harbor at Mevagissey in Cornwall

apart, a harsh place to make a living on a small farm or in small-scale fishing. Yet it possesses much weatherbeaten beauty and a sandy, cliff-walled coast. The Southwest Coast Path runs along the coast's perimeter, offering unforgettable views and steep up-and-down climbing. Swimming is superb, from beaches as expansive as the 3-mile Penhale Sands to the most diminutive cove. Inland there are more delights: prehistoric standing stones and tombs, hidden villages and sheltered valleys where subtropical gardens flourish.

But it is that tremendous, storm-carved coast, narrowing to the final full stop of Land's End, that really holds the spirit of this dramatic outpost of the West Country.

West Country Flavors

The West Country boasts some culinary delights, too. This is the home of the traditional cream tea: scones served with strawberry preserves and piled high with "clotted" cream (thick Devonshire or Cornish cream), accompanied by a pot of tea. Fudge also is excellent here, and ice cream is some of the best you'll find anywhere in Britain. Of course, seafood abounds in every town and village along the coast, from traditional fish and chip shops to top-quality, elegant fish restaurants. Try the local cheeses, such as cheddar and Somerset brie. The county of Somerset also is famed for its cider, an alcoholic drink made from apples. Stop at a village pub for a "ploughman's lunch" consisting of cheese, pickles and fresh bread, and taste a glass of the locally brewed ale.

Artists and Craftsmen

If you're looking for local crafts, St. Ives in south Cornwall is a magnet for artists and craftspeople. Don't miss Dartington Glass, on the Dartingon Hall estate, located just outside the Devon town of Totnes. A wonderful collection of glass, pottery and wood-carvings made by local craftsmen is sold here. The hall itself is home to an arts and education center, set up by American millionairess Dorothy Elmhirst in 1925. There is a program of movies, concerts, plays and talks here during the summer months.

BATH

Bath is Britain's best-known small city, famous worldwide for the glories of its Georgian architecture. The beauty of Bath is framed to perfection in its setting among seven hills where the Cotswold and Mendip ranges converge. It is the underlying oolitic limestone, a building material with a lovely gold finish, that lends Bath its unique good looks.

The city was fortunate to experience its 18th-century apex of prosperity as a spa resort at a time when British architecture also had reached a high point in the clean lines and symmetry of the Palladian style. In Bath it attained its peak, transforming an unremarkable market town into the supreme example of classic Georgian elegance.

From Leper King to Social Dictator

Bath's hot springs have had a long history of healing. Back in the mists of mythology it was the leper Bladud, a king turned swineherd, who discovered their powers in about 850 BC, when he noticed his pigs wallowing in the mud to ease their itchy skins. Following their example, Bladud found himself cured. When the Romans arrived in about AD 44 they built magnificent baths here. Their spa city of Aquae Sulis flourished.

But it was the 18th-century preoccupation with "taking the waters" that really launched Bath into prosperity as Britain's premier spa town. The social side of this activity, far more important to most spa-goers than anything medical, had its origin here under the benign dictatorship of

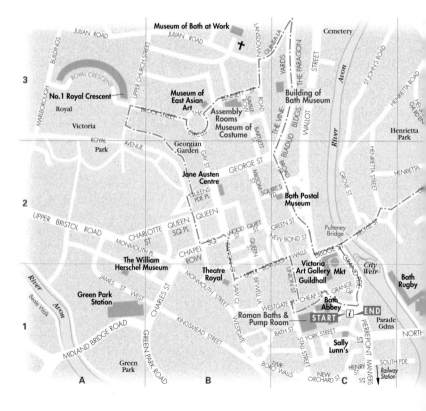

Beau Nash (see page 77). Soon the rich, famous and marriageable all came flocking.

Delectable Small City

With its graceful crescents, squares and terraces rising and falling across the hillsides, Bath is an absolute must for any visitor to Britain. The city has controlled modern development effectively and retains a low-rise, human scale. As one of the country's most delectable small cities, it has attracted a well-heeled and sophisticated set of inhabitants. Bath is an ideal size for strolling, although it can become horribly crowded on holidays and sunny weekends.

Lay of the Land

Orienting yourself in the city is not difficult. Bath Abbey, the Pump Room and the Roman Baths all lie flanking Abbey Courtyard, the lively focus of the city. East of here the River Avon flows south under Pulteney Bridge, then curves west by the railroad station to mark the southern boundary of the city center. North of Abbey Courtyard a warren of little streets gives way to Milsom Street, where you'll find Bath's most exclusive shops. North of Milsom Street are the Assembly Rooms; to the west lies the elegant Circus, and then the incomparable sweep of Royal Crescent at the crown of Royal Victoria Park.

Park and Ride

If you bring a car into the city center, park in the big Charlotte Street parking lot. For on-street parking you'll need to buy a permit from a shop showing the permit sign, and display it in your vehicle. Alternatively, leave your car at one of the big "park and ride" lots on the city's outskirts, and make your way to and from the center aboard one of the frequent special buses.

The historic sections of Bath can be seen comfortably in an hour or so. The train station at the south end of

The West Country

American Museum
ROAD
A36
BATHWICK STREET
BECKFORD
ROAD
Sydney Gardens
DANIEL STREET
SYDNEY PL
Holburne Museum of Art
SUTTON ST
SYDNEY
MEWS
STREET
SYDNEY WHARF
POULTENEY EDWARD ST
VANE ST
PULTENEY MEWS
Cricket Ground
PULTENEY
BATHWICK
Kennet & Avon Canal
Recreation Ground
PO
SYDNEY BUILDINGS
HILL
Sports & Leisure Centre
Magistrates Court
ROAD
N
PARADE
ROAD
BATH
Bath Cricket Club
0   100   200 metres
0   100   200 yards
D
E

Festival!

The Bath International Music Festival brings the cream of the musical world to Bath for two weeks in late May and early June. Classical, traditional, jazz, ethnic and blues music mix with art shows and theater, both formally staged and erupting in the street. This is Bath at its liveliest, and also at its most crowded.

Reserving accommodations and tickets well in advance is essential.

For information and tickets contact the Bath Festivals Box Office (☎ 01225 463362).

The West Country

Manvers Street is a 10-minute walk from Abbey Courtyard.

Try a Bath Bun

Bath has plenty of elegant restaurants, as you'd imagine, and many intimate bistros that come and go in the wink of an eye. Lunch at the Moon and Sixpence, in secluded Shire's Yard off Milsom Street, or satisfy your hunger with a giant Sally Lunn Bun, baked according to a secret recipe, at Sally Lunn's in North Parade Passage. Take tea in the Pump Room to the tinklings of a piano trio; it will wash away the bad-egg flavor of the healing hot-spring mineral waters.

Shopping and Street Entertainment

Shoppers will find upscale establishments – antiques, jewelry, clothes – on and around Milsom Street, and cheaper and more cheerful shops in the narrow warrens around Abbey Courtyard.

For entertainment, the 18th-century Theatre Royal on Barton Street has been superbly restored and offers plays, concerts and tours of the interior. There are lunchtime music recitals in the abbey.

A weekly listings publication, *Venue*, gives full reviews and details of what's on in Bath and Bristol. Entertainment, often baffling or hilarious, is provided by street performers around Abbey Courtyard. It comes free, but a coin in the hat is appreciated.

Cycling the Railroad

If the crowds of sightseers are getting you down, why not try a bicycle ride along the Bristol and Bath Railway Path (for information, ☎ 0117 922 4325)? The long-abandoned railroad track between Bath and Bristol has been turned into a 12.5-mile bicycle path through attractive countryside, perfect for a bike ride or a country hike.

Bicycles can be rented from Bath and Dundas Canal Company (☎ 01225 722292).

ESSENTIAL INFORMATION

BATH TOURISM TOURIST INFORMATION
✉ Abbey Chambers, Abbey Churchyard
☎ 09067 112000 (there is a charge of 50p per minute for this call); www.visitbath.co.uk

URBAN TRANSPORTATION
Bath Spa railroad station is on Dorchester Street, a 10-minute walk from the city center. There are regular train services to London's Paddington station and other destinations in Britain. For information and reservations, ☎ 08457 484950. National Express operates regular long-distance buses from Bath to London Victoria station (some services stop at Heathrow airport).

For information, ☎ 08705 808080. Buses in and around Bath start from the bus station on Dorchester Street; ☎ 08706 082608 for details. The Bath Shopmobility Centre (✉ 4 Railway Street, ☎ 01225 481744) rents out wheelchairs and scooters.

AIRPORT INFORMATION
Bristol International Airport is located 15 miles southwest of the city center (✉ Lulsgate, near Bristol, ☎ 08701 212747; www.bristolairport.co.uk). There is a regular bus link to central Bristol for onward connections to Bath.

CLIMATE – Average highs and lows

JAN.	FEB.	MAR.	APR.	MAY	JUN.	JUL.	AUG.	SEP.	OCT.	NOV.	DEC.
8°C	7°C	10°C	12°C	17°C	19°C	22°C	21°C	18°C	14°C	11°C	8°C
46°F	45°F	50°F	54°F	63°F	66°F	72°F	70°F	64°F	57°F	52°F	46°F
3°C	3°C	5°C	6°C	9°C	12°C	14°C	14°C	12°C	9°C	6°C	4°C
37°F	37°F	41°F	43°F	48°F	54°F	57°F	57°F	54°F	48°F	43°F	39°F

Georgian splendor: The Theatre Royal in Bath

BATH SIGHTS

Key to symbols

➕ map coordinates refer to the Bath map on pages 72–73; sights below are highlighted in yellow on the map.

✉ address or location ☎ telephone number
🕐 opening times 🍴 restaurant on site or nearby
🍷 admission charge: $$$ more than £6, $$ £2–£6, $ less than £2 ℹ️ information

AMERICAN MUSEUM

At 19th-century Claverton Manor on Bath's eastern fringe is the American Museum, not a trivial Disneyfication but a very well thought-out series of reconstructed interiors. They show the development of American home life from early pioneer rooms, with their plain handmade tables and chairs, through elegant 18th-century woodwork that compares favorably with some of the best that Bath itself offers, to overblown 19th-century grandeur.

There are displays of venerable quilts, needlework samplers, severe Shaker furniture, indigenous American art, and cookies baked on the premises to original pioneer recipes.

The grounds of Claverton Manor, which include an arboretum, are beautiful; don't miss the painstaking reconstruction of the garden George Washington tended at Mount Vernon.

➕ E3 ✉ Claverton Manor, Claverton Down
☎ 01225 460503 🕐 Tue.–Sat. noon–5:30 (museum: 2–5:30), late Mar.–late Oct. (also Mon., in Aug.); check with museum for hours mid-Nov. to mid-Dec. 🍴 Café
🍷 $$$ (grounds only $$)

ASSEMBLY ROOMS

The Assembly Rooms were built in 1769–71 by John Wood the Younger at the height of his fame. His father, John Wood the Elder, died in 1754. The Woods were the most illustrious architects of their day, and between them they shaped the face and character of Georgian Bath.

The Assembly Rooms were the hub of the social whirl. They consist of three harmonious rooms – a lofty, chandelier-lit ballroom, a tearoom and a galleried, octagonal card room. Here all fashionable Bath would gather in the evenings to play cards, dance and size up potential lovers.

Downstairs in the basement is the Museum of Costume, a display of dress that spans 400 years from Elizabethan hand embroidery to modern synthetics. Some of the 18th- and 19th-century gowns are breathtakingly beautiful examples of master craftsmanship.

Assembly Rooms and Museum of Costume

➕ B3 ✉ Bennett Street ☎ 01225 477785 🕐 Daily 11–6, Mar.–Oct.; 11–5, rest of year 🍷 Assembly Rooms free; museum $$ ℹ️ Audio-guided tours of museum

BUILDING OF BATH MUSEUM

If you want to appreciate what you see as you stroll around the city, you can't do better than to start with a visit to the Building of Bath Museum, housed in an old chapel behind the beautiful curved terrace of the Paragon. It relates the story of how the medieval wool-trading town of Bath was transformed into the most chic and elegant resort in Britain, chiefly at the hands of the talented father and son team of John Wood the Elder and John Wood the Younger.

    Fascinating details include the nitty-gritty of plumbing, heating and lighting in the Georgian era, and how the Woods designed and built the most harmonious and carefully balanced facades for their terraces and crescents while leaving the body of each house to the design whim of individual builders. Disciplined order without, multiple eccentricities within: Bath stands as a metaphor of sorts for the British personality.

🚌 C3 ✉ The Countess of Huntingdon's Chapel, The Vineyards ☎ 01225 333895 🕐 Tue.–Sun. 10:30–5, mid-Feb. through Nov. 30 🎟 $$

PULTENEY BRIDGE

This is one of the finest town bridges in Britain, built across the River Avon to link the city center with the east bank of the river, which Sir William Pulteney intended to develop into a grand residential area in the 1770s. He called in the eminent Scottish architect Robert Adam, who finished the bridge in 1774 in splendid Italianate style with two rows of flanking shops and dwellings supported above a terraced weir on three great round arches. Pulteney's funds would not stretch to accomplishing his ambitious plans, however. Today he is remembered through Great Pulteney Street, the one wide and handsome thoroughfare that was completed on the east bank, and by the remarkably beautiful bridge that carries his name.
🚌 C2

The Italianate-style Pulteney Bridge, set above a terraced weir

A 19th-century street scene re-created in the Museum of Costume, housed in the Assembly Rooms

The West Country

LIFE IN GEORGIAN BATH

A morning stroll along Milsom Street, with one eye on the shop windows and the other on one's fellow strollers, followed by a glass or two of warm mineral water fresh from the hot springs in the Pump Room to the genteel sound of a string ensemble. In the afternoon, a saunter along the gravel walks of the park to display one's new walking gown, before tea and civilized conversation in the drawing room of one of Mr. Wood's elegant new houses. And at night, perhaps a game of cards and a few dances in the Assembly Rooms, with the chance to indulge in a little flirtation while – of course – observing the strict rules of etiquette laid down by that arbiter of good taste, Beau Nash...

When Richard "Beau" Nash became Bath's Master of Ceremonies in 1704, he wisely saw that when strangers gathered together for pleasure in one small town – lords and ladies, prosperous farmers, London swells, local traders all cheek by jowl – they needed some agreed-on rules to abide by if they were all to get along

amicably. Most of Beau Nash's rules were common-sense recommendations: no swearing or smoking in public places, no wearing of swords, and entertainments such as balls to end by 11 o'clock at night.

There was plenty of gossip in Georgian Bath, and plenty of ritual. This was Britain's premier spa, unsurpassed for elegance and gentility. Good manners and an obligation to conform were imposed on all who stayed at Bath. Visitors came under the civilizing influence of superb architecture, plenty of green spaces and a social life with unwritten but very definite rules.

The daily round of family walks, taking the waters in the Pump Room, courting in the public gardens, tea drinking, visiting, and card parties and dances in the Assembly Rooms suited almost everyone. It was easy and pleasant to follow the set course, which gave maximum opportunity to flirt, make and break alliances, secure one's next step up the social ladder – and, of course, exchange endless gossip.

The Roman Baths in the shadow of Bath Abbey

PUMP ROOM

The cornerstone of the Georgian social scene in Bath faces the south side of Abbey Churchyard and was built in the 1790s in Classical style. Five glasses of mineral water a day was the recommended dose for liverish Georgians, although once you have choked down a single glass of the warm spring water (which tastes like a combination of iron, soap and long-boiled eggs) you may wonder how anyone completed the course. The water wells up from the King's Spring and jets down through spouts from a handsome stone samovar.

A statue of Beau Nash, Bath Master of Ceremonies in the early 18th century and ultimate arbiter on all matters of taste and behavior, keeps a stern eye on water drinkers, cream tea guzzlers and lunchers as they browse and quaff to the tinkling of the Pump Room's music ensemble. Through a side window you can look down to view the sacred spring of the Romano-Celtic goddess Sulis-Minerva, steaming and bubbling in the King's Bath.

✚ C1 ✉ Stall Street ☎ 01225 444477 ⊙ Daily 9:30–5:30, Jun.–Aug.; 9:30–4:30, rest of year
🍽 Restaurant 🎟 Free

ROMAN BATHS

This is one of Britain's prime Roman relics, and a very popular tourist attraction. If crowds in narrow spaces bother you, don't visit on summer holiday weekends.

These splendid baths, 2,000 years old, were built around AD 65–75, shortly after the Romans came to Britain. With their departure in the early fifth century the baths gradually fell into disrepair and lay all but forgotten 20 feet beneath the ground until excavation brought their secrets to light beginning in 1878.

The elevated terrace with statues of Roman heroes that overlooks the Great Bath is a Victorian addition, but the baths themselves are much as the Romans would have known them. The lead-lined Great Bath itself, measuring 39 feet by 78 feet, is fed with steamy green water at a constant 115 degrees Fahrenheit from the largest of the three hot springs, welling

The Royal Crescent: Georgian Bath's supremely elegant sweep of houses

from 10,000 feet deep in the earth. The stumps of masonry that surround it would have supported columns holding up a great barrel roof, but nowadays the bath lies open to the sky.

In chambers off the Great Bath are other baths and rooms – a little circular bath for medicinal bathing, a sauna whose heat came from a well-stocked furnace blowing hot air beneath the floor, and the handsome Norman structure known as the King's Bath, built above a Roman reservoir around 1100.

In locating their baths at the hot springs, the Romans made the wise diplomatic decision to incorporate the locally worshiped water goddess Sulis in their dedication of the spring, as well as to their own Minerva. The Baths Museum holds fascinating relics from the temple to Sulis-Minerva that the Romans built here, chief among them a beautiful gilt bronze head of the goddess and a giant stone sculpture of the head of a Gorgon-like god, wildly bearded and fiercely staring, that once adorned the pediment of the temple.
✚ C1 ✉ Stall Street ☎ 01225 477785 🕐 Daily 9 a.m.–10 p.m., Jul.– Aug.; 9–6, Mar.–Jun. and Sep.–Oct.; 9:30–5:30, rest of year. 🍴 Restaurant in Pump Room 💰 $$$ (includes audio guide)

ROYAL CRESCENT

This wonderful sweep of 30 houses bends in a superbly graceful golden bow of stone, closing the vista at the upper end of Royal Victoria Park. John Wood the Younger, its architect, was not quite 40 when building started in 1767. The crescent, completed in 1774, is the finest in Britain and the jewel in the crown of Wood's achievements. It was a hollow triumph, literally, since Wood followed his general practice in constructing only the facade: Speculative builders completed the dwellings as they saw fit. Number One is open to the public, and its elegant refurbished reception rooms and cheerful basement kitchen give a good idea of the lifestyle of visitors to Bath, who would rent houses like this one for the season.
No. 1 Royal Crescent ✚ A3 ✉ Royal Crescent ☎ 01225 428126 🕐 Tue.–Sun. 10:30–5, mid-Feb. to late Oct.; Tue.–Sun. 10:30–4, late Oct.–late Nov. and first two weekends in Dec. 💰 $$

The courtyard outside Bath Abbey: Starting point for a walk around the city

WALK: AROUND BATH

Refer to route marked on city map on pages 72–73

Bath is just the right size for a stroll, and this walk passes a great number of interesting sites and museums – if you want to visit some of these the excursion could easily last all day.

Start at the Tourist Information Centre on Abbey Courtyard.

Stop to explore the adjacent Bath Abbey, a beautiful Tudor church, completed in 1499 by Bishop Oliver King after a dream about angels. The abbey is fan-vaulted inside, with a wonderful collection of memorials and inscriptions from Bath's Georgian heyday.

Walk across Abbey Courtyard past the Pump Room, turn right onto Union Street, then left along Upper Borough Walls to Barton Street.

To your left is the Theatre Royal, a beautiful late Georgian building dating from 1805, plush and well gilded within. There are regular plays performed here, and it is the hub of the city's cultural life.

Turn right to reach elegant Queen Square. This beautiful square was built in 1728–34 by John Wood the Elder.

Walk up the left-hand side of the square, cross to the steps and continue ahead beside fine stone gateposts to the Gravel Walk, which curves to the left through Royal Victoria Park. This 57-acre park is a good place to stop for refreshments in the café.

Veer to the right to reach Royal Crescent. Leave the east end of the crescent along Brock Street to get to The Circus. There are 30 houses, as in the Royal Crescent; but these form a stylish circle with a frieze of magical symbols, instruments and animals.

Continue along Bennett Street (the Assembly Rooms and Museum of Costume are to your right), turn left onto Lansdown Road (enjoy the views behind you), and right down Guinea Lane, before turning right onto the Paragon. Jane Austen lived at No. 1 in 1801; the Building of Bath Museum (see page 76) is in the Old Chapel halfway along the curve.

Continue past the traffic lights and then down Broad Street. Have a pint at the Saracen's Head pub on the left, the oldest pub in Bath.

Bear right at the bottom of Broad Street, then left over graceful Pulteney Bridge and along Argyle Street, and then the grand avenue of Great Pulteney Street to the Holburne Museum of Art in Sydney Gardens, at the end of the street. The museum contains fine furniture, silver and paintings.

Return over Pulteney Bridge, turning left along the river. Grand Parade and Grange Grove bring you back to the tourist office. Try a restorative Bath Bun at Sally Lunn's (Bath's oldest house), to your left in North Parade Passage.

Bath Abbey ✚ C1 ✉ Abbey Courtyard ☎ 01225 422462 ◷ Mon.–Sat. 9–6, Sun. 1–2:30 and 4:30–6, Easter–late Oct.; Mon.–Sat. 9–4:30, Sun. 1–2:30, rest of year ⓤ Free (suggested donation $$)

Holburne Museum of Art ✚ D3 ✉ Great Pulteney Street ☎ 01225 466669 ◷ Tue.–Sat. 10–5, Sun. 11–5, mid-Jan. to mid-Dec. 🍴 Café ⓤ $$

Jane Austen Centre ✚ B2 ✉ 40 Gay Street ☎ 01225 443000 ◷ Mon.–Sat. 10–5:30, Sun. 10:30–5:30 ⓤ $$

Jane Austen's City

Jane Austen enjoyed several family vacations in Bath before coming to live at No. 1, The Paragon, in 1801. The Austens moved around the city from house to house during the next five years, and Jane could observe the rituals, pleasures and pretensions of Bath society. She wrote about them in the novels *Persuasion* and *Northanger Abbey*. In *Persuasion*, for example, Anne Elliot meets Captain Wentworth in the octagonal room of the Assembly Rooms; she is both intrigued and repelled by her creepy cousin Mr. Elliot in the concert room, and declines to accompany him to the tearoom.

Austen enthusiasts can imagine themselves present at Miss Elliot's side as they explore these same rooms today, and guided walking tours, which begin at the Jane Austen Centre, will help visitors follow in Jane's footsteps around Bath.

The West Country

A waitress serves Bath Buns at Sally Lunn's tea house

The West Country

The Clifton Suspension Bridge spanning the Avon at Bristol

REGIONAL SIGHTS

Key to symbols

⊞ map coordinates refer to the West Country map on pages 68–69; sights below are highlighted in yellow on the map.

⊠ address or location ☎ telephone number
☉ opening times 🍴 restaurant on site or nearby
🍷 admission charge: $$$ more than £6, $$ £2–£6,
$ less than £2 ⓘ information

BRADFORD-ON-AVON

Set beside the River Avon in northwest Wiltshire, Bradford-on-Avon is a charming stone-built town whose name derives from "broad ford." Its crooked streets, lined with old wool merchants' houses, rise to fine hillside churches, and down along the river are handsome water mills. West of town on the south bank of the Avon is a splendid 14th-century tithe barn at Barton Farm, built to store the tenth of the tenants' produce that was due to the local abbey. Afternoon tea is served here. Toward the town center north of the river is a complete Saxon church, a great rarity. It functioned as a school and then a cottage, until recognized for what it was in the 1850s by the Vicar of Bradford.

⊞ E3

Tourist information ⊠ 50 St. Margaret's Street ☎ 01225 865797; www.bradfordonavon.co.uk

BRISTOL

Bristol is the West Country's biggest and liveliest city, where hilly streets slope down past Georgian sea captains' houses to a center with attractive harbors and old docks. Here you will find the Watershed and Arnolfini art centers; both display art exhibitions and show regular movies.

Attractions include the beautiful 14th-century church of St. Mary Redcliffe, which has an imposing spire. The elegant Regency district of Clifton perches on the lip of the Avon Gorge beside engineer Isambard Kingdom Brunel's handsome Clifton Suspension Bridge, finished in 1864. In the dock area sits Brunel's great pioneering steamship, the SS *Great Britain*, which is nearing the completion of long-term restoration.

Also on the waterfront is At Bristol, an interactive attraction featuring "Wildwalk," "Explore" and a giant IMAX screen.

⊞ D3

Tourist information ⊠ The Annexe, Wildscreen Walk, Harbourside ☎ 09067 112191 (there is a charge of 50p per minute for this call); www.visitbristol.co.uk

SS *Great Britain* ⊠ Great Western Dock, Gas Ferry Road ☎ 0117 926 0680 ☉ Daily 10–5:30, Apr.–Oct.; 10–4:30, rest of year 🍷 $$$

At Bristol ⊠ Anchor Road ☎ 08453 451235 ☉ Daily 10–6 🍷 $$

Opposite: The view over Exmoor from Dunkery Beacon in Somerset

Slabs of stone were assembled in prehistoric times to form Clapper Bridge at Postbridge on Dartmoor

DEVONSHIRE MOORS

The county of Devon, broad and deep, possesses two national parks, Exmoor and Dartmoor. The two moors are twins, but entirely dissimilar ones. Exmoor is the more northerly, with the Devon/Somerset border dividing it into an eastern and a western half (two-thirds of the park actually lies within Somerset). The moor is founded on red sandstone from which it takes a light and open character, with rounded hills blanketed with grass or heather. Deep wooded valleys known as "combes" fall to a varied coast – sandy surfing beaches and dunes along the Atlantic-facing west, pebbly shores under high sloping cliffs on the north coast that looks at Wales across the Bristol Channel.

Arlington Court, between Barnstaple and Lynton, is a fine house worth visiting for its collection of objets d'art, woodland walks and horse carriage rides. Your Exmoor reading list must include R.D. Blackmore's famous romantic novel *Lorna Doone* (1869), set on the moor.

Dartmoor, in southern Devon, is associated with the classic Sherlock Holmes tale *The Hound of the Baskervilles* (1902). In this exciting fable, Sir Arthur Conan Doyle caught the grimly fascinating atmosphere of Dartmoor and its misty granite moorland. The standing stones and beehive huts of primitive pre-Roman moor dwellers only serve to highlight the lonely aspect of the landscape in these parts.

Southeast of Dartmoor is historic Dartmouth, tucked away up the Dart estuary. This is a good base for exploring the area; it's packed with restaurants and inns, and pretty shops to browse.

In the southwest, beyond Plymouth, is Morwellham Quay, a former copper-mining village on the River Tamar. Here visitors can explore a reconstructed mine, a Victorian schoolroom, draft horse stables and other places in the company of guides dressed in period costume.

Exmoor National Park Authority ✚ C2–C3 ✉ Exmoor House, Dulverton, Somerset ☎ 01398 323665; www.exmoor-nationalpark.gov.uk

Dartmoor National Park ✚ C1–C2 ✉ Parke, Haytor Road, Bovey Tracey, Newton Abbot, Devon ☎ 01626 832093; www.dartmoor-npa.gov.uk

Arlington Court ✚ C3 ✉ Arlington, near Barnstaple, Devon ☎ 01271 850296 🕐 Sun.–Fri. 10:30–5 (house opens at 11), late Mar.–late Oct.; garden only also Sat. 10:30–5, Jul.–Aug. 🍴 Café 🎫 $$$; garden only $$

Combstone Tor: A granite outcrop on Dartmoor

Buildings huddle around the harbor at Fowey

The West Country

THE END OF ENGLAND

At the southwest tip of the West Country peninsula lies Cornwall, a county famous for its superb seaside – sandy beaches, beautiful granite cliffs and coves, fishing villages piled into clefts in the cliffs. The south coast is rich in fishing villages such as Polperro, Mevagissey, Portloe, Portscatho and Mousehole, and in delightfully old-fashioned gray stone towns – Fowey, St. Mawes, Falmouth – sheltered in deep-cut estuaries.

The local specialty: Cornish pasties

In the north the settlements, like the coastline itself, tend to be less cozy. Here you will find windswept villages such as Zennor, which has a fascinating church. The biggest and cheeriest resort is Newquay, set behind fine beaches. The atmospheric little town of Padstow has an internationally renowned waterside fish restaurant and hosts a ceremonial "Mayday" of madness on May 1, when thousands pack the narrow streets to cheer a comical prancing horse ("Obby Oss") through town in a festive parade originally designed to celebrate the defeat of winter.

The mild Cornish climate encourages the growth of beautiful gardens. Many feature exotic species, such as the gardens in Trelissick and Trewithen, both near Truro, and farther west at Glendurgan and Trengwainton. Other delights include the causeway island of St. Michael's Mount, near Penzance, crowned with a magnificent house and church; and beautiful St. Ives, on the north coast. An artists' haunt, St. Ives also contains the Barbara Hepworth Museum, where you can stroll through the gardens among works by this celebrated sculptress. And don't forget the historic sites inland, chief among them the tiny Iron Age houses and gardens preserved at Chysauster, near St. Ives.

Trelissick Garden ✚ A1 ✉ Feock, near Truro ☎ 01872 862090 ◷ Daily 10:30–5:30, mid-Feb to late Oct.; daily 11–4, late Oct.–Dec. 25; Tue.–Sun. noon–4, Dec.26–Jan. 1; Thu.– Sun. 11–4, rest of year. Closes at dusk if earlier 🍴 Restaurant and café 🎫 $$

St. Michael's Mount ✚ A1 ✉ Marazion, near Penzance ☎ 01736 710507 ◷ Sun.–Fri. 10:30–5:30, late Mar.–Oct. 31; variable hours rest of year (call for details). Last admission 45 minutes before closing 🍴 Restaurant and café 🎫 $$

Barbara Hepworth Museum ✚ A1 ✉ Barnoon Hill, St. Ives ☎ 01736 796226 ◷ Daily 10–5:30, Mar.–Oct.; Tue.–Sun. 10–4:30, rest of year. Garden closes at 4:30 (or dusk if earlier) 🎫 $$

Chysauster Ancient Village ✚ A1 ✉ B3311, near Gulval ☎ 07831 757934 ◷ Daily 10–6, Jul.–Aug.; 10–5, Apr.–Jun. and in Sep.; 10–4, in Oct. 🎫 $$

Charming thatched cottages near the parish church in Milton Abbas

DRIVE: THOMAS HARDY'S DORSET

Distance: 80 miles

It is a fact that novelist-poet Thomas Hardy still dominates the psyche of his native county. Dorset's most celebrated son, Hardy captured the landscape, people and moody character of the county. This 80-mile drive around Hardy-related sites takes in many of the most interesting and beautiful parts of Dorset. Note: The names that Hardy gave to various locations in his famous "Wessex novels" appear in parentheses after their real names.

Start in Dorchester ("Casterbridge"). Dorchester is the county capital, and the excellent Dorset County Museum preserves the manuscript of *The Mayor of Casterbridge* and a mock-up of Hardy's study. Don't forget to visit Max Gate on Alington Avenue, which Hardy designed and lived in from 1885 until his death in 1928.

Proceed east along A35 to Stinsford. Hardy's heart lies buried in the churchyard in the grave of his first wife, Emma. The National Trust maintains Hardy's Cottage, the author's birthplace, at nearby Higher Bockhampton. Bockhampton and Stinsford together form "Mellstock" in *Under the Greenwood Tree.*

Continue east along A35.
Puddletown ("Weatherbury" in *Far From The Madding Crowd*) is where Hardy's grandfather played bass viol in the local church. A little farther on is Tolpuddle, from where the six iconic "Tolpuddle Martyrs" were transported to Australia in 1834 for membership in a "secret society." They were, in fact, poor farm laborers trying to form a union. The pine-covered heathland south of the road hereabouts is "Egdon Heath," whose dour presence brooded over *The Return of the Native.*

Continue along A35.
The village of Bere Regis ("Kingsbere-sub-Greenhill" in *Tess of the D'Urbervilles*) has a Saxon church with tombs and a stained-glass lion crest of the Turbervilles, the name that inspired Hardy.

Go north on minor roads via Milborne St. Andrew to Milton Abbas.
This charming thatched estate village used to be next to the Gothic mansion and 14th-century abbey church of Milton Abbey a mile away, but in 1780 the house's owner, the Earl of Dorchester, had the village removed and rebuilt so that it did not intrude on his view.

From Milton Abbas proceed west to Hilton, then north to Bulbarrow Hill.
Standing atop the hill are the ramparts of the

Iron Age hill fort of Rawlsbury Camp; to the northwest is Blackmoor Vale.

> *From Bulbarrow Hill, work your way southwest on minor roads past Melcombe Bingham, Cheselbourne and Piddletrenthide to Cerne Abbas.*

A 2,000-year-old chalk outline on the hillside depicts a priapic giant wielding his club.

> *Continue southwest via Sydling St. Nicholas to Maiden Newton, then turn northwest along the ridgeback A356. After 6 miles, bear left to Beaminster.*

Look out for the beautiful medieval church.

> *A3066 brings you south to the town of Bridport; from here, B3157 ambles southeast near the coast of Lyme Bay.*

Here stretches pebbly Chesil Beach, which shelters brackish Fleet lagoon. Abbotsbury is a charming golden stone village; its attractions include the longest tithe barn in Britain, a subtropical garden and a Swannery, where swans have been kept since monastic days.

> *From Abbotsbury minor roads bring you back to Dorchester by way of the enormous and spectacular Iron Age ramparted hill fort of Maiden Castle.*

The Swannery at Abbotsbury

Dorchester ✚ D2
Tourist information ✉ 11 Antelope Walk ☎ 01305 267992; www.westdorset-dc.gov.uk
Dorset County Museum ✉ High West Street, Dorchester ☎ 01305 262735 ⏰ Daily 10–5,

Jul.–Sep.; Mon.–Sat. 10–5, rest of year ✋ $$
Max Gate ✉ Alington Avenue, Dorchester ☎ 01305 262538 ⏰ Sun.–Mon. and Wed. 2–5, late Mar.– late Sep. ✋ $$
Hardy's Cottage ✚ E2 ✉ Higher Bockhampton, near Dorchester ☎ 01305 262366 ⏰ Thu.–Mon. 11–5 or dusk if earlier, mid-Mar. through Oct. 31 ✋ $$
Abbotsbury Swannery ✉ New Barn Road, Abbotsbury ☎ 01305 871858 ⏰ Daily 10–6, mid-Mar. to early Oct.; 10–5 early to late Oct. 🍴 Café ✋ $$

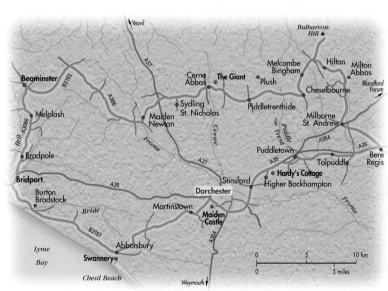

The West Country

The West Country

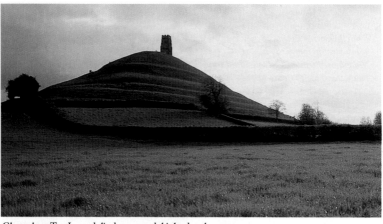

Glastonbury Tor: Legends lie deep around this landmark

GLASTONBURY

Few places in the British Isles have attracted so many legends as Glastonbury. This unremarkable town sits amid the flat peat moors of the Somerset Levels, which some say is the location of the Vale of Avalon, legendary valley of healing and rebirth. Above the town rises Glastonbury Tor, a dragon-shaped mass of rock crowned with a landmark church tower. Legend recalls how King Arthur, mortally wounded after his final battle, was rowed to Glastonbury in a dark barge to be healed. The king is said to lie with his knights under the Tor in an enchanted sleep, from which all will be roused to save England from some calamity yet to come.

The last abbot in England, Richard Whytyng, was hanged on the Tor in 1539; his abbey and monastery buildings lie in scenic ruin in the center of Glastonbury. The 14th-century, octagonal-roofed Abbot's Kitchen still stands, and the former monastic tithe barn now houses the excellent Somerset Rural Life Museum. Here, displays illustrate traditional rural ways of life such as cider- and cheese-making, thatching and farming.

Another legend tells how Joseph of Arimathea brought Jesus Christ to Glastonbury as a boy. In about AD 60, as a very old man, Joseph allegedly returned to Avalon with either the chalice used at the Last Supper, or the holy cup that caught the blood from Christ's side at the

Crucifixion. On Wearyall Hill just outside town you can see the Glastonbury Thorn tree, a type of hawthorn found in England said to bloom twice a year, at Easter and Christmastide. Legends also say the tree is a cutting from a hawthorn tree that took root from the spot where Joseph of Arimathea struck his staff – made of a piece of Christ's cross – into the ground. Below the Tor lies the Chalice Well, a garden from which healing water springs; some say the holy cup lies buried here.

✚ D3

Tourist information ✉ The Tribunal, 9 High Street ☎ 01458 832954; www.glastonburytic.co.uk
Glastonbury Abbey ✉ Magdalene Street ☎ 01458 832267 🕓 Daily 9–6, Jun.–Aug.; 9:30–6, Apr.–May and in Sep.; 9:30–5:30, in Mar.; 9:30–5, in Oct.; 10–5, in Feb.; 9:30–4:30, in Nov.; 10–4:30, rest of year 🎫 $$
Somerset Rural Life Museum ✉ Abbey Farm, Chilkwell Street ☎ 01458 831197 🕓 Tue.–Fri. 10–5, Sat.–Sun. 2–6, Apr.–Oct.; Tue.–Sat. 10–5, rest of year 🍴 Café 🎫 Free

LACOCK

Lacock is an 18th-century gray stone village that has been preserved by the National Trust, the country's conservation organization. Among the Elizabethan, Jacobean and Georgian houses stands the 15th-century Church of St. Cyriac, with the vast, elaborate tomb of Sir William Sharington, who bought up the estate in 1539. As old as the church is the village pub, The Sign of the Angel (see page 261).

Longleat House stands on grounds designed by Capability Brown

Lacock's chief attraction, however, is the abbey complex, which has many medieval features. Here you can see reproductions of a smeary photograph of the bay window in the abbey's south gallery, snapped in 1835 by William Henry Fox Talbot and claimed to be the first photograph ever taken. An exhibition in the Photographic Museum, located in the barn near the entrance, tells the story.

✠ E3
Lacock Abbey ✉ High Street ☎ 01249 730227
🕐 Wed.–Mon. 1–5:30, mid-Mar. to late Oct. 🎟 $$$
Photographic Museum ✉ High Street ☎ 01249 730176 🕐 Daily 11–5:30, late Feb.–late Oct.
🍴 Restaurants and cafés in the village 🎟 $$

LONGLEAT

Sir John Thynne bought an Augustinian priory, Abbey Farm and more than 900 acres of land in 1541 on which he then built the grand Elizabethan mansion of Longleat. Today you can visit the great hall, with its hammerbeam roof, seven libraries containing more than 40,000 books, and an art collection that includes Titian's *Holy Family*. There also are murals painted by the present owner, the 7th Marquess of Bath, who has continued his father's unorthodox approach to tourism. The 6th Marquess was the first homeowner in Britain to open his house to the public on a fully commercial basis, and the first to establish a drive-through wildlife safari park on the Capability Brown-landscaped grounds. Amusement park attractions now dominate the scene.

✠ E3
Longleat ✉ Longleat, Warminster, Wiltshire
☎ 01985 844400 🕐 Safari Park: Mon.–Fri. 10–4, Sat.–Sun. 10–5 (also Mon.–Fri. during summer school holidays), mid-Feb. to early Nov. Other attractions: daily 11–5:30. House: 10–5:30 (tours at 10 and 11), Easter–Sep. 30; 11–3 (guided tours only), rest of year
🍴 Restaurant and café 🎟 $$$

All set for dinner at Longleat

SALISBURY

The symbol, pride and glory of Salisbury is its wonderful cathedral, set beautifully among the meadows of the River Avon in a hollow of the Wiltshire downs. The most famous part of this very famous building is its immense spire, a graceful slim javelin of stone rising 404 feet into the sky. Salisbury Cathedral was completed in less than 40 years (1220–58), a tight timeframe that lent a unity of design and purpose so often lacking in medieval cathedrals that evolved through several centuries.

One of Britain's most agreeable small cities offers far more than one great church. But any visit should start there, at the heart of Salisbury. Stand outside the cathedral, looking up at the tip of the spire with clouds scudding above, and you may feel the whole structure leaning and toppling over you. That seeming illusion is actually real: The foundations of the church go down no more than 6 feet into the soft alluvial soil of the river valley, and the top of the spire leans forward 2 feet.

Statues of saints and kings adorn the ornate west front. Inside the church seems austere, its clustered marble pillars framing the tall emptiness of the nave. A glance upward reveals pillars bowed like bananas under the 6,000-ton weight of tower, spire and roofs, all built of solid stone. The late 13th-century cloisters, the most spacious in Britain in their day, are handsomely vaulted. In the late 13th-century Chapter House are biblical sculptures and one of only four surviving copies of England's seminal Bill of Rights, the 1215 Magna Carta. There is a glorious 13th-century Tree of Jesse in stained glass in the south aisle (installed as the cathedral was built), and a delicate little fan-vaulted Tudor chantry (chapel) in which Masses were sung for the soul of Bishop Edmund Audley.

The cathedral stands at the center of the Close, a tranquil green space of trees and grass surrounded by fine buildings. The Bishop's Palace, the Deanery and the crooked old Wardrobe are all more than 700 years old. Mompesson House, dating from 1701, displays a collection of late 18th-century furniture and furnishings.

Salisbury itself was laid out in a grid pattern in early medieval times, as witnessed by the functional yet evocative

Above: The Palladian bridge at Wilton House
Left: Salisbury Cathedral with it's graceful spire

street names: Fish Row, Salt Lane, Butcher Row. A walk around town will show you the Poultry Cross, where laying birds were sold, and the strange display of a gambler's severed hand in a wall niche at the Haunch of Venison pub on nearby Minster Street. In the Church of St. Thomas carved angels hold up the 15th-century roof, and demons drag down sinners in a vividly painted Day of Judgment mural from Tudor times. There are bookstores and craft stores to explore, and every Tuesday and Saturday a market is held on Market Square. The city also is a lively cultural center for theater and concerts, crowned by the annual Salisbury International Arts Festival for two weeks from late May to mid-June.

Two other notable sights are just outside of town. On the western outskirts stands the splendid baroque Wilton House, re-created by celebrated architect Inigo Jones for the Earl of Pembroke out of the ashes of a previous house, which burned in a fire in 1647. The art treasures inside are impressive (Rembrandt, Breughel, Van Dyck, Poussin, Rubens), and on the grounds is a stylish Palladian bridge. There also is an excellent display about "Tudor kitchens and Victorian laundry," neatly bringing the history of ordinary people to life.

The town of Wilton itself gained world fame for its Wilton and Axminster carpets. You can see them being made using traditional methods at the Wilton Carpet Factory. And you can browse for bargains afterward at the Wilton Shopping Village, set in old factory buildings on the riverside.

North of Salisbury you can climb the ramparts of the Iron Age hillfort of Old Sarum. This was where the Normans first built a cathedral in 1092; a hundred years later, lack of water and space forced the inhabitants down to the river meadows.

E2

Tourist information Fish Row 01722 334956; www.visitsalisbury.com

Cathedral Ladywell, The Close 01722 555120 Mon.–Sat. 7:15–7:15, Sun. 7:15–6:15, Jun.–Aug.; daily 7:15–6:15, rest of year Restaurant $$ donation requested Access may be restricted during concerts and services

Mompesson House The Close 01722 335659 Sat.–Wed. 11–5, late Mar.–late Oct. Café $$; garden only $

Wilton House Wilton 01722 746729 Sun.–Fri. 10:30–5:30, late Mar.–late Oct. (open Sat. on Public Holidays) Café $$$

Wilton Carpet Factory King Street, Wilton 01722 744919 Tue.–Fri. 10–5, late Mar.– late Oct. $$ Tours at 11, 12:30, 2 and 3:30

Wilton Shopping Village Minster Street, Wilton 01722 741211 Mon.–Sat. 9:30–5:30, Sun. 10–4 Restaurant and café Free

Old Sarum Castle Road 01722 335398 Daily 9–6, Jul.–Aug.; 10–5, Apr.–Jun. and in Sep.; 10–4, in Mar. and Oct.; 10–3, rest of year $$

The sun casts its rays through the ancient stones at Stonehenge

STONEHENGE AND PREHISTORIC WILTSHIRE

The chalk downs of Wiltshire teem with prehistoric monuments, the richest collection in Britain. Best known of all is Stonehenge, 10 miles north of Salisbury, a remarkable 5,000-year-old double ring of stones that attracts the fanatical devotion of hippies, archeologists, druids, New Age dreamers and historians. The earliest stones in the structure came from Wales, 200 miles away. The great trilithons, or "doorways," which still stand on the site are built of stones brought here from Marlborough Downs to the north. A great effort of organization, labor and willpower, sporadically rekindled over the centuries, must have been required to transport and erect such enormous slabs of stone. What was the structure actually for? The answer to that question has eluded the investigations of curious minds for many centuries. Some say that Stonehenge is akin to a vast computer, built to calculate the cycle of the seasons: This is perhaps the most likely theory.

A few miles west of Marlborough is Avebury, a village literally surrounded by prehistory. A giant circle 1,400 feet in diameter encloses the settlement with great bulbous stones, around which dark legends have gathered. One of the stones is said to spit smoke if sat on; others roll off for a drink at certain times. Under one was discovered the flattened skeleton of a medieval surgeon-barber, complete with scissors and leather purse, who may have been caught unaware and crushed when the stone was toppled by superstitious locals.

The story of the stones is told in Avebury's excellent Alexander Keiller Museum, maintained by the National Trust. Also here are displays relating to other nearby monuments, including a ceremonial avenue of standing stones; the notable chambered tomb of West Kennet Long Barrow, dating from around 3250 BC; and the enigmatic, flat-topped Silbury Hill, built 130 feet high from chalk blocks that conceal a remarkable interior shaped like a spoked wheel.

Stonehenge ✚ E3

✉ Off A303, near Amesbury, Wiltshire ☎ 08703 331181 ⏰ Daily 9–7, Jun.–Aug.; 9:30–6, mid-Mar. through May 31 and Sep. 1 to mid-Oct.; 9:30–4, rest of year 🍴 Café 💵 $$ (includes tour)

Avebury ✚ E3

Tourist Information ✉ Avebury Chapel Centre, Green Street ☎ 01672 539425; www.kennet.gov.uk

Alexander Keiller Museum ✉ High Street ☎ 01672 539250 ⏰ Daily 10–6, Apr.–Oct.; 10–4, rest of year. Closes at dusk if earlier 🍴 Restaurant 💵 $$

STOURHEAD

Rich banker Henry Hoare built the splendid Palladian mansion of Stourhead, in western Wiltshire, between 1721 and 1725. Wings were added later, and in 1840 a grand portico completed the house. The fine Chippendale furniture was made specifically for the house. Landscape paintings by Nicolas Poussin and Claude Lorrain influenced Hoare's son, Henry Hoare "the Magnificent," when he was laying out gardens, lakes and temples on the grounds. Strolling among the rhododendrons, tulip trees and beeches, venturing into a cave to pay your respects to the sculpture of the Spirit of the River Stour, or visiting the Pantheon or the Temple of the Sun, you'll get an idea of the high style in which the rich and powerful set themselves up in 18th-century England.

✚ E2 ✉ Stourton, near Warminster, Wiltshire ☎ 01747 841152 ⏰ Garden: daily 9–7; house: Fri.–Tue. 11–5, mid-Mar. through Oct. 31. Closes at dusk if earlier 🍴 Restaurant 💵 House or garden $$ (house and garden $$$)

WELLS

The pride of Wells is its magnificent Gothic cathedral, begun in 1180. The twin-towered west facade, with its 300 statues of saints, priests and kings, is considered the finest in Europe. Inside, the daring design of the scissor arch under the central tower strikes many visitors as thoroughly modern, although it was installed nearly seven centuries ago. There is a fine astronomical clock dating from

The scissor arch in Wells Cathedral

1392 with animated knights on horseback who joust as each hour strikes, and a beautiful 14th-century Chapter House.

Also worth seeing in Wells are the moated Bishop's Palace; the 14th-century Vicar's Close, opposite the cathedral (the oldest intact medieval street in Europe); and the Wells Museum alongside it.

The Mendip Hills north of the city are made of limestone riddled with caves; some of the most impressive can be seen on a guided underground walk at Wookey Hole, a couple of miles west.

✚ D3

Tourist Information ✉ Town Hall, Market Place ☎ 01749 672552; www.wells.gov.uk

Cathedral ☎ 01749 674483 ⏰ Daily 7–7, Apr.–Sep.; 7–6, rest of year 🍴 Restaurant 💵 $$ donation requested 🎫 Tours at 10, 11, 1, 2 and 3, Apr.–Oct.

Bishop's Palace ✉ The Close ☎ 01749 678691 ⏰ Mon.–Fri. 10:30–6, Sun. noon–6 (also often open Sat.), Apr.–Oct. 💵 $$

Wookey Hole Caves ✚ D3 ✉ Wookey Hole ☎ 01749 672243 ⏰ Daily 10–5, Apr.–Oct.; 10–4, rest of year. Closed Dec. 20–26 🍴 Café 💵 $$$

EASTERN ENGLAND

*"**E**NORMOUS skies, half-timbered medieval houses, a gently undulating landscape, the finest parish churches in Britain and a coast of lonely beauty – you'll find all of this and more in slow-paced East Anglia."*

Opposite: A half-timbered house in Suffolk with herringbone brickwork

Eastern England

SOUTH YORKSHIRE
M180
Brigg
Grimsby ■ Cleethorpes
Waltham
Gainsborough
Market Rasen
Ludborough
Louth
Mablethorpe
Sutton on Sea
Dunholme
Wragby
Alford
Ulceby
Ingoldmells
■ Lincoln
LINCOLNSHIRE
Horncastle
Waddington
NOTTINGHAMSHIRE
Mareham le Fen
Skegness
Billinghay
Leadenham
Sibsey
Sleaford
Old Leake
Scolt Head Island
Wells-ne-the-s
No
Hunstanton
Boston
The Wash
Burnham Market
Hol Hal
Grantham
Swineshead
Donington
Sutterton
Gedney Drove End
Dersingham
Heacham
Colsterworth
Bourne
Holbeach
Walpole St. Peter
Castle Rising
Sandringham House
Fakenhar
Houghto Hall
NORFO
LEICESTERSHIRE
RUTLAND
Market Deeping
The Fens
Wisbech
King's Lynn
Castle Acre
Oakham
Stamford
Crowland
Guyhirn
Walsoken
Nar
Swaffh
Uppingham
Rutland Water
Burghley House
Thorney
Nene
March
Downham Market
Oxburgh Hall
Watto
Peterborough
Wissey
Mundfo
Ramsey
Chatteris
Ely
Brandon
Grime's Graves
NORTHAMPTONSHIRE
CAMBRIDGESHIRE
Huntingdon
Lakenheath
Mildenhall
Thetford
Ixwort
Brampton
Godmanchester
Wicken Fen
Girton
Anglesey Abbey
Ickworth
Newmarket
Bury Edm
St. Neots
Cambridge
Great Shelford
Olney
Bedford
Wimpole Hall
Sawston
Haverhill
Kentwell Hall
Lave
Milton Keynes
BEDFORDSHIRE
Biggleswade
Royston
Duxford Air Museum
Saffron Walden
Cavendish
Melford Hall
Lo Me
Gainsborough's House
Sud
Buckingham
M1
Woburn Abbey
Letchworth
Baldock
Buntingford
Halstead
Nayle
Claydon House
Leighton Buzzard
Hitchin
A1(M)
M11
Thaxted
Great Dunmow
Braintree
Copfo
Wissir
BUCKS Dunstable
Luton
Stevenage
Knebworth
HERTFORDSHIRE
Bishop's Stortford
Stansted
Coggeshall
Waddesdon Manor
Luton Hoo
Whipsnade
Welwyn Garden City
Hertford
Witham
T
Aylesbury
Tring
Harpenden
ESSEX
Mala
Wendover
Shaw's Corner
St. Albans
Harlow
Chelmsford
Princes Risborough
Hemel Hempstead
Hatfield House
Hoddesdon
Danbury
OXFORDSHIRE
West Wycombe
Milton's Cottage Museum
Watford
M25
Epping
Greensted
Burnham-on-Cro
Crouch
Stonor Park
High Wycombe
Chalfont St. Giles
Barnet
Brentwood
Southend-on-Sea
Marlow
Beaconsfield
GREATER LONDON
Basildon
Canvey Island
M25
Stanford le Hope
Tilbury

A   B   C

EASTERN ENGLAND

England's eastern side is a vast area of country extending from the fringes of London as far north as Yorkshire, defined by a coast as rounded as a rump that stretches south into tatters of creeks and north to a smooth straight line of crumbling low cliffs and marshes. The country's major highways all lie west of this region, as do the big manufacturing cities. In many ways it is England's least "touristy" rural area, a region of small towns and villages rooted in agriculture. The landscape is undramatic, flat in the western part of the district, gently rolling as you travel farther east. It takes time and tuning to appreciate the east of England for what it is: a subtle, slow-paced kind of place where villages, pubs, paths, woods and beaches lie tucked away for the traveler to discover a little off the beaten track.

Undiscovered Delights

The Chiltern Hills, that rampart of beechwood downs that guard London to the northwest, offer a taste of the east in the chalk and flint that underlie them, and in the vast flat claylands of Bedfordshire over which they look. Essex is generally considered as too flat and too built-up to be of interest, but that is only really true of the towns that sprawl out eastwards along the main

A ford crosses the main street in Kersey, Suffolk

roads from London. Away from this urbanized area you come upon a coast of quiet, muddy creeks and bird-haunted marshes, dotted with flat islands that are the cruising ground of boaters, bird-watchers and painters. Inland, too, there are delights such as the charming medieval buildings in Thaxted, Saffron Walden and Coggeshall; the great Jacobean mansion of Audley End; and footpaths through ancient, carefully tended woodlands.

Riches from Wool

North of Essex lie the twin counties of Suffolk and Norfolk, the heart of East Anglia. These were the most populous and prosperous counties in medieval England, thanks to the excellence of the wool they produced and the talent of the weavers who brought their skills from continental Europe when they arrived as refugees from religious persecution. The splendor and magnificence of the lifestyle of East Anglian wool merchants and landowners in the Middle Ages is reflected in the sumptuous architecture of the parish churches they paid for (see page 116). It also is seen in the rich beauty of the timber-framed houses they built and the even grander redbrick halls their heirs so proudly constructed in the 16th, 17th and 18th centuries. The churches at Long Melford and Blythburgh (Suffolk) and Salle and Cley (Norfolk) are good examples, as are the great houses of Kentwell Hall and Ickworth House (Suffolk), and Blickling Hall and Holkham Hall (Norfolk).

Lonely Coasts

The Suffolk coastline is windblown, lonely and beautiful, with an outstanding bird reserve at Minsmere and the quaint little coastal towns of Aldeburgh and Southwold. The composer Benjamin Britten founded the Aldeburgh Festival in 1948, and now the Maltings concert hall (in the village of Snape) is the focus for a series of East Anglian musical events, held in churches throughout the region.

Norfolk's coast curves as clay cliffs north and west to charming Cromer, an easy-paced resort with a pier and good beaches, then along a strange shore with little villages stranded inland by the growth of the marshes. The area offers superb bird-watching and boating; it also is renowned for amber, still collected on the beaches and featuring in locally made jewelry.

Local crafts are available all over the region – "Made in Cley" is worth a stop (next door to the smokehouse in Cley next the Sea). A craft co-operative, it comprises six potters and a jeweler; the gallery and workshop is open all year.

Fenland Heritage

The broad, horizon-filling acreage of grain crops in northern Cambridgeshire and southern Lincolnshire is not the only feature of fenland. Windmills are regularly visible on the horizon, and great cathedrals, churches and monastic ruins still straddle their islets of silt, dominating the level landscape – among them Ely, Ramsey, Thorney, Crowland and Boston. The churches in the fens are the setting for some wonderful musical events, crowned by the Festival of Lessons and Carols, held on Christmas Eve in King's College Chapel, Cambridge. The world-famous

Sunset at Blyth estuary near Southwold

university town of Cambridge has a wonderful cluster of medieval colleges, chapels and grounds. It's a great place to walk around, and small enough to explore on foot. Just north of the city, in the nature reserve at Wicken Fen, you can enjoy an unspoiled green corner of genuine old Fenland as the whole region would have looked before the drainers got to work. This little haven for wildlife is of ever-increasing value considering the implacable march of mechanized and intensive agriculture across eastern England since World War II.

Little-known Lincolnshire

Farther north lies Lincolnshire, its southern fens rising into the limestone uplands of the Lincolnshire Wolds. This is one of Britain's most overlooked counties – all the better for discerning travelers who seek out the delightful Georgian town of Stamford; the unfrequented coast; the town of Boston, with its immense church tower known as the "Boston Stump"; and the city of Lincoln itself, where there is a magnificent Norman cathedral.

Draining the Fens

Until the Middle Ages, the counties of Cambridgeshire and Lincolnshire were one vast fen, or reed-filled swamp, flooded regularly by rivers and by inward surges from the sea over an unprotected coast.

Monasteries were established on the silty low islands that rose above the swamp, and it was their inhabitants who organized the area's first big drainage efforts. Dutch engineers completed the job in the 17th century, bringing into being a huge, flat region of farmland that still produces excellent crops today.

NORWICH

Norwich, the capital of Norfolk and of East Anglia, is one of the most agreeable cities in Britain. Yet surprisingly few visitors have really explored the city's delights, perhaps because it is located beyond the reach of the country's major highway systems. Like East Anglia itself, Norwich has remained a little behind the times, and is all the better for that. But the city is far from being run-down or boring. On the contrary, it has a well-looked-after medieval center, more fascinating medieval churches than any other British city of comparable size, and a thriving arts scene thanks to the lively University of East Anglia.

A shopping arcade in Norwich city center

Past Riches

There was a market at Norwich in Saxon times, more than 1,000 years ago. The Normans thought it an important enough place to build a castle here; the great keep still looms on its mound.

In the Middle Ages an influx of emigrants from the Low Countries just across the North Sea helped Norwich become the most prosperous town in England, as local wool was woven and decorated with the skills passed on by these Flemish and Dutch settlers. The city's rich monastic communities and merchants built dozens of fine churches, scores of handsome flint and timber-framed houses, and a truly magnificent cathedral with an ornate, 315-foot spire.

Norwich's location gave it a trading advantage with the rest of Europe, and the town scarcely needed to glance back over its shoulder at London and the rest of the country.

Marooned in Time

But for exactly these geographic and economic reasons, Norwich languished when the Industrial Revolution got under way early in the 18th century. Suddenly the well-to-do city – still confined within medieval walls – was isolated and out on a limb when the woolen and textile trades moved north to the new factories. Norwich had no mineral resources to exploit, and a big decline set in as it sank into a geographical and cultural backwater.

One happy effect of this was that the city was too poor to replace its old churches and townscape with modern architecture. It has therefore retained a great deal of its medieval character, in spite of a recent return to prosperity thanks to the establishment of high-tech industry and the university.

Getting your Bearings

Finding your way around Norwich can be a bit of a puzzle, since the city still retains a haphazard jumble of streets. But you soon get used to the shape of the center, defined by the great Norman keep and the wide open space of the market square, the latter indicated by the landmark clock tower that is part of City Hall. From here the most interesting medieval streets run north to meet the River Wensum as it curls around the north and east flanks of the old city. Norwich Cathedral is northeast of the city center, but well inside the loop of the river. The bus station is a five-minute walk south of the market, while the railroad station lies just across the river to the east, about a 10-minute walk.

Dining and Shopping

Eating in Norwich can be as cosmopolitan as you like, with a choice of French, Italian, Chinese, Thai, Mexican, Indian and more. You can dine in a floating restaurant housed in a barge on the River Wensum, or lunch in the Refectory of Norwich Cathedral. Be sure to try the pungent Colman's mustard, made in town. Use it sparingly to start with; it is fierce enough to sting your tongue unless approached with caution. In fact it is so hot that the founder of the firm used to claim that he became rich on the mustard that people left on their plates!

At Colman's Mustard Shop in the Royal Arcade you can buy tiny square cans of the stuff. Another characteristic purchase in Norwich is an antique or

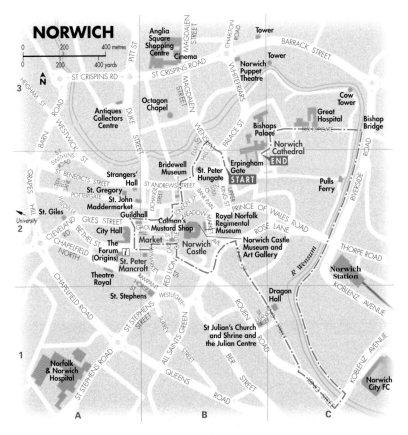

Eastern England

Colman's famous Mustard Shop in Norwich city

piece of bric-a-brac from one of the many antique shops on picturesquely medieval Elm Hill. And don't forget to browse under the "tilts" of Norwich market (see page 103–104) while enjoying the ambience and gossip.

As for entertainment, the presence of the university guarantees a lively atmosphere. For theater, try the Norwich Theatre Royal on Theatre Street, or the Norwich Puppet Theater in the converted St. James' Church in Whitefriars, just across the river to the north with performances for children and adults. There is live music at the Norwich Arts Centre in Reeves Yard, off St. Benedict's Street. The Norfolk and Norwich Festival is held during May and features performances in a wide range of arts from classical music to comedy; events are staged all over the city.

ESSENTIAL INFORMATION

TOURIST INFORMATION
✉ The Forum, Millennium Plain
☎ 01603 727927; www.norwich.gov.uk or www.visitnorwich.co.uk

 URBAN TRANSPORTATION
Norwich's railroad station is on Thorpe Road. For information and reservations, ☎ 08457 484950 (24hrs). The bus station is between Surrey Street and Queen's Road. For information ☎ 08453 006116. There are taxi stands outside the bus and train stations and in front of the Guildhall.

AIRPORT INFORMATION
Norwich International Airport (☎ 01603 411923) is north of the city on Cromer Road. "Park and ride" service provides a frequent, quick (about 15 minutes) bus link to the city center.

CLIMATE – Average highs and lows

JAN.	FEB.	MAR.	APR.	MAY	JUN.	JUL.	AUG.	SEP.	OCT.	NOV.	DEC.
7°C	7°C	10°C	12°C	16°C	19°C	22°C	22°C	19°C	14°C	10°C	8°C
45°F	45°F	50°F	54°F	61°F	66°F	72°F	72°F	66°F	57°F	50°F	46°F
2°C	2°C	3°C	4°C	7°C	10°C	13°C	12°C	10°C	7°C	4°C	3°C
36°F	36°F	37°F	39°F	45°F	50°F	55°F	54°F	50°F	45°F	39°F	37°F

Cobbles create character along medieval Elm Hill

NORWICH SIGHTS

Key to symbols

➕ map coordinates refer to the Norwich map on page 101; sights below are highlighted in yellow on the map.

✉ address or location ☎ telephone number

🕐 opening times 🍴 restaurant on site or nearby

💷 admission charge: $$$ more than £6, $$ £2–£6, $ less than £2 ℹ information

ELM HILL AND MEDIEVAL NORWICH

West of Norwich Cathedral the picturesque cobbled thoroughfare of Elm Hill rises as it runs south from Wensum Street. This is the best preserved of Norwich's many medieval streets, its crooked buildings overhanging the sidewalks – perfect for photography. Fragments of medieval Norwich are thickly scattered. Dragon Hall on King Street (southeast of the market) and Strangers' Hall on Charing Cross both retain handsome 15th-century halls. In Bridewell Alley is the Bridewell, once a prison; its crypt (not usually open to the public), with massive vaulting, dates back to 1325 and is now a fascinating museum of local trades and industries. The cathedral close (grounds) exhibits some fine medieval architecture; the most striking is the entryway, Erpingham Gate. In a niche

above the archway kneels Sir Thomas Erpingham in full armor. He directed the fire of the English archers as they crushed their French foes at the 1415 Battle of Agincourt, and built the gateway in 1420 as a thanksgiving – and to laud his own achievements, too.

Elm Hill ➕ B2

Dragon Hall ➕ C1 ✉ 115–123 King Street ☎ 01603 663922 🕐 Mon.–Sat. 10–4, Apr.–Oct.; Mon.–Fri. 10–4, rest of year 💷 $$

Strangers' Hall ➕ B2 ✉ Charing Cross ☎ 01603 667229 🕐 Wed. and Sat. 10:30–4:30 💷 $$

Bridewell Museum ➕ B2 ✉ Bridewell Alley ☎ 01603 629127 🕐 Mon.–Sat. 10–5, late Jul.–Aug. 31 (also Easter and during school semester breaks); Tue.–Fri. 10–4:30, Sat. 10–5, Apr.–Jun. and Sep. 1–late Oct. 💷 $$

MARKET AND ST. PETER MANCROFT CHURCH

Norwich Market is a phenomenon. The market has been a fixture in the big, sloping Market Place west of the castle for 900 years, having been moved there from its Saxon site in Tombland, near the cathedral. Here is another place where you will quickly feel an ache in your camera finger, for the market stalls are covered with dozens of awnings known as "tilts," each tilt striped in bright colors contrasting with its neighbors. Under the

Eastern England

Eastern England

tilts you will find a bustling collection of stalls selling everything from dried fruit to underwear and tools to animal feed. The narrow lanes between the stalls are as crowded as an Oriental bazaar; the atmosphere buzzes with jokes and gossip.

Market Place is surrounded on all sides with notable buildings. On the west side is the plain-faced, 20th-century City Hall, with its 200-foot clock tower; on the north side is the fine 15th-century Guildhall, patterned in black knapped (cut) flint and white freestone to form a striking checkerboard pattern (access only to Caley's Cocoa Café within). East across Gentlemen's Walk is the art nouveau elaboration of the Royal Arcade, which connects market and castle.

It is the medieval church of St. Peter Mancroft, dominating the south side of the square, that takes the breath away. Inside, carved angels hold up the hammerbeam roof. In the east window, beautiful pre-Reformation stained glass depicts the Nativity, Crucifixion and Resurrection, with many of the characters resplendent in 15th-century costume.

Church of St. Peter Mancroft ✚ A2–B2 ✉ Market Place ☎ 01603 610443 🕐 Mon.–Fri. 9:30–4:30, Sat. 10–12:30 💲 $ donation requested

Guildhall ✚ A2 ✉ Gaol Hill 🕐 Café Mon.–Sat. 9–5

NORWICH CASTLE

Norwich's Norman castle keep was built around 1100. The smooth facade seen today is the result of an 1834 facelift. Guided tours show you around the massive walls, battlement walkways and chambers of one of the most complete Norman castles in Britain. It was the county jail for nearly 700 years, and the dungeons and cells are grim.

You can enjoy a fine collection of paintings – mostly of 19th-century East Anglian landscapes by open-air painters of the Norwich School – in the castle's museum gallery. There are ceramics here, too, and a collection of archeological treasures, unearthed all over Norfolk.

Below the castle is the Royal Norfolk Regimental Museum, which narrates the battles fought by the regiment since 1685.

Castle ✚ B2 ✉ Castle Meadow ☎ 01603 493625 or 493648 (recorded information) 🕐 Mon.–Sat. 10–5:30, Sun. 1–5, late Jul.–Aug. (also Easter and during school semester breaks); Mon.–Fri. 10–4:30, Sun. 1–5, rest of year. Last admission 30 minutes before closing 🍴 Café 💲 $$–$$$ 🛈 Guided tours

Royal Norfolk Regimental Museum ✚ B2 ✉ Market Avenue ☎ 01603 493650 🕐 Mon.–Sat. 10–5, late Jul.–Aug. (also Easter and during school semester breaks); Tue.–Fri. 10–4:30, rest of year 🍴 Café in castle 💲 $$

Colorful tilts cover the stalls in Norwich's bustling Market Place

Illuminated at night: St. Peter Mancroft with the castle beyond and the cathedral in the distance

CHURCHES OF NORWICH

Like any self-respecting bunch of rich and successful medieval men, the wool and trade merchants of Norwich expressed their gratitude to God and proclaimed their self-satisfaction through the building of fine churches. Norwich is well endowed with medieval churches: more than 30 survive inside the old city, most in decent states of repair. In these more secular days, over half are now out of commission as religious buildings; some are now used as arts venues, museums, shops or community centers. Together they make a fascinating display of the art of medieval church architecture in East Anglia, particularly in their use of the local flint, either in cobble form or cut smooth and black to lie level with the surrounding stonework in a style known as flushwork.

St. Peter Mancroft, in the market (see pages 103–104), is the finest of them all, but there are many others worth visiting. West of the market, on the corner of St. Giles Street and Upper St. Giles Street, stands St. Giles under its great tower, with an impressive angel roof. North of the market are St. Gregory's (just off St. Benedict Street), which has

pre-Reformation frescoes, and St. John Maddermarket (built beside the market square, where madder, a Eurasian herb, was sold for the dyeing of cloth), boasting a beautiful tower and some fine monuments.

To the northeast, near the top of Elm Hill, is St. Peter Hungate. South of the market, off the intriguingly named Rampant Horse Street, the tower of St. Stephen's displays good flushwork, and there is brilliantly colored 16th-century glass from Germany in the east window.

A poignant oddity is St. Julian's Church, in St. Julian's Alley, a small lane between King Street and Rouen Road, where St. Julian of Norwich had her reclusive cell (see page 107). Next door, The Julian Centre is a study center dedicated to St. Julian.

Check hours of operation with the tourist office (see page 102) before visiting any of Norwich's churches.

St. Julian's Church and Shrine ☒ St. Julian's Alley, Rouen Road 🕐 Daily 7:30–7:30, Apr.–Sep.; 7:30–4, rest of year 🎟 Free

The Julian Centre ☒ St. Julian's Alley, Rouen Road ☎ 01603 767380 🕐 Mon.–Sat. 11–4, Apr.–Sep.; 11–3, rest of year 🎟 Free

Norwich Cathedral and its soaring spire

NORWICH CATHEDRAL

Norwich Cathedral was built of beautiful silvery-white French stone in Norman times. The blunt east end is supported by graceful flying buttresses. The spire, soaring 315 feet, is the second tallest in Britain after Salisbury (see pages 90–91).

Inside, delicate columns rise to the nave roof to burst out in fan vaulting and resemble stone-carved treetops. This is a place to bring your binoculars, to admire the beautiful ornamental carving in the roof. They unroll the entire biblical story, from the Garden of Eden through the Flood (Mr. and Mrs. Noah and family, peeping out of the Ark in company with a smiling unicorn), the infant Moses in a golden basket, the terrified Pharaoh's army drowning in the Red Sea, and on to scenes from the New Testament.

There are more richly carved roof bosses in the very well preserved cloisters, too, much closer above your head for ease of inspection; they incorporate several sly-eyed, faun-like Green Men (see page 122) peering out of thickets of leaves. There also is 20th-century artistry to admire in the Stations of the Cross, inlaid in wood.

The most remarkable artwork in the cathedral, however, is the haunting *Despenser Reredos* in St. Luke's Chapel at the east end, a 14th-century depiction of Christ's Passion and Resurrection. We see Christ being scourged by brutish guards, hanging helpless but with dignity on his cross while his mother swoons into the arms of St. John, and stepping purposefully out of his tomb over the heads of cringing soldiers. During the 17th century this rare treasure was used as a table, its painted face downward, to hide it from the Puritan zealots who would have destroyed it.

Outside, nestling near the cloisters, is the grave of Edith Cavell, a Norfolk-born nurse who tended both friend and foe alike while working in Belgium during World War I, but was executed by the Germans in 1915 for helping Allied prisoners to escape the occupied country.

✚ B2–B3 ✉ The Close ☎ 01603 218321 🕐 Daily 7:30–7, mid-May to mid-Sep.; 7:30–6, rest of year 🍴 Restaurant 💲 $$ donation requested 🚶 Guided tours: Mon.–Sat. at 10:45, noon and 2:15 (donation suggested) depart from the west end of the cathedral

The Norman keep of Norwich Castle towers over the city center

WALK: CENTRAL NORWICH

Refer to route marked on city map on page 101

This stroll around the best parts of Norwich could be completed in a couple of hours, but half a day would be better if you want to visit the cathedral or stop at any of the sights en route.

Starting at Erpingham Gate west of the cathedral, turn down Wensum Street and left up medieval Elm Hill (see page 103). Browse among the enticing shops here.

Turn right onto Princes Street at the top of the hill, and cross St. Andrew Plain to turn left up narrow Bridewell Alley. The Bridewell Museum (see page 103) is here.

Continue across Bedford Street and up Swan Lane, then go right down London Street to the market, Guildhall and St. Peter Mancroft. Bear left through Royal Arcade, past the Colman's Mustard Shop, to Norwich Castle. Bear right out of the arcade to curve left around the castle by Farmer's Avenue and Cattle Market Street. Turn right onto King Street; on

your left you pass Dragon Hall. Opposite the hall is St. Julian's Alley, leading to St. Julian's Church (see page 105). This plain and over-restored flint building houses a shrine to a remarkable woman, Mother Julian of Norwich, who spent 43 years voluntarily confined to a tiny cell here after receiving heavenly visions. Her writings about them, published later as *The Revelations of Divine Love*, mark the first book written in English by a woman and speak directly. She sees Christ crucified, a pure white baby rising to heaven out of a dead body, and a demon with "a young man's face, long and lean, the colour of a tilestone newly fired, and a foul and nauseating stench." Mother Julian is unsure about their meanings, but asserts, "All I know is that the joy I saw surpasses all the heart could wish for, or the soul desire."

Continue along King Street for a quarter-mile, then bear left over Carrow Bridge to cross the River Wensum. Turn left up the riverside path that skirts the city. Pass the medieval watergate of Pulls Ferry. Bear left across the ancient, triple-arched Bishop Bridge, dating from 1340. Proceed up Bishopgate back to the cathedral.

REGIONAL SIGHTS

Key to symbols

⊕ map coordinates refer to the Eastern England map on pages 96–97; sights below are highlighted in yellow on the map.

✉ address or location ☎ telephone number

🕐 opening times 🍴 restaurant on site or nearby

⛴ ferry

🎫 admission charge: $$$ more than £6, $$ £2–£6, $ less than £2 ℹ information

ALDEBURGH AND THE SUFFOLK COAST

The Moot Hall at Aldeburgh

Aldeburgh is a delightful small resort-cum-fishing town, where local fishermen still launch their boats off the shingle beach and sell their catch fresh from the sea. The Tudor church contains a fine stained-glass window honoring Benjamin Britten, one of England's most celebrated 20th-century composers, who lived in the town for many years and lies buried in the churchyard. His house on the beach is marked by a commemorative plaque. On the street a block off the beach, you'll find cafés, restaurants and shops (the local fish and chip shop is particularly good – you can tell by the line of people outside on weekend evenings). There also are art galleries featuring watercolor paintings of the regional landscape.

Music lovers can attend concerts just inland at Snape Maltings, converted by Britten into a splendid concert hall in the 1960s. It plays host to the annual Aldeburgh Festival in June. The town also is busy in November when the international poetry festival takes place.

South of town stands Orford Castle, with a polygonal 12th-century keep overlooking Aldeburgh; it is now separated from the sea by a 10-mile-long shingle spit. Take a boat over to the "elbow" of the spit, Orford Ness, for a wonderful nature walk among seabirds and old military buildings.

North of Aldeburgh you will find the Royal Society for the Protection of Birds' superb reserve at Minsmere (don't forget your binoculars!), as well as remnants of magnificent monastic buildings on the cliffs at Dunwich, once the finest town in Suffolk but long since eaten by the sea. A good local museum tells the story.

A shingle beach leads farther north to Walberswick, beloved by landscape painters, and the small upscale resort of Southwold, with its lovely color-washed houses and picturesque bay. There are plenty of pubs to choose from in Southwold, and Adnams Bitter (an uncarbonated, dark beer) is brewed in the town. Some say it's the tastiest in the country; don't leave without sampling it.

Aldeburgh ⊕ E2

Tourist information ✉ 152 High Street ☎ 01728 453637; www.suffolkcoastal.gov.uk

Snape Maltings ✉ Snape, Saxmundham ☎ 01728 688303

Orford Castle ✉ Orford ☎ 01394 450472 🕐 Daily 10–6, Apr.–Sep.; daily 10–5, in Oct.; Wed.–Sun. 10–1 and 2–4, rest of year 🎫 $$

Orford Ness ⊕ E2

Orford Ness National Nature Reserve ✉ Quay Office, Orford Quay, Orford ☎ 01394 450900 🕐 Tue.–Sat., 10–5, late Jun.–early Oct.; Sat. 10–5, late Mar.–late Jun. and early Oct.–late Oct. 🎫 $$ ℹ Access only by boat from Orford Quay 10–2, every 15 minutes; last boat returns at 5 p.m.

Southwold ⊕ E3

Tourist information ✉ 69 High Street ☎ 01502 724729; www.visit-southwold.co.uk

Opposite: Marbled opulence in the entrance hall of the Fitzwilliam Museum in Cambridge

Dutch gables, corner turrets and a dominant clock tower mark Blickling Hall

BLICKLING HALL

This is one of north Norfolk's finest country houses, a redbrick Elizabethan mansion altered and extended in Jacobean times with curly-edged gables and tall chimneys, its wings flanked by square-built towers. The long approach drive offers a superb view. The ceiling of the long gallery is a triumph of plasterwork, set with allegorical figures. If there is a ghost around, it is probably Anne Boleyn, ill-fated second wife of King Henry VIII, who spent part of her childhood here.

✚ D4

✉ Blickling, Aylsham, Norfolk ☎ 01263 738030
🕐 House: Wed.–Sun. 1–5, mid-Mar. to early Oct.; 1–4, early Oct.–late Oct. Garden: Wed.–Sun. (also Tue. in Aug.) 10:15–5:15, mid-Mar. to late Oct.; Thu.–Sun. 11–4, rest of year 🍴 Restaurant 💷 $$$ (garden only $$)

BURGHLEY HOUSE

A mile south of Stamford (see page 123) stands Burghley House, in a vast deer park centered on a lake and laid out by the 18th-century landscape architect, Capability Brown. A five-story central gatehouse is enhanced by domes, cupolas, pediments and towers that bristle from the heights of Burghley.

The house – much altered in subsequent centuries – was built 1555–87 in the grandest possible style for William Cecil, 1st Lord Burghley, who was confidant and favored counselor to Queen Elizabeth I. The 240-room house contains much fine artwork, notably the fresco paintings by 17th-century artist Antonio Verrio. His Hell staircase depicts the grisly fate of sinners, while his Heaven Room shows gods and nymphs from classical mythology indulging themselves.

✚ B3

✉ On B1443, 1 mile east of Stamford, Lincolnshire
☎ 01780 752451 🕐 Sat.–Thu. 11–5, Apr.–Oct.
🍴 Restaurant 💷 $$$

BURY ST. EDMUNDS

Bury St. Edmunds is a charming market town with fine ecclesiastical buildings. The abbey (now ruined) was built to house the shrine of the martyred St. Edmund, the last Saxon king of East Anglia, slain in AD 870. The abbey gardens, peppered with the abbey ruins, run down to the River Lark. In town, the Angel Hotel is famous for being featured in Charles Dickens' *Pickwick Papers*, while The Nutshell is said to be the world's tiniest pub.

✚ D2

Tourist information ✉ 6 Angel Hill ☎ 01284 764667; www.stedmundsbury.gov.uk

NORFOLK BROADS

Long thought to be natural, these interconnected lakes in the flat country east of Norwich are in fact flooded medieval peat diggings. When locals connected them with a network of water channels, a unique way of life came into being. The marshmen made a subsistence living out of fishing, shooting wildfowl, and cutting reed and sedge for thatching. It was a lonely, idiosyncratic lifestyle that persisted until Victorian pleasure boaters "discovered" the Broads. Soon the area became a playground for yachtsmen and riverboat parties – not so bad during the days of sail, but once diesel engines came on the scene the Broads quickly became grossly polluted.

Over the last two decades the Broads have been restored to their former glory, and the area is now one of the most popular inland waterways in Europe, offering around 125 miles of wonderful boating, both sail and motor.

The Broads are Britain's only national wetlands, famous for the rich variety of plants, animals and birds that can be found there. At nature reserves such as Ranworth Broad, Hickling Broad and Horsey Mere you can see rare water spiders, swallowtail butterflies, marsh harriers and hen harriers, reed buntings and other thriving wildlife. The Broads are a unique ecosystem, which is explained as you wander the boardwalk trails at The Broads Wildlife Centre in Ranworth.

The main boating centers include Wroxham and Potter Heigham, where you can rent a boat or take a boat tour. Stalham is home to the Museum of the Broads, with displays on the history of the area and the local crafts.

There are plenty of churches and pubs to divert you on your voyages around the area. Visit the Broads to enjoy huge skies spread over a flat horizon, pierced by windmills, willows and the sails of boats.

Broads Information Centre ✚ E3 ✉ The Staithe, Ranworth ☎ 01603 270453; www.broads-authority.gov.uk ⏰ Daily 9–5, Easter–Oct. 31 ⛴ Ferry tours and river trips operate from the Information Centre to the Broads Wildlife Centre

Broads Wildlife Centre ✚ E3 ✉ Ranworth ☎ 01603 270479 ⏰ Daily 10–5, Apr.–Oct. 🍴 Café 🚹 Good disabled access along boardwalk

Norfolk Broads Direct ✚ E3 ✉ The Bridge, Wroxham ☎ 01603 782207 🚹 Boat tours

Museum of the Broads ✚ E4 ✉ The Staithe, Stalham ☎ 01692 581681 ⏰ Mon.–Fri. (also Sat.–Sun., late Jul. and Aug.), 11–5, Easter–Oct. 31 ♿ $$

Right: A windmill at How Hill, near Stalham
Below: Boats for rent on the Norfolk Broads

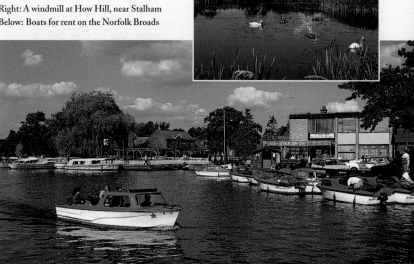

Punting along the Cam toward the Bridge of Sighs

CAMBRIDGE

Probably the best way to see the city of Cambridge is by renting the most sedate mode of transport known to man – a slow and creaky wooden punt. A soporific June afternoon spent poling one of these flat-bottomed boats gently along the River Cam – with university undergraduates basking on the green lawns on one hand and the stately towers and pinnacles of mellow chapels and colleges on the other – will soon convince you that Cambridge is heaven. It is a conclusion reached by many through the centuries.

This almost perfect medieval university town originated when disgruntled scholars and teachers from Oxford University established a settlement by the river in the early 13th century. A whole range of splendid and beautiful colleges came into being over the ensuing centuries, endowed by the pious or seriously rich. Most are laid out along traditional monastic lines: a quadrangle (known here as a "court") surrounded by chapel, cloisters, dining and sleeping quarters. Radical politics and cutting-edge research have always been the hallmarks of Cambridge University.

Here Protestant bishop-martyrs Thomas Cranmer, Hugh Latimer and Nicholas Ridley were educated; here Isaac Newton calculated the speed of sound; and here in the 20th century the atom was split by Ernest Rutherford and the DNA double helix structure was identified by James Watson (an American geneticist) and Francis Crick (an English biophysicist).

Cambridge contains upwards of 30 colleges spread out over a considerable area. But all the finest and oldest are concentrated along the east bank of the River Cam (except Magdalene, pronounced "Maudlin," which is on the west bank). Their elegant gardens are connected to the green meadows and lawns (known as The Backs) on the other side of the river by an assortment of bridges. Phone ahead to check opening times if you plan to visit any of the colleges, since schedules vary during the school year.

Walking south from Magdalene Bridge, the first college you'll come to is St. John's, founded in 1511 by the mother of King Henry VII, with a turreted and tabernacled gateway leading to beautiful courts. The Bridge of Sighs, a covered bridge of pale stone, was built in 1831 to connect St. John's with its new extension across the river. The

Visitors admire the fan-vaulting in the chapel at King's College

bridge was named after the original in Venice (although it's not a faithful copy). The Church of the Holy Sepulchre, just across Sydney Street from St. John's, was built with a round nave in imitation of the original, which had been admired in Jerusalem by Crusaders.

Trinity College boasts Great Court, the scene of a traditional undergraduate race against the clock (famously re-enacted in the film *Chariots of Fire*), and Nevile's Court, where Isaac Newton stamped his foot and timed the echo to calculate the speed of sound. Clare College, whose lovely Jacobean buildings and courts stand in beautifully tended grounds, has one of the oldest and most graceful of the city's bridges – Clare Bridge, which is a perfect place to stand and survey the surrounding glories.

King's College has an internationally renowned chapel, built 1446–1515, with glorious fan-vaulting and Tudor stained glass. It is the site of an internationally broadcast Christmas Eve service.

Queens' College is one of Cambridge's most memorably beautiful, with its Tudor courts and gatehouse, and the charming, half-timbered President's Lodge. Mathematical Bridge, built in 1749,

connects Queens' College with The Backs.

If you tire of the colleges, Fitzwilliam Museum on Trumpington Street is one of the world's great small museums, whose granite and marble halls contain paintings by Old Masters (Titian, Hals), English landscape artists (Gainsborough, Constable, Wilson), Impressionists (Renoir, Monet, Cézanne, Gauguin) and modernists (Modigliani, Picasso, Spencer, Hockney). There also are superb collections of antiquities, illuminated manuscripts, folios, ceramics and armor.

And as if all this intellectual stimulation weren't enough, Cambridge also boasts an impressive range of cafés, pubs and nighttime entertainment.

✚ C2

Tourist information ✉ Wheeler Street
☎ 09065 862526 (there is a charge of 60p per minute for this call); www.cambridge.gov.uk

St. John's College ✉ St. John's Street
☎ 01223 338600

Trinity College ✉ Trinity Street ☎ 01223 338400

Clare College ✉ Trinity Lane ☎ 01223 333200

King's College ✉ King's Parade ☎ 01223 331100

Queens' College ✉ Queens' Lane ☎ 01223 335511

Fitzwilliam Museum ✉ Trumpington Street
☎ 01223 332900 ⏰ Tue.–Sat. 10–5, Sun. noon–5
💷 Free

Paradise found: John Milton's cottage

CHILTERN HILLS

The Chiltern Hills arch like a bent bow around the northwestern outskirts of London, a great wall of high downland with a fine escarpment sloping down and out into the lower lands of Oxfordshire, Bedfordshire and Hertfordshire. They grow superb stands of beech and oak, and nourish many kinds of wildflowers.

Chiltern villages are kept smart and snug by their proud residents. Among the most charming are Hambleden, West Wycombe (cared for by the conservation organization, the National Trust) and Chalfont St. Giles, with its beautiful church and the cottage where John Milton finished writing *Paradise Lost.* All are located in Buckinghamshire. In Hertfordshire are the fine villages of Aldbury and Much Hadham, and tiny Ayot St. Lawrence, where George Bernard Shaw lived at Shaw's Corner; the house is preserved as a shrine to the playwright.

Chilterns tourist information 🔲 A1 ✉ Paul's Row, High Wycombe ☎ 01494 421892
Milton's Cottage 🔲 B1 ✉ Dean Way, Chalfont St. Giles ☎ 01494 872313 🕔 Tue.–Sun. 10–1 and 2–6, Mar.–Oct. 👆 $

Shaw's Corner 🔲 B1 ✉ Ayot St. Lawrence, near Welwyn, Hertfordshire ☎ 01438 820307
🕔 Wed.–Sun. noon–5:30 (house: 1–5), mid-Mar. to late Oct. 👆 $$

COLCHESTER

"The oldest recorded town in Britain" is Colchester's proud boast, and you can see below the Norman castle the foundations of the fort established here by the Romans in AD 44 – the year after they invaded – and burned by Queen Boudicca in AD 61. The castle, set above a beautiful park, is now an excellent museum that tells the story of the town. Evidence of the centuries lies all around: sections of 2,000-year-old city wall; the Saxon tower of Holy Trinity Church; ruins of the Norman Priory of St. Botolph; the medieval Dutch Quarter, where refugee weavers started up the cloth trade that would enrich the town; and dozens of handsome Georgian and overblown Victorian buildings. The Town Hall is a nice specimen of the latter. On the culinary front, Colchester's oysters are famed. The Colchester Arts Centre hosts a program of music and dance.
🔲 D2
Tourist information ✉ 1 Queen Street
☎ 01206 282920; www.colchester.com
Colchester Castle Museum ✉ Castle Park, High Street ☎ 01206 282939 🕔 Mon.–Sat. 10–5, Sun. 11–5
👆 $$

The Norman castle at Colchester

Ely's unusual tower beyond the Porta gatehouse

Ely

Ely is a beautiful small town in the middle of the black Cambridgeshire peat fenlands, its crooked medieval streets running off the summit of a low "island" and down into the surrounding flat corn-growing country. From 1636 to 1646 – through the years of the English Civil War – Oliver Cromwell's family, and occasionally the great man himself, were based in a black and white 14th-century house in the town. Part of Oliver Cromwell's House is now in use as Ely's Tourist Information Centre. The rest is given over to an exhibition about the domestic life of this serious-minded but far from curmudgeonly parliamentary leader who became Lord Protector of England – king in all but name – after ordering the execution of King Charles I in 1649.

Ely Cathedral is a mighty Norman edifice that literally overshadows and dominates the town. From whichever direction you approach Ely, the cathedral looms on the skyline like an enormous ship. It is a glorious building from the outside, sporting a 217-foot tower at the west end and an enormous central wooden octagon with a 62-foot lantern on top, which was hoisted to its crowning position

in 1348. Inside, solid rounded Norman arches contrast with a couple of delicately ornate Tudor chantry chapels. There is beautiful Victorian painting on the nave roof, and a fascinating Stained Glass Museum with examples of the craft from the early Middle Ages onwards. And as a testimony to the subversive wit of the medieval woodcarvers, there are dozens of "Green Men" to spot: strange, often savage faces sprouting from or consumed by foliage, peeping out from roof trusses.

The cathedral gardens make a pleasant place to stroll, and the market square is usually bustling with stalls.

✚ C3

Tourist information ✉ Oliver Cromwell's House, 29 St. Mary's Street ☎ 01353 662062; www.ely.org

Oliver Cromwell's House ✉ 29 St. Mary's Street ⏰ Daily 10–5:30, Apr.–Oct.; Sun.–Fri. 11–4, Sat. 10–5, rest of year ♿ $$

Ely Cathedral ✉ The College ☎ 01353 667735 ⏰ Daily 7–7, Easter–Oct 31; Mon.–Sat. 7:30–6, Sun. 7:30–5, rest of year 🍴 Restaurant and café (free to all on Sun.) ♿ $$ ℹ Guided tours

Stained Glass Museum ✉ South treforium, Cathedral ☎ 01353 660347 ⏰ Mon.–Fri. 10–5, Sat. 10–5:30, Sun. noon–6, Easter–Oct. 31; Mon.–Sat. 10:30–5, Sun. noon–4:30, rest of year 🍴 Restaurant and café ♿ $$

Eastern England

The remarkable parish churches of East Anglia, more than 2,000 of them, came into being literally on the backs of sheep. It was the enormous wealth generated by the woolen cloth trade during the Middle Ages that allowed merchants, abbots and wealthy Londoners to build these sumptuous "wool churches." Some used imported limestone, but most were built of the local flint and chalky rubble, ragstone, brick, abandoned Roman tiles or whatever was available. Embellishment was the key to a successful trumpeting to God and your peers of just how well you had done in business.

Stained-glass glory at Lavenham

THE "WOOL CHURCHES" OF EAST ANGLIA

these days to fill the front row of pews, let alone to raise the mighty shout of praise to God for which these splendid buildings were so obviously intended. The dedication of the small bands of volunteer parishioners who clean, maintain and raise funds for them is a remarkable thing in its own right.

Wandering from village to village through Essex, Suffolk and Norfolk you are bound to discover your own particular favorite among the parish churches of East Anglia. Following are some suggestions; each has special features over and above its general beauty.

The darkness of beautifully knapped (cut) flint was contrasted with the whiteness of limestone, pinnacles were raised from the corners of towers, and one's initials were set into the fabric of tower or porch. Statues, frescoes, painted screens and clerestory windows would flood the church with clear East Anglian light. Stained-glass windows were set in flowing stone frames; wonderfully balanced hammerbeam roofs were seemingly upheld by sublime wooden angels; and pulpits were carved in slender-stemmed "wineglass" style. Eternity would be spent in an elaborate tomb of marble, surmounted by one's effigy lying or kneeling with hands piously folded and every intricate crinkle of lace or link of chain mail faithfully depicted.

The first-time visitor to East Anglia marvels at the sheer number, size and quality of parish churches, and the fact that so many of them grace tiny villages that can hardly muster enough worshipers

Essex

St. Michael's, Copford (southwest of Colchester): fine early medieval wall and roof paintings.

St. Peter-on-the-Wall, Dengie (3 miles east of Bradwell Waterside): a seventh-century Saxon church in a beautiful, bleak coastal location.

St. Andrew's, Greensted (off A414 east of Harlow): log-built 11th-century nave, reputedly the oldest in the world.

St. John's, Thaxted: a mighty spire and a riot of medieval stone carvings.

Suffolk

Holy Trinity, Blythburgh (on A12 near Southwold): "The Cathedral of the Marshes" is filled with light, has a wooden angel roof and features the Seven Deadly Sins bench-ends offering humorous warning.

St. Michael's, Framlingham: a striking

collection of elaborate Tudor tombs, chiefly of the Howard family.

St. Peter and St. Paul, Lavenham: Tudor church with memorable carved screens, crowning Suffolk's purest medieval town.

Holy Trinity, Long Melford: probably the county's finest church. How did such wonderful stained glass survive the Reformation and Puritan vandalism?

St. Mary and St. Andrew, Mildenhall: astonishing carved roof with angels, saints, beasts and foliage.

St. Edmund's, Southwold: ship-like church with impressive flushwork.

St. Peter's, Wenhaston (just west of Blythburgh): a dramatic medieval painting of the Last Judgment.

St. Mary's, Wissington (pronouned "Wiston"; off A134 near Nayland): Norman arches, very early medieval wall paintings.

The fine interior at Salle in Norfolk

Norfolk

St. Nicholas', Blakeney (on A149 north Norfolk coast road): a really welcoming church, with local produce for sale and friendly helpers; the light in its extra tower guided sailors and travelers at night.

St. Margaret's, King's Lynn: full of character, this church's architecture is spread over eight centuries; medieval stone carvings, elaborate wooden screens.

St. Helen's, Ranworth (off B1140 northeast of Norwich): superb medieval painted screen; great view across the Broads from the tower.

St. Peter and St. Paul, Salle (off B1145 near Reepham): finest of all the Norfolk churches – flooded with light and beautified with stone carvings and glorious wood-carving in the roof.

St. Peter's, Walpole St. Peter (off A47 between Wisbech and King's Lynn): the "Queen of the Marshlands," with many treasures; ancient screens and pews.

The ancient timber church at Greensted

Eastern England

Statues survey the immaculate knot garden at Hatfield House

HATFIELD HOUSE

William Cecil, 1st Lord Burghley, close confidant and adviser to Queen Elizabeth I, built Burghley House in Lincolnshire (see page 110); it was his son Robert, 1st Earl of Salisbury, who built the splendid Jacobean mansion Hatfield House in Hertfordshire from 1607–11. Robert had become Elizabeth's adviser after his father's death in 1598 and went on to be secretary of state to the new king, James I. All the power and prestige of the man are reflected in the giant C-shaped house with its domes, pinnacles, chimneys and enormous cupola-crowned entrance. The gardens have been restored to reflect their Jacobean origins.

Nearby stands the mellow redbrick remnant of Hatfield Palace, where Queen Elizabeth I spent much of her childhood. Inside the house are portraits of her in later life as the mightiest of the Tudor monarchs.

✚ B1

✉ Hatfield, Hertfordshire   ☎ 01707 287010

🕓 Sat.–Wed. noon–4 (park and gardens 11–5:30, East Gardens Mon. only), Easter–Sep. 30   🍴 Restaurant

💵 $$$ (park and gardens only $$, park only $$)

ℹ️ Guided tours of house only Mon. except Bank Holidays ($$ extra)

LAVENHAM

Lavenham was one of Suffolk's most prosperous wool towns until Tudor times, but slumped into a depression when the trade moved north. Lavenham's loss is the visitor's gain, however, for there was never enough money in the town to replace the crooked old timber-framed houses with anything more convenient or up-to-date. Thus Lavenham survives as the finest collection of medieval vernacular buildings in Britain, an absolute feast of leaning walls, carved timbers, crooked doorframes and overhanging upper storys. Particularly notable are the half-timbered Swan Inn, the handsome church (see page 117), 14th-century Little Hall, the Priory in Water Street, and the elaborately carved 1529 Guildhall in the marketplace, which houses an exhibition on the wool industry.

✚ D2

Tourist information ✉ Lady Street   ☎ 01787 248207; www.visit-suffolk.org.uk   🕓 Daily, Easter–Oct. 31; Sat.–Sun. in Mar. and Nov.–Dec.

Guildhall ✉ Market Place   ☎ 01787 247646

🕓 Daily 11–5, Jun.–Sep.; Wed.–Sun. 11–5, Easter–May 31 and in Oct.; Sat.–Sun. 11–4, early Mar.–Easter and in Nov.   🍴 Café   💵 $$

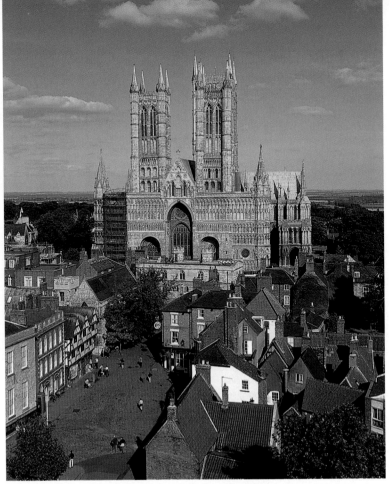

The broad west front of Lincoln Cathedral overlooks the rooftops of the city

LINCOLN

Lincoln Cathedral stands superbly on a 200-foot rocky eminence dominating the town, a position it shares with Lincoln Castle, both encircled within the old city walls. The cathedral dates mostly from the 13th century, with two great towers flanking the broad west front and a third soaring behind. Don't miss the 13th-century rose windows with their original glass, the slim arcades and the graceful Chapter House. Up at the top of a column squats the cheeky Lincoln Imp, supposedly turned to stone for flirting with the 30 angels that hold up the wonderful 1280 choir roof.

The Norman castle offers an interesting if rather chilling time-trip. In the prison chapel the pews are so tall that felons could not see or hear each other.

Halfway up cobbled Steep Hill an appropriately named second-hand bookshop – The Reader's Rest – gives visitors an excuse to catch their breath before continuing uphill to the cathedral, past some arts, craft and jewelry shops. For a taste of local cuisine, stop for a game pie at the Wig and Mitre (see page 263).

🔢 B5

Tourist information ✉ 9 Castle Hill ☎ 01522 873213 ✉ 21 The Cornhill ☎ 01522 873256; www.lincoln.gov.uk

Lincoln Cathedral ✉ Minster Yard ☎ 01522 544544 🕐 Mon.–Sat. 7:15 a.m.–8 p.m., Sun. 7:15– 6, May–Sep.; Mon.–Sat. 7:15–6, Sun. 7:15–5, rest of year 🍴 Café 🥤 $$ (free to all on Sun. and after services) ℹ️ Guided tours

Lincoln Castle ✉ Castle Hill ☎ 01522 511068 🕐 Mon.–Sat. 9:30–5:30, Sun. 11–5:30, Apr.–Oct.; Mon.–Sat. 9:30–4, Sun. 11–4, rest of year 🍴 Café 🥤 $$

Eastern England

DRIVE: CONSTABLE COUNTRY

Distance: 85 miles

If you're a fan of British painter John Constable, this drive through the low-lying countryside of the wide Stour Valley, on the borders of Suffolk and Essex, may give an odd sense of *déja vu*. If several of the artist's landscapes and scenes seem surprisingly similar to the real thing, it was because Constable celebrated so effectively the unemphatic richness and subtle beauty of his native East Anglian countryside and its trees, mills, river, wheatfields and big, cloud-filled skies.

Just east of the sprawling town of Haverhill you join A1092, a lazy road with plenty of bends that winds eastward along the north bank of the Stour.

The River Stour rises across the county border in Cambridgeshire, and winds down into Suffolk as a stream almost big enough to step over, then wends its way through a string of lovely old-fashioned villages enriched and beautified by medieval wool wealth.

First comes Stoke by Clare. Then you pass through Clare, with its castle mound, little Nethergate Brewery, priory remains and richly pargeted (plasterworked), 15th-century former priest's house on the churchyard corner. Cavendish is next, its thatched houses exuding pink-faced charm. Then comes Long Melford and its great church (see page 117).

At Long Melford turn right on B1064, passing the broad village green to navigate a straggling main street lined with handsome old houses.

Set back from the road are two magnificent Tudor houses, Kentwell Hall and Melford Hall.

Continue south on A131 to Sudbury.

The 18th-century portrait and landscape painter Thomas Gainsborough was born here; his house is now a museum.

From Sudbury, B1508 wanders south along the east bank of the Stour (or you can take an even prettier and narrower road along the west bank) for 5 miles to Bures, one of the smallest and sleepiest of the Stour Valley towns. From Bures, you remain just within the southernmost

border of Suffolk as you take the 5-mile local road east along the north bank of the river.

This is a really beautiful stretch in a shallow, rolling valley. Don't forget to look into the Norman church at Wissington (pronounced "Wiston"), with its ancient wall paintings.

Cross A134 to reach Nayland.

There are picturesque old houses, and an altarpiece by John Constable in the village church.

Continue on B1087 to Stoke-by-Nayland.

This village has a commanding church tower on the ridge. The Angel Inn (see page 264), at the crossroads here serves superb bar food.

From Stoke-by-Nayland, bear right on B1068 toward the A12 highway. Turn left onto A12, then immediately take B1070 to East Bergholt, John Constable's birthplace. Turn right in the village (watch for the sign) to reach a parking lot and walk down to Flatford Mill.

Scenes from Constable paintings surround you here: *Flatford Mill* (1817), *Boat-building near Flatford Mill* (1815), and at the end of the lane, the whitewashed gables of Willy Lott's Cottage and the tree-hung pool by the mill as shown in dappled sunlight in *The Hay Wain* (1821).

From the Flatford parking lot retrace your journey to Stoke-by-Nayland. From here,

Flatford Mill – inspiration for Constable paintings

a local road leads north past Polstead and its village pond. Turn right along A1071 (in the direction of Hadleigh), leaving it after a short distance to take a local road on the left that dips through Kersey, an unspoiled and enchanting medieval village. Just north of here, turn left on A1141 to much-visited Lavenham (see page 118). Leave the village along B1071, Great Waldingfield/Sudbury road; in a mile a local road on the right returns you to Long Melford, and then A1092 back to Haverhill.

Kentwell Hall ✚ D2 ✉ Long Melford, near Suffolk ☎ 01787 310207 ⏰ Daily noon–5, mid-Jul. through Aug. 31; Sun.–Wed. noon–5, Apr. 1 to mid-Jun. and in Sep.; Sun. noon–5, in Oct. Gardens and farm only: phone for details 🍴 Restaurant and café 💲 $$$ (gardens and farm only $$)

Melford Hall ✚ D2 ✉ Long Melford ☎ 01787 379228 ⏰ Wed.–Sun. 2–5:30, May–Sep.; Sat.–Sun. 2–5:30, in Apr. and Oct. 💲 $$

Gainsborough's House ✚ D2 ✉ 46 Gainsborough Street, Sudbury ☎ 01787 372958 ⏰ Mon.–Sat. 10–5 (bank holiday Sun. and Mon. 2–5), early Jan.–late Dec. 💲 $$ (free to all in Dec.)

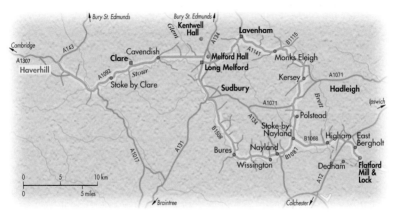

The beach and pier at Cromer

NORTH NORFOLK COAST

A strange thing has happened to many of the seaside settlements along the coast of north Norfolk. They have been left high, dry and up to 2 miles from the sea by the growth of marshes on the rich silt brought down by rivers. At the same time, the phenomenon known as longshore drift has dragged silt and pebbles westward to form 3-mile spits at Blakeney Point and Scolt Head Island. Wildfowl flock here to spend the winter, and pass through in their millions while migrating – hence the area's reputation for bird-watching.

Gems along this lonely coast include the easy-paced seaside resorts of Cromer, Sheringham and Hunstanton. There are notable churches at Salthouse, Cley-next-the-Sea, Blakeney and Snettisham. Burnham Thorpe is the birthplace of Admiral Lord Nelson, the hero of the 1805 Battle of Trafalgar – enjoy mementos of this great sailor in the church, and a glass of "Nelson's Blood" in the local pub. South of Snettisham is the Royal Family's country residence of Sandringham. There is an exhibition of royal memorabilia in the house, and there are attractive grounds.

Cromer ✚ D4
Tourist information ✉ Prince of Wales Road
☎ 01263 512497; www.north-norfolk.gov.uk
Sheringham ✚ D4
Tourist information ✉ Station Approach ☎ 01263 824329 ⓘ Daily, mid-Mar. to late Oct.; www.north-norfolk.gov.uk
Sandringham House ✚ C4 ✉ Sandringham, Norfolk ☎ 01553 772675 ⓘ House: daily 11–4:45, Apr.–Sep.; 11–3, in Oct. Museum: daily 11–5, Apr.–Sep.; 11–4, in Oct. Garden: daily 10:30–5, Apr.–Sep.; 11–4, in Oct. Closed last week in Jul.
🎟 $$$ (museum and gardens only $$)

Green Men

As you're exploring Norfolk, look out for the "Green Man." He can be found vomiting tendrils of leaves or wreathed in foliage, staring out with a troubled frown or a salacious leer from church roofs and pillars, or from pew ends and screens. But he is not confined exclusively to churches. You can spot him painted on pub signs and carved into old inn paneling. He is thousands of years old. Who is he? A representation of man's untamed inner nature? A wild god from the woods? Christ giving the Word of God? No one knows.

Timber-framed houses in Saffron Walden

✚ C2

Tourist information ✉ 1 Market Place ☎ 01799 510444; www.uttlesford.gov.uk

SAFFRON WALDEN

Saffron Walden is certainly the best-looking small town in Essex. An excellent *Town Trail* booklet is available from the tourist office in the Market Place. For sale each August from the tourist office and the museum on Museum Street are the saffron crocus bulbs that made the town's fame and fortune in the Middle Ages – they produced yellow dye ideal for the woolen cloth spun all over East Anglia then.

You'll also find the saffron crocus flower honored in carved stone in the Church of St. Mary. From Gold Street there is a memorable exterior view of the church with its 193-foot spire. Take a look inside to admire the angel roof. Other sights include the medieval houses along Bridge Street and in Myddylton Place; the peaceful haven of Bridge End Gardens, with lawns, rose pergolas and trees; and the rich plasterwork molding (known as pargeting) that adorns the old Sun Inn. There are a number of book and antique shops on Church Street, and a network of alleyways and shops around the Market Place.

Don't leave without trying the brick-paved maze on the town common; it has baffled people for 800 years!

STAMFORD

Stamford, down in the southwest corner of Lincolnshire, is a beautifully preserved town of 17th- and 18th-century buildings constructed from attractive cream-colored limestone. Filmmakers love to set period costume dramas here, and no wonder. There are many cobbled lanes, and on Barn Hill and Broad Street are rows of dignified stone door and window frames, porches and chimneys. Several church spires rise from the roofscape.

Stamford Museum contains a wax effigy of Daniel Lambert (1770–1809), who rejoiced in the title of "Britain's Fattest Man": he weighed 628 pounds when he died. Lambert is buried in the graveyard of the Church of St. Martin's. Inside the church is an alabaster effigy of William Cecil, adviser to Queen Elizabeth I and builder of Burghley House (see page 110), just south of town.

✚ B3

Tourist information ✉ Stamford Arts Centre, 27 St. Mary's Street ☎ 01780 755611; www.southwestlincs.com

Stamford Museum ✉ Broad Street ☎ 01780 766317 🕐 Mon.–Sat. 10–5, Sun. 1–5, Apr.–Sep.; Mon.–Sat. 10–5, rest of year 🎟 Free

HEART OF ENGLAND

"IN the rural landscape of the "Heart of England" – commonly referred to as the Midlands – is the oldest university in the country, the mightiest non-royal palace, the stoutest castle and three of the country's most beautiful cathedrals."

Opposite: The narrow Church Lane at Ledbury

HEART OF ENGLAND

Heart of England

"Heart of England" is essentially a tourist board label, intended to soften the unflattering image of grimy manufacturing cities called up at the mention of the traditional reference to England's central area: the Midlands. It is certainly true that this region was the birthplace of Britain's

0	10 20 30	40 km
0	10	20 miles

CHESHIRE

STOKE-ON-TRENT

DERBYSHIRE

DERBY

4

Ellesmere

Market Drayton

STAFFORDSHIRE

East Midlands ✈

Oswestry

SHROPSHIRE

Shawbury

Newport

Ashby-de-la-Zouch

Shepshed

Nesscliffe

TELFORD

Coalville

Shrewsbury

Telford

M54

Brownhills

M42

Snailbeach

Severn

Ironbridge Gorge

Walsall

Sutton Coldfield

Atherstone

3

The Long Mynd

Church Stretton

Wolverhampton

West Bromwich

M6 Toll

Hinckley

Hope Bowdler

Bridgnorth

Dudley

Great Barr

Coleshill

Nuneaton

Clun Forest

Kingswinford

Birmingham

✈

M6

Bedworth

Craven Arms

Stourbridge

Halesowen

Solihull

Coventry

Stokesay Castle

Kidderminster

Kenilworth

Rugby

Ludlow

Bewdley

Bromsgrove

M42

Leamington Spa

WALES

Croft Castle

Tenbury Wells

Stourport-on-Severn

Redditch

M40

Warwick Castle

Eardisland

Leominster

Lower Broadheath

WORCESTERSHIRE

Alcester

WARWICKSHIRE

Kington

Pembridge

Stoke Lacy

Worcester

M5

Avon

Stratford-upon-Avon

2

Willersley

Weobley

Great Malvern

Pershore

Banbury

Hay-on-Wye

Wye

HEREFORDSHIRE

Little Malvern

Evesham

Chipping Campden

Ledbury

Malvern Hills

Broadway

Moreton-in-Marsh

Hook Norton

Hereford

Much Marcle

M50

Tewkesbury

Stanton

Great Tew

Abbey Dore

Kilpeck

Winchcombe

Stanway

Stow-on-the-Wold

Chipping Norton

Ross-on-Wye

Bishop's Cleeve

Cleeve Hill

Lower Slaughter

Woodstock

Symonds Yat

Gloucester

Cheltenham

Bourton-on-the-Water

Blenheim Palace

Cinderford

Forest of Dean

GLOUCESTERSHIRE

Northleach

Burford

Witney

Coleford

Painswick

Chedworth

Bibury

OXFORDSHIRE

Stroud

Cotswolds

Cirencester

Filkins

Bampton

1

Wye

Slimbridge Wildfowl Trust

Nailsworth

Minchinhampton

Fairford

Lechlade

Kelmscot

Berkeley Castle

Dursley

Faringdon

M48

M5

Wotton-under-Edge

Westonbirt Arboretum

Shrivenham

Uffington

Wantage

SOUTH GLOUCESTER-SHIRE

Chipping Sodbury

WILTSHIRE

M4

A   B   C

Industrial Revolution. And the growth of huge manufacturing conurbations such as Birmingham and Leicester and their accompanying roads, railroads and canals have detracted from the rural idyll in some places. But the Heart of England covers a lot of ground. Here, too, are the beautiful Cotswold Hills with their perfect little limestone villages; the lift and sweep of the Herefordshire and Shropshire hills along the Welsh border; and the green lowlands of woods and fields in Warwickshire, where William Shakespeare was born and spent his formative years.

Rivers and Hills

Toward the western part of the region you will find the most dramatic landscapes, the red stone that underpins the Welsh border hills and the red earth that covers them. The sister rivers of Severn and Wye wind a lazy course through much of this countryside. The River Severn flows from Wales through Shropshire and on through Worcestershire, widening toward the start of its mighty estuary that splits the edges of southern Gloucestershire. The River Wye snakes to meet the Severn through the lush cattle-grazing country of Herefordshire.

Shropshire has the fine whaleback uplift of the Long Mynd, and to the east a succession of narrow gorges along the River Severn. Here in 1709 an iron-master named Abraham Darby discovered how to smelt iron cheaply with coke, and this set in motion the monstrous juggernaut of the country's Industrial Revolution.

Worcestershire looks to its mini-mountain chain of the Malvern Hills, aptly nicknamed the "English Alps." Gloucestershire and neighboring Oxfordshire share the Cotswolds, a low rolling range of hills considered by many to be the most appealing stretch of country in southern England.

Heart of England

Sherwood Forest Visitor Centre
Ollerton
Mansfield
ton-in-Ashfield
Hucknall
Southwell
Trent
NOTTINGHAMSHIRE
LINCOLNSHIRE
Nottingham
Loughborough
Melton Mowbray
LEICESTERSHIRE
RUTLAND
Birstall
Leicester
Wigston
utterworth
Oundle
Corby
Market Harborough
Desborough
Nene
Thrapston
Kettering
NORTHAMPTONSHIRE
CAMBRIDGESHIRE
Wellingborough
Rushden
Daventry
Althorp
Northampton
Weedon
Towcester
MILTON KEYNES
Sulgrave
Silverstone
BEDFORDSHIRE
Brackley
BUCKINGHAMSHIRE
Bicester
LUTON
Marston
Waterperry
HERTFORDSHIRE
OXFORD
Thame
Chilterns
Abingdon
Dorchester
Stonor Park
Marlow
GREATER LONDON
Goring
Henley-on-Thames
Cookham
Pangbourne
Mapledurham
D
E

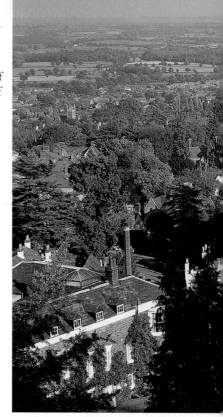

Regional Architecture

These southern regions of the Heart of England show very distinctive styles of building that reflect the underlying stone in some parts, the growth of brick-making in others. Shropshire, Herefordshire and Worcestershire are famous for their black-and-white, half-timbered houses that look as if they have existed since medieval times – as many have, in fact. Around Weobley (pronounced "Webley") and Leominster (pronounced "Lemster") in west Herefordshire, you can follow a special signposted trail through the best of these "black-and-white" villages.

Many of the churches in this region are built of dark red sandstone, with squat fortress-like towers that are reminders of bitter Anglo-Welsh conflict in days gone by. Other fortified buildings include castles and sturdy manor houses; Stokesay Castle, just north of Ludlow in Shropshire, is the oldest and finest in England. Grand and graceful ecclesiastical buildings are here, too, notably the "three cathedrals" of Hereford, Gloucester and Worcester that encircle the Malvern Hills.

The buildings of east Gloucestershire and west Oxfordshire are of a different order, for here they are made mostly of the limestone that underlies the Cotswolds, varying from palest silver to the deepest gold. The buildings in the university city of Oxford, far and away the most stunning city in the Heart of England region, exemplify the beauty of this Cotswold stone.

Cotswold Delights

The Cotswold towns and villages are havens for antique shops and local crafts – Stow-on-the-Wold and Broadway are particular hotspots. The idyllic village of Chipping Campden boasts its own group of "Morris Men" who perform the traditional English Morris Dance in the market square on May Day (May 1) and some summer weekends. Dressed in white, and decorated with bells and ribbons, they dance to the fiddle and accordion. There are lovely pubs all through this region; the Falkland Arms in Great Tew is one of the most characterful. The city of Cheltenham has elegant shopping streets decorated with flower-filled hanging baskets; it also plays host to the Cheltenham Music Festival in July and the National Hunt festival in March, one of Britain's best steeplechase events.

Rivers and Waterways

North of the Cotswold belt lies green and pleasant Warwickshire, bisected by the slow-flowing River Avon, on whose banks William Shakespeare grew up in Stratford-upon-Avon. The shadow of

Great Malvern, with houses nestling around the Priory

Shakespeare lies long in his home town, which draws millions of visitors each year, and it is an undisputed center for theater. Warwick Castle, north of Stratford, is another immensely popular tourist attraction – a magnificent, grim medieval stronghold.

The River Thames threads and loops its way through the region, passing through Oxford before heading off to London. It is dotted with the villages and their accompanying pubs that grew up along its banks, and it is alive with boats. The crowning event of the river's year is the Royal Regatta in June at Henley-on-Thames, an international rowing event that also is firmly on the social calendar.

Canals crisscross this region, a legacy of the days before the railroads. You can go boating on the placid Grand Union Canal as it winds from London to Birmingham. Farther north stretches the open countryside of Leicestershire, prime hunting territory, and the semi-agricultural, semi-industrial county of Nottinghamshire, where the leafy remnants of Robin Hood's Sherwood Forest rub shoulders with gritty coal-mining country.

Such scenes provide a hint of what you find when you arrive in the West Midlands – the sprawling industry of Birmingham and the neighboring towns of the appropriately named Black Country. This region is home to a lively and enjoyable multicultural society which has enriched the area through the music, arts, cuisine and indigenous culture of a dozen nations. There is a "can-do" atmosphere in Birmingham, where you will meet friendly people speaking with an accent as distinctive as a birthmark.

OXFORD

Any visitor to Britain who aims further than London should have Oxford at the top of the agenda. This is a truly extraordinary city, the seat of the most famous university in the world and one of Europe's richest ensembles of medieval architecture. The 19th-century poet Matthew Arnold wrote seductively of a "sweet city with her dreaming spires," a magnetic image in the minds of so many visitors making their way to Oxford. Yet one's first impressions are generally disappointing. So powerful are those images of timeless towers and dignified colleges that it will come as something of a

"The High," as Oxford's High Street is known

shock to find yourself navigating the housing subdivisions, ring roads and shopping malls with which Oxford has gradually become surrounded. But press on, and cheer up! The dreaming spires and the glorious architecture are still there, once you make your way to the very heart of the city.

The Early University

Oxford developed around a ford on the Thames, and had probably already become a seat of learning by 1167, when English scholars cast out by the University of Paris settled here. The colleges were built more or less to a conventional monastic pattern of chapel, dormitories and refectory around a quadrangle. Until Elizabethan times college residence was reserved for dons (tutors) and graduates, and the students continued to lodge all over town. Pre-Reformation traditions persisted for centuries; for example, until 1877 dons were not permitted to marry, and women were not awarded degrees until as late as 1920.

Town and Gown

Church influence over the thinking of the undergraduates and dons did not last as long, however. During the Middle Ages Oxford became a hothouse for intellectual liberty, which at times translated into anarchic behavior on the part of students – hence the number of "town-versus-gown" confrontations that not infrequently led to serious injury or death. Before the colleges admitted undergraduates into residence, these disputes were exacerbated by the famously loose morals of the student lodgers around Oxford.

These days things are a lot quieter and less confrontational. Don't expect to see all the undergraduates in "Oxford bags" (loose flannel trousers), long scarves and billowing black gowns – this is the 21st century, after all! By their bicycles shall ye know them. Don't be fooled by their casual appearance, either. An Oxford degree is no longer the absolute "open sesame" to success in politics, business or the church that it once was, but Oxford and Cambridge between them continue even now to be the goal of the brightest pupils.

Getting Your Bearings

All the chief Oxford sights are within a 20-minute walk of the city center. You can stroll around them independently (see page 137), or join an official guided walking tour departing from the Tourist Information Centre on Broad Street (daily at 11 and 2 lasting 2 hours; additional tours during busy periods). The train station is a 10-minute walk west of the center (shuttle buses make the journey in five minutes).

Orienting yourself is not difficult. The old city is bounded by water – the River Cherwell on the east and the Oxford Canal on the west. Carfax Tower is the city's hub, with High Street (known as "The High") running east from the tower to Magdalen Bridge over the Cherwell. The High neatly divides the center into south and north; there are colleges on both sides, but most of the other attractions are north of The High.

Eat, Drink and Enjoy

Given the number of undergraduates in Oxford, it's not surprising that there are dozens of inexpensive eateries in town – and some are quite good. The Covered Market off The High just north of

Heart of England

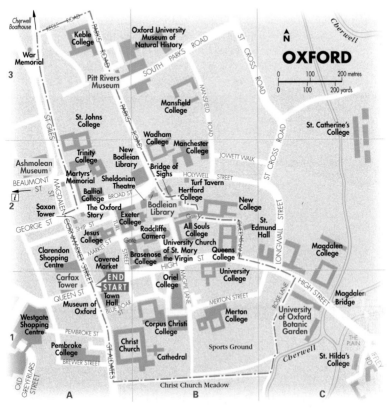

Popular transportation outside Balliol College

boat) to work it all off. Oxford's pubs range from the tacky to the atmospheric – of the latter, try the Eagle and Child on St. Giles (known locally as the "Bird and Baby") or the diminutive Turf Tavern, on Bath Place off Holywell Street, not far from the Bodleian Library.

The Covered Market is good fun for impromptu bric-a-brac purchases, too. When in Oxford, buy books – new ones at Blackwell's on Broad Street, *the* Oxford bookstore, or secondhand in various emporia (ask for a free leaflet at the Oxford Information Centre). Secure an unearned but authentic-looking university sweater, scarf or mug from the University of Oxford Shop on The High.

Carfax Tower is a good bet for pleasant café-style nibbling, and on The High itself you'll find numerous places for tea and cakes. You can eat well by the river at the Cherwell Boathouse on Bardwell Road, then rent a punt (flat-bottomed

At night, try the college chapels or the venerable Sheldonian Theatre for a concert, or the lively Oxford Playhouse on Beaumont Street for plays, opera, a concert or whatever else is going on. In summer, undergraduates sometimes put on open-air performances on the grounds of their colleges.

ESSENTIAL INFORMATION

 TOURIST INFORMATION
✉ 15–16 Broad Street ☏ 01865 726871; www.visitoxford.org

 URBAN TRANSPORTATION
The main railroad station is on Botley Road, half a mile west of the center. There also is a frequent bus link. For information and reservations contact the national rail information service, ☏ 08457 484950. The bus station at Gloucester Green is where the longer distance buses terminate. Most city buses leave from St. Aldates, Magdalen Street or Queen Street. For further details on local travel contact

The Oxford Bus Company, ☏ 01865 785400. For long-distance bus services, contact Stagecoach Oxford, ☏ 01865 772250, or National Express, ☏ 08705 808080. There are taxi stands outside the railroad station and at Gloucester Green (by the market).

 AIRPORT INFORMATION
Oxford is linked directly by bus to Heathrow, Gatwick, Luton and Stansted airports. For Heathrow and Gatwick contact Oxford Express, ☏ 08706 082608. For Luton and Stansted contact Jetlink, ☏ 08705 747777.

CLIMATE – Average highs and lows

JAN.	FEB.	MAR.	APR.	MAY	JUN.	JUL.	AUG.	SEP.	OCT.	NOV.	DEC.
6°C	6°C	9°C	12°C	16°C	18°C	21°C	21°C	17°C	13°C	9°C	7°C
43°F	43°F	48°F	54°F	61°F	64°F	70°F	70°F	63°F	55°F	48°F	45°F
1°C	1°C	2°C	3°C	6°C	9°C	12°C	11°C	9°C	6°C	3°C	2°C
34°F	34°F	36°F	37°F	43°F	48°F	54°F	52°F	48°F	43°F	37°F	36°F

The Ashmolean Museum, which houses a vast and varied collection

OXFORD SIGHTS

Key to symbols

⊞ map coordinates refer to the Oxford map on page 131; sights below are highlighted in yellow on the map.
⊠ address or location ☎ telephone number
◉ opening times ⏹ restaurant on site or nearby
⚲ admission charge: $$$ more than £6, $$ £2–£6, $ less than £2 ⏹ information

ASHMOLEAN MUSEUM

The museum was founded in 1683 around the utterly catholic collection of explorer John Tradescant, and has been growing ever since then. The melange of exhibits encompasses Michelangelo and Raphael, Egyptian mummies and Islamic ceramics, Impressionists and pre-Raphaelites, Oliver Cromwell's death mask and the lantern Guy Fawkes was holding when he was arrested plotting to blow up London's parliament buildings.

⊞ A2 ⊠ Beaumont Street ☎ 01865 278000 ◉ Tue.–Sat. 10–5 (also Thu. 5–7, Jun.–Aug.), Sun. noon–5 ⏹ Café ⚲ Free

BODLEIAN LIBRARY

Founded in Tudor times, this library contains more than 7 million books. The fan-vaulted, 15th-century Divinity School housed the English Parliament during the Civil War (1642–46) and is still used for university ceremonies. The most precious manuscripts are stored securely away, but frequent exhibitions display many of the library's treasures. The cylindrical room and dome of the Radcliffe Camera, now the Bodleian's reading room, were built in the mid-18th century with a bequest of the royal physician Sir John Radcliffe to house his scientific books. Admire the exterior; it is not open to the public.

Bodleian Library ⊞ B2 ⊠ Broad Street ☎ 01865 277224 ◉ Mon.–Fri. 9–4:45, Sat. 9–12:30 ⚲ Free ⏹ Guided tours ($$) available

The Radcliffe Camera reading room

Heart of England

Although not all the colleges of Oxford University are crammed together in the center of the old city, the most interesting ones are. Brief descriptions of the best follow, in the order in which they are encountered during the course of the Oxford walk (see page 137).

Colleges are becoming increasingly unpredictable in the hours they are open to the general public, but remember that these are educational establishments, not museums. Opening times (mainly afternoons) are displayed on boards at each college entrance. Carry cash so that you can pay whatever entrance fee (generally moderate) is suggested, and try to phone in advance the colleges you wish to visit, to avoid disappointment if they happen to be closed.

Wren's sundial at All Souls College

OXFORD COLLEGES

Christ Church was founded in 1525 by Cardinal Thomas Wolsey. The college chapel doubles as Oxford's cathedral; it retains some Saxon work and a 12th-century nave and choir, along with 15th-century vaulting. The arcaded Tom Quad is the chief quadrangle; the gallery in Canterbury Quad contains paintings by Renaissance masters. "Great Tom" bell is rung 101 times beginning at 9:05 each evening from the Sir Christopher Wren-designed Tom Tower over the gateway, a ritual curfew disregarded by today's less tradition-bound undergraduates.

Magdalen, pronounced "Maudlin," has a foundation dating from 1458, with some truly grotesque gargoyles around the cloisters, a fine paneled 15th-century hall and a beautiful tower rising over The High. On May Day (May 1) morning the choir sings hymns at sunrise (6 a.m.) from the tower top, a fine Oxford tradition.

University College is largely composed of handsome buildings from the mid-17th century. Tradition says this was the site of the first learned community in Oxford, established in AD 872 by King Alfred.

Queen's College consists of a 14th-century foundation rebuilt in the 17th and 18th centuries in fine baroque style, with input from Sir Christopher Wren and his pupil Nicholas Hawksmoor.

New College was founded in 1379 by William of Wykeham, Bishop of Winchester, who had founded Winchester College four years previously. He wished to ensure a supply of well-educated priests to fill in the gaps in the ranks of the clergy caused by the disastrous Black Death plague some 30 years before. The college chapel contains the bishop's jeweled crozier, a study of St. James by El Greco, a stained-glass Nativity in the west window designed by Sir Joshua Reynolds, and a 1951 statue by Sir Jacob Epstein of Lazarus awakening from the slumber of death.

All Souls is unique in that it has no undergraduates, but only fellows (graduates elected for periods of research). A very fine restored 15th-century facade fronts The High. The chapel contains beautiful 15th-century stained glass and a handsome hammerbeam roof. Sir Christopher Wren was a fellow, and designed the colored sundial in the quad.

Trinity, set in beautiful grounds, was founded in 1555, the same year as the martyrdom of Bishops Latimer and Ridley. Wren designed its lovely Garden Quad. In the chapel are exquisite late 17th-century carvings by master carver Grinling Gibbons.

Ancient gateway to Magdalen College

Punts for rent on the Cherwell by Magdalen Bridge

Merton traces its origins back to 1264. It was the first college to bring pupils and tutors together under one roof. Mob Quad, dating from the 14th century, has the oldest library in England. Beautified with Tudor woodwork, it contains an astrolabe (an instrument used for navigating by the stars) once owned by Geoffrey Chaucer. In the chapel is more stained glass from the 13th and 14th centuries.

Christ Church ✉ St. Aldates ☎ 01865 286573
Magdalen ✉ High Street ☎ 01865 276000
University College 🕐 Closed to visitors
Queen's College 🕐 Closed to visitors except on official tours (ask at the tourist office)
New College ✉ New College Lane ☎ 01865 279555
All Souls ✉ High Street ☎ 01865 279379
Trinity ✉ Broad Street ☎ 01865 279900
Merton ✉ Merton Street ☎ 01865 276310

The Pitt Rivers Museum is housed in the Oxford University Museum of Natural History

CARFAX TOWER

The tower, all that remains of the 14th-century St. Martin's Church, is located in the center of town where Cornmarket Street and St. Aldates meet The High. Animated figures known as quarterjacks strike out the quarter-hours. You can climb 99 steps to the top for a superb view over all of central Oxford.

🕂 A1–A2 ✉ The High ☎ 01865 792653 🕓 Daily 10–5:30, Apr.–Oct.; 10–3:30, rest of year 🎟 $

PITT RIVERS MUSEUM

This is a wonderfully anachronistic place, the absolute antithesis of the modern, high-tech, interactive museum. Here are case upon case of ethnic artifacts and scientific and archeological curiosities – including some South American shrunken heads – brought to Oxford from the corners of the earth during the great halcyon days of the British Empire.

🕂 B3 ✉ South Parks Road (enter from interior of the Oxford University Museum of Natural History, see page 137) ☎ 01865 270927 🕓 Daily noon–4:30 🎟 Free 🛈 Audio-guided tours ($) available

UNIVERSITY OF OXFORD BOTANIC GARDEN

The great greenhouse backing onto the River Cherwell near Magdalen Bridge was established nearly 400 years ago, the first garden in Britain devoted to the scientific study of plants. The formal flower beds and yew tree date from the garden's inception.

It is from the parapet on Magdalen Bridge that you can rent a punt, and also from where undergraduates ritually launch themselves into the Cherwell after learning the results of their final examinations.

🕂 C1 ✉ Rose Lane ☎ 01865 286690 🕓 Daily 9–6 (last admission at 5:15), May–Sep.; 9–5 (last admission at 4:15), Mar.–Apr. and in Oct.; 9–4:30, rest of year 🎟 $$

Punting

This is the way to savor Oxford's atmosphere at a laid-back pace. The River Cherwell is a good choice; rent a punt (flat-bottomed boat) at Magdalen Bridge or at the Cherwell Boathouse (restaurant), on Bardwell Road north of the center, and pole gently downstream. The pole acts as a source of forward movement (push gently on the river bottom) and as a steering device (like the rudder on a boat). It is blissfully simple– unless you forget to withdraw the punting pole from the riverbed in time.

🕂 C1 ✉ Bardwell Road ☎ 01865 515978 🕓 Daily, mid-Mar. to mid Oct. 🍴 Restaurant 🎟 Punting $$$

The Museum of Oxford: Place of learning for visitors

WALK: CENTRAL OXFORD

Refer to route marked on city map on page 131

Allow a whole day for this walk, since there are many museums, libraries and college buildings to explore. Some of the best-known and most enjoyable are described on pages 133–136, but you are bound to discover others along the way.

Start at Carfax in the center of town.
Be sure to climb Carfax Tower before setting off to see Oxford's treasures.

Walk south down St. Aldates to the Town Hall, housing the Museum of Oxford.
The museum gives an entertaining and informative trot through the history of Oxford since Roman times, and is a good precursor to a walk around the city.

After visiting the museum, continue along St. Aldates past Christ Church College and turn left onto Broad Walk through meadows to the River Cherwell, then proceed across Merton Field and up Rose Lane to The High.
Ahead is Magdalen College; to the right is the University of Oxford Botanic Garden and Magdalen Bridge.

Turn left onto The High and proceed until you turn right onto Queen's Lane. New College soon appears on the right, as the road becomes New College Lane.
Bath Place is on the right, with the Turf Tavern

beckoning – one of Oxford's best small pubs.

Proceed on New College Lane under the Bridge of Sighs until you reach Catte Street. Turn right on Catte Street to cross Broad Street, with the Sheldonian Theatre on your left.
The theater was an early design by Sir Christopher Wren. Inside, a ceiling painting shows Ignorance and Jealousy cast out by Art and Science. Degree ceremonies and concerts are held here. Ahead on the right along Parks Road, past Wadham College, is the Oxford University Museum of Natural History with the Pitt Rivers Museum (see page 136) inside. Displays are in a huge, glass-roofed hall and range from dinosaur skeletons to fossils.

Continue on Parks Road and turn left past Keble College onto Keble Road, then left onto broad St. Giles. Pass between the Ashmolean Museum on your right and Trinity College on your left.
On the corner of Broad Street is The Oxford Story, an interesting exhibition about the university, its history and its personalities.

Turn right, and then left onto Cornmarket Street and return to Carfax Tower.

Museum of Oxford ➕ A1 ✉ Town Hall, St. Aldates ☎ 01865 252761 ⏰ Tue.–Fri. 10–4, Sat. 10–5, Sun. noon–4 ♿ \$\$ 🛈 Audio tours

Oxford University Museum of Natural History ➕ B3 ✉ Parks Road ☎ 01865 272950 ⏰ Daily noon–5 ♿ Free

The Oxford Story ➕ A2 ✉ 6 Broad Street ☎ 01865 728822 ⏰ Daily 9:30–5, Jul.–Aug.; Mon.–Sat. 10–4:30, Sun. 11–4:30, rest of year ♿ \$\$\$

REGIONAL SIGHTS

Key to symbols

✚ map coordinates refer to the Heart of England map on pages 126–127; sights below are highlighted in yellow on the map.

✉ address or location ☎ telephone number
◷ opening times 🍴 restaurant on site or nearby
🥤 admission charge: $$$ more than £6, $$ £2–£6,
$ less than £2 ℹ️ information

ALTHORP

Until 1980, Althorp was only vaguely known as a pleasant Georgian country house in Northamptonshire with an interesting collection of portraits of the Spencer family by artists Thomas Gainsborough and Sir Joshua Reynolds. Then came the announcement of the engagement of Lady Diana Spencer to Charles, Prince of Wales, and Althorp suddenly became one of the best-known houses in the country. Diana's tragic early death in 1997 has fixed her childhood home firmly in the public imagination, for it is here that she lies buried on an island in a lake. An exhibition, "Diana: A Celebration," commemorates this glamorous and tragic person.

✚ D2
✉ Off A428, 6 miles northwest of Northampton
☎ 01604 770107 ◷ Daily 11–5, Jul.–Sep.; closed Aug. 31 🍴 Café 🥤 $$$ (house $$ extra)

BLENHEIM PALACE

The Royal Manor of Woodstock in Oxfordshire, a former royal hunting lodge, was presented to John Churchill, 1st Duke of Marlborough, as a token of the nation's gratitude for thrashing the French at the Battle of Blenheim in 1704. Over the next 20 years the duke (and after his death in 1722, his widow Sarah) oversaw the construction of a baroque residence so large and grand that it could properly be termed a "palace" – the only non-royal one in the land. Sir John Vanbrugh and Wren's pupil Nicholas Hawksmoor were the chief architects. From the front, with its colonnaded portico, great wings stretch back to enclose a Great Court. Among the 200 rooms are the 183-foot Long

Blenheim: Birthplace of Winston Churchill

Library, the frescoed Saloon, and state rooms rich with Old Master paintings, tapestries and Grinling Gibbons carvings. Several rooms are dedicated to Sir Winston Churchill (prime minister of Britain during World War II), who was born here in 1874 and lies buried in nearby Bladon church.

Outside you can wander around 2,100 acres of beautiful parkland landscaped by Capability Brown. You also can try the maze and visit the Butterfly House. The handsome town of Woodstock, standing at the gates of the estate, holds plenty of interest, with a number of tearooms and restaurants, and some interesting antiques, souvenir and jewelry shops.

✚ D1
✉ On A44 at Woodstock, 8 miles northwest of Oxford
☎ 08700 602080 ◷ Park: daily 9–4:45. House: daily 10:30–4:45, mid-Feb. to mid-Dec. Pleasure Gardens, Marlborough Maze and Butterfly House: daily 10–5:30, mid-Feb. to mid-Dec. 🍴 Restaurants and cafés
🥤 $$$ ℹ️ Guided tours of house every 5–10 minutes

Opposite: Warwick Castle stands beside the River Avon

Regency splendor in Cheltenham: Pittville Pump Room

CHELTENHAM

Cheltenham's medicinal spring was discovered in 1718, and by the time of King George III's visit in 1788 it had become an important spa town. But it was the patronage of the king's son, the fun-loving dandy George, Prince of Wales, that really set the town in the firmament of inland resorts. You can admire the Regency elegance of the green-roofed Rotunda and stroll down the wide Promenade with its range of exclusive shops.

The Art Gallery and Museum has an exhibition on William Morris, one of the leading lights of the English arts and crafts movement in the late 19th century.

Round off your afternoon in Regency Cheltenham with a cup of tea and a delicate cucumber sandwich at one of the numerous tearooms, then saunter to Pittville Park to take the rather nasty-flavored waters under the blue domed roof of the Pittville Pump Room.

✚ C1–C2

Tourist information ✉ 77 The Promenade ☎ 01242 522878; www.visitcheltenham.com

Cheltenham Art Gallery and Museum ✉ Clarence Street ☎ 01242 237431 🕐 Mon.–Sat. 10–5:20 (opens at 11, first Thu. of each month) 🍴 Café 💰 Donation requested

CIRENCESTER

Cirencester is the capital of the Cotswolds, and its market, on Mondays and Fridays, draws many people from the surrounding rural region. There are fashionable boutiques, as well as antiques shops; a converted Victorian brewery, Brewery Arts, off Crickland Street, is a good place to purchase art and crafts. It's run by a co-operative of local artists – you can watch them at work in their studios.

The 15th-century parish church of St. John Baptist has a heavily buttressed tower and a mighty three-story south porch rich in fan vaulting. Wool wealth built and beautified the church, as it did the rest of Cirencester. Along Cecily Hill are the very grand town houses of Jacobean and Georgian wool merchants.

The Romans named the town they built here Corinium, and bits and pieces are continually being excavated. Many of the best – including some touching and evocative mosaics – are on display in the Corinium Museum.

✚ C1

Tourist information ✉ The Corn Hall, Market Place ☎ 01285 654180; www.cotswold.gov.uk

Corinium Museum ✉ Park Street ☎ 01285 655611 🕐 Mon.–Sat. 10–5, Sun. 2–5 🍴 Restaurant 💰 $$

Early morning sun warms the glowing stone in Chipping Campden

COTSWOLD VILLAGES

The Cotswolds owe their reputation among lovers of the subtler forms of English landscape to the beautiful limestone that underlies them, so productive when it comes to making attractive dips and hollows, so eye-catching when used for building. Oak and beech woods clothe the Cotswolds, interspersed with cornfields and open grazing land. These hills nurtured sheep to enrich medieval wool masters, and the wool men, in gratitude and self-advertisement, built beautiful churches. Chipping Campden, Cirencester, Fairford, Northleach, Painswick and Winchcombe are among the best. The wool masters also built fine gabled and mullioned houses for themselves, and handsome wool barns that still stand under stone-tiled roofs. The landscape is cross-hatched by mile upon mile of drystone walls (built without mortar), some of them tumbledown nowadays, others kept in wonderful repair.

Of the dozens of gorgeous Cotswold towns and villages you should at least try to see Bourton-on-the-Water, the "Venice of the Cotswolds," with its tiny bridges and plentiful antiques shops and tearooms. Chipping Campden is perhaps the most appealing small town in the Cotswolds. The villages of Broadway, Stanton and Stanway are heavenly.

Broadway ➕ C2
Tourist information ✉ Cotswold Court ☎ 01386 852937; www.cotswold.gov.uk
Bourton-on-the-Water ➕ C1
Tourist information ✉ Victoria Street ☎ 01451 820211; www.cotswold.gov.uk
Chipping Campden ➕ C2
Tourist information ✉ The Old Police Station, High Street ☎ 01386 841206; www.cotswold.gov.uk

Cheese Rolling

Six miles southwest of Cheltenham, Coopers' Hill is the venue for one of central England's oddest events. The annual Cheese Rolling festival takes place on the second public holiday in May; it involves a large Double Gloucester cheese being rolled down a steep hill, followed by dozens of villagers in hot pursuit. It's a serious matter, however; the prize goes to the first one to grab the cheese!

The cloisters at Gloucester Cathedral

DRIVE: THREE CATHEDRALS COUNTRY

Distance: 65 miles

This drive leads you in a ragged circle around some very typical south Midlands countryside, green and rolling, and takes in three outstanding medieval cathedrals, an abbey church and a beautiful Saxon chapel along the way – not to mention England's own "mini-Alps" and the one-time home of American poet Robert Frost.

Start in the city of Worcester.

Worcester has a sandstone cathedral occupying a superb location on the bank of the River Severn. The early Norman chapter house is worth seeing, as is the big Norman crypt and the marble effigy of King John, who died

in 1216 and lies buried here. Worcester is one of three neighboring cathedrals – Gloucester and Hereford are the others – which host the famous Three Choirs Festival each August. On Worcester's Severn Street you can visit the factory and showroom of the Royal Worcester porcelain company, makers of fine china since 1751.

From Worcester A449 runs southwest and skirts the Malvern Hills.
The Malverns are a 9-mile-long chain of miniature mountains. Malvern spring water is famed for its purity, and there are still spa wells here where you can taste the water.

A449 continues to Ledbury.
Ledbury is a charming small town, with its ancient Market Hall standing proud on tall wooden legs in the center. Cobbled Church Lane, a feast of black-and-white medieval buildings, leads to the Church of St. Michael and All Angels. This is a splendid building with a detached tower and spire, a handsome Norman west front and an interior full of fine stonemasonry and memorials. Hereford (see page 144) is 15 miles west along A438.

From Ledbury, take A449 (in the Ross-on-Wye direction) southwest. After 1 mile you'll reach B4216 (toward Dymock) branching off to the left; pass this and take the second left, a winding lane. After 1 mile you'll pass a black-and-white farmhouse on your right at the brow of a short hill.
This farmhouse was Little Iddens, where Robert Frost came to stay as a young unpublished poet just before World War I. For a few golden months in the summer of 1914 Little Iddens was a powerhouse of poetry, with eminent poets gathering under the charming spell of Frost. They included Rupert Brooke, Lascelles Abercrombie, Wilfred Gibson, Eleanor Farjeon and the soon-to-be-celebrated Edward Thomas, who died in the Battle of Arras in 1917, leaving behind some exquisite rural poetry. Collectively, they were known as the "Dymock Poets."

Continue along the lane to Dymock, then follow B4215 through Newent to Gloucester.
Here Gloucester's glorious Norman cathedral stands under a graceful 225-foot spire. Inside are wonderful 14th-century fan-vaulting in the cloisters, plenty of fine medieval stained glass and the tomb of King Edward II, gruesomely murdered with a red-hot poker in nearby Berkeley Castle in 1327.

The half-timbered Market Hall at Ledbury

Take A417 (the Ledbury road) north from Gloucester. After 5 miles, at Hartpury, bear right on a series of local roads through Ashleworth.
Here a medieval farm and a fine riverside pub, the Boat, are down a side lane.

After Hasfield, turn right on B4213 to cross the River Severn at Haw Bridge. After 1 mile turn left, pass through Apperley and continue to the Saxon church at Deerhurst, a mile farther on. A minor road joins Deerhurst with B4213 and then A38; turn left at A38 to reach Tewkesbury.
This handsome town has a superb abbey. The Norman structure is rich in fan-vaulted chantry chapels and tomb effigies. You can climb the tower for views over the countryside.

Return to Worcester via A38 or M5.

Worcester ✚ B2
Tourist information ✉ The Guildhall, High Street ☎ 01905 726311; www.visitworcester.com
Worcester Cathedral ✉ College Green ☎ 01905 28854 🕐 Daily 7:30–6 🍽 Café 🎟 Donation ($$) requested ℹ Tours May–Aug.
Gloucester ✚ B1
Tourist information ✉ 28 Southgate Street ☎ 01452 396572; www.gloucester.gov.uk/gloucester
Gloucester Cathedral ✉ College Green ☎ 01452 528095 🕐 Daily 7:30–after Evensong (Mon.–Fri. at 5:30, Sat. at 4:30, Sun. at 3) 🍽 Restaurant 🎟 $$ donation requested ℹ Guided tours available

Heart of England

A medieval bridge crosses the River Wye near Hereford Cathedral

HEREFORD

Like most important communities along the border with Wales, Hereford suffered numerous sackings and burnings throughout the turbulent Middle Ages. During the 17th century it entered quieter times, and this more prosperous era is reflected in the solid furnishings and handsome decoration of The Old House, a museum of Herefordshire life in Stuart times. Nearby stands the city's pink sandstone cathedral, with its Norman interior, and Tudor chantry with elaborate fan-vaulting. The most outstanding feature is the Mappa Mundi ("map of the world"), drawn by Richard de Bello in 1289. The big circular map writhes with beasts both real and legendary – rhinoceros and unicorn, centaur and salamander, men and monsters, Minotaur and Golden Fleece. Mappa Mundi shows an imagination stimulated and stretched by the tension between the certainties of Holy Scripture and tales of the voyages of brave adventurers in that medieval flat-earth world.

➕ B2

Tourist information ✉ 1 King Street ☎ 01432 268430; www.herefordshire.gov.uk

Hereford Cathedral and Mappa Mundi ✉ Cathedral Close ☎ 01432 374202 🕐 Cathedral: daily 9:15–Evensong. Mappa Mundi: Mon.–Sat. 10–5, Easter–Oct. 31. (also Sun. 11–4, May–Sep.); Mon.–Sat. 10–4, rest of year 🍴 Café 🎟 Cathedral (donation suggested) $$; Mappa Mundi $$

The Old House ✉ High Town ☎ 01432 260694 🕐 Tue.–Sat. 10–5, Sun. 10–4, Apr.–Sep. 🎟 Free

LUDLOW

Ludlow is south Shropshire's showpiece town, straddling a sharp-spined ridge and dominated by the Church of St. Laurence. Ludlow Castle overlooks a patchwork of ancient gardens and meadows collectively known as the Linney. A permanent, traditional market under striped awnings is held in the streets between the castle and the church. On Corve Street you can admire ornate black timberwork on the front of the early 17th-century Feathers Hotel, so named because of an old local industry making feathered arrows. Enjoy a drink in the bar or tea in the lounge. To appreciate the flavor of this ancient town, wander down Broad Street, up Raven Lane or along Old and Corve streets.

Robin Hood

The legends of Robin Hood and his Merry Men, who stole from the (usually wicked) rich to give to the (invariably hard-working and good) poor, have survived and been elaborated through seven centuries of storytelling, but even today it is not known for certain whether they have a basis in fact, or are pure fiction. Perhaps because of the durability of the folk tale, it is possible that there was such a character as Robin Hood who lived the life of an outlaw in Sherwood Forest, poaching the king's deer. More likely his character and story is a mix of many such real-life outlaws, heroes of medieval ballads.

Robin Hood statue in Sherwood Forest

✚ B3

Tourist information ✉ Castle Street ☎ 01584 875053; www.ludlow.org.uk

Ludlow Castle ✉ The Square ☎ 01584 873355 🕐 Daily 10–7, in Aug.; daily 10–5, Apr.–Jul. and in Sep.; daily 10–4, Feb.–Mar. and Oct.–Dec.; Sat.–Sun. 10–4, rest of year. Last admission 30 minutes before closing 👋 $$

NOTTINGHAM AND SHERWOOD FOREST

Nottingham is a historic town with a great sense of its past. Nottingham Castle stands on a wonderfully dramatic site, a great crag overlooking the town. The building is forever associated with the epic archery contests, imprisonments and escapes of folk hero Robin Hood in his struggles with the satisfyingly wicked Sheriff of Nottingham. Another tale of daring, dating from 1330, has King Edward III leading a band of friends through a 300-foot-long passage in the rock below the castle in order to capture his mother, Isabella, and her dastardly lover Sir Roger Mortimer. Certainly there are eerie and ancient tunnels through the rock which can be explored during a tour of the castle. Hacked from the walls beneath the castle is England's oldest pub, Ye Olde Trip

to Jerusalem – dating from 1189, it was in use during the 13th-century Crusades to the Holy Land.

The city also is famous for its lace-making, and you can see beautiful examples in the Lace Centre directly opposite the castle gates.

Sherwood Forest is only a shadow of its medieval self after many centuries of tree felling. But you can still find enough of it around Ollerton, 20 miles north of Nottingham, to get yourself happily lost among the trees.

✚ D4

Tourist information ✉ 1–4 Smithy Row ☎ 0115 915 5330; www.nottinghamcity.gov.uk or www.nottinghamshiretourism.co.uk

Nottingham Castle ✉ Off Friar Lane ☎ 0115 915 3700 🕐 Daily 10–5 (last admission at 4:30), mid-Feb. through Oct. 31; 10–4 (last admission at 3:30), rest of year. Castle grounds: daily 8–dusk 👋 Mon.–Fri. free, Sat.–Sun. and public holidays $$

Sherwood Forest Country Park and Visitor Centre ✚ D4 ✉ Edwinstowe, near Mansfield ☎ 01623 823202; www.sherwood-forest.org.uk 🕐 Country park: daily dawn–dusk. Visitor Centre: daily 10–5, Apr.–Oct.; 10–4:30, rest of year 👋 Free

Lace Centre ✉ Castle Road ☎ 0115 941 3539 🕐 Daily 10–5, Apr.–Oct.; 10–4, rest of year 👋 Free

Stained glass in St. Mary's Church, Shrewsbury

OUNDLE

Oundle is a harmonious old town of silver-gray buildings. The mostly 13th-century Church of St. Peter has a fine spire 203 feet high. The spire's crockets (decorative projections) are set just far enough apart to tempt rash boys from Oundle School to climb to the summit and touch "Peter," the weathercock at the tip. One lad achieved the feat in 1880, but when he reached ground level again it was to find his headmaster waiting grimly for him. He was first soundly thrashed for disobeying the school rules, then presented with a golden sovereign to reward his daring: a peculiarly English administration of justice.

In the 17th-century Talbot Inn there is a wide staircase, said to have been brought here from nearby Fotheringhay Castle and to be the one that Mary, Queen of Scots descended on her way to execution at Fotheringhay in 1587. A painting of the scene hangs in the Talbot. On the bank of the River Nene just downstream from Oundle stands a grassy mound, all that remains of the castle, its flat top aptly covered with thistles (the Scottish national emblem) – a poignant reminder of the most tenacious of Scottish queens.

✚ E3

Tourist information ✉ 14 West Street ☎ 01832 274333; www.east-northamptonshire.gov.uk

SHREWSBURY

The capital of Shropshire county lies in a bend of the River Severn, a hunched defensive position appropriate to such an important Welsh Border town. Shrewsbury was attacked, sacked and burned numerous times during the Middle Ages strife between Wales and England. There are some handsome old buildings, notably the twin timber-framed Elizabethan houses of Owen's Mansion and Ireland's Mansion on High Street, reminders of the prosperity that the wool trade once brought to the town.

Shrewsbury Castle dates mostly from the 14th century, as does much of the wonderful stained glass in St. Mary's Church. A statue on the library's grounds opposite the castle commemorates naturalist Charles Darwin, born here in 1809. Shrewsbury Abbey, dating from the 11th century, was originally dedicated to St. Peter and St. Paul.

✚ B3

Tourist information ✉ The Music Hall, The Square ☎ 01743 281200; www.shrewsbury.com
Shrewsbury Castle and the Shropshire Regimental Museum ✉ Castle Street ☎ 01743 358516 🕐 Mon.–Sat. 10–5, Sun. 10–4, Jun.–Sep.; Tue.– Sat. 10–5, day before Easter–May 31 ; Tue.–Sat. 10–4, mid-Feb. through Easter and Oct. 1 through Dec. 25 💷 Castle grounds free; museum $$
Shrewsbury Abbey ✉ Abbey Foregate ☎ 01743 232723 🕐 Daily 10–4:45, Easter–Oct. 31; 10–3, rest of year 💷 $$ donation requested

What is astonishing about the English language's greatest playwright is not so much the sheer volume of brilliant work he produced – 37 plays over a 20-year period, not to mention dozens of sonnets – but that such sustained genius could have flourished in a sketchily educated boy from an obscure Warwickshire market town.

Sign marking the Bard's birthplace

WILLIAM SHAKESPEARE

William Shakespeare was born in a timber-framed house in Stratford-upon-Avon on April 23, 1564. He probably attended the local grammar school, and may have had scrapes with the law and with local landowners over poaching expeditions. In 1582, while still a teenager, he married his pregnant girlfriend Anne Hathaway, a yeoman farmer's daughter from nearby Shottery. They quickly produced a son and two daughters. Then, at some time between 1585 and 1592, William left his young family and moved away to London to carve out a career for himself as an actor-manager and playwright in the lively theater scene then thriving in the raffish red-light district of Southwark.

Within a few years Shakespeare had become joint owner of the wooden-walled Globe Theatre (see page 41), which saw many of his plays launched. In 1603, shortly after the death of Queen Elizabeth I and the accession of King James I, he became patron of the royal theater troupe, the King's Men, a welcome opening of the door of royal approval. But in 1610 Shakespeare sold the theater, moved back to Stratford and hung up his quill. On his own birthday six years later he died, comfortably well off and respected but not lionized, and was buried in the town's Holy Trinity Church, where he had been baptized 52 years before.

These bald facts are what we know for certain about the Bard. After his death Shakespeare's reputation languished in the shadows for well over a century until the actor David Garrick inspired a rekindling of interest in the playwright's works in the 1760s and '70s.

Anne Hathaway's cottage in Shottery, childhood home of Shakespeare's wife

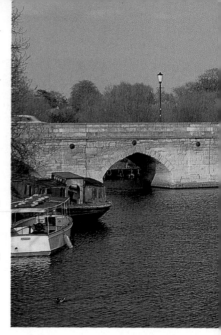

STRATFORD-UPON-AVON

Stratford-upon-Avon lies some 20 miles south of Birmingham, and most of the town itself has no particular claim to interest or beauty. That its Shakespearean associations make it England's most popular tourist destination after London is a testament to the internationally effective magic of the Bard's genius.

Everyone who comes here wants to seek out the Shakespeare sites. These are very well kept and of great intrinsic interest, and a day's stroll will allow you to cover all that are within the town boundaries. If you prefer a guided tour, a number of tour buses take in most of these sites – ask at the tourist office for details. One word of warning, though: You will greatly increase your enjoyment if you can avoid visiting on

The Grammar School numbers Shakespeare among its former pupils

holiday weekends, and especially the months of July and August.

If you want to take in a play, there are three theaters to choose from – the Royal Shakespeare Theatre (a modern building on the riverside), the lovely, galleried Swan Theatre, and The Other Place (a small studio theater). The prestigious Royal Shakespeare Company stages performances at each one. The repertoire ranges from classical playwrights to modern drama, so take your pick. There are a number of restaurants on the riverside, and many offer good-value pre-theater dinners.

On Henley Street stands Shakespeare's Birthplace, a handsome half-timbered building that must have been nearly new when John Shakespeare, William's wool-merchant father, moved in. In subsequent centuries it did duty as a pub, the Swan and Maidenhead. It was bought for the nation in 1847 and refurbished. The "birth room" may not be the actual room in which Shakespeare entered the world. Apparently David Garrick, while in Stratford in 1769 to fan some flames of interest in the long-neglected playwright, arbitrarily chose the room in time for the Shakespeare Festival he was organizing. Famous signatures scratched with diamond rings on a windowpane include Sir Walter Scott, Henry Irving and Ellen Terry.

On the corner of High Street stands Judith Shakespeare's House (now a shop), where the playwright's daughter lived. A bit farther along High Street is Harvard House, built in Tudor times, where the mother of Harvard University founder John Harvard was born.

Nash's House stands on Chapel Street next to the site of Shakespeare's retirement home, New Place, where he died in 1616. New Place was torn down

The Clopton Bridge, built in the 1480s, stretches across the river at Stratford-upon-Avon

in the 18th century on the orders of its owner, who was tired of Shakespeare fans knocking on his door. There is a beautiful Knot Garden on the site of the house itself, just down Chapel Street on the left.

Chapel Street soon becomes Church Street; on the left is the handsome old King Edward VI Grammar School, where Shakespeare probably studied as a boy. It also is possible to visit the beautiful medieval house of Hall's Croft, where Shakespeare's daughter Susanna lived after her marriage to Dr. John Hall. Here you can wince over a display of medical practices back in those primitive days.

Holy Trinity Church on Trinity Street is where Shakespeare lies buried beside his wife within the altar rails. The walk from here back along the Avon is pretty, passing the looming Royal Shakespeare Theatre before reaching Clopton Bridge, where you bear left along Bridge Street to return to Henley Street.

Two other notable sites lie outside Stratford-upon-Avon. Mary Arden's House, a Tudor farmhouse where Shakespeare's mother was born, including the Shakespeare Countryside Museum, is in Wilmcote, 4 miles north of town. At Shottery, 2 miles west of town, stands Anne Hathaway's Cottage, charmingly thatched and half-timbered, where you can view the wooden bench on which William proposed to Anne – perhaps!

➕ C2

Tourist information ✉ Bridgefoot ☎ 08701 607930; www.shakespeare-country.co.uk

Shakespeare's Birthplace ✉ Henley Street ☎ 01789 201823 🕐 Mon.–Sat. 9–5, Sun. 9:30–5, Jun.–Aug.; daily 10–5, Apr.–May and Sep.–Oct.; Mon.–Sat. 10–4, Sun. 10:30–4, rest of year 💷 $$$

Harvard House ✉ High Street ☎ 01789 204016 🕐 Wed.–Sun. noon–5, early Jul.–early Sep.; Wed. and Sat.–Sun. noon–5, late May–early Jul. and early Sep.–Oct. 31 💷 $$

Nash's House and New Place ✉ Chapel Street ☎ 01789 292325 🕐 Mon.–Sat. 9:30–5, Sun. 10–5, Jun.–Aug.; daily 11–5, Apr.–May and Sep.–Oct.; daily 11–4, rest of year 💷 $$

Hall's Croft ✉ Old Town ☎ 01789 292107 🕐 Same as Nash's House and New Place 🍴 Café 💷 $$

Holy Trinity Church ✉ Trinity Street, Old Town ☎ 01789 266316 🕐 Mon.–Sat. 8:30–6, Sun. 12:30–5, May–Sep.; Mon.–Sat. 8:30–5, Sun. 12:15–5, in Apr. and Oct.; Mon.–Sat. 9–4, Sun. 12:15–5, rest of year 💷 Church free, Shakespeare's grave $

Mary Arden's House ✉ Wilmcote, 4 miles north ☎ 01789 293455 🕐 Daily 9:30–5, Jun.–Aug.; 10–5, Apr.–May and Sep.–Oct.; 10–4, rest of year 🍴 Café 💷 $$

Anne Hathaway's Cottage ✉ Shottery, 2 miles west ☎ 01789 292100 🕐 Mon.–Sat. 9–5, Sun. 9:30–5, Jun.–Aug.; Mon.–Sat. 9:30–5, Sun. 10–5, Apr.–May and Sep.–Oct.; daily 10–4, rest of year 🍴 Café 💷 $$

Imposing Warwick Castle rises from grounds landscaped by Capability Brown

WARWICK CASTLE

One of the mightiest and most impressive of Britain's great medieval fortresses, Warwick Castle looms over the River Avon like a statement of strength, impregnability and permanence, set literally in stone. No castle in England so perfectly epitomizes the power and influence of medieval nobility – and also their dinosaur-like vulnerability to social change, which simply bypassed them and left them behind.

The original Norman castle was captured and burned in 1264 by Simon de Montfort, leader of the rebellious barons. The remains still stand on their mound within the castle precincts. But it is the solid, gray stone towers and outer walls, added in a 14th-century rebuilding, that are seen today, outward and visible signs of the glory of the Beauchamp and Neville families, Earls of Warwick. The most powerful of all the Earls of Warwick was Richard Neville, who as "Warwick the Kingmaker" tried to serve both sides during the 15th-century Wars of the Roses.

There is a mighty turreted gatehouse pierced with arrow slits; it also holds concealed "murder holes" for the anointing of attackers' heads with boiling oil. The original portcullis still hangs high over the gateway. Five-story battlemented towers rise at the corners of the outer wall: Caesar's Tower, Guy's Tower and Watergate Tower, the last likely walked by the restless ghost of Sir Fulke Greville. Sir Fulke was murdered in 1628 by a servant who believed (mistakenly, it turned out) that his master had left him nothing in his will. In the dungeon of Caesar's Tower is an *oubliette*, a tiny cell where prisoners, brought back from the battlefields of France, were forgotten and left to perish.

There are several exhibitions and displays in the castle, including an armory that contains pieces of Oliver Cromwell's armor, a collection of ghastly looking torture instruments and a display telling the story of Warwick the Kingmaker.

Parts of the medieval castle were refurbished during the 17th and 18th centuries and turned into state rooms with fine carved fireplaces, plasterwork, furniture and paintings. The castle is part of the Tussaud's Group, and features several tableaux of waxwork models.

In the 1750s Capability Brown landscaped the very extensive grounds; on some summer weekends jousting contests are staged here, for those who are happy to risk life and limb or to watch others do it for their amusement.

➕ C2

✉ Castle Hill, Warwick ☎ 08704 422000 (24 hours)
🕐 Daily 10–6, Apr.– Sep.; 10–5, rest of year. Last admission 1 hour before closing 🍴 Restaurants and cafés 💵 $$$

The Royal Regatta at Henley-on-Thames is an annual sporting and social occasion

DAYS ON THE RIVER THAMES

Between Oxford and London the River Thames passes through its most delectable stretch, winding through meadows and soft green lowlands.

Abingdon is the first place of any size you come to, a pretty old town with a lovely riverfront and some notable buildings, especially the 17th-century County Hall, which houses a museum about the area. A few miles downriver is Dorchester (not to be confused with the county town of Dorset), where the Norman abbey church has glorious east windows full of early medieval stained glass.

Moving on south and east, you pass through the villages of Goring and Pangbourne, on a beautiful, thickly wooded stretch of the river. Kenneth Grahame, author of the children's classic *The Wind In The Willows* (1908), lived the last few years of his life here. Grahame had this section of the Thames in mind as a setting for his tales of Ratty, Mole, Mr. Toad and friends. Artist Ernest Shephard used scenes here for his charming illustrations for the book.

Mapledurham's lock, weir and mill make a picturesque setting for a picnic, and the manor house of Mapledurham is worth a visit for its Elizabethan staircase, Jacobean plaster ceilings, Georgian private chapel and beautiful grounds. Farther along are the town of Henley, site of the annual Royal Regatta rowing events, and the village of Cookham, with a gallery celebrating local artist Sir Stanley Spencer and displaying his *Christ Preaching At Cookham Regatta*, an eccentric masterpiece with the river as its setting.

Mapledurham House ✚ D1 ✉ Mapledurham ☎ 0118 972 3350 🕐 Sat.–Sun. 2–5:30, Easter–Sep. 30 🍴 Café 💷 $$

Stanley Spencer Gallery ✚ E1 ✉ The Kings Hall, High Street, Cookham ☎ 01628 471885 🕐 Daily 10:30–5:30, Easter–Oct. 31; Sat.–Sun. 11–4:30, rest of year 💷 $

Boaters are the headgear on the water at Henley

Wales

WALES

"WALES is a land apart, rich in mountains and wild coasts, churches and castles, with a language and tradition all its own."

Opposite: Lake and mountain scenery in Snowdonia

Wales

0 10 20 30 40 km
0 10 20 miles

5

4

3

2

1

Carmel Head • Amlwch
Holyhead
Bay • Holyhead
Anglesey Great Ormes
Head
Llandudno
Holyhead • Oriel Ynys Môn Beaumaris Colwyn Bay
Holy Llangefni Conwy Bodnant
Island Llanfairpwll Penrhyn
Bryn Celli-Ddu Bangor **CONW**
Newborough • Bethesda
Caernarfon Llanrwst
Llanberis Capel Cu
3560ft Snowdon
Snowdon ▲ Mountain Betws-y-co
Caernarfon Railway
Bay Nant Gwynant Sygun Copper Mine
Beddgelert Blaenau
Ffestiniog Railway Ffestiniog
Nefyn Porthmadog Portmeirion
Lleyn Peninsula Trawsfynydd Snowdonia
Porthmadog National
Pwllheli Harlech Park
Aberdaron Abersoch **GWYNEDD**

Bardsey Barmouth Dolgellau
2927ft Mallwy
Cader Idris Centre f
Castell y Bere Alternat
Technolc

Tywyn
Aberdyfi Machynll
Dovey Dylife

Cardigan 2467ft
Bay Plynlimon

Rheidol
Aberystwyth
Devil's
Bridge

Claerwen
Reservoir
Aberaeron **CEREDIGION**
New Quay Tregaron

Temple Bar
Aberporth
Cardigan Lampeter
Llanwrty
Dinas Wel
Strumble Head *Head*
Pembrokeshire Coast *Myny Preseli* Newcastle *Teifi*
National Park **Fishguard** Pentre Ifan Emlyn
Porthgain *Foel Eryr* Llandovery
Abereiddy Trefin
St David's Head **St. David's** **CARMARTHENSHIRE**
Whitesand Bay Solva
Ramsey St. Non's Newgale Llandeilo *Brecon*
Chapel Carmarthen *Towy* Carreg
St. Brides Bay **Haverfordwest** Cennen Dan-yr-Ogof
Narberth St. Clears Castle Caves
Skomer **PEMBROKESHIRE** Laugharne Pontyberem Ammanford
Skokholm Dale Milford Haven Kidwelly Pontarddulais *Tawe*
Carew Burry Port **NEAT**
Pembroke Castle **Llanelli** **& POR**
Pembrokeshire Coast Manorbier **Tenby** *Carmarthen* Gorseinon **Neath** TALBO
National Park Bosherston *Bay* Killay Swansea
Caldey Llanrhidian **SWANSEA** **Port**
St. Govan's Rhossili *Gower* Mumbles Talbot
Chapel Oxwich Head
Worms Head Port *Swansea Bay*
Einon **BRIDGEND**
Porthcawl

A   B   C

*IRISH
SEA*

Rhyl
Prestatyn
Rhuddlan
Dee
St. Asaph
Clwyd
Flint
Denbigh
FLINTSHIRE
CHESHIRE
1821ft
Moel Famau
Mold
DENBIGHSHIRE
Llyn
Brenig
Ruthin
Gresford
Cerrigydrudion
Horseshoe
Pass
Erddig
Wrexham
Valle Crucis Abbey
Pontcysyllte
Aqueduct
n
yn
Corwen
Llangollen
Dee
WREXHAM
Bala
Berwyn Mts
Plas Newydd
Llyn
Tegid
Pistyll
Rhaeadr
Llyn
Vyrnwy
Llanymynech
Llanfyllin
Vyrnwy
Welshpool
Llanfair
Caereinion
Powis Castle
Carno
Montgomery
SHROPSHIRE
Caersws
Severn
*Offa's
Dyke*
Newtown
Llanidloes
Llangurig
POWYS
Rhayader
Knighton
Elan
Village
*Radnor
Forest*
Llandrindod Wells
Presteigne
ewbridge
on Wye
Old Radnor
Beulah
Builth Wells
Gladestry
Llangammarch Wells
HEREFORDSHIRE
Erwood
Hay-on-
Wye
Talgarth
*Offa's
Dyke*
ennybridge
Brecon
k
Mountain Centre
Black
Llanthony Priory
acons
2907ft
Pen-y-Fan
Mountains
Park
Ystradfellte
Tretower
Crickhowell
Abergavenny
Brynmawr
Big Pit : National Mining
Museum of Wales
Monmouth
Tredegar
Ebbw
Vale
Blaenavon
Raglan
Aberdare
Merthyr
Tydfil
Abertillery
MONMOUTH
SHIRE
Tintern
Abbey
ountain Ash
Bargoed
Usk
RHONDDA
CYNON
TAFF
CAERPHILLY
Pontypool
Cwmbran
Chepstow
Pontypridd
M4
Caerphilly
Newport
Caldicot
Castell Coch
NEWPORT
ridgend
CARDIFF
St. Fagans
Llandaff
VALE OF
GLAMORGAN
CARDIFF
Severn
NORTH
SOMERSET
BRISTOL
antwit
Major
Barry
D
E

WALES

There is a new mood afoot in Wales to suit the new millennium, a fresh self-confidence and sense of "Welshness" that will be very apparent to anyone visiting this beautiful and characterful country. Wales is a country in its own right, as well as a part of Britain along with England and Scotland. It has its own language, entirely distinct from English, as well as its own culture, literature, mythology and history.

Dramatic Landscapes

Wales is hilly, rising to the north and west toward Snowdonia National Park. The Welsh coastline is mostly steep and craggy, cut with great sandy estuaries and sheltered fishing havens. In Snowdonia, at the upper end of the great westward-opening pincer of Cardigan Bay, are some of the oldest rocks in Britain, volcanic solidifications mixed with hard slates and schists pushed up in titanic upheavals some 400 million years ago. Wind and weather have shaped them into mountain ranges, superb for walking and climbing, whose slate hearts were intensively quarried during the British Industrial Revolution for building materials.

Slate quarrying in the north, sheep and cattle raising in the interior, coal mining and iron smelting in the south, fishing along the coast: Wales' traditional industries defined its regions for hundreds of years. But no longer. Most of the slate quarries have closed, and all of the coal mines except one. Farmers are having hard times, and

Wales

inshore fishing is on the decline. Even the "soft" fifth mainstay industry, seaside tourism, has lost out to cheaper, sunnier vacations abroad. It would be enough to crush the spirit of a less resilient people, but the Welsh have fought back energetically.

Transformation and Tourism

The semi-derelict Cardiff docklands, for example, are being transformed by an ambitious plan into an extensive waterside development for work, leisure and residence. The coal-mining valleys have taken on new, lighter industry, some of it very high-tech. Black spoil heaps and scummy reservoirs are being converted into green hillocks and lakes for water

The lovely curve of beach at Rhossili, Gower Peninsula

recreation, and many of the former coal pits and blast furnaces are being turned into tourist attractions. The same is true of the giant abandoned slate mines in Snowdonia. Former industrial railway lines now haul visitors behind diminutive steam locomotives.

In 1997 the Welsh voted to have their own National Assembly, located in the capital city of Cardiff. It wields only limited powers at present, although it is expected to have more say in national affairs in the near future. This move toward autonomy reflects a new optimism in Wales. It is partly a brave and necessary response to adversity, but indicative as well of a new feeling of nationalism that also is resurgent in Scotland.

Strong Traditions

Adversity historically came from centuries of skirmishing between the Welsh and English. Evidence of the tensions is still scattered thickly across Wales in the form of castles and fortifications. But despite the depredations of English oppressors from across the border, you can't keep a good man down, and the roots of

Males of Wales

The macho ethic of heavy labor in the valleys of South Wales during the Victorian era contributed to two very Welsh cultural icons – the male voice choir and the no-holds-barred village rugby team.

The Welsh still love their rugby; a flood tide of men, women and children pours into the national stadium in Cardiff whenever Wales is playing at home, and each town in the valleys has its own fanatically supported team.

Male voice choirs, strongly influenced by the tradition of singing in chapel, could be heard from one valley to the next in their heyday in the 19th century. But the echo of their unique sound still reverberates. Performances are advertised locally, and heavily attended; if you can secure a place, you will experience the power and emotion generated by dozens of male voices in multi-part harmony, from quiet as a whisper to exultantly loud.

indigenous Welsh culture have proved extremely deep and enduring. The language itself continued to live in the rural west; so did the tale-telling and the strong traditions of poetry, song and independent religious thought. Meanwhile, radical politics flourished in the hothouse atmosphere of the crowded, vigorous coal and steel towns of southern Wales. They spawned a hard-working, hard-playing society of choral singing, rugby playing, beer-drinking masculinity, left wing in politics and nonconformist in religion.

As for the English castles, fortified towns and Offa's Dyke (a massive earth bank and trench dug in the eighth century along the border) – they remain part of the Welsh landscape, historic monuments to be explored for fun by visitors, but powerful reminders of a turbulent past.

Welsh Culture and Language

Today the Welsh language is in good health and widespread. It appears on every road sign and map, and you'll see it the moment you enter Wales, on the welcoming sign "Croeso i Cymru" (Welcome to Wales). Your enjoyment and appreciation of Wales will be greatly enhanced if you learn the meaning of the country's highly descriptive and poetic place names (see page 283). In northern and central Wales you will frequently hear the language spoken, but English is understood everywhere. The Welsh, with their lilting voices, are famously musical, and the country has produced some well-known musicians, poets and actors. Singers, dancers, musicians, actors, artists and writers all participate in *eisteddfods* – celebrations of culture – that culminate in the National Eisteddfod, held in early August.

Seafood and Oatcakes

On the culinary front, Wales has some dishes all its own. Roast lamb with mint sauce, served with leeks, is traditionally Welsh, but so are salmon, trout and shellfish. Try laverbread for breakfast (an oatmeal and seaweed cake, often served with a cooked breakfast); Welsh cakes for tea (flat dough pancakes with raisins); and Welsh rarebit for lunch (bread topped with grilled, crumbly Caerphilly cheese and beer).

Wales

CARDIFF

Cardiff is a lively, friendly city with a variety of interesting architecture. There is a warren of intriguing Victorian shopping arcades in the center. The Edwardian-style Civic Centre in Cathays Park encompasses the National Museum and Gallery Cardiff, City Hall, Law Courts and the University of Wales science building, a fine assemblage of neoclassic structures. Cardiff Castle, on the other hand, boasts one of Britain's

truly eccentric interiors. Nearby rises the futuristic bulk of the Millennium Stadium, home to Wales' much-worshiped national rugby team as well as the football (soccer) team. Llandaff Cathedral contains wonderful craftsmanship and artistry spanning eight centuries, while along Cardiff Bay modern architects have let their imaginations rip – to varied effect.

Mapping the City

Orientation in Cardiff is mostly a matter of north and south. The spine of

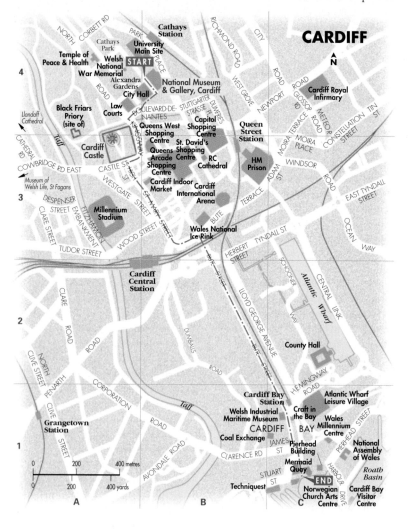

Cardiff City Hall, which forms part of the Civic Centre at Cathays Park

the city center is the street that starts as St. Mary Street and changes to High Street as it runs north, throwing off famous Victorian shopping arcades left and right, until it reaches the gates of Cardiff Castle. Farther north is the Civic Centre, while Llandaff Cathedral is 2 miles northwest – a nice hour's stroll along the banks of the River Taff. The Millennium Stadium is a couple of blocks west of St. Mary Street.

Cardiff Cuisine

Cardiff has long been a cosmopolitan city with a wide range of ethnic cuisines. You can find anything from Thai to Japanese to classic French in or near the city center, with cheap curry houses toward Roath, just east of the center. Along the Cardiff Bay waterfront are smart cafés and brasseries, old ones closing and new ones opening regularly. Genuine Welsh cooking with regional ingredients is not hard to find. Try Welsh lamb or Welsh black beef, sewin (a delicious fish), Penclawdd cockles (small shellfish) from the Gower Peninsula in south Wales, or laverbread, made from

seaweed. Cardiff-brewed Brains SA is a popular beer.

Arcades and Cafés

The main shopping district is right in the city center, a maze of pedestrianized streets, Victorian and Edwardian arcades and brand-name shops. St. Mary Street/High Street

Welsh Pronunciation

If you're asking for directions in Wales, your one stumbling block could be in the pronunciation of place names.

Here are a few hints:

c is always hard, as in *c*ow

dd is *th*, as in *th*at

ch is similar to the Scottish lo*ch*

ll is similar to the Scottish lo*ch*, followed by an *l* sound

f is *v* as in *v*ole

s is *s*, never *z*

y at the end of a word is *ee* as in Mar*y*; *y* elsewhere, or by itself, is *er* as in m*y*rtle

w, as a consonant, is *w* as in *w*ater

w, as a vowel, is *oo* as in b*oo*t or c*oo*k

Wales

forms its left flank; Duke Street/ Queen Street is the northern boundary. The arcades are fun, narrow alleyways with high glass and cast-iron roofs; shops tend to be either frothy gift emporia or boutiques. The Royal Arcade is best for antiques, and the best cafés and bars are in Castle

Lovespoons

Welsh arts and crafts traditionally rely on available natural materials (clay, wood, slate, wool and gold) and often reflect the country's traditions and folklore. The intricately designed wooden lovespoons are one of the best examples of this. Made from a single piece of wood, the entwined spoons are patterned with images from old myths and poems: keys, ships, dragons, hearts and flowers. The spoons originated in the 17th century and were made by men as a gift for a sweetheart. If the spoon was accepted, it was a sign that an offer of marriage would be, too.

Arcade. You can watch crafts being made, and then purchase them, at the bustling Cardiff Indoor Market (Monday to Saturday) off High Street and at Craft in the Bay, a shop at the lower end of Bute Street. Welsh gold is always a good bet, as well as the traditional, intricately carved wooden lovespoons (see sidebar). At Jacob's Market you can buy period clothes, furniture and curios, and for food exotica, try the splendid Wally's, a Polish delicatessen in the Royal Arcade.

Sport and Singing

Cardiff's Millennium Stadium hosts both international rugby and football (soccer) matches, where up to 72,500 ardent fans singing in unison can be quite an experience. You can enjoy Welsh singing at lower levels and in greater comfort at the Welsh National Opera in its new home in the Wales Millennium Centre on Cardiff Bay, or by attending one of the stirring male voice choir performances frequently advertised around the city.

ESSENTIAL INFORMATION

TOURIST INFORMATION
Cardiff Gateway Visitor Centre ✉ The Old Library, The Hays ☎ 029 2022 7281 www.visitcardiff.info
Cardiff Bay Visitor Centre ✉ "The Tube," Harbour Drive ☎ 029 2046 3833; www.visitcardiff.info

484950. Cardiff Bus Station also is centrally located (✉ Wood Street). Cardiff Bus (Bws Caerdyy) serves the city; for information on schedules, ☎ 08706 082608. There are frequent buses servicing all areas of the city and suburbs. Taxi stands are at both the rail and bus stations.

URBAN TRANSPORTATION
From Cardiff Central Railway Station there are regular services to London Paddington (2 hours), and to other destinations in Britain. For rail information or rail reservations in Wales, ☎ 08457

AIRPORT INFORMATION
Cardiff International Airport is 10 miles southwest of the city at Rhoose. For information, ☎ 01446 711111. Regular buses serve central Cardiff.

CLIMATE – Average highs and lows

JAN.	FEB.	MAR.	APR.	MAY	JUN.	JUL.	AUG.	SEP.	OCT.	NOV.	DEC.
7°C	7°C	9°C	12°C	15°C	18°C	20°C	20°C	17°C	13°C	10°C	8°C
45°F	45°F	48°F	54°F	59°F	64°F	68°F	68°F	63°F	55°F	50°F	46°F
3°C	2°C	3°C	4°C	7°C	10°C	12°C	12°C	11°C	8°C	5°C	4°C
37°F	36°F	37°F	39°F	45°F	50°F	54°F	54°F	52°F	46°F	41°F	39°F

CARDIFF SIGHTS

Key to symbols

⊞ map coordinates refer to the Cardiff map on page 158; sights below are highlighted in yellow on the map.

✉ address or location ☎ telephone number

🕐 opening times 🍴 restaurant on site or nearby

🚍 nearest bus or tram route

🎫 admission charge: $$$ more than £6, $$ £2–£6, $ less than £2 ℹ information

CARDIFF CASTLE

An object lesson in what happens when a clever and dreamy 18-year-old inherits a lot of money and a whole castle to spend it on, Cardiff Castle's overblown Victorian Gothic grotesqueries will not be to everyone's taste. But this unique exercise in mock-medieval, over-the-top style is one of the highlights of any visit to Cardiff.

The 3rd Marquess of Bute was bright, brooding and fabulously rich through inherited coal and docks money. In 1867, while still a teenager, he commissioned the singular architect William Burges – not much over 4 feet tall, and given to carrying a parrot on his shoulder – to "do up" the castle, already a mishmash of building styles spanning 800 years. Together the two men spent eight years letting their imaginations and the Marquess' money go.

The guided tour will take you through lavishly decorated apartments, many of them cramped in size and exuding more than a whiff of claustrophobic paranoia. The Winter Smoking Room in the clock tower is painted with signs of the zodiac, the Labors of the Seasons, songbirds and satyrs, with a splendid black-faced devil leering down from the ceiling of the entrance lobby. The Summer Smoking Room has a gold-painted gallery and a sumptuously inlaid floor. In the nursery, handpainted wall tiles depict fairy tales. There is a heavily Moorish "stalactite" ceiling in the Arab Room (decorated by imported Arab craftsmen with gold leaf, marble and lapis lazuli), and a beautiful wooden angel roof over the banqueting hall. This genuine medieval hall was given the full Burges treatment with a castle-

The Arab Room with its amazing Moorish ceiling

like fireplace telling the story of King Stephen's struggle with his cousin Matilda in three-dimensional relief sculpture.

The Marquess' bedroom has a mirrored ceiling – "to reflect the beauty of the furnishings," grins the guide – and a unifying religious theme based around St. John (the 3rd Marquess also was named John). The blood-red dining room contains one nice human touch: unsophisticated but beautiful wood-carvings on the backs of the window shutters, executed by the 14-year-old son of Bute's master carver.

A stretch of the original Roman wall can be seen by the Black Tower on Castle Street, with modern three-dimensional murals providing a glimpse of everyday life in a Roman fort.

⊞ A3 ✉ Castle Street ☎ 029 2087 8100 🕐 Daily 9:30–6, Mar.–Oct.; 9:30–5, rest of year. Last admission 1 hour before closing. Times may change due to events; call ahead 🍴 Café 🎫 Castle $$$ (grounds only $$)

The Law Courts building, which forms part of Cardiff's Civic Centre

CATHAYS PARK AND THE CIVIC CENTRE

The grand cluster of Edwardian civic buildings laid out in spacious style in the formal setting of Cathays Park, just north of the city center, is a monument to the aspirations of Cardiff around the turn of the 20th century, when the city's prosperity was at its height.

On the southern side of this great square of white stone buildings stand the Law Courts and the National Museum and Gallery, Cardiff (see page 164). They flank City Hall, which has an enormous clock tower, a sculptured exterior celebrating worldwide trade, and a Marble Hall full of statues of Welsh heroes.

The buildings of the University of Wales dominate the other sides of the park, with the Welsh Office and the pretty Temple of Peace and Health (both built in 1938) set between them. Within the square of buildings are the formal and beautiful Alexandra Gardens, with the national War Memorial – a circular colonnade – at the center.

🔲 A4 ✉ Cathays Park

Cardiff Bay

Modern housing developments, marinas and small businesses have sprouted all around the rejuvenated shoreline of Cardiff Bay. There are smart wine bars and brasseries, waterside walkways and high-tech museums such as Techniquest, a science discovery center incorporating a planetarium and excellent interactive displays. Atlantic Wharf and Mermaid Quay are "leisure villages" complete with movie theaters, bowling alleys and nightclubs. The Wales Millennium Centre hosts music and dance performances and is the home of the Welsh National Opera, while the Welsh government, the National Assembly of Wales, also has its home here. This whole area lies about a mile south of the city center at the foot of Bute Street, reached by Lloyd George Avenue, a pleasant tree-lined boulevard, a 20-minute stroll from the city center. Among the shiny new buildings around the bay are some interesting older ones; the Norwegian Church is an arts center conversion of a weatherboarded church once used by Scandinavian seamen docked at Cardiff. The big redbrick and terra-cotta Pierhead Building on the Inner Harbour and the giant Coal Exchange (now an arts center) tucked away in the heart of Butetown are both monuments to Victorian pride and prosperity.

🔲 C1

Cardiff Bay Visitor Centre ✉ "The Tube," Harbour Drive ☎ 029 2046 3833; www.visitcardiff.info

Museum of Welsh Life, St. Fagans

Wales

The Museum of Welsh Life, St. Fagans is set in the 100-acre grounds of St. Fagan's Castle, an Elizabethan manor house built on the site of a ruined Norman castle on the western outskirts of Cardiff. The castle is worth exploring in its own right, as are its well-kept gardens. The museum's collection was started in 1946, when ordinary buildings redolent of Welsh life were being demolished all over Wales with little appreciation of their historic value. The museum opened two years later on July 7, 1948. More than 30 reconstructed buildings provide fascinating snapshots of life in Wales over the centuries.

Home, School and Chapel

There are grand farmhouses furnished in Jacobean and Edwardian style, which contrast with the basic amenities of humble farm laborers' cottages. A severe Victorian school is the scene of many a mock-terrifying lesson re-enacted for young visitors by stern "school mistresses." The tiny 18th-century chapel from northern Pembrokeshire evokes the stark simplicity of nonconformist religion in rural Wales. A tollhouse from 1772 once stood on the road to Aberystwyth.

A particularly imaginative touch is shown in a terrace of ironworkers' houses from Merthyr Tydfil, in the valleys; each of the six cramped cottages has been furnished in the style of a different decade between the early 19th century (open fires, no running water) and the late 20th century (electricity and plastic). A row of 19th-century shops evocatively displays the simple goods of those days.

Living History

Costumed guides are on hand to get you into the mood of the "good old days." There also are a number of craft experts demonstrating coopering, clogmaking and other skills, and the workings of such small-scale industrial concerns as a corn-mill, a tannery and a blacksmith's forge.

✚ A3 ✉ St. Fagans, 4 miles west of the city center
☎ 029 2057 3500 🕐 Daily 10–5 🍴 Restaurant and cafés 🚌 Bus Number 320 and 325 (at least hourly) from Cardiff Central Bus Station 🎫 Free

One of the houses that has been reconstructed as part of the museum

The war memorial outside Llandaff Cathedral

LLANDAFF CATHEDRAL

Half-hidden in a hollow in the quiet suburb of Llandaff, 2 miles northwest of the city center, Llandaff Cathedral is a strikingly diverse building. It has undergone hard times in its 900 years of existence, including a long period of dereliction in the 17th and 18th centuries. Oliver Cromwell's soldiers drank and gambled in the nave during the 1642–51 English Civil War, and John Wood (Georgian architect of the city of Bath) built a complete Italianate temple within its ruined walls in 1734. The cathedral was lovingly restored by the Victorians. A German land mine shattered whole sections of it in 1941, and the long work of restoration was finally completed in 1960.

Drama grabs you as soon as you enter the west door, with Sir Jacob Epstein's elongated aluminum statue of *Christ in Majesty* floating on a bold, modern concrete arch at mid-nave level. Other notable highlights are medieval and Victorian stone carvings; pre-Raphaelite stained-glass windows by William Morris, Edward Burne-Jones and Ford Madox Brown; and a painted triptych by Dante Gabriel Rossetti. Above the chancel arch a 1959 John Piper window and round ornamental panel are full of rich, burning colors.

✚ A4 ✉ Cathedral Green, Llandaff ☎ 029 2056 4554 ⏰ Daily 7:30–7 🚌 25, 33, 33A and 62 from Cardiff Central Bus Station 💵 Donation sugggested

NATIONAL MUSEUM AND GALLERY, CARDIFF

Housed in a splendid Portland stone building on the south side of Cathays Park, these collections are divided between two floors. Downstairs is an absorbing "Evolution of Wales" exhibition, with plenty of animated prehistoric creatures and dinosaur skeletons. Here, too, is the "Man and the Environment" gallery, a natural history display about animals and plant life from around the world.

Upstairs is the archeology section, featuring gold, bronze and stonework from Wales' deep past, and an impressive collection of paintings and sculpture. The sculpture ranges from Rodin (a version of *The Kiss*) and Degas (a dancer gracefully balanced) to work by Barbara Hepworth and Henry Moore. Paintings include classic 18th- and 19th-century land and seascapes by painters such as Thomas Gainsborough, J.M.W. Turner and Wales' own Richard Wilson; pre-Raphaelite scenes; and modern abstract art. A highlight is the collection of Impressionists – Monet views of the Thames, Renoir's *La Parisienne*, Alfred Sisley river views along the Seine, Cézanne in Provence – and a despairing *Rain at Auvers* by Vincent van Gogh shortly before his suicide.

✚ B4 ✉ Cardiff Civic Centre, Cathays Park ☎ 029 2039 7951 ⏰ Tue.–Sun. 10–5 🍴 Restaurant and café 💵 Free ℹ Self-guiding audio tour (donation suggested)

WALK: CENTRAL CARDIFF

Refer to route marked on city map on page 158

Cardiff's city center is compact, and you could see all the sights on this tour within an hour's stroll. It would be a 2- to 3-hour trip to walk through parks and meadows out to Llandaff and have a look around the cathedral. Cardiff Bay is a 20-minute stroll along Bute Street.

Cardiff Castle in Bute Park

Starting among the grand civic buildings of Cathays Park (see page 162), cross the Boulevard de Nantes just south of City Hall to reach the Hilton Cardiff Hotel. Continue along the pavement, with the walls of Cardiff Castle (see page 161) rising across Kingsway on your right. A pedestrian crossing takes you over to the castle gates if you want to visit, and a few hundred yards farther along Castle Street you'll reach a lodge from which footpaths lead through Bute Park and then through gardens and fields beside the River Taff to Llandaff Cathedral.

If you don't want to visit the castle and cathedral, turn left opposite the castle gates down High Street/St. Mary Street, detouring down any of the Victorian and Edwardian shopping arcades (mostly on your left). At the bottom of St. Mary Street turn left onto Custom House Street. The so-called Café Quarter is on the left here, if you feel in need of a cappuccino and a croissant.

Then it's a right turn onto Bute Street, which leads straight as an arrow to Cardiff Bay. At the foot of Bute Street you will emerge on the Inner Harbour beside the grand Pierhead Building, with Cardiff Bay spread right and left. If you have done enough walking by now, a Number 6, 7, 8 or 35 bus will return you to the city center.

Spring flowers make a colorful display in Cathays Park

REGIONAL SIGHTS

Key to symbols

🔲 map coordinates refer to the Wales map on pages 154–155; sights below are highlighted in yellow on the map.

🔲 address or location ☎ telephone number
🔘 opening times 🍴 restaurant on site or nearby
🍺 admission charge: $$$ more than £6, $$ £2–£6,
$ less than £2 ℹ️ information

ABERYSTWYTH AND AREA

The friendly seaside town of Aberystwyth (pronounced "Aber-rist-with") stands right at the center of the immense Cardigan Bay coastline. It is the unofficial capital of Welsh culture and language ("Welsh Wales"), harboring one of the colleges of the University of Wales, the National Library of Wales, and the headquarters of both the Welsh Language Society and the Welsh Books Council. Here are bookstores, pubs and record shops where Welsh is the only language read, heard or sung. Big, gloomy chapels loom among the houses. There is an excellent town museum, the Ceredigion Museum, in the Coliseum, a former Edwardian music hall and cinema on Terrace Road, just inland from the seafront.

You can ride in one of the little wooden carriages of the Aberystwyth Electric Cliff Railway ("a conveyance for gentlefolk since 1896," in operation daily mid-March to early November) up Constitution Hill north of town, and survey Aberystwyth stretched out below around its bay – either with the naked eye, or through the Camera Obscura (claimed to be the world's biggest) that stands at the top of the hill.

Devil's Bridge, 12 miles east of town, is a spot famed for its beauty, where the rivers Mynach and Rheidol fall thunderously between sheer rock walls spanned by a three-in-one bridge – a 20th-century road bridge jammed on top of an 18th-century one, with an ancient 11th-century bridge beneath them.

The little locomotives of the Vale of Rheidol Railway, belching steam and smoke, depart from the center of Aberystwyth for Devil's Bridge via the

The coastal town of Aberystwyth

Rheidol Valley. For details on the variable train schedules in the area, contact the tourist office or call 01970 625819.

🔲 C3

Tourist information 🔲 Terrace Road
☎ 01970 612125; www.ceredigion.gov.uk
Ceredigion Museum 🔲 Coliseum, Terrace Road
☎ 01970 633088 🔘 Mon.–Sat. 10–5 🍴 Café
🍺 Free

Devil's Bridge station on the Vale of Rheidol Railway

Opposite: Pistyll Rhaeadr – the most spectacular waterfall in Wales (see page 173)

Conwy Castle approached from a suspension bridge

CONWY

Conwy stands on an estuary at the northern tip of Snowdonia National Park, a tiny town comprised of medieval and later buildings drawn tight inside the protective circle of an astonishingly complete set of late 13th-century town walls. Even without the picturesque castle rising from the southeastern angle of the walls, Conwy would be breathtakingly attractive in its setting between mountains and sea. In the cobbled Old Town, Plas Mawr is a superb Elizabethan mansion, and St. Mary's Church a pleasing jumble of architecture, part monastic.

You can walk a circuit of the walls and their regularly spaced guard towers before turning your attention to the castle, one of eight built after 1283 by King Edward I to form an "Iron Ring" around the mountainous retreats of the rebellious Welsh. The castle is massively built, with eight round towers forming vantage points around its walls. A walkway lets you look down into the interior of the roofless Great Hall, as well as the king's bedroom and drawing room. Some of the towers conceal dungeons, a chapel and a baking oven of suitable proportions to feed a hungry garrison. Children will love the high walkway, and the warren of hide-and-seek passages within the walls.

🚩 D5
Tourist information ✉ Conwy Castle Visitor Centre ☎ 01492 592248; www.visitconwy.org.uk
Conwy Castle ✉ Castle Square ☎ 01492 592358 🕐 Daily 9:30–6, Jun.–Sep.; daily 9:30–5:30, Apr.–May and in Oct.; Mon.–Sat. 9:30–4:30, Sun. 11–4, rest of year 👜 $$

GOWER PENINSULA

The Gower Peninsula, ragged-edged and irregular, poking west from the underbelly of the south Welsh coast, is one of Britain's special places – popular but seldom crowded, peaceful and blessed with a mild climate, green and pastoral. The coast boasts some spectacular sandy beaches, particularly at Oxwich, where there also is a fine nature reserve. Mumbles, in the southeast, is a nice old seaside resort.

At Rhossili Bay the Gower is at its best, with 4 miles of beautiful sand, a spectacular cliff and ridge coastline, and the strange double-humped promontory of Worm's Head ("worm" is Norse for dragon). You can scramble along the promontory's causeway at low tide (it is covered at high tide) to a thrilling perch at the seaward tip among seabirds and wave spray.

🚩 C1
Swansea tourist information ✉ Plymouth Street, Swansea ☎ 01792 468321; www.visitswanseabay.com

Water for the Talyllyn Railway steam engine

LLANGOLLEN

Llangollen lies deep in the valley of the River Dee in northeastern Wales, a slate-roofed town beside a rushing river. It is renowned for the Llangollen International Musical Eisteddfod of music, dance and poetry, which takes place during the first week in July, attracting competitors from around the world. During the festival, performances are held at venues all over town, both indoors and out. The green slopes of the Berwyn Hills look down on Llangollen from the south. The dramatic limestone crags of Creigiau Eglwyseg (now there's a challenging Welsh pronunciation – "craig-ee-igh egg-loo-iss-egg") rise to the north, overlooking the ruins of Castell Dinas Brân, a 12th-century castle perched on a knoll.

Take a ride through the Dee valley on the steam-hauled Llangollen Railway, or on one of the horse-drawn barges that clip-clop along the Llangollen Canal. And don't forget a visit to Plas Newydd, the fascinating house where the celebrated Ladies of Llangollen, the eccentric Lady Eleanor Butler and Sarah Ponsonby, lived their chosen life of "friendship, celibacy and the knitting of blue stockings." They lived here from 1780, transforming the cottage into a handsome house, and were visited by William Wordsworth, Sir Walter Scott, the Duke of Wellington and everyone who was anyone around the turn of the 19th century.

➕ E4
Tourist information ✉ Town Hall, Castle Street ☎ 01978 860828; www.borderlands.co.uk **Plas Newydd** ✉ Hill Street, Llangollen ☎ 01824 708223 🕐 Daily 10–5, Easter. through Oct. 31 🍴 Café 💰 $$

Great Little Trains of Wales

Wales is a mecca for steam railroad enthusiasts, with more than a dozen lines operating. Many of these are narrow-gauge, using the trackbeds of long-abandoned industrial railroads. Among the best known Welsh steam railways are:

- The Llangollen Railway (☎ 01978 860979)
- The Snowdon Mountain Railway, a rack-and-pinion railway stretching from Llanberis to the summit of Wales' highest mountain (☎ 01286 870223)
- The 13-mile Ffestiniog Railway, a scenic former slate-quarrying line between Porthmadog and Blaenau Ffestiniog (☎ 01766 516000)
- The Vale of Rheidol Railway, 12 miles from Aberystwyth to Devil's Bridge (☎ 01970 625819)
- The Talyllyn Railway, a 27-inch gauge line traversing wonderful mountain scenery near Cader Idris (☎ 01654 710472)
- The tiny one-foot gauge Fairbourne and Barmouth Steam Railway, connecting Fairbourne and Barmouth on opposite sides of the Mawddach Estuary with the help of a ferry (☎ 01341 250362)

Caerphilly – one of the biggest castles in Europe

GREAT CASTLES OF WALES AND THE BORDERS

It was the Lords Marcher, powerful independent barons sent to control the Welsh shortly after the 1066 Norman Conquest of England, who initiated castle-building in Wales and along the Welsh border with England. Their first efforts were of wood, but as their power and confidence grew they began to build in stone. Some of these "private" castles were more like fortified houses than mighty strongholds. Many saw their final moments of action during the Civil War of 1642–46. Typical is Hopton Castle near Knighton, some 4 miles from the English border, a crumbling stone keep on a diminutive mound in a field, peaceful yet poignant in its all-but-forgotten circumstances. Hopton had a most dramatic swan song, when a three-week siege by Royalist forces in 1644 ended in the capture of the castle and the slaughter of all but one of the 33-member Parliamentarian garrison. The captives were allegedly tied back to back in pairs and thrown in the moat to drown.

It is the great classic castles of Wales that draw visitors, however – and deservedly so, for these complex, cleverly designed mini-townships are truly fascinating places. They, like the smaller castles, are in varying states of repair; their condition mostly depends on what befell them during the English Civil War. Those that were held by supporters of the king, and had to be captured, were mostly "slighted" after the war – blown up or torn down to the point where they were considered sufficiently ruinous to be militarily useless. A good example is Raglan Castle in Monmouthshire, built during the 15th and 16th centuries; another is sturdy Denbigh Castle, on the crest of a hill in northeast Wales, built at the end of the 13th century to exert further control over natives already crushed by the onslaught of King Edward I. But the Welsh turned out to be not so thoroughly crushed after all; the castle had not even been completed when they captured it (albeit

Wales

briefly) in 1294. It was abandoned at the end of the English Civil War after holding out against a Parliamentary siege that lasted almost a year.

Many of the stronger stone castles were built by the barons during the uprisings earlier in the 13th century, before Edward I launched his decisive campaign. In this category falls Caerphilly Castle near Cardiff, a sprawling complex inside an enormous moat that was begun in 1268 in response to raids by Prince Llewellyn the Last. White Castle is another, a fortress built in the 1260s when Llewellyn allied himself with Earl Simon de Montfort in the Barons' Rebellion. White Castle's great curtain walls and drum towers are all the more impressive for its isolation in lonely country west of Monmouth. Chepstow Castle predates these two by a couple of centuries; it is the oldest stone-built castle in Britain, begun immediately after the Normans had arrived. Its location on a clifftop perch near the mouth of the River Wye provided very visible proof of the new order.

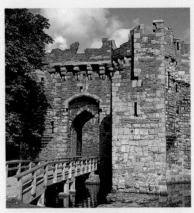

The gatehouse at Beaumaris Castle

But the most impressive of all the Welsh castles are those built under orders of King Edward I from 1283 onward to form the Iron Ring around Welsh western and northern strongholds. Eight were constructed, of which four are in excellent repair. Harlech, on Cardigan Bay, has 40-foot walls and a dominant position atop a crag; Conwy (see page 168) has a superb walkway circuit of its walls and a breathtaking backdrop of mountains. Caernarfon, on the Menai Strait, is the biggest and most impressive of them all, a grim and strong fort. Across the Menai Strait on the island of Anglesey is Beaumaris, the last of the Iron Ring to be built – strategically situated, eye-catchingly symmetrical and brilliantly engineered to snuff out an attack from any quarter.

The ramparts of Caernarfon Castle

Beaumaris ✚ C5 ☎ 01248 810361
Caernarfon ✚ C5 ✉ Y Maes ☎ 01286 677617
Caerphilly ✚ D1 ☎ 029 2088 3143
Chepstow ✚ E1 ☎ 01291 624065
Conwy ✚ D5 ✉ Castle Square ☎ 01492 592358
Harlech ✚ C4 ✉ Castle Square ☎ 01766 780552
Raglan ✚ E1 ☎ 01291 690228

Caernarfon Castle on the Menai Strait

Wales

OFFA'S DYKE

Offa, King of Mercia (a southern region of what is now England) between AD 757 and 796, had an uneasy relationship with the Welsh on the western border of his kingdom. So he ordered the building of an 80-mile-long dyke (embankment) and ditch to delineate the boundary between the two peoples, and to keep the rabble-rousing Welsh out of Mercia. Sited on western-facing slopes and ridges, it was easily patroled. Offa's Dyke has survived for more than 1,200 years. Some sections are all but intact; others have been reduced to ground level.

The actual political border between England and Wales, although it is now settled a little farther east at the northern end of the dyke, largely follows its course, the two boundaries crossing and recrossing like tangled threads all along the Welsh Borders.

A 177-mile footpath, Offa's Dyke National Trail, was established along the course of the dyke in the early 1970s, linking the southern coast of Wales at Chepstow with the northern coast on the Dee estuary at Prestatyn. In the course of its northward run the route encompasses such delights as the Wye Valley and Tintern Abbey; the Black Mountains and Llanthony Abbey; the beautiful tumbled country of the Herefordshire, Shropshire and Powys border counties; the towns of Knighton and Montgomery; the cliffs and bluffs of the Dee Valley at Llangollen; and the airy uplands of the Clwydian Hills.

The market town of Knighton, located at the halfway point along the route, is a good base from which to explore the area (and to stop for tea), and the friendly and helpful Offa's Dyke Centre there can supply visitors with maps, guidebooks, and details of the history and geography of the area.

✚ E3

Offa's Dyke Centre ✉ West Street, Knighton
☎ 01547 528753; www.offasdyke.demon.co.uk
🕐 Daily 9–5:30, Easter–Oct. 31; Mon.–Fri. 9–5, rest of year 💷 Free, donation requested

Walking along the Offa's Dyke National Trail near Knighton

Italianate styles peer over a rocky ledge in the intriguing village of Portmeirion

PISTYLL RHAEADR
WATERFALL

Four miles northwest of the village of Llanrhaeadr-ym-Mochnant ("the church by the falls of the stream where the pigs are"), the River Disgynfa pours over a rock lip in the eastern flank of the Berwyn Hills and crashes down in the most spectacular waterfall in Wales. Its upper stage is a straight tumble of more than 100 feet into a rock pool, from which it gushes out under an arch of rock to leap on down in spray and thunderous noise into a frothing pool at the foot of the fall. A footbridge near the bottom is a prime spot from which to view the full 240 feet of fall, a stupendous sight at any time but particularly so after heavy rain.

✚ D4

PORTMEIRION

Portmeirion is a bizarre place, reflecting its creator's sense of fun and feeling for the theatrical. It was after World War I that architect Clough Williams-Ellis began to install pieces from buildings in danger of demolition or decay all over the world on a peninsula between the rivers of Glaslyn and Dwyryd, in the northern part of Cardigan Bay. His idea was to prove that the beauty of man-made architecture could enhance rather than diminish the beauty of nature. Over the next half-century a strange, surrealistic little Italianate town slowly took shape, with a stylistic shock or surprise around every corner.

You enter Portmeirion through the Triumphal Arch to find more than 50 displaced buildings tightly huddled around a central square, or scattered along the hillside and shore. There's a telescopic-looking Italian bell tower, a splendid colonnade from a Georgian bath house in Bristol, temple furnishings from India and the Far East, a Jacobean town hall with Hercules featured in its ceiling, classical Greek columns, rococo plasterwork, and a hotel with a bar fitted out in Rajastani opulence.

You can rent a vacation cottage in Portmeirion, stay at the Hotel Portmeirion on the waterfront, or just come for the day to wander the streets and hillside gardens beautifully laid out with eucalyptus and cypress trees. You can enjoy a cup of tea and a Welsh cake at one of the cafés, and browse the shops selling Portmeirion pottery.

✚ C4 ✉ Minffordd, 2 miles east of Porthmadog
☎ 01766 770000 ⏲ Daily 9:30–5:30 🍴 Cafés 💰 $$$

Monastic magnificence: The ruins of Tintern Abbey

DRIVE: THE SOUTHERN BORDERS

Distance: 150 miles

You will dip in and out of Wales and England during this drive through the southernmost Welsh Borders: up the Wye Valley by Tintern Abbey and across to Raglan Castle; a glimpse of the famed Welsh valleys; on through the mountainous Brecon Beacons; and skirting the Black Mountains to descend to the gentle landscape of the "Golden Valley."

> *Begin the drive in Chepstow.*

This is an old river port where the River Wye flows down to meet the River Severn under the high walls of Chepstow Castle. The castle contains some of the earliest Norman stonework in Britain.

> *Follow A466 up the thickly wooded Wye Valley, with England on the east bank and Wales on the west, to Tintern.*

Here you will find one of the glories of monastic architecture, the roofless but still magnificent ruins of Tintern Abbey. The tall east, west and south windows frame beautiful woodland views.

> *From Tintern take the side road to the left, marked "Raglan," and follow these crooked lanes past Star Hill and Llansoy to cross over the A449 highway to reach Raglan.*

Visit Raglan's ruined castle (see page 170).

> *Head west along A40, turning left just before Abergavenny to continue west on A465.*

To the left are a series of once-industrial valleys, along with their ex-mining and steelmaking towns. The Big Pit: National Mining Museum of Wales at Blaenavon allows visitors to experience conditions at the coal face 300 feet below ground.

> *A465 skirts the northern edge of the former mining town of Merthyr Tydfil, then A470 heads north through the heart of Brecon Beacons National Park.*

These hills are not quite mountains, but they are certainly impressive – particularly the neighboring summits of Cribyn, Corn Du and Pen y Fan (at 2,907 feet the highest summit in southern Wales). To climb all three, start by way of the minor road to Pontsticill and the Neuadd Reservoir, which climbs north from the junction of A465 and A470 just northwest of Merthyr Tydfil. Up at the reservoir parking lot you'll have conifers, hills and water for company; a beautiful, silent place.

Stay on A470 north to Brecon, a small market town.

The Brecknock Museum and Art Gallery here has a superb display of Welsh lovespoons (see page 160).

Proceed northeast on A470/A438 to Talgarth. Leave Talgarth on A4078 for 1 mile, then bear right on a minor road to Hay-on-Wye.

Hay-on-Wye is famous for its second-hand books. You should certainly stop and browse.

B4348 curves east and then southeast from Hay-on-Wye, to descend the "Golden Valley" of the River Dore.

Here there is a string of medieval churches: St. Peter's at Peterchurch, St. Bartholomew's at Vowchurch and the lofty Norman remnant of Dore Abbey at Abbey Dore.

At the village of Pontrilas you reach A465. For a diversion, turn left toward Hereford and proceed for 3 miles, then turn right at Wormbridge to reach Kilpeck village.

The 12th-century Church of St. Mary and St. David at Kilpeck contains the most expressive church sculpture in Britain. The south doorway is embellished with dragons, huntsmen and intricate patterns, and a corbel table is finely carved with the personification of sins.

Backtrack to Pontrilas and take the B4347 past Grosmont Castle and Rockfield to Monmouth, before returning to Chepstow.

Chepstow ⊞ E1

Tourist information ✉ Castle Car Park, Bridge Street ☎ 01291 623772; www.visitwyevalley.com or www.monmouthshire.gov.uk

Chepstow Castle ✉ Bridge Street ☎ 01291 624065 🕒 Daily 9:30–6, Jun.–Sep.; daily 9:30–5, Apr.–May and in Oct.; Mon.–Sat. 9:30–4, Sun. 11–4, rest of year 🎟 $$

Tintern Abbey ✉ 5 miles north of Chepstow ☎ 01291 689251 🕒 Daily 9:30–6, Jun.–Sep.; daily 9:30–5, Apr.–May and in Oct.; Mon.–Sat. 9:30–4, Sun. 11–4, rest of year 🎟 $$

Big Pit: National Mining Museum of Wales ⊞ E1 ✉ Blaenavon, Torfaen ☎ 01495 790311 🕒 Daily 9:30–5 (tours 10–3:30), mid-Feb. through Nov. 30 🍴 Café (peak season) 🎟 Free

Brecknock Museum and Art Gallery ⊞ D2 ✉ Captain's Walk, Brecon ☎ 01874 624121 🕒 Mon.–Fri. 10–5, Sat. 10–1 and 2–5, Sun. noon–5, Apr.–Sep.; Mon.–Fri. 10–5, Sat. 10–1 and 2–5, rest of year 🎟 $

Hay-on-Wye ⊞ E2

Tourist information ✉ Unit 3, Oxford Road ☎ 01497 820144; www.hay-on-wye.co.uk

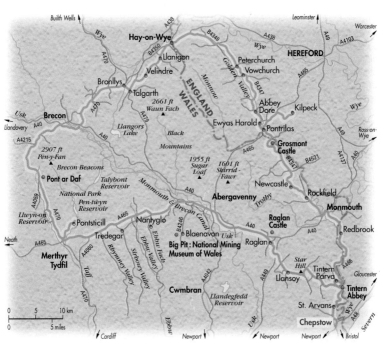

Mist is trapped among the folds of Snowdonia National Park looking toward Nant Gwynant

ST. DAVID'S AND PEMBROKESHIRE COAST NATIONAL PARK

St. David's is Britain's smallest city. No larger than a village, it is the ecclesiastical center of Wales, and as such it was officially granted city status in 1995. The squat but beautiful cathedral lies half-buried in a hollow. Inside the cathedral, the shrine to Wales' patron saint is always decorated with fresh flowers, and music recitals and concerts are sometimes played here.

The city itself is a charming place to stroll around; there are plenty of tearooms, cafés, shops and art galleries. The enchanting setting attracts many artists, and you will find pottery, weaving and wood-carvings for sale.

St. David's is within Pembrokeshire Coast National Park, 225 square miles of beautiful and unspoiled coastline encompassing the southwest tip of Wales. The Pembrokeshire Coastal Path traces the ins and outs of this coast for nearly 200 miles, through seaside towns as charming as Tenby and Fishguard and villages as picturesque as Manorbier and Little Haven, or you can explore it via the Puffin coastal bus services.

St. David's ✚ A2

Pembrokeshire Coast National Park Visitor Centre ✉ The Grove, St. Davids ☎ 01437 720392; www.pembrokeshirecoast.org.uk

Tenby ✚ B1

Tourist information ✉ The Croft ☎ 01834 842404; www.visitpembrokeshire.com

SNOWDONIA NATIONAL PARK

The most impressive mountain scenery south of the Scottish Highlands is found in Snowdonia National Park – 840 square miles of high country, lakes, mountains, dramatic valleys and coastline that fill the northwest corner of Wales. The pride of the region is Snowdon, at 3,560 feet the tallest mountain in England and Wales. You can ascend Snowdon from the town of Llanberis the lazy way, aboard the steam-hauled rack-and-pinion Snowdon Mountain Railway; or you can climb it in three to four hours by one of six routes.

Snowdonia's main industry these days is tourism, but a century ago it was slate quarrying. Many of these enormous and gloomy caverns are open to the public, such as Llechwedd Slate Caverns in Blaenau Ffestiniog, where you can try your hand at the art of splitting slate. From Blaenau Ffestiniog the steam trains of the Ffestiniog Railway descend for 13 twisty and dramatic miles to the coast at Porthmadog, only a couple of miles from Portmeirion (see page 173).

Blaenau Ffestiniog ✚ C4

Tourist information ✉ Unit 3, High Street ☎ 01766 830360; www.eryri-npa.gov.uk

Betws-y-Coed ✚ D5

Tourist information ✉ Royal Oak Stables ☎ 01690 710426; www.eryri-npa.gov.uk

Llechwedd Slate Caverns ✚ C4 ✉ Crimea Pass, Blaenau Ffestiniog ☎ 01766 830306 🕐 Tours daily 10–5:15, Mar.–Sep.; 10–4:15, rest of year 🖐 $$$

A drive northward through the central Welsh Borders from Hay-on-Wye up to Welshpool reveals a string of charming market towns in the heartland of this pastoral but wild region, so attractive to the visitor who loves landscape, legend and history intertwined.

Hay-on-Wye is famous for its second-hand bookshops, which have proliferated since the so-called "King of Hay," Richard Booth, established a business in Hay Castle over 20 years ago. The town also hosts the Hay Festival of Literature at the end of May to early June.

The Victorian clock tower at Knighton

MARKET TOWNS

North of Hay the border snakes around as it leaves the broad River Wye for the tighter little valleys of the River Arrow. Around Gladestry it enters a landscape filled with history, from the ancient standing stones and hill forts around Old Radnor to the broad back of Hergest Ridge. Under shelter of the ridge are two notable houses: Hergest Croft, with beautiful gardens painstakingly tended by three generations of the Banks family; and medieval Hergest Court, whose erstwhile owner, wicked Black Vaughan, is said to haunt the area in the guise of a hellish black dog.

Black Vaughan was beheaded in 1469 after suffering defeat at the Battle of Banbury during the Wars of the Roses. But legend maintains that he continued to roam the Borders in ghostly form. It was in St. Andrew's Church at nearby Presteigne – so the stories say – that 13 clergymen gathered to exorcise the troublesome spirit. The clerics managed to shut him in a snuffbox for 100 years, but he eventually escaped.

Presteigne itself is an agreeable little town with Edwardian wood-and-glass fronts to its shops and a fine old beamed coaching inn, the Radnorshire Arms.

Knighton, to the north, has steep streets with a number of antiques shops and tearooms, an oversized clock tower, and a former school converted into the Offa's Dyke Centre (see page 172).

North of Knighton the border takes a big westward bulge, bequeathing a wide swath of lonely uplands to England. Offa's Dyke twists and turns like a rollercoaster toward Welshpool, site of stunning Powis Castle. This charming market town has held a Monday livestock market for more than 500 years. It also has an ornate Victorian railroad station and a canal-side wharf. The steam-hauled Welshpool and Llanfair Light Railway makes an 8-mile jaunt from here to the friendly village of Llanfair Caereinion.

The 17th-century bridge over the Lugg at Presteigne

NORTHERN ENGLAND

"IN the north the folk are friendlier, the land is fairer and the grass greener; beer tastes better, the lads are bolder and the lasses prettier. So northerners say ..."

Opposite: Taking a stroll along The Shambles in York

NORTHERN ENGLAND

Northern England

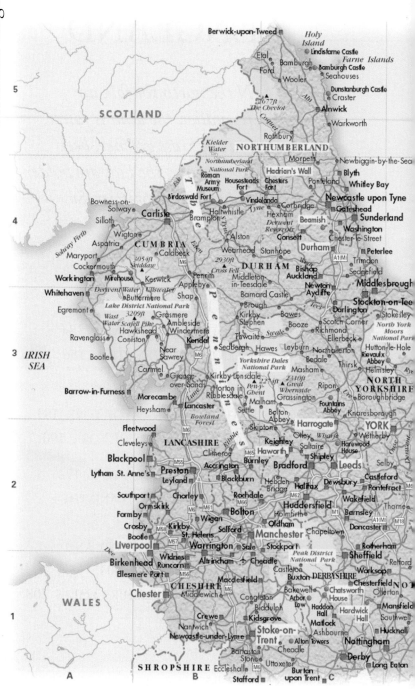

Northern England

There are many preconceptions about the north of England. To many a southerner, the idea of the north is still bound up with images that were true of large parts of this region only a generation ago, but have since become obsolete. Slate-roofed, redbrick rows of workers' houses, tall factory chimneys pumping out smoke, the great factories and textile mills themselves, coal mines and spoil heaps, shipyards and steelworks – all can be attributed to the man-made ugliness and environmental degradation of heavy industry bequeathed to the North by the British Industrial Revolution of the 18th and 19th centuries. And the no-nonsense character attributed to "The Northerner" – bluff, honest, blunt but neighborly, impatient with frills and courtesies – is fixed in the southerner's mind as well, with the approval of some northerners themselves who are happy to foster this "plain but proud" image. If Britain is in part a divided society, it is less along class lines these days than along this north–south fault line, illusory though it may be.

The Modern North
It is certainly true that Britain largely owed to the heavy industries of the north the prosperity on which its Georgian and Victorian feats of empire-building were founded. It is true, too, that industry blighted sizable chunks of England between Liverpool and Leeds, and around the coalfields of South Yorkshire and County Durham.

Any traveler with an eye for industrial architecture will have a field day in the north. But times have moved on in a very big way. The palls of smoke and grime that used to overhang the region's cities are long gone. Steelmaking, coal mining, textile manufacturing and shipbuilding are either gone or on their way out, swept aside by foreign competition or the redundancy forced on them by modern technology. The big urban areas – Liverpool, Leeds, Bradford, Manchester, Newcastle upon Tyne – take pride in their industrial heritage and are turning it to their advantage, creating hands-on museums telling the stories of their industries to visitors who may arrive skeptical, but who stay to become fascinated.

Mountains and Castles

And then, of course, there are those parts of the north that have never been industrial – hills, moors, valleys and coasts. There are the mini-mountains of the Lake District, the rugged glories of the Peak District, the Yorkshire Dales and Moors, the lonely Pennine hills and the wild uplands of Northumberland. There are fewer crowds in the north, more space, more elbow room for those who like to travel and explore.

The cultural and architectural delights of the north are wide-ranging, from the huge temples of commerce – warehouses, mills, factories – of Liverpool and Manchester to the great ruined abbey churches of Yorkshire (Fountains Abbey, Rievaulx, Whitby, Bolton Abbey) and the splendid cathedrals of York Minster, Durham and Beverley Minster. There are famous residences to visit – country mansions such as Castle Howard and Burton Agnes Hall in Yorkshire, and Northumbrian castles like those at Bamburgh, Dunstanburgh and Warkworth. Beamish The North of England Open Air Museum in County Durham is the best of its kind in Britain, a fascinating reconstruction of community life as it was before the world wars of the 20th century. Two very different annual events take place in this region, too: Early April sees the Grand National steeplechase at Aintree, near Liverpool, while York hosts the Jorvik Viking Festival in February, complete with a "long ships" race, folk dancing and Viking feasts.

Regional Flavors

As you travel through the northern counties, you'll encounter subtle differences in accents and dialects and a (usually) friendly rivalry between the regions. Different cities and counties boast their own brands of beer and ales, and there are distinct local dishes. Cumberland sausages are delicious, accompanied by mashed potatoes and gravy. For tea, try a piece of rich fruit cake with some crumbly white Wensleydale or Cheshire cheese, or a Derbyshire Bakewell pudding (jam pastry with cake). Yorkshire's most famous lunch is roast beef and Yorkshire pudding, served with hot horseradish sauce – a meal that you will see on pub menu boards across Britain. This also is the county where Harry Ramsden set up his first fish and chip "restaurant," an innovation for two items that had traditionally been served as a takeout in a paper wrapper. Today there is a chain of Harry Ramsden restaurants across the country.

Many northern cities – particularly Leeds, Bradford and Manchester, with their strong Asian communities – have excellent Indian restaurants and takeouts. Mild chicken curry was supposedly invented in Bradford to cater to those unfamiliar with spicy foods, and curry has now overtaken fish and chips as Britain's premier takeout. However, a curry takeout is really for

Cottages near the beach at Robin Hood's Bay

taking to your own kitchen, where you can assemble the components of the meal (rice, meat and sauce, nan bread, etc.) on a plate. For impromptu refueling on park benches, stick to fish and chips, or the ubiquitous burgers and pizzas. Enjoy your curry in an Indian restaurant – usually very inexpensive and tasty.

Take Your Time

Probably the best way to get into the heart and spirit of the north is to spend a few relaxed days wandering – on foot in the Peak District or along the Pennine Way; by train along the wonderfully scenic Settle and Carlisle Railway through the heart of the Pennines; or by car along the back roads and country lanes of the Yorkshire Dales or the Northumbrian hills.

Don't forget to stop at a pub or two to savor some locally brewed beer and engage in conversation. Northerners are famously friendly: That part of the cliché, at any rate, is true.

YORK

York is the best-known small city in northern England. It draws flocks of visitors, and it's easy to see why – the magnificent York Minster cathedral is second to none, and the 2 miles of almost complete medieval walls that encircle York are the finest of their kind anywhere in Britain. The hour-long strolling circuit of the walls and their four great fortified gates, or "bars," is one of Europe's classic town walks. The city is laid out along a photogenic tangle of medieval streets with enchanting names – Goodramgate, The Stonebow, Whip-Ma-Whop-Ma-Gate – which are attractively lined with an array of houses ancient and not quite so ancient. Everything within the walled city, including a large number of excellent museums and some beautiful medieval churches, is within a 10-minute stroll of the center. Residents tend to be friendly and to take time for strangers, when not carried away by the tides of tourism that sweep through the city at peak vacation periods.

Leadership Confirmed

York stands on one of the main through routes between England and Scotland, and as such has been an important stronghold and center for trade since the Romans established their garrison town of Eboracum here in AD 71. Through its Saxon incarnation as Eoforwic, and later a Danish phase as Jorvik, the town prospered. The Normans built two castles here, and the fortified circle of city walls was added and improved upon in later centuries. With the building of the great Minster cathedral (see page 188), York confirmed its spiritual as well as its military and commercial leadership. Later, in Georgian times, York became

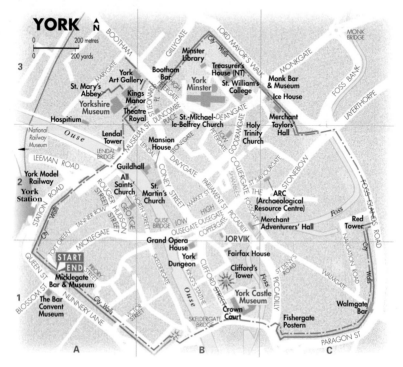

Stained-glass rose window in York Minster

as fashionable an inland resort for northerners as Bath did for southerners. In the Victorian era the city was the base for the powerful North-Eastern Railway company. Nowadays tourism keeps the money flowing through the coffers of this ancient city.

Traffic-Free Center

If you arrive by car, you will find parking lots only sporadically interspersed along the medieval walls. Since the city center is a vehicle-free zone it is advisable to use one of the "park and ride" parking lots on the approach roads (well marked by signs). From there an inexpensive bus will take you right into the center. The train station is just outside the western angle of the city walls, the bus station just inside on Rougier Street – both a 10-minute walk from the center.

The old city can be walked across in 20 minutes. With its narrow, crooked streets it is ideal for exploring on foot. Getting your bearings can be a problem at first because of the tangled nature of those streets. Keep in mind that the city walls form a diamond shape, with the Minster within the northern angle, the York Castle Museum within the southern angle and JORVIK on a

Minster

The word "minster" was first used in medieval England as a version of the word "monastery." It was often applied simply to describe the church attached to a monastery, which was used for worship by the monks.

Through time the word became associated with certain cathedral churches, like York Minster.

straight line between these two points. Davygate, Parliament Street, Piccadilly and Fishergate progress generally north to south through the center;

Rise and Fall

Two famous men in York's history, both gamblers who rode their luck to wild success and then to downfall, were Dick Turpin and George Hudson. Turpin, a butcher's apprentice from London, had a notoriously productive career as a highway robber in the 1730s. Eventually he fled to York, where he was arrested for the workaday crime of shooting a pheasant. Then his previous crimes came to light. Turpin was hanged in York on April 7, 1739, and took five long minutes to die. George Hudson, the "Railway King," became a towering figure in York as Lord Mayor and also as the immensely rich boss of a giant railway empire in early Victorian days. The crash, prompted by Hudson's dodgy business dealings, came in 1849, and he found himself a broken pauper in the city's prison.

Micklegate, Bridge Street, Ousegate, High Ousegate, Pavement, The Stonebow and Peaseholme Green progress roughly west to east. The River Ouse flows through the city from Lendal Bridge, at the northwestern section of the walls, to Skeldergate Bridge in the southern part. If in doubt, you can always find north by looking for the towering Minster. Don't forget that a "bar" here means an arched gate in the old city wall, and a "gate" is a street.

Eating and Drinking

Walking around York will make you hungry and thirsty, two states of mind and body well catered to in the city center. There are plenty of restaurants along Micklegate and Goodramgate, as well as dozens of pubs for a snack and a drink. Try the King's Arms on King's Staithe, near the Ouse Bridge in the center, where you can sit outside and watch the river. York's own York Brewery produces a tasty bitter beer. For afternoon tea, try Taylor's on Stonegate, which is nicely refurbished. Another good choice is Betty's Café Tea Rooms, on St. Helen's Square at the top of Davygate.

ESSENTIAL INFORMATION

TOURIST INFORMATION
De Grey Rooms, Exhibition Square, and York Railway Station ☎ 01904 621756; www.visityork.org

URBAN TRANSPORTATION
York's main railroad station is on Station Road. For rail information and reservations, contact the 24-hour national inquiry line (☎ 08457 484950). York's bus station is on Rougier Street; the information line is ☎ 01904

551400. The main taxi stand is outside the railroad station. Visitors can obtain transportation information from the tourist offices in the De Grey Rooms or York Railway Station.

AIRPORT INFORMATION
Leeds/Bradford Airport (☎ 0113 250 9696), 11 miles northwest of Leeds, is about an hour's drive from York. Manchester Airport (☎ 0161 489 3000) is 56 miles southwest by road, but has direct train service to York.

CLIMATE – Average highs and lows

JAN.	FEB.	MAR.	APR.	MAY	JUN.	JUL.	AUG.	SEP.	OCT.	NOV.	DEC.
7°C	7°C	9°C	11°C	16°C	18°C	20°C	19°C	17°C	13°C	9°C	8°C
45°F	45°F	48°F	52°F	61°F	64°F	68°F	66°F	63°F	56°F	48°F	46°F
3°C	2°C	4°C	5°C	8°C	11°C	13°C	13°C	10°C	8°C	5°C	4°C
37°F	36°F	39°F	41°F	46°F	52°F	55°F	55°F	50°F	46°F	41°F	39°F

Northern England

YORK SIGHTS

Key to symbols

◆ map coordinates refer to the York map on page 184; sights below are highlighted in yellow on the map.

✉ address or location ☎ telephone number
◷ opening times ⏸ restaurant on site or nearby
▣ admission charge: $$$ more than £6, $$ £2–£6,
$ less than £2 ⓘ information

THE SHAMBLES AREA

The Saxons called them "shamel," and medieval Englishmen "shambles" – the word meant slaughterhouses, places that in most towns were confined to one bloody and stinking quarter. The Shambles of York, at the heart of the city, is no longer a scene of dung and death. Far from it: This is York's most picturesque and photogenic street, much too narrow for any wheeled vehicle, where crazily bent and leaning timbered houses jut their upper storys so far over the flagstoned sidewalk that occupants could almost shake hands across the roadway. Today antiques emporia and bookstores fill the ground floors of the old butchers' shops, but fixed in the beams above you can still see the hooks from which carcasses and cuts of meat were hung.

From The Shambles, the charmingly narrow and bent streets of York spread out along their haphazard medieval layout. Here the suffix "gate," legacy of ninth-century Danish settlers, means a street; a snickelway, or snicket, is an even narrower alley. Such is Whip-ma-whop-ma-gate, a needle's eye of a snickelway off Fossgate, southeast of The Shambles. Farther along Fossgate stands the 14th-century Merchant Adventurers' Hall, a cavernous structure 40 feet wide under a really magnificent timber roof. The wool dealers, known as Merchant Adventurers, formed York's most influential guild during the Middle Ages, and this fine building reflects their prosperity.

Colliergate runs northwest from Fossgate toward the Minster, soon meeting Goodramgate. Here stands the

Impish red devil at Stonegate

delightful Holy Trinity Church, its 14th-century pillars and 18th-century box pews leaning this way and that. Next to the church is a little row of early medieval houses, Our Lady's Row – constructed in 1316, they are York's oldest dwellings. A little west of Goodramgate runs Stonegate, built along the course of one of the roads the Romans laid out in their garrison town. Look high up to spot the red-skinned, horned devil chained by his waist to a wooden post, some medieval carver's little joke.

◆ B2

The Shambles after an evening rain shower

York Minster dominates the city

York Minster

This magnificent cathedral, the largest medieval church in northern Europe, dominates York from its position in the northern angle of the city walls. It seems that from every vantage point in town you catch a glimpse of its great square central tower and rocket-like west towers, soaring high above roofs and walls. By sheer bulk and length – 534 feet – it draws the eye, yet the whole effect is light and graceful.

Take binoculars inside to appreciate the beauty and fine workmanship on display. York Minster was begun in 1220 and took 250 years to complete, so the mixture of architectural and aesthetic styles is fascinating. The 100-foot-high nave and the octagonal Chapter House are full of carvings on roof bosses and the capitals of the slender pillars. Those in the Chapter House include funny beasts (one is of a monkey making a ridiculous face) and even funnier grotesques of church figures. The choir screen, carved in 1461 at the end of the long construction process, shows English kings from William the Conqueror to Henry VI, with wild hair and luxuriant beards. Downstairs in the undercroft and crypt you can see the sturdy columns and vaulting that upheld the Norman cathedral which predated the Minster.

The glory of this church, though, is in its stained-glass windows, a collection unmatched in Britain for size, color and antiquity. In the great west window, 54 feet tall, the 14th-century glass is held in delicate stonework tracing the form of a heart. The north transept's big window, made in 1250 shortly after work started on the building, contains more than 100,000 pieces of grisaille (gray-tinted) glass, of great although muted beauty. The south transept holds a beautiful Tudor rose window in glowing reds and blues.

But all eyes in the end turn to the east window, the size of a tennis court (78 feet by 31 feet), where between 1405 and 1408 the stories of creation and of doomsday were depicted in glorious color and detail. It is the largest display of medieval stained glass in the world, a breathtaking spectacle.

🚩 B3 ✉ Minster Yard ☎ 01904 557216 🕐 Minster: Mon.–Sat. 7–6:30, Sun. noon–6:30. Undercroft, Treasury and Crypt: Mon.–Sat. 9–5, Sun. noon–5, Easter–Oct. 31; Mon.–Sat. 9:30–5, Sun. noon–5, rest of year. Tower: Mon.–Sat. 9–5:30, Sun. noon–5:30, Easter–Oct. 31; Mon.–Sat. 9:30–30 minutes before dusk, Sun. 12:30–30 minutes before dusk, rest of year. Restricted access during services 🍴 Restaurant 🎟 Minster $$ (cheaper admission after 4:45 p.m. and 5:30–6:30); Undercroft, Treasury and Crypt $$; Tower $$

Northern England

Monsters from the age of steam in the National Railway Museum

MUSEUMS OF YORK

York is particularly well endowed with excellent museums, and you could happily spend hours in them. Four of the best are:

JORVIK

The crowds are often large, but this most popular of York's museums offers an enjoyable glimpse into everyday life in Viking York some 1,000 years ago. You travel on a "time-car" through tableaux complete with appropriate sounds and smells – wattle huts, dirty streets, cooking smoke, animals and children everywhere.

JORVIK ✚ B2 ✉ Coppergate ☎ 01904 643211 🕓 Daily 10–5, Apr.–Oct.; 10–4, rest of year 🍴 Café 🎫 $$$

Yorkshire Museum

The Crucifixion scene beautifully etched in the gold of the 15th-century Middleham Jewel is only one of the archeological treasures here. Also on display are Roman mosaics, carvings and artifacts, Viking silver bowls and fossils from the Yorkshire coast.

Yorkshire Museum ✚ A3 ✉ Museum Gardens ☎ 01904 687687 🕓 Daily 10–5 🍴 Café 🎫 $$ ℹ️ Events and changing exhibitions at various times (opening times may vary)

York Castle Museum

Here are reconstructed Victorian streets, shops and houses, agricultural work and crafts, and archeological finds, including the best preserved Saxon helmet in the country. A wide-ranging collection of everyday domestic objects, housed in the former Debtors' and Women's Prisons, is a poignant flashback to simpler days.

York Castle Museum ✚ B1 ✉ The Eye of York, Tower Street ☎ 01904 687687 🕓 Daily 9:30–5 🍴 Café 🎫 $$

National Railway Museum

The best railroad museum in Britain is a guaranteed delight for all, railroad enthusiasts or not. More than 60 juggernauts of steam loom large amidst all the posters, signs, models and memorabilia. Here you can view the *Mallard*, holder of the world speed record for steam locomotives – 126 mph, set back in 1938 and as yet unbroken. Take a look at how royalty used to travel in the "Palaces on Wheels" display of royal saloons.

National Railway Museum ✚ A2 ✉ Leeman Road ☎ 01904 621261 🕓 Daily 10–6 🍴 Restaurant and café 🎫 Free (charge for special exhibitions)

Northern England

WALK: THE WALLS OF YORK

Refer to route marked on city map on page 184

The 2-mile circuit of the medieval city walls of York is fascinating, not just for the completeness and historical interest of the walls themselves, but also for the stunning views they offer across the tight huddle of medieval streets within their orbit. York Minster, moored to the northernmost angle of the walls, inevitably dominates.

The walkway surface of the walls is even underfoot, suitable for ordinary shoes. Be warned, however, that there are some steep flights of steps to negotiate, and that there are unguarded drops of up to 20 feet at many points inside the walls. Young children get endless fun out of this walk, but they should not be allowed to dash ahead unsupervised.

The walls form a rough diamond shape, with York Minster at the top or northern angle, and York Castle toward the bottom or southern angle. They are pierced with four great medieval "bars," or gates, from which roads radiate out to the intermediate points of the compass.

Micklegate Bar, on the southwestern side of the diamond, is a good place to start the walk.

Micklegate Bar is flanked by two tall 14th-century drum towers on Norman foundations. In the days of robust punishments the severed heads of traitors would be displayed on spikes on the top of the bar as a grisly example to others.

From Micklegate Bar turn north along the raised walkway inside the ramparts of the wall, which seems to ripple like a ribbon of pale stone as it runs toward Lendal Bridge across the River Ouse.

These city walls follow much the same shape as the walls built by the Romans around their city of Eboracum, but they are immensely stronger, a forbidding girdle of stone built on the orders of King Edward III to protect the medieval city from attacks by the then-insurgent Scots. From Lendal Bridge there is a great view ahead to York Minster.

Beyond the river the original walls

disappear. A very pleasant stroll through the Yorkshire Museum Gardens leads to the Multangular Tower, which stands on a Roman base next to the graceful arches of the ruined Abbey of St. Mary. The abbey was founded around 1080, and Benedictine monks left from here to found Fountains Abbey (see page 208).

Micklegate Bar at the start of your walk

Rejoin the wall at Bootham Bar and continue above the lovely green parkland of the gardens behind York Minster, with the giant towers and walls of the Minster standing majestically on your right.

Your perspective of the church will change almost 180 degrees between Bootham Bar on the west and Monk Bar on the east.

Monk Bar, tall and grim, displays dummy soldiers at the parapets of its twin flanking towers, seemingly threatening to hurl missiles down on anyone contemplating attack. From here you walk on to the southeast, looking inward across the jumbled roofs of medieval York and outward to the domed roof of the city's Ice House. Built around 1800, it held tons of ice collected each winter and insulated in straw until needed during the heat of summer.

Beyond the Ice House the walls disappear once more. Here you find the River Foss, and the small lake created for William the Conqueror that is still called the King's Pool.

A short stretch of road reaches a brick-built Tudor watchtower, the Red Tower, where the wall reappears to take you on to Walmgate Bar.

Walmgate is the only bar to retain its barbican, or defensive courtyard – the others were pulled down in the 1820s and '30s to improve traffic flow. The bar contains a Calvary Chapel with a café which is open on Saturdays.

Next comes the tall outlook tower of Fishergate Postern, and then York Castle, next to the moody-looking Clifford's Tower, a 13th-century stronghold atop a knoll.

From the tower it is a short stroll back to Micklegate Bar.

From the walkway, the towers of York Minster rise beyond the Lendal Bridge across the Ouse

Northern England

A tram in a re-created early 20th-century street scene at Beamish

REGIONAL SIGHTS

Key to symbols

✚ map coordinates refer to the Northern England map on pages 180–181; sights below are highlighted in yellow on the map.

✉ address or location ☎ telephone number

🕐 opening times 🍴 restaurant on site or nearby

🚌 nearest bus route

🖐 admission charge: $$$ more than £6, $$ £2–£6, $ less than £2 ℹ information

BEAMISH, THE NORTH OF ENGLAND OPEN AIR MUSEUM

There is unashamed nostalgia in the air at Beamish, where a complete township has been laid out on 300 acres of parkland. High Street contains authentic early 20th-century shops, a pub, a dentist's office, a candy shop and a motor and cycle works. The workers' accommodations are typical of those once found in the Durham coalfield, including a terrace row of miners' houses complete with outside toilets ("netties") and vegetable plots, a mining company school and a chapel. You also can tour the Mahogany Drift Mine with guides who have themselves worked in coal mines and speak from direct personal experience.

Beamish boasts its own railroad with steam engines and old-fashioned carriages. All told, this is one of northern England's best day trips.

✚ C4

✉ Beamish, County Durham ☎ 0191 370 4000
🕐 Daily 10–5, late Mar.–late Oct.; Tue.–Thu. and Sat.–Sun. 10–4, rest of year. Closed mid-Dec. to early Jan. Last admission at 3 p.m. 🍴 Café 🖐 $$$ (admission reduced late Oct.–late Mar.)

CASTLE HOWARD

This Palladian mansion near York was built between 1699 and 1712 by then untried architect Sir John Vanbrugh (with the help of Sir Christopher Wren's pupil Nicholas Hawksmoor), and is one of the country's most impressive houses. It was commissioned by Charles Howard, 3rd Earl of Carlisle, and his descendants still live in the east wing. There is a giant north facade topped by a cupola, which forms the roof for the enormous great hall. State rooms contain portraits, furniture, china and glassware of great beauty. There is pre-Raphaelite stained glass in the chapel, and a collection of costumes and court regalia.

The grounds contain a lake as well as a whole array of follies and fancies: obelisks and towers; the Temple of the Four Winds, complete with four porticoes; and the circular Howard family mausoleum.

Evelyn Waugh's tale of degeneration and conceit, *Brideshead Revisited*, was filmed for TV at Castle Howard.

✚ D3

✉ Malton, near York ☎ 01653 648333 🕐 Daily 10–4 (house opens at 11), Mar. 1–early Nov. 🍴 Cafés 🖐 $$$

Opposite: Old houses sit above modern shops in Chester

Chatsworth House is set on a beautiful landscaped park of 1,000 acres

CHATSWORTH HOUSE

By far the finest house in Peak District National Park, Chatsworth, a classic baroque mansion near the town of Bakewell, was built between 1687 and 1707 for the 1st Duke of Devonshire. Impressive Palladian facades look to all quarters of the compass, but it is the west front and its giant pediment that dominates the long driveway approach.

In the state rooms hang paintings by Anthony van Dyck, Rembrandt and Frans Hals. There are richly frescoed ceilings by Louis Laguerre and Antonio Verrio, and a clever *trompe l'oeil* fiddle painted by Jan Van der Vaart as if hanging on the back of a door. You can view grand table settings as once laid for King George V and Queen Mary in the great dining room.

The 1,000-acre park was landscaped by Capability Brown in the 1760s. Nearer at hand are superb formal gardens with beautiful water features. Joseph Paxton, who designed the Crystal Palace in London for the Great Exhibition of 1851, was head gardener here; his 1848 "Conservative Wall," a line of iron-framed greenhouses, still flourishes at Chatsworth. ⊞ C1

✉ 8 miles north of Matlock, off the B6012, Derbyshire ☎ 01246 565300 ⏰ House: daily 11–5:30, mid-Mar. to mid-Dec. Garden: daily 10:30–6, Jun.–Aug.; 11–6, mid-Mar. through May 31 and Sep. 1 to mid-Dec. Park: daily dawn–dusk, all year 🍴 Restaurants and cafés 💷 $$$ (garden only $$); Park free

CHESTER

Chester, capital of Cheshire, is a small city the right size for strolling around, with carved medieval woodwork adorning its buildings. Take one of the themed guided walking tours (including a "ghost" tour) arranged by the tourist office. Be sure to see the partly excavated Roman amphitheater and the Dewa Roman Experience to discover what life was like in Roman Chester. Also visit Chester Cathedral, with stonework and wood-carvings dating from Norman times.

The medieval Rows is a galleried arcade of enticing shops, while Watergate Street has plenty of antique shops. Stop for afternoon tea at Katie's (a real Old World tea shop), or enjoy a light lunch served in the 13th-century monks' dining room in the cathedral refectory. ⊞ B1

Tourist information ✉ Vicar's Lane; also Town Hall, Northgate Street ☎ 01244 402111; www.chestertourism.com

Roman amphitheater ✉ Little St. John Street ⏰ Daily 24 hours 💷 Free

Dewa Roman Experience ✉ Pierpoint Lane, off Bridge Street ☎ 01244 343407 ⏰ Daily 9–5, Feb.–Nov.; 10–4, rest of year 💷 $$

Northern England

Visiting the Brontë Parsonage Museum at the top of Haworth's steep, Church Street, it is hard to imagine the currents of creation that swirled through this plain sandstone West Yorkshire house in the 1830s and '40s. But it was here that Charlotte, Emily and Anne Brontë wrote their childhood chronicles of the imaginary lands of Angria and Gondal. Then, in the pivotal year of 1847, each published a first novel that would immortalize their names: Charlotte's *Jane Eyre*, Emily's *Wuthering Heights* and Anne's *Agnes Grey*.

The museum is in the former home of the Brontës

HAWORTH AND THE BRONTËS

The Parsonage Museum contains a priceless archive of Brontë papers, as well as items of memorabilia such as Charlotte's dress, a bracelet of Anne's hair and a watercolor by Emily of her dog, along with amateurish portraits by their brother Branwell, a sad victim of drink and consumption (tuberculosis). It was consumption that killed Emily and Anne, too, within two years of publishing their books. Charlotte outlived them by a few years, but died in 1855 at the age of 38, recently married and newly pregnant, after catching cold.

To see where so much of the sisters' inspiration came from, you should step out across the wild moors that roll west of the village. From the cobbled lane outside the parsonage, a paved path marked "Haworth Moor" crosses a field to join West Lane through a narrow stone stile. After about 130 feet, fork left and follow the road beneath a slab of rock engraved "Penistone Hill Country Park." Cross the Stanbury-to-Oxenhope road. Step over a metal grid

designed to prevent cattle straying and follow a lane signed "Brontë Waterfalls," which becomes a track that leads you to the falls. This was a favorite place of the sisters – the water tumbles down under a stone clapper bridge known as Brontë Bridge, overlooked by the Brontë chair, a rock with a natural seat shape. West of here stands a ruined farmhouse that gave Emily Brontë the inspiration for Heathcliff's dour dwelling, Wuthering Heights. Ask at the tourist office for directions or a map.

You can travel to Haworth by steam train aboard the Keighley and Worth Valley Railway. The 5-mile route runs between Keighley and Oxenhope.

✚ C2

Tourist information ✉ 2–4 West Lane, Haworth ☎ 01535 642329; www.visithaworth.com

Brontë Parsonage Museum ✉ Church Street, Haworth ☎ 01535 642323 🕐 Daily 10–5:30, Apr.–Sep.; 11–5, Feb.–Mar. and Oct.–Dec. Closed Dec. 25 💰 $$

Keighley and Worth Valley Railway ☎ 01535 645214 ✉ The Railway Station, Haworth 🕐 Schedules vary over the year; call for details 💰 $$$

Shops, galleries and cafés line the main street in Haworth

Northern England

Durham

On a high bluff over the River Wear stand Durham's cathedral and castle, commanding the slate roofs below in lofty grandeur. There are splendid views of both from many places around Durham. All reinforce the impregnability of the site, a steep-sided peninsula caught in a tight loop of the Wear. Durham Cathedral is the finest and most handsomely sited Norman building in Britain. Combined with the castle, it radiates both magnificence and a sense of defiance, fitting for an ensemble that Sir Walter Scott memorably described as "half church of God, half castle 'gainst the Scot."

Symbol of Power

The city's modest size and the region's recent history of workaday heavy industry might lead one to wonder why such a grand cathedral was built here. One reason was the turbulence of northern England after the Norman Conquest. In an effort to bring order into the region, the king granted the "Prince Bishops" of Durham almost unlimited powers, which were wielded freely and ruthlessly all through the Middle Ages. They controlled the garrison at Durham Castle to such effect that the city was never captured, and peace of a kind lay over this volatile corner of northeast England. They also minted their own money, made their own laws and built a cathedral to trumpet forth their power and prestige.

Most of Durham's sights are on or near the short peninsula on which the cathedral and castle stand. The cathedral looms over Palace Green, on the spine of the peninsula. Begun in 1093, it was built in classic Norman style. The nave is flanked by immensely sturdy, squat round pillars, their surfaces incised with wide chevrons and dogtooth patterns. Some arches are rounded in true Norman fashion; others are pointed, reflecting the changes in building style that took place before the completion of the cathedral in 1274. The choir reaches high, its aisle roofs ribbed in stone. Everything here is bulky, massive and built to last forever.

In contrast are the two elegantly beautiful chapels at either end of the building. At the east end in the Chapel of the Nine Altars lies St. Cuthbert, hermit and reluctant bishop, who died in AD 687 and whose well-preserved body was brought here three centuries later by disciples from the island of Lindisfarne, off the Northumbrian coast (see page 206). In the delicately carved and constructed 12th-century Galilee Chapel at the west end is buried the Venerable Bede, a learned monk who wrote Cuthbert's life story.

Cathedral Treasures

In the Cathedral Treasury you can see, among many treasures from the cathedral's long life, the bejeweled pectoral

Dominant Durham Cathedral overlooks the River Wear

cross that St. Cuthbert wore when he was buried, and the wooden coffin in which he was first interred. There are some superbly decorated manuscripts, and it is hoped that the Lindisfarne Gospels – exquisitely illuminated gospels dating from St. Cuthbert's time and presently housed in the British Library in London – will some day find a permanent home here.

The castle is worth a tour for the woodwork in its Tudor chapel, a really fine 17th-century staircase, and the ancient kitchen with fireplaces big enough to roast an entire ox. The old streets around the castle and cathedral, packed with shops, pubs and cafés, are fascinating to explore.

On the east bank of the river below the cathedral, the University of Durham's excellent Museum of Archaeology is housed in a medieval mill. From here you can either walk a riverside footpath around the peninsula, or take a river cruise or rowboat ride, and enjoy the memorable views of the cathedral and castle.

✚ C4

Tourist information ✉ 2 Millennium Place ☎ 0191 384 3720; www.durhamtourism.co.uk

Durham Cathedral ✉ Palace Green ☎ 0191 386 4266 🕐 Mon.–Sat. 9:30-8, Sun. 12:30–6, Apr.–Sep.; Mon.–Sat. 9:30–6, Sun. 12:30–5, rest of year 💲 Donation requested

Museum of Archaeology ✉ Old Fulling Mill, The Banks ☎ 0191 334 1823 🕐 Daily 11–4, Apr.–Oct.; Fri.–Mon. 11:30–3:30, rest of year 🚻 $

Looking along Hadrian's Wall toward Housestead's Crag in Northumberland

HADRIAN'S WALL

Hadrian's Wall was built across the neck of northernmost England from AD 120 on the orders of the Roman Emperor Hadrian to keep the trouble-making Scots out of England. Originally it stood some 20 feet high, with observation and signal turrets spread evenly along its 73-mile length. A garrisoned fort, or "milecastle," was located at the point of every Roman mile. The wall ran from the North Sea at Wallsend in the east to Solway Firth in the west.

For 1,500 years after the Romans left Britain, Hadrian's Wall was seen only as a source of ready-shaped building stone. Now it has been restored and is treated with the respect it deserves. You can walk its length along the 84-mile-long National Trail, or explore the excavated forts and associated museums at Chesters, Housesteads (the best of the lot), Vindolanda and Birdoswald. The Hadrian's Wall bus (No. AD122) links each of the sites.

✚ B4–C4

Hadrian's Wall Information ✚ B4 ✉ Railway Station, Station Road, Haltwhistle, Northumberland ☎ 01434 322002; www.hadrians-wall.org

Hadrian's Wall Bus (AD122) ✚ B4–C4

✉ Wallsend–Bowness-on-Solway ☎ 01434 322002 🕐 Daily 7:30–4:30, mid-May to late Sep.; on Sun. rest of year 🚌 $$

HARDWICK HALL

Second only to Chatsworth House (see page 194) among Peak District houses, Hardwick Hall in eastern Derbyshire is a fine Elizabethan mansion set in well-wooded and rolling parkland. "Hardwick Hall, more glass than wall," so the saying goes, is a reference to the house's large windows. The real fascination about Hardwick Hall is the story of the remarkable woman who had it built between 1591 and 1597. Elizabeth Hardwick, Countess of Shrewsbury – better known as "Bess of Hardwick" – possessed a will and a temper fully as strong as her sovereign, Queen Elizabeth I. Having hauled herself up from humble origins through a series of advantageous marriages, Bess used the money of her last husband, the Earl of Shrewsbury, to build Hardwick Hall as a temple to herself. Her initials, E.S. (Elizabeth Shrewsbury), appear in stonework, woodwork and tapestries all over the house.

Tapestries embroidered by Bess and her staff hang in nearly every room, claustrophobically thick and dark. The portraits of her, imperious and cold under her scraped-back red hair, reveal an iron-hard egotist who built a house that was more of a showpiece than a home.

sulphurous water guaranteed to sort out any insubordination on the part of your digestive system.

Harrogate is a great strolling town, with an abundance of handsome Victorian architecture. You also can take a Turkish bath in the Royal Baths building or just continue a pleasurable piling on of the pounds with afternoon tea at elegant Betty's Tea Rooms on Parliament Street, which serves irresistible local bakery goodies.

✚ C2

Tourist information ✉ Royal Baths, Crescent Road
☎ 01423 537300; www.harrogate.gov.uk
Betty's Tea Rooms ✉ 1 Parliament Street ☎ 01423 502746
Royal Baths (Turkish Baths) ✉ Parliament Street
☎ 01423 556746 ⏰ Daily 9–9 🍴 Café 💷 $$$
Royal Pump Room Museum ✉ Crown Place
☎ 01423 556188 ⏰ Mon.–Sat. 10–5, Sun. 2–5, Apr.–Oct.; Mon.–Sat. 10–4, Sun. 2–4, rest of year
💷 $$

✚ C1
Hardwick Hall ✉ Doe Lea, near Chesterfield
☎ 01246 850430 ⏰ House: Wed.–Thu. and Sat.–Sun. noon–4:30, Apr.– Oct. Garden: Wed.–Sun. 11–5:30, Apr.–Oct. 🍴 Restaurant 💷 $$$ (garden only $$)

HARROGATE

As a spa, Harrogate appeared very late on the scene. It was not until the late Victorian era that this pleasant gray stone town in central Yorkshire had its heyday. Sufferers and pleasure-seekers alike flocked to taste the waters in the Pump Room, to sweat in a Turkish bath at the Royal Baths, and to dance and flirt at parties in the Assembly Rooms.

The healing springs were discovered in 1571 on The Stray, a big, grassy common south of the town center. Almost 100 additional springs were unearthed over the following centuries, with a greater or lesser infusion of sulphur, magnesium or iron. Strolling on The Stray, or in Valley Gardens west of the town center, you can see the temple-like structures erected over these scores of well heads over the years.

These days the Royal Pump Room houses a museum with exhibits depicting Harrogate's healing past, as well as a jet which will deliver you a glass full of eggy,

The Settle–Carlisle Railway

The Settle–Carlisle Railway, opened in 1875, is England's most spectacular and exciting line. The building of the 72-mile track through the inhospitable moorlands and uplands of the Pennines was dangerous work, costing the lives of dozens of construction workers. The 24-arch Ribblehead Viaduct, north of Horton-in-Ribblesdale, is a triumph of Victorian engineering.

The journey takes an hour and 40 minutes; there are regular daily scheduled trips as well as occasional steam-hauled trains, or you can drive the by-roads that follow the line. The pleasant towns of Settle, Kirkby Stephen and Appleby each have stations, and make good bases from which to explore the Pennine hills.

✚ B3–B4
The Settle–Carlisle Railway Stations
☎ 08457 484950

Northern England

LAKE DISTRICT

The tight little circle of the Lake District, England's best-known piece of mountainous country, measures only about 30 miles from side to side as the crow flies. It contains nearly 200 fells (the local word for high hills or small mountains) that top 2,000 feet, but only four over 3,000 feet. These are statistics that instantly give you an idea of the lay of the land in this national park – a tumbled, undulating mass of fells pressed close together, with deep dales (valleys) between them. Lakes, long and thin, are scattered in the dales; tarns (small lakes) lie in hollows of the upper fells. None of the fells has the majesty of a full-blown Alpine mountain, but they have something better – intense individual character, so that a visitor who falls in love with the Lake District returns again and again as if to familiar friends.

This is prime walking country, from the cultivated grazing fields of the dale bottoms to the wild moorland that clothes the upper slopes of the fells. Farming hamlets and individual farms of gray stone are sprinkled throughout the district, and there are several villages – Ambleside, Grasmere, Hawkshead – as well as a couple of well-appointed small towns, Windermere and Keswick. These places are thoroughly geared to catering to visitors who want to explore the fells and dales that surround them. In Windermere in the south and Keswick in the north you can buy all the gear, footwear, clothing and maps that you will need to get out and about on foot. And you'll certainly see Kendal Mint Cake for sale – a very sweet, strongly flavored mint candy, the perfect energy-booster for walkers.

Windermere in the southeast is the largest and longest lake, with the tourist-ridden town of the same name on its east bank. On the opposite side of the lake is Near Sawrey, where Beatrix Potter lived from 1905 to 1913. Here she wrote and illustrated *Tom Kitten*, *Samuel Whiskers*, *Jemima Puddle Duck* and other much-loved children's tales. Just north is Hawkshead, whose grammar school William Wordsworth attended as a boy.

The shadow of Wordsworth lies long over Grasmere (northwest of Ambleside), where England's great Romantic poet came to live in 1800. You can look around Dove Cottage, where he began his Lake District sojourn with sister Dorothy, and Rydal Mount, where he lived toward the end of his life, before paying your respects at his grave in St. Oswald's churchyard.

Helvellyn, 3,116 feet tall and one of the Lake District's best-known fells, is north of Grasmere. Farther northwest is Cockermouth, where Wordsworth was born in 1770 – his birthplace, now called Wordsworth House, is a museum.

Visitors can go out across Derwent Water in a motorboat or power themselves in a rowboat

A view of Lake Windermere near Troutbeck Bridge

It is south of Keswick that the main excitements of the Lake District await you. The steep and narrow B5289 road that loops southward through Borrowdale brings you to the feet of the highest fells – Haystacks, Great Gable, Scafell Pike – and the high passes that connect them. Farther on are Buttermere and Crummock Water, heavenly twin lakes framed by fells of breathtaking beauty.

In the southwestern section of the Lake District are the wild and lonely valleys of Wasdale, with its dark lake, and rugged Eskdale, where the miniature steam-hauled Ravenglass and Eskdale Railway will take you down to the coast.
➕ A2–B2

Lake District at Brockhole Visitor Centre ➕ B3 ✉ Brockhole, Windermere ☎ 01539 446601 🕐 Daily 10–5, late Mar.–late Oct. Grounds and gardens open all year 🍴 Café 💲 Free

Beatrix Potter Gallery ➕ B3 ✉ Main Street, Hawkshead ☎ 01539 436355 🕐 Sun.–Thu. 10:30–4:30, mid-Mar. to late Oct. (timed ticket) 💲 SS

Dove Cottage and the Wordsworth Museum ➕ B3 ✉ Grasmere ☎ 01539 435544 🕐 Daily 9:30–5:30, early Feb.–early Jan. 🍴 Restaurant 💲 SS

Wordsworth House ➕ A4 ✉ Main Street, Cockermouth ☎ 01900 824805 🕐 Mon.–Sat. 11–4:30, late Mar.–late Oct. 🍴 Cafés nearby 💲 SS

Walking in the Lake District

Common sense walking rules apply; the fells are not dangerous places, but you should treat them – and the rapidly changeable weather – with respect. Find out the local weather forecast (☎ 017687 75757), and equip yourself properly with weatherproof clothes and good boots.

If climbing the fells, take food and a hot drink, a compass and a map. Tell someone where you are going, and stick to your plan.

There are mountains of guidebooks to walks in the Lake District, but still the best (although now a couple of decades old) are the seven pocket-size books in the *Pictorial Guide to the Lakeland Fells* series by master fellwalker Alfred Wainwright – hand-drawn and written, bossy but knowledgeable, and absolutely reliable.

Liverpool's skyline, with the twin towers of the Liver Building, seen across the Mersey from Birkenhead

LEEDS

The city of Leeds reached the peak of its prosperity during the height of the 19th-century wool trade, and the wealth of that era is evident in the massive Victorian civic buildings that grace the city center. The grand, colonnaded facade of Town Hall dominates the Headrow; inside, ornate Victoria Hall plays host to classical music concerts. The neighboring City Art Gallery has a good selection of 19th- and 20th-century British art, including some curvaceous Henry Moore sculptures, while the Royal Armouries, once displayed in the Tower of London, have been rehoused in an excellent, custom-built museum.

Leeds is home to the eminent Opera North company, and offers a multitude of restaurants and some excellent shopping. The prestigious London department store Harvey Nichols has a branch in the city, and the glass-roofed Victorian arcades are a pleasure to wander through. The renovated Corn Exchange is graced with a two-tiered gallery of shops; craft and clothes stalls fill its huge central hall.

➕ C2

Tourist information ✉ The Arcade ☎ 0113 242 5242; www.leeds.gov.uk

City Art Gallery ✉ The Headrow ☎ 0113 247 8248 🕐 Mon.–Sat. 10–5 (also Wed. 5–8), Sun. 1–5 🍴 Café 🖐 Free

Royal Armouries Museum ✉ Armouries Drive ☎ 08700 344344 🕐 Daily 10–5 🍴 Restaurant and café 🖐 Free

LIVERPOOL

Liverpool is one of Britain's great seaports. It was natural for docks and wharves to develop along the deepwater estuary of the River Mersey, which faces the Atlantic. Rum, tobacco, cotton and sugar poured in from Britain's Caribbean and American colonies in the 17th and 18th centuries, and from here the manufactured goods of the Industrial Revolution cities went out to the rest of the world. The slave trade flourished, too, as did emigration to the United States and Canada by the poor and disillusioned seeking a fresh start.

These aspects of the city's colorful history are explored in the Merseyside Maritime Museum and the Museum of Liverpool Life. The giant Port of Liverpool Building, Cunard Building and Royal Liver Building – grand expressions of Liverpool's importance – stand at the Pierhead, where you can board one of the famous Mersey ferries for a river cruise.

The Walker houses a superb and wide-ranging collection of paintings, including European masters, pre-Raphaelites and modern British art. Tate Liverpool also is an impressive showcase of modern art.

Liverpool also is famous for its successful musicians. Tour the sites made famous by the Beatles and other Liverpool beat groups in the '60s – Cavern City Tours (☎ 0151 709 3285) will set you on the right track. Its two-hour Magical Mystery Tour takes visitors on a journey aboard a customized bus to visit Strawberry Fields, Penny Lane and other Fab Four-related sites.

➕ B1

Tourist information ✉ Queen Square ☎ 0151 709 5111 or 09066 806886 (there is a charge of 25p per minute for this call); www.visitliverpool.com

Merseyside Maritime Museum ✉ Albert Dock ☎ 0151 478 4499 🕐 Daily 10–5. Ships and docksides closed during the winter 🍴 Café 🎟 Free

Museum of Liverpool Life ✉ Pier Head ☎ 0151 478 4080 🕐 Daily 10–5 🎟 Free

The Walker ✉ William Brown Street ☎ 0151 478 4199 🕐 Mon.–Sat. 10–5, Sun. noon–5 🎟 Free

Tate Liverpool ✉ Albert Dock ☎ 0151 702 7400 🕐 Tue.–Sun. 10–5:50 🍴 Café 🎟 Free; special exhibitions $$

MANCHESTER

Manchester slid a long way downhill when its textile trade collapsed in the mid-20th century. But this great northern city has pulled itself back up to celebrate a heritage of magnificent Victorian industrial architecture. The Museum of Science and Industry in Manchester has undergone a massive expansion. The highlight of Manchester Art Gallery, which reopened in 2002 after renovation, is its collection of paintings by pre-Raphaelite artists. The Lowry at Salford Quays houses the "matchstick men" paintings by L.S. Lowry, whose figures were inspired by the city's factory workers.

The Castlefield area boasts trendy canal-side bars and chic eateries. For a taste of the Orient, seek out Chinatown (between Princess and York streets) for its excellent restaurants. The Royal Exchange is bursting with shops. Opposite G-Mex (a huge conference center), is Bridgewater Hall, completed in 1996 and admired by concertgoers for its clarity of sound. Soccer fans can pay homage at Old Trafford Stadium, home of the Manchester United Football Club.

➕ B2

Tourist information ✉ Town Hall Extension, Lloyd Street ☎ 0161 234 3157; www.visitmanchester.co.uk

Museum of Science and Industry in Manchester ✉ Liverpool Road, Castlefield ☎ 0161 832 2244 🕐 Daily 10–5 🍴 Café 🎟 Free; charge for special exhibitions

The Lowry ✉ Pier 8, Salford Quays ☎ 0161 876 2001 🕐 Sun.–Fri. 11–5, Sat. 10–5 🚃 Metrolink tram to Harbour City 🍴 Café 🎟 Free

Barton Arcade shopping mall in Manchester

The great potteries of Staffordshire are known the world over. Wedgwood, Spode, Minton and Royal Doulton have become household names; their best and most venerable pieces – superbly delicate, painstakingly hand-crafted and painted – change hands for a fortune these days.

Josiah Wedgwood statue in
Stoke-on-Trent

Pottery Towns

The potteries of the six neighboring Staffordshire towns of Tunstall, Burslem, Hanley, Stoke, Fenton and Longton – known collectively as Stoke-on-Trent – operated throughout the 18th and 19th centuries. Stoke-on-Trent owed its prosperity to a location atop rich deposits of marl clay suitable for pottery-making, as well as

FINE POTTERY AND ELEGANT CHINA

coal, sandstone, gravel and sand. Excellent transportation links by canal and later by railroad meant that fragile pottery could be taken to the ports and then onto ships taking it to the export markets of the world without risk of being broken by jolting on the rough roads of those times.

Classic Designs

Josiah Wedgwood (1730–1795) was the king of the pottery-owners, producing celebrated stoneware designs of white classical scenes in relief on a blue, green or black background. The region's other famous potters included Josiah Spode, who produced coveted bone china dining services painted with an old Chinese "willow-pattern" legend, and later Henry Doulton and his beautiful Royal Doulton ware.

You can take a fascinating tour around Wedgwood and Spode to see just how hard-earned skills are put to work creating masterpieces of fine china. A brown-signposted Heritage Trail will guide you around the potteries of the towns. Fabulously expensive and more affordable pieces rub shoulders in the showrooms maintained by each pottery along the museum trail.

✚ B1

The Wedgwood Visitor Centre ✉ Barlaston
☎ 01782 282986 🕓 Mon.–Fri. 9–5, Sat–Sun. 10–5
🍴 Restaurant and café 💲 $$$ (includes audio-guided factory tour)

The Courtyards at Spode Visitor Centre
✉ Church Street, Stoke ☎ 01782 744011
🕓 Mon.–Sat. 9–5, Sun. 10–4 💲 Free
ℹ Factory tours ($$$) available Mon.–Thu. at 10, 11, 1;30 and 3, Fri. at 10 and 11

Classic Spode pottery in the Spode Visitor Centre

Still majestic, the ruins of Rievaulx Abbey

NORTH YORK MOORS

The Yorkshire coast runs north from the seaside resort of Scarborough for some 30 miles, with Whitby as its jewel. This little seaport is protected by the moors on all sides, except where its harbor looks out over the North Sea. Spectacular abbey ruins stand high on a cliff, and you can visit the house where South Seas explorer Captain James Cook lodged as an apprentice. You also are following in Dracula's footsteps around here: Bram Stoker based some of the scenes in his novel in Whitby – ask at the tourist office about the Dracula Trail. South of town is Robin Hood's Bay, a fishing village tumbling charmingly down a cleft in the cliffs. Visitors must park in the parking lot at the top of the village. The steep main street, lined with tearooms and shops, heads down to the little bay.

Inland, the atmosphere of the North York Moors can be very bleak in rain or the not infrequent sea mists, but beautiful in fair weather. The town of Pickering, on the southern edge of North York Moors National Park, is a good base for exploring; from here the steam-hauled North Yorkshire Moors Railway will take you north through the moors for 18 miles to Grosmont. West of Pickering is the big moorland village of Helmsley; the fine ruined abbey of Rievaulx (pronounced "Ree-voe") is in Ryedale, a few miles beyond. Hutton-le-Hole has an idyllic village green and boasts the Ryedale Folk Museum, which includes a reconstruction of a glassworks and a blacksmith's shop. ✚ D3

North York Moors National Park Authority ✚ D3 ✉ The Old Vicarage, Bondgate, Helmsley, York, ☎ 01439 770657

North Yorkshire Moors Railway ✚ D3 ✉ Pickering Station, Park Street, Pickering ☎ 01751 472508 or 01751 473535 (recorded timetable) 🕐 Daily, mid-Mar. to late Oct. and 2 weeks in Feb. 🖐 $$$

Ryedale Folk Museum ✚ D3 ✉ Hutton-le-Hole ☎ 01751 417367 🕐 Daily 10–5:30, early Mar.–early Nov. 🖐 $$

Whitby ✚ D3

Tourist information ✉ Langborne Road ☎ 01947 602674; www.scarborough.gov.uk

Pickering ✚ D3

Tourist information ✉ Ropery House, The Ropery ☎ 01751 473791; www.ryedale.gov.uk

End of the line at Grosmont station

Northern England

NORTHUMBERLAND

Much of Northumberland is a national park, a region of moors and coniferous forests. The beaches are largely deserted. Two castles sit atop the low cliffs: Dunstanburgh, a grim 14th-century ruin, and Bamburgh, sited on a crag a few miles farther north, with a Norman keep and the extensive remains of a curtain wall. The castle looks out on the Farne Islands, shelves of volcanic rock inhabited by seals and seabirds. Bamburgh village, where the Northumbrian kings were crowned, is a nice place to stop; the Lord Crewe Arms (see page 269) has a welcoming fire in winter. Also here is the Grace Darling Museum, which tells the tale of a Longstone lighthouse keeper's daughter who in 1838 spotted a ship aground. Grace, age 23, and her father rowed out to the rescue, saving nine passengers – 43 were drowned. The lighthouse still stands on Longstone.

Lindisfarne, or Holy Island, is 5 miles up the coast and accessible by a causeway over the sands. This is submerged at high tide; contact the tourist office at Alnwick for tide times. On Holy Island you will find another castle and the impressive ruins of Lindisfarne Priory, built in Norman times on the site of the monastic community led by St. Cuthbert in the seventh century. The ancient tradition of brewing mead (an alcoholic drink made from honey and herbs) is still carried out on the island.

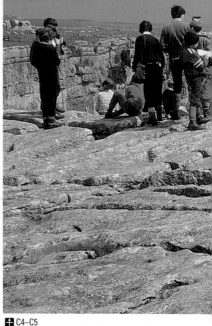

✚ C4–C5

Alnwick tourist information ✚ C5
✉ 2 The Shambles ☎ 01665 510665;
www.alnwick.gov.uk

Northumberland National Park Authority ✚ C4
✉ Eastburn, South Park, Hexham ☎ 01434 605555;
www.nnpa.org.uk

Bamburgh Castle ✚ C5
✉ Bamburgh ☎ 01668 214515 ⏰ Daily 11–5, mid-Mar through Oct. 31 🎫 $$

Lindisfarne Castle ✚ C5
✉ Lindisfarne (Holy Island) ☎ 01289 389244
⏰ Tue.–Sat. 10:30–3 or noon–4:30 (depending on tides), mid-Feb. to late Oct. 🎫 $$

Dunstanburgh Castle ✚ C5
✉ Craster, Alnwick ☎ 01665 576231 ⏰ Daily 10–6, Apr.–Sep.; daily 10–4, in Oct.; Thu.–Mon. 10–4, rest of year 🎫 $

Grace Darling Museum ✚ C5
✉ Radcliffe Road, Bamburgh ☎ 01668 214465
⏰ Mon.–Sat. 10–5, Sun. noon–5, Easter–Oct. 31
🎫 Donation requested

Bamburgh Castle standing sentinel by the beach

PEAK DISTRICT

The Peak District is yet another of northern England's splendid national parks. The Dark Peak, or more northerly section of the park, takes its atmosphere from the brooding heather uplands of the Derbyshire/South Yorkshire border between Sheffield and Manchester. Here you can stride the lonely moors along the most southerly section of the Pennine

Admiring the view from the limestone cliffs at Malham in The Pennines

Way. There are spectacular caves at nearby Castleton, where feldspar was once mined in deep caverns.

Buxton, to the south, is a charming small spa town with some notable Georgian buildings, while neighboring Bakewell is famous for Bakewell pudding, a jam-and-almond cake. East of these towns is the great mansion of Chatsworth (see page 194); to the south are the water-cut limestone dales of the White Peak, marvelous for walking. Dovedale, the best known and most photogenic, has mighty rock pinnacles; also seek out Lathkilldale, south of Bakewell, where medieval Haddon Hall waits to be discovered.

➕ C1–C2

Peak District National Park Authority ➕ C1

✉ Aldern House, Baslow Road, Bakewell, Derbyshire ☎ 01629 816200; www.peakdistrict.org

Haddon Hall ➕ C1

✉ Bakewell, Derbyshire ☎ 01629 812855 ⏱ Daily 10:30–5, Apr.–Sep.; Thu.–Sun. 10:30–5, in Oct.
🍴 Restaurant 💲 $$$

Buxton ➕ C1

Tourist information ✉ The Crescent ☎ 01298 25106; www.highpeak.gov.uk

THE PENNINES

The Pennine chain of hills forms the north-south backbone of northern Britain. Apart from one or two serious hills, this is mostly a rolling, undulating landscape. The Pennine Way National Trail runs the entire length of the chain, starting in Derbyshire on the Dark Peak moors between Sheffield and Manchester, and ending up just across the Scottish Border 268 miles to the north.

You can travel through the hills and see some of its loneliest landscapes aboard the Settle–Carlisle Railway (see page 199). Towns along the railroad line include Settle, Brough, Appleby and Penrith, all bleak-looking but friendly settlements. It also is possible to stop in one of the villages near the line, such as Hawes, Kirkby Stephen or Alston. They are great places to spend a few hours, shopping or just chatting with the locals in a shop or pub.

There are uplands around Malham, where there is a spectacular curved cliff formation, and in Upper Teesdale near Middleton-in-Teesdale, where the River Tees plummets over a lip of rock and becomes High Force waterfall. Farther north in western County Durham are moors and dales around Weardale and Derwent Dale, where the village of Blanchland boasts one of Britain's most authentic inns, the Lord Crewe Arms (see page 269).

➕ B2–B4

Landscape at Swaledale, typical of the Yorkshire Dales

DRIVE: THE YORKSHIRE DALES

Distance: 200 miles

Yorkshire Dales National Park has legions of admirers who love the beauty of this patchwork landscape. The classic view of a Yorkshire dale is of a fertile valley bottom set with stone barns and farm buildings and divided up by distinctive "drystone" walls (built without mortar). These walls snake up the sides of the dale and over the clearly defined boundary where pasture meets moorland. It is this mixture of uses – rough grazing on the upper slopes and intervening hills, pastureland down in the valleys – that gives the Yorkshire Dales their character. This drive will show you some of the loveliest places in the dales, but there are others waiting to be discovered up side roads and in odd corners. Take your time – you could drive it in a day, but it would be better to stop overnight in beautiful Swaledale or Wharfedale.

Skipton, a bustling market town a few miles north of Haworth and the Brontë moors (see page 195), is the starting point. Proceed east along A59 to

Blubberhouses; 2 miles farther, turn left on B6451/B6165 to Pateley Bridge.
If you have a couple of hours to spare, bear left along Nidderdale and past the long Gouthwaite Reservoir to the village of Lofthouse. The narrow cleft of How Stean gorge is just beyond. Beautiful Nidderdale attracts few visitors along this wild road, but the 16-mile detour is worth the extra effort.

Continue from Pateley Bridge on B6265 toward Ripon, turning right before you reach the town.
Here are the impressive remains of Fountains Abbey, a 12th-century monastery, and the beautiful water gardens and landscaped grounds at nearby Studley Royal.

Ripon itself has a glorious late Norman cathedral. If you arrive in the evening, attend the blowing of curfew on the Wakeman's horn in the market square at 9 p.m.

From Ripon, A6108 takes you to Masham.
Stop and tour the traditional Theakston's Brewery in Masham.

Richmond, the next town, is one of Yorkshire's most appealing, with its huge Norman castle and steep streets.

From Richmond, proceed along A6108, bear west toward Swaledale via B6270 and continue to Reeth.
Here you can make a counterclockwise loop on the minor road through the valley of Arkengarthdale, with its intriguingly named settlements of Booze and Whaw, then on

Northern England

through rugged moorland scenery through the valley of Swaledale, passing the villages of Keld and Muker on the way back to Reeth.

From Reeth, turn south on the moorland road over the fells to the villages of Redmire and Wensley in broad, green Wensleydale, famous for its cheese.

From Wensley a side road runs up ever-narrowing Coverdale, a little-visited dale under the bulk of Great Whernside hill.

Drop steeply into the village of Kettlewell and turn right on B6160 to Buckden, then bear left to Hubberholme.

At Hubberholme there is an excellent inn, The George. The little Church of St. Michael and All Angels stands next to a hump-backed bridge. It contains a fine Tudor rood screen and wooden pews made by the celebrated craftsman Robert Thompson; look for his trademark – long-tailed mice – carved into the furniture.

Continue from Hubberholme up the glorious valley of Langstrothdale beside the River Wharfe, admiring the distinctively elongated farmhouses. Eventually the moorland road takes you back to Wensleydale at the cheerful market town of Hawes. Turn right down Wensleydale on A684 to Aysgarth.

Stop here to admire the waterfalls.

Turn right on B6160 up Bishopdale; then descend the full length of Wharfedale, passing again through the village of Kettlewell and onward through Threshfield and Burnsall.

Near the foot of the dale, park and take a stroll upriver from the scenic ruins of Bolton Abbey to the Strid, a dramatic, rocky narrows where the river comes boiling through.

Return to your car and turn right on A59 for the 5-mile drive back to Skipton.

🔲 B3–C3

Yorkshire Dales National Park Authority ✉ Colvend, Hebden Road, Grassington, North Yorkshire ☎ 01756 752748; www.yorkshiredales.org.uk

SCOTLAND

"WHETHER it is mountains or seacoasts you seek, whiskey or haggis, wild music or solitude – Scotland has it."

Opposite: Eilean Donan Castle

Scotland

SCOTLAND

Scotland, more than any other region of Britain, projects itself in the minds of visitors in a series of

ATLANTIC
OCEAN

Orkney
Islands

5

Butt of Lewis
Port of Ness

Durness   Scrabster
Thurso   John
O'Groats

North Minch

Tongue

W

Stornoway

Laxford
Bridge

Lewis

Lochinver

3146ft
Ben Kilbreck

Latheron

A9

3274ft
Ben More Assynt

Lairg

Helmsdale

Outer Hebrides

Harris

Tarbert

Ullapool

Dornoch

North Uist

Rodel

Dundonnell
Gairloch   Inverewe
Garden

Lairg

Moray Firth

Lossiemou

Lochmaddy

Little Minch

Kilmuir

Kinlochewe

3428ft
Ben Wyvis

Cromarty

Elgin

Ke

A96

4

Benbecula

Uig

Dunvegan

Strathcarron

Torridon   Achnasheen   Dingwall

Nairn

Culloden

Dufftown

Hun

South Uist

Portree

Kyle of
Lochalsh

3773ft
Sgurr na
Lapaich

Inverness

A9

Grantown-
on-Spey

Eilean
Donan
Castle

Skye

Kyleakin

A87

Loch
Ness

Invermoriston

Aviemore

Spey

Strathdon

Cairngorm Mis

Canna

Ardvasar

A82

Kingussie

Invergarry

Ballo

Barra

Rum

Mallaig

A830

Laggan
Bridge

Braemar   **Balmoral
Castle**

Eigg

Muck

**Fort
William**

4406ft
Ben Nevis

Blair
Atholl

A9   Pitlochry

Brech

Coll

Tobermory

Glencoe

Aberfeldy

Glamis

Fort

3

Tiree

Lochaline

Mull

Tyndrum

Blairgowrie

Arbroc
Carnoustie

Iona

Fionnphort

Oban

3842ft
Ben More
The Trossachs

Crieff   A85   Perth

Dund

St. Andre

Inveraray

Auchterarder
Callander

A85

Colonsay

Arrochar   Aberfoyle

M90

Glenrothes

Oronsay

Lochgilphead

A83

Loch
Lomond

Stirling

Kinross

Kirkcaldy

Dunfermline

Port Askaig

Jura

Tarbert

Dunoon   **Dumbarton**

Falkirk

Firth of Fo

2

Islay

Bute

Greenock

Linlithgow

Dunb

Firth of Clyde

GLASGOW

EDINBURGH

Dalkeith

Paisley

M8

Motherwell

A702

East Kilbride

A71

M74

Lauc

Ardrossan

Lanark

Peebles

Brodick

Troon

Kilmarnock

Abington

Melrose

Arran

Prestwick

Tarbolton

*Ettrick
Forest*

Drybur

Jedburg

Campbeltown

Ayr

Mauchline
Cumnock

A76

Ha

*Mull of
Kintyre*

Culzean Castle

Turnberry

**Burns National
Heritage Park**

Southern Uplands

A74(M)

Moffat

Scottish Borders

Girvan

A77

New
Galloway

Lockerbie
Gretna
Green

1

**NORTHERN
IRELAND**

Newton
Stewart

Dumfries

Langholm

Stranraer

Castle
Douglas

Carlisle

A75

Kirkcudbright

Drummore

Whithorn

Solway Firth

A   **B**   **C**

Scotland

strong and clearly defined images – red-bearded men in kilts and bonny women in tartan, bagpipes and wild step-dancing, whiskey and haggis, empty glens sweeping up to mountains purple with heather. Scots are dour, reliable, close with the pennies but open-handedly hospitable, quick to anger, practical, hardy and endlessly antagonistic to the English, the "Auld Enemy."

The Proud Scots

So run the stereotypes – and there is a grain of truth in them. You will indeed find elements of all these characteristics if you peer and probe hard enough. But there is a whole lot more to Scotland and the Scots than a string of picture-postcard views and an inclination to take a gloomy relish in the darker episodes of the nation's history. For Scotland is indeed a nation again; it has had its own parliament, vested with significant powers, since 1997 (although central British government is still based in London). Scottish national pride is currently running high, and the mood among Scots is to look forward rather than back. Scotland remains within the United Kingdom for the time being, but the old ties seem to be loosening.

Highlands and Lowlands

Just as there is a "north-south divide" in England, one also exists in Scotland, although the Scottish divide is more geographical than social. Everyone seems to have heard of the Scottish Highlands (although exactly where they begin and end is a moot point, even among Scots), and most visitors, once they have "done" Edinburgh, tend to gravitate north and west as quickly as possible to get to the mountains, castles, islands, red deer and golden eagles. That the lowlands

and border regions also contain more than their share of beautiful, dramatic landscapes, quiet and tucked-away places, wild animals and birds, and romantic lakes and castles is a fact unknown to many of those who come to Scotland. And just as well, think lowland enthusiasts who treasure the peace and absence of tourists in these southerly regions of Scotland.

History's Bloody Conflicts

The national boundary between England and Scotland stretches northeast from Carlisle to Berwick-on-Tweed through the tumbled, lonely country of the Borders. Ownership of these parts was disputed with fire and sword for many centuries between English and Scots, who took and retook the Border towns and valleys, and also between Scottish landowners themselves. These conflicts led their retainers into many a bloody skirmish and siege with neighbors in dispute over cattle and land, and their "pele towers" (defensive strongholds, half house and half castle) dot the landscape.

The little Border towns – Peebles, Kelso, Melrose, Hawick (pronounced "Hoik"), Moffat, Jedburgh – are neat, orderly places where shopkeepers delight in offering personal service and local gossip. West Ayrshire is Robert Burns country, where Scotland's humorous national poet enjoyed his short life at the end of the 18th century with bottle and bedchamber – there are Burns sites galore here.

Cities and Mountains

Across the neck of southern Scotland, like two jewels on a choker, sit Edinburgh and Glasgow, the country's two biggest and liveliest cities. North of them is a rising landscape of high hills and broken ridges, vigorous country full

of lakes and fast rivers. There are the wild moors of Rannoch and the fearsome canyon of Glencoe in the west, the long lakes and hills of the Trossachs, and lumped together in the center the Grampians, rising to the most formidable mountains of all, the Cairngorms, famous among skiers and climbers. Compared with the great ranges of the world the Cairngorms may be only toy mountains – the highest peaks barely top 4,000 feet – but conditions on top can be as tough as anywhere, especially in winter when sub-arctic temperatures and fierce blizzards make them worthy of any mountaineer's respect.

Lochs and Islands

Even here, some would say, the real Highlands have yet to be reached. For diehard romantics the Highlands really start north and west of the Great Glen, that decisively straight slash of the geological sword from northeast to southwest, from the North Sea up on the Moray Firth to the Atlantic Ocean down on Loch Linnhe, below Fort William. Beyond dark Loch Ness (with its mythical monster) spread the wide glens and sweeping mountain landscapes beloved by every Scottish calendar photographer, but far more beautiful, impressive and mournful when seen in person. You have to leave your car and walk here, along the glen rivers and into valleys where the ruins of abandoned farms and settlements still lie, to experience fully the silence and emptiness of this landscape, cleared of its people and its Gaelic way of life in the 18th and 19th centuries.

Then there are the islands, where tough and practical people still make a precarious living in unbelievably bare but beautiful surroundings. Four great archipelagos shelter mainland Scotland – the Inner Hebrides off the west coast,

The steam cruiser *Sir Walter Scott* conveys visitors across Loch Katrine, just east of Loch Lomond

the Outer Hebrides 30 miles farther out, and Orkney and Shetland stretching north from the northernmost tip of the mainland. Here you will find the wildest scenery and music, the coldest winds and seas, and the warmest hearths and hospitality in Britain.

Scottish Culture

The Scottish accent and dialect changes perceptibly between regions. Visitors will find that English is spoken everywhere, although Gaelic is still spoken in the far north and Outer Hebrides (see page 283). The language survives in place names, poetry and also song, which you'll encounter frequently in Scotland. Many pubs offer live folk music, while "ceilidhs" (pronounced "kay-lees," dances accompanied by fiddle and pipe music, usually at a cracking pace) take place year-round.

Visitors invariably choose to visit Scotland during the warmer months of summer (May through August); because of the country's northern latitude, this time of year is blessed with long days and short nights. It also is the season for Highland Games, held countrywide, where you watch Scottish dancing and "tossing the caber" (a "caber" is a log that is thrown as far as possible).

The Real Taste of Scotland

Watch out for the "Taste of Scotland" sign in restaurant windows if you're looking for authentic food cooked with the best of local produce. Aberdeen Angus beef and wild salmon are both of high quality here, and you'll see game on the menu in many pubs and restaurants.

For the hungry, huge fried breakfasts can include hot porridge (oatmeal cooked in milk and seasoned with a pinch of salt), eggs, bacon, square slice (a type of flat beef sausage), black pudding (blood sausage), potato cakes and tomatoes.

Haggis is Scotland's most famous dish; it consists of sheep's offal cooked in spices and oatmeal and boiled in a sheep's stomach – vegetarian varieties are available for the less adventurous!

Scotland

EDINBURGH

Whatever the pretensions and aspirations of Glasgow, its near neighbor and rival, Edinburgh is unquestionably Scotland's premier city, the capital of the Scottish nation. You feel an air of grandeur the moment you reach the city center. Edinburgh Castle is every inch the dark and dominant fortress, perched high over the city atop a basalt crag as it frowns down the Royal Mile to the Palace of Holyroodhouse, while Princes Street is a splendidly wide Georgian thoroughfare with handsome civic buildings and a solidly impressive layout of Georgian town houses, terraces and squares under its influence.

Two Faces of the City

Castle and palace reflect the older, historic side of this split-personality city. Along the Royal Mile you will see ancient tall houses, cramped little courts, churches and bent old inns that made up "Auld Reekie," the atmospheric but unsanitary medieval city where Mary, Queen of Scots plotted, traitors and honest men alike rotted in the castle's dungeons, John Knox preached Reformation, and Scottish Presbyterian Covenanters signed a declaration of religious dissent in their own blood. The student pubs and clubs that buzz here today have a strange ambience, both deeply historical and completely modern.

But along Princes Street and streets farther north Edinburgh shows another face. This part of town was built clean and new in the late 18th century, when Auld Reekie became too old and reeking to be tolerated any longer. This New Town had a grand and visually pleasing building scheme, with its galleries, monuments and academy buildings, its spacious layout, its gardens and solid, prosperous-looking architecture. It exudes a solemnity and gravitas that used to make Edinburgh, along with its mannerly and upright citizens and their rather precise accents, seem stiff and pompous. No longer, however – there are enough students, visitors, media and arty types around to give the city an agreeably light and positive atmosphere, boosted by the ever-growing popularity of the annual summertime Edinburgh International Festival and its irreverent "Fringe" offshoot.

Center of Attractions

The layout of central Edinburgh is simple to grasp. The west side of the city center is bounded by the Water of Leith, the east by Holyrood Park and the fine basalt rampart of Salisbury Crags. The Old Town clusters along the Royal Mile, which runs from Edinburgh Castle east to the Palace of Holyroodhouse. Below

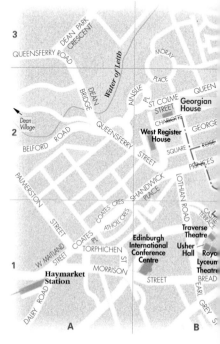

Looking down the Royal Mile toward the Palace of Holyroodhouse

and to the north of the Old Town (and separated from it by Waverley railroad station and some sunken gardens) lies the New Town; the main artery, Princes Street (parallel to the Royal Mile), runs east to Calton Hill.

All the city's main attractions are within a 20-minute walk of Waverley Station. However, there are so many that you may want to save your feet and take one of the frequent red Lothian buses that serve the city center.

Hunger for a High Tea

As you would expect from a major capital city, Edinburgh has a great number of cafés, restaurants and pubs. Cafés tend to be for tea and light snacks; hotels and restaurants may also serve the famous Scottish high tea. Consider your state of hunger honestly before ordering this, as it consists of biscuits, jam, cakes and pastries, plus a cooked dish of eggs, ham, kippers and haddock.

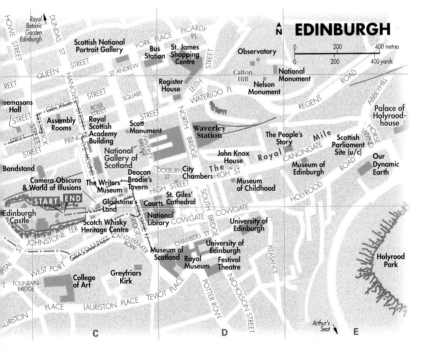

Scotland

The once-rowdy dock area of Leith, a mile north of the center, has cleaned up its act and become a trendy place to enjoy a brasserie-style meal with a view over the Firth of Forth. As for pubs, noisy student hangouts are along the Royal Mile and around the Grassmarket. If you want to see beautiful Victorian "high-pub" decor and sample some good beer, step into one of the pubs along Rose Street, just north of Princes Street.

Edinburgh Festival

The Edinburgh International Festival is one of the world's biggest arts festivals. Held during the last two weeks in August and the first week in September, opera, dance, theater and music are performed at venues across the city. The Edinburgh Festival Fringe (last three weeks of August) is a more irreverent event featuring student theater companies and some excellent comedy. If you're visiting Edinburgh during the festivals, make sure you book any accommodations well in advance.

For information on the Edinburgh International Festival call ☎ 0131 473 2000.

For information on The Edinburgh Festival Fringe call ☎ 0131 226 0026.

Music and Dancing

Princes Street has the standard chain stores, and some that are more elegant. Tourist-oriented but amusing Scottish goods – haggis, kilts, sporrans (a leather pouch worn over a kilt), tam-o'-shanters, malt whiskey (spelled "whisky" in Scotland) and the like – are plentiful along the Royal Mile. Edinburgh Rock is a crumbly, fruit-flavored candy-stick that comes in various pastel colors.

Music is big in Edinburgh – everything from classical concerts, opera, jazz and traditional Scottish music at Queen's Hall to jangly guitar and dancing in dozens of small clubs. Traditional Scottish music also is played in many bars – try the Hebrides Bar on Market Street or the Tron Ceilidh House on Hunter Square.

ESSENTIAL INFORMATION

ⓘ TOURIST INFORMATION
Edinburgh and Scotland Information Centre ✉ 3 Princes Street ☎ 08452 255121 (in the U.K.); 001 44 1506 832121 (from the U.S.); www.edinburgh.org

URBAN TRANSPORTATION
The main railroad station is Waverley Station on Princes Street, in the heart of the city. For schedule information and reservations ☎ 08457 550033. There are numerous city buses; for information contact Lothian Buses ✉ 2 Cockburn Street ☎ 0131 555 6363 (24 hrs.). The main taxi stands are at Waverley Station. You can also hail a cab on the street or call ☎ 0131 229 2468 or 0131 228 1211.

✖ AIRPORT INFORMATION
Edinburgh is served by Edinburgh International Airport, 8 miles west of the city center (☎ 08700 400007). There is a tourist and airport information desk in the main hall. Frequent buses (every 10 minutes in daytime) go to and from Waverley Station (journey time 20 minutes), and taxis can be hired right outside the terminal.

CLIMATE – Average highs and lows

JAN.	FEB.	MAR.	APR.	MAY	JUN.	JUL.	AUG.	SEP.	OCT.	NOV.	DEC.
5°C	6°C	7°C	10°C	13°C	16°C	18°C	17°C	15°C	12°C	9°C	6°C
42°F	43°F	45°F	50°F	55°F	61°F	64°F	63°F	59°F	54°F	48°F	43°F
1°C	1°C	2°C	4°C	6°C	9°C	11°C	11°C	9°C	6°C	4°C	2°C
34°F	34°F	36°F	39°F	43°F	48°F	52°F	52°F	48°F	43°F	39°F	36°F

The view across Edinburgh from the Dugald Stewart Monument on Calton Hill

Edinburgh Sights

Key to symbols

✚ map coordinates refer to the Edinburgh map on pages 216–217; sights below are highlighted in yellow on the map.

✉ address or location ☎ telephone number

🕐 opening times 🍴 restaurant on site or nearby

🎫 admission charge: $$$ more than £6, $$ £2–£6, $ less than £2 ℹ️ information

Calton Hill

The eastern end of Princes Street is cut off by the volcanic upthrust of Calton Hill, a green and tree-covered mound that you can climb for some excellent views across Edinburgh toward Arthur's Seat and Edinburgh Castle. Below the south slope of Calton Hill stand the grand old Royal High School and a round classical temple dedicated to the memory of Robert Burns.

The upper slopes of the hill are adorned with a splendidly motley collection of mainly 19th-century monuments, none of which quite attained the dignity they strove for. The Dugald Stewart Monument of 1837 resembles the upper tiers of a sandstone wedding cake and commemorates a professor of philosophy at Edinburgh University who left no other trace behind him.

The National Monument, "Edinburgh's Disgrace," was an attempt (begun in 1822) to build a replica of the Parthenon to honor Scotland's dead from the Napoleonic Wars. Money and enthusiasm ran out after the erection of the 12 columns that stand here today. The Nelson Monument, constructed 1807–15 and based on the appropriate design of an upturned and extended telescope, purports to honor Admiral Horatio Nelson, who fell at the Battle of Trafalgar in 1805. You can climb the 143 steps of the monument for more stunning city views. Note: This site should be avoided at dusk and after dark.

✚ D2, D3, E2, E3

Nelson Monument ✉ Calton Hill ☎ 0131 556 2716 🕐 Mon. 1–6, Tue.–Sat. 10–6, Apr.–Sep.; Mon.–Sat. 10–3, rest of year 🎫 $$

Dean Village

Down below Thomas Telford's four-arched bridge (built in 1832) and huddled in the narrow, wooded valley of the Water of Leith, Dean once was an industrial settlement with 11 mills driven by the river. Today this secret and charming little village, reached from the city center end of the bridge by way of steep Bell's Brae, has become a desirable place to live. The handsome old mill buildings here have been converted into smart apartments.

✚ A2

Dramatic Edinburgh Castle, guarding the city from its high crag

EDINBURGH CASTLE

Standing in lordly disdain on its volcanic crag high above both Old and New Town, this is one of Britain's really great castles. The site can't be bettered for dramatic effect – nor for military effectiveness, as one quickly discovers when looking over the ramparts from the King's Bastion and down impregnable cliffs. The surrounding view commands nearly 100 miles, from the hills of the Borders to the distant Grampian peaks. Encapsulated here, from the grim cells and dungeons in the bowels of the castle to the ramparts and their all-embracing view of any approaching friend or foe, are eight centuries of Scotland's history.

The obvious defensive site of the castle's crag has been fortified since Bronze Age times, and the present castle's datable structure (going back to the 12th-century Chapel of St. Margaret) probably conceals far older and earlier buildings. Sieges have been many, and it changed hands several times in the Anglo-Scots wars of the Middle Ages.

The castle houses various regimental museums, as well as the venerable 15th-century bombard, or siege cannon, called Mons Meg – "the great iron murderer, Muckel Meg."

The beautifully simple chapel, high up in the castle, is a must-see, as are the Honours of Scotland, a collection of royal regalia that includes the priceless crown, scepter and sword of the monarchs of Scotland. After 100 years in obscurity following the 1707 Act of Union between England and Scotland, it was the patient detective work of Sir Walter Scott that brought them to light in 1818, locked away and forgotten in the castle. Scott might have written that romantic denouement himself in one of his Waverley novels.

Displayed nearby is the Stone of Destiny, also called the Stone of Scone, a sandstone block on which Scottish monarchs traditionally rested their feet during the coronation ceremony. It was returned to Scotland in 1996 after 700 years in Westminster Abbey following its abduction by the English King Edward I.

⊞ B1, C1

✉ Castlehill ☎ 0131 225 9846 ⏰ Daily 9:30–6, Apr.–Oct.; 9:30–5, rest of year. Last admission 45 minutes before closing ⏚ Cafés 💲 $$$ ⏚ Guided tours and self-guiding audio tours available

Georgian architecture in Charlotte Square

THE GEORGIAN HOUSE

In 1796 Robert Adam designed Charlotte Square to be the New Town's architectural masterpiece. No. 7, The Georgian House, has been refurbished to show the lifestyle of its first owner, John Lamont, chief of clan Lamont, a typical citified gentleman. His dining room and parlor are furnished with Wedgwood and Spode china and you can see the wine cellar and kitchens. Fine portraits by contemporary Scottish artists Henry Raeburn and Allan Ramsay hang among others on the walls.

✚ B2 ✉ 7 Charlotte Square ☎ 0131 226 3318
🕐 Daily 10–7, Jul.–Aug.; 10–5, Apr.–Jun. and Sep.–Oct.; 11–3 in Mar. and Nov. Last admission 30 minutes before closing 📷 $$

Greyfriars Bobby on the lookout for his master

Greyfriars Bobby

Descending the Royal Mile from Edinburgh Castle, turn right at the first crossroads, onto George IV Bridge. You will soon reach Greyfriars Kirk on the right. In the churchyard dissenting Presbyterians signed the National Covenant in 1638 (some in their own blood), pledging to keep their religion free from monarchical taints and the doctrines of the Roman Catholic Church. Thousands of Covenanters died in the ensuing persecutions.

The churchyard's most famous recumbent incumbents are "Auld Jock" Gray and his Skye terrier, Bobby. Jock died in 1858, and for the next 14 years, rain or shine, Greyfriars Bobby stayed on guard beside his grave. The people of Edinburgh lovingly tended the little dog. He was granted the Freedom of the City and became an international celebrity before his own death and burial in the churchyard in 1872.

"Auld Jock" lies under a pink granite tombstone beside the path northeast of the church; Bobby lies near the gate. On top of a memorial drinking fountain just outside the gate is an effigy of Bobby, his face alertly cocked for his master's voice.

Inside the National Gallery of Scotland

NATIONAL GALLERY OF SCOTLAND

The National Gallery of Scotland stands in an impressive location on The Mound, off Princes Street. Renaissance Italians here include Raphael, Filippino Lippi, Tintoretto and Veronese; Flemish and Dutch masters are represented by Frans Hals, Rembrandt, Van Dyck and Vermeer. There are notable collections of J.M.W. Turner watercolors, landscapes by John Constable, and some fine American landscapes and portraits. Scottish painters have their own wing, with seascapes by Alexander Nasmyth and portraits by Allan Ramsay. The one everyone loves, for the affectionate humor and dignity of its composition as well as its subject matter, is Sir Henry Raeburn's *Rev. Robert Walker Skating on Duddingston Loch* – a sublimely skating clergyman dressed all in black.

✚ C2

✉ The Mound ☎ 0131 624 6200 ⏱ Daily 10–5 (also Thu. 5–7); extended hours during Edinburgh International Festival ✋ Free; special exhibitions $$

PALACE OF HOLYROODHOUSE

The grand Palace of Holyroodhouse stands at the bottom of Canongate (the final descent of the Royal Mile) against a backdrop of the rock curtain of Salisbury Crags. This is the official Edinburgh residence of the British monarch, part country house and part palace, built from 1500 by the kings of Scotland around the nucleus of the guesthouse of Holyrood Abbey. The abbey was founded in 1128 by King David I of Scotland, after he had seen a vision of a cross, or "rood," between the antlers of a stag he was hunting here.

Grand ironwork gates and a fountain are your introduction to the palace. Inside are ornamental ceilings with intricate plasterwork and frescoes, and beautiful antique furniture. Up a winding staircase you can view the antechamber of Mary, Queen of Scots. Here the Queen's jealous husband Lord Darnley had her Italian secretary, David Rizzio, stabbed to death on March 9, 1566. Behind the palace lie the open spaces of Holyrood Park. You can climb from Dunsapie Loch to the summit of Arthur's Seat for a fine view.

✚ E2

✉ Canongate, Royal Mile ☎ 0131 556 5100 ⏱ Daily 9:30–6, Apr.–Oct.; 9:30–4:30, rest of year. Last admission 45 minutes before closing. Closed for some state functions ✋ $$$

The so-called "Royal Mile" is composed of four streets – Castlehill, Lawnmarket, High Street and Canongate, which run in that order downhill from Edinburgh Castle to the Palace of Holyroodhouse. This was the spine upon which the body of the Old Town was built.

Some features of the Royal Mile, in order as you descend, are:

Taste the history of whiskey along the Royal Mile

THE ROYAL MILE

Scotch Whisky Heritage Centre
Regular tours show visitors how whiskey is made. You can sample a few of the different malts before you decide to buy.
✚ C1 ✉ 354 Castlehill ☎ 0131 220 0441 ⏰ Daily 9:30–6:30, May–Sep.; 10–6, rest of year. Last tour 1 hour before closing 🍴 Restaurant 🎫 $$$

Camera Obscura & World of Illusions
Upper stories were added to this 17th-century building in 1853 when it first housed a camera obscura. From the heights a panoramic view of the city is displayed on a table in front of visitors.
✚ C2 ✉ Outlook Tower, Castle Hill ☎ 0131 226 3709 ⏰ Daily 9:30–7:30, Jul.–Aug.; 9:30–6, Apr.–Jun. and Sep.–Oct.; 10–5, rest of year. Last presentation 1 hour before closing 🎫 $$$

Gladstone's Land
This is a cramped, crowded and fascinating restoration of a six-story "land," or apartment building, of 1617.
✚ C2 ✉ 477B Lawnmarket ☎ 0131 226 5856 ⏰ Daily 10–7, Jul.–Aug.; Mon.–Sat. 10–5, Sun. 2–5, Apr.–Jun. and Sep.–Oct. Last admission 30 minutes before closing 🎫 $$

The Writers' Museum
Displays and memorabilia pertaining to poet Robert Burns and writers Sir Walter Scott and Robert Louis Stevenson are exhibited in a house dating from 1622.
✉ Lady Stair's House, Lawnmarket ☎ 0131 529 4901 ⏰ Mon.–Sat. 10–5 (also Sun. noon–5 during the Edinburgh International Festival) 🎫 Free

Deacon Brodie's Tavern
Murals tell the story of Councillor William Brodie, respectable by day but a burglar by night. Brodie had the grim distinction of designing the very gallows he was hanged on in 1788, and of inspiring Robert Louis Stevenson with the idea for his classic 1886 tale *The Strange Case of Dr. Jekyll and Mr. Hyde.*
✚ C2 ✉ 435 Lawnmarket ☎ 0131 225 6531 ⏰ Mon.–Sat. 10:30 a.m.–1 a.m., Sun. 12:30 p.m.–midnight

St. Giles' Cathedral
The cathedral is a treasure house of stained glass and monuments.
✚ C2, D2 ✉ Off High Street ☎ 0131 225 9442 ⏰ Mon.–Fri. 9–7, Sat. 9–5, Sun. 1–5, May–Sep.; Mon.–Sat. 9–5, Sun. 1–5, rest of year 🍴 Restaurant 🎫 Free (donation requested) ℹ Guided tours (free)

John Knox House
This finely carved 16th-century house once was the home of John Knox, who was the minister at St. Giles' from 1559–72 and spearheaded the Protestant Reformation in Scotland.
✚ D2 ✉ 43–45 High Street ☎ 0131 556 9579 ⏰ Mon.–Sat. 10–6, Sun. noon–6 🎫 $$

The People's Story
The lives of ordinary citizens from the 18th century to the present are represented with audiovisual displays.
✚ E2 ✉ Tolbooth, 163 Canongate ☎ 0131 529 4057 ⏰ Mon.–Sat. 10–5 (also Sun. noon–5 during the Edinburgh International Festival) 🎫 Free

The Museum of Edinburgh
The city's life over the centuries is traced through a display of artifacts.
✚ E2 ✉ Huntly House, 142 Canongate ☎ 0131 529 4143 ⏰ Mon.–Sat. 10–5 (also Sun. noon–5 during the Edinburgh International Festival) 🎫 Free

Scotland

Reflected glory in Georgian Charlotte Square

WALK: CENTRAL EDINBURGH

Refer to route marked on city map on pages 216–217

Allow at least three hours for this walk, more if you spend time at the attractions along the way.

Starting at Edinburgh Castle (see page 220), walk down Castlehill at the top of the Royal Mile.

You'll see the Edinburgh Old Town Weaving Company, with kilts and tartan material for sale. The Outlook Tower is on the left, housing a camera obscura that provides a panoramic preview of your journey (see page 223).

Turn right at Lawnmarket along George IV Bridge, with the National Library of Scotland on your left. Soon Chambers Street runs off to the left, with the striking new Museum of Scotland on the

Transportation matches the era of architecture

right, and the Royal Museum next door.

The modern museum tells Scotland's story, while the Victorian structure contains art and scientific displays from all over the world.

Return to George IV Bridge and turn left down Victoria Street.

Take time to browse among the second-hand bookshops. You'll also see a cheese shop and an indoor market called Byzantium that sells antiques, comic books and 1960s ephemera.

From Grassmarket, the square at the bottom of Victoria Street, it is a short walk below the castle and through West Princes Street Gardens to Princes Street, Edinburgh's showplace boulevard. Turn left and walk to the end of Princes Street, then cross and turn right up Hope Street to reach Charlotte Square.

The square is designer Robert Adam's Georgian masterpiece, with The Georgian House (see page 221) on the north side.

From the east side of Charlotte Square turn left onto Rose Street.

Pop into one of the Victorian pubs here – the Abbotsford or the Rose Street Brewery, perhaps – for a pint or other refreshment.

Turn left at Frederick Street and then right along elegant George Street in the heart of the New Town. At Hanover Street, turn right. Cross Princes Street, traverse The Mound, and then climb back to the Royal Mile and Edinburgh Castle.

Museum of Scotland and Royal Museum 🔢 D1
✉ Chambers Street ☎ 0131 247 4422 🕐 Mon.–Sat. 10–5 (also Tue. 5–8), Sun. noon–5 🍴 Restaurant and cafés 🎫 Free 🛈 Guided tours (free)

Opposite: Princes Street in the early evening

Scotland

GLASGOW

In the 1970s anyone comparing the merits of Edinburgh and Glasgow would have had no hesitation placing Glasgow far below the Scottish capital. In contrast to Edinburgh's solidity and atmosphere of cultural self-confidence, there was a real air of depression and decay about the shipbuilding city on the River Clyde, just 30 miles east. The shipyards and heavy engineering industries were in terminal decline, and fine old warehouses and commercial buildings were in disrepair. But there has since been a remarkable upswing in Glasgow's image. Today the city projects renewed self-confidence, loudly trumpeting its unquestionably superb galleries and museums, lively nightlife, rash of new trendy eateries and watering holes, and legacy of Georgian and Victorian architecture. There are walkways along the banks of the Clyde and newly refurbished urban green spaces. Tall sailing ships docked at the city wharves wait to be visited, and architectural and heritage trails take visitors to the best pockets of the city. While Glaswegians have always loudly acclaimed their own worth, there now seems to be a genuinely exciting buzz about this once run-down city.

Glasgow celebrates its new image

Scotland

Boom and Decline

An initial flourishing of culture and self-confidence took place in the 18th century, when the merchants of Glasgow became rich through trans-Atlantic trade. Streets, squares and fine Georgian churches sprang up. During the 19th century shipbuilding boomed, bringing with it a market in financial services. Ornate offices and warehouses were the temples of commerce in the city center. As long as iron foundries, shipyards and engineering works along the river continued to roar – which they did until after World War I – it was boom time for Glasgow.

The long, slow decline in the 20th century, exacerbated by industrial slumps in the 1930s and '70s and by intense wartime bombing, was hard to bear and had a dramatic effect on the morale of city residents.

All of which makes the renaissance of an attractively buoyant Glaswegian spirit all the more astonishing. Glasgow, in fact, was designated the Cultural Capital of Europe in 1990 and the U.K. City of Architecture and Design in 1999.

Seeing the Sights

This is a sprawling place, and orientation is a matter of remembering that the grid of streets around the

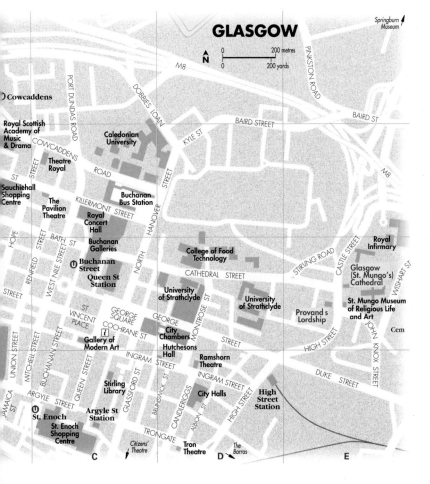

Scotland

center run east-west (the wide ones) and north-south (the narrower ones). Almost every sight worth seeing is located north of the River Clyde. The center's hub is George Square (Buchanan Street metro station), with the elegant streets and squares of the 18th- and 19th-century city to the west. To the north is the Glasgow School of Art, high above Sauchiehall (pronounced "Sockie-hall") Street (Charing Cross railroad station); farther north is The Tenement House on Buccleuch ("B'cloo") Street.

Farther west, Kelvingrove Park (Kelvinhall or Hillhead subway stations), has a wonderful clutch of museums and art galleries. A 10-minute walk east of George Square (High Street railroad station) is another, older cluster of attractions – St. Mungo's Cathedral and its museum, and the ancient house of Provand's Lordship. Finally, 3 miles southwest of the city and a half-mile walk from Pollokshaws West railroad station, The Burrell Collection in Pollok Country Park is a must-see, brimming with art and artifacts from around the world.

Shopping and Entertainment

By far the best shopping fun you'll have is at the stalls of The Barras, the busy weekend market near Glasgow Green (High Street railroad station).

Entertainment varies from mainstream music at Glasgow Royal Concert Hall on Sauchiehall Street to adventurous plays at the Citizens' Theatre on Gorbals Street (just south of the river) to the perpetual theater of loud and friendly Glasgow pubs. For great live traditional music, check out Molly Malones on Hope Street.

Brasserie-style bar/restaurants abound; try Albion Street or Brunswick Street, both a five-minute walk southeast of George Square.

ESSENTIAL INFORMATION

TOURIST INFORMATION
✉ 11 George Square ☎ 0141 204 4400; www.seeglasgow.com

URBAN TRANSPORTATION
Strathclyde Passenger Transport provides a comprehensive travel center within Buchanan Bus Station on Killermont Street. For information call ☎ 08706 082608. It has information about local bus, rail, subway and ferry services. It also sells tickets for long-distance bus tours. Glasgow Central railroad station is on Argyle Street. For train schedules and reservations ☎ 08457 550033. A subway (metro) system ensures smooth travel around the city. Four types of travel tickets provide unlimited use of local transportation. For rail services (including the subway) within about 10 miles of the city center, the Roundabout Ticket is valid for one day (Mon.–Fri. after 9 a.m. and all day Sat.–Sun. and public holidays). The Discovery Ticket, for the subway only, is valid for one day (Mon.–Sat. after 9:30 a.m. and all day Sun. and public holidays). The FirstDay Tourist Ticket is valid for one day for any First bus within Greater Glasgow. The Daytripper Ticket, valid for one day (Mon.–Fri. after 9 a.m. and all day Sat.–Sun.) is for families (either for two adults and up to four children, or for one adult and up to two children). It includes rail services (including the subway), most buses and some ferries for unlimited travel throughout the region of Strathclyde. To arrange a taxi ☎ 0141 429 4900.

AIRPORT INFORMATION
Glasgow International Airport, in Paisley, is 8 miles west of the city center. For the tourist information desk ☎ 0141 848 4440; for flight inquiries ☎ 08700 400008. Shuttle buses link the airport to Glasgow. There also is a bus/rail link. For airport taxis ☎ 0141 848 4900 (dial 4900 from free phones in the airport).

CLIMATE – Average highs and lows

JAN.	FEB.	MAR.	APR.	MAY	JUN.	JUL.	AUG.	SEP.	OCT.	NOV.	DEC.
6°C	7°C	8°C	11°C	15°C	17°C	19°C	18°C	16°C	12°C	9°C	7°C
43°F	45°F	46°F	52°F	59°F	63°F	66°F	64°F	61°F	54°F	48°F	45°F
1°C	1°C	2°C	3°C	6°C	9°C	11°C	11°C	8°C	6°C	3°C	2°C
34°F	34°F	36°F	37°F	43°F	48°F	52°F	52°F	46°F	43°F	37°F	36°F

A visitor ponders over Rodin's *The Thinker* in The Burrell Collection

GLASGOW SIGHTS

Key to symbols

✚ map coordinates refer to the Glasgow map on pages 226–227; sights below are highlighted in yellow on the map.

✉ address or location ☎ telephone number

🕐 opening times 🍴 restaurant on site or nearby

🚌 nearest bus or tram route Ⓜ nearest metro/tube/subway station(s)

💷 admission charge: $$$ more than £6, $$ £2–£6, $ less than £2 ℹ️ information

THE BURRELL COLLECTION

Any city in the world would be proud to claim this astonishing collection of art and artifacts, the fruit of one man's obsession with amassment. It was Sir William Burrell, enormously well-off thanks to ship-owning interests, who in 1944 presented his native city with 6,000 items, continuing to add to them until his death in 1958. Burrell's only stipulation was that the collection be displayed in a rural setting, far enough from Glasgow to escape pollution. Those conditions were met in 1967, when Mrs. Maxwell Macdonald gave the Pollok Estate (now Pollok Country Park) to the city.

The collection is housed in a low, modern building, 4 miles from the city center. There are striking pieces of European art from the early Middle Ages onward; entire church doorways; medieval German religious carvings in beautiful limewood; very well-lit stained glass; and tapestries, glass and silver.

Paintings include a self-portrait by Rembrandt, as well as other portraits by William Hogarth, George Romney and Frans Hals; some beautiful Impressionist paintings by Monet, Cézanne, Degas and Alfred Sisley; and earlier masterpieces such as *Judith* by Lucas Cranach the Elder (1530).

Items in the Ancient Civilisations section include Etruscan mirrors and Greek perfume bottles, a giant Roman bowl, mosaics and beautifully modeled Egyptian busts. Outstanding exhibits in the Oriental Art collection are Persian carpets and Islamic tiles, delicate Chinese porcelain and jade, Japanese prints and a set of Tang dynasty tomb guardians.

There are re-creations of three of the rooms at Hutton Castle near Berwick-upon-Tweed, which Burrell bought in 1916 to house his then much smaller collection – all heavy antique furniture and dark draperies. Bronzes by Auguste Rodin (including *The Thinker*) and Jacob Epstein stand sentinel over the collection.

✚ A1

✉ Pollok Country Park, 2060 Pollokshaws Road ☎ 0141 287 2550 🕐 Mon.–Thu. and Sat. 10–5, Fri. and Sun. 11–5 🍴 Café Ⓜ Train: Pollokshaws West – half-mile walk 🚌 45, 47, 48, 57 💷 Free ℹ️ Guided tours (free)

Scotland

A Mackintosh chair at the Glasgow School of Art

GLASGOW SCHOOL OF ART

This fine sandstone building – still in use as Glasgow's prestigious art school – is a prime example of the style of its art nouveau architect, Charles Rennie Mackintosh (see page 232). In 1896 he won a competition to design the building and embarked on the project with confidence and vigor.

Entry is by guided tour only, led by well-informed student guides. The tour explains how Mackintosh strove to utilize every space to the utmost, to emphasize with dark-colored wood the brilliance of light pouring down from above or through tall windows, and to bring the vivid colors of Scottish nature and the smooth elegance of uncluttered lines to each corner of his building.

Mackintosh completed the art school in two stages, the eastern facade in a stern Scottish baronial style from 1897 to 1899, and the western end of the building in a less severe fashion between 1907 and 1909. The second phase saw the installation of a two-story library where angular dark wood columns support the reading galleries and light floods down on readers at the central tables from brightly colored lamps suspended on long cables.

The Furniture Gallery contains a collection of stored Mackintosh artifacts, from his trademark tall-backed chairs to a model for a "House for an Art Lover" – which was finally built in 1996 in Bellahouston Park, south of the river.

✚ B3 ✉ 167 Renfrew Street ☎ 0141 353 4526 ⏰ Daily 10–5 (guided tours at 10:30, 11, 11:30, 1:30, 2 and 2:30), Apr.–Sep.; Mon.–Fri. 10–5 (guided tours at 11 and 2), Sat. 10–3 (guided tours at 11 and 2), rest of year ⑪ Café 🅿 $$$

KELVINGROVE PARK: MUSEUMS AND GALLERIES

Kelvingrove Park, 1.5 miles west of the city center, houses the Gothic mini-palace of Glasgow University in addition to a number of first-class museums.

The university itself, dominating the north side of the park, is home to the Hunterian Art Gallery and Hunterian Museum. The Hunterian Art Gallery, in Mackintosh House, contains fine examples of Scottish oil and watercolor painting, as well as paintings and drawings by James McNeill Whistler. Upstairs is a reconstruction of several rooms in the house of Charles Rennie Mackintosh. The Hunterian Museum, across University Avenue, contains archeological finds and zoological material, as well as a display on the Roman occupation of Scotland.

The Kelvingrove Art Gallery and Museum (closed until June 2006), on the southern edge of the park, is housed in a huge red Edwardian mock castle. There are sections on natural history and Scotland's wildlife, and arms and armor. But it is the paintings that most visitors come to see. Here are Scottish works galore, with the Massacre of Glencoe a popular subject, along with pre-Raphaelite and 19th-century genre paintings. The "Glasgow Boys" – late 19th-century outdoor realists, disliked by the art establishment of the time but now seen as innovators in the same mold as the Impressionists – are well represented. Also here are fine Constable and Turner landscapes, some French Impressionist works, and plenty of Dutch and Flemish landscapes and portraits by such artists as Rembrandt, Lely and Van Dyck.

The red-brick Gothic building of Glasgow University overlooks the north side of Kelvingrove Park

Just across Argyle Street is the Museum of Transport. It's great fun to wander among the gleaming steam engines, trams and buses, ship models, highly polished roadsters and a tableau of a Glasgow street scene circa 1938.

Kelvingrove Park ✚ A4 ✉ Otago Street ☎ 0141 334 6363 ⊙ Daily dawn–dusk

Hunterian Art Gallery ✚ A4 ✉ University of Glasgow, 82 Hillhead Street ☎ 0141 330 5431 ⊙ Mon.–Sat. 9:30–5 🍴 Café 💷 Free

Hunterian Museum ✚ A4 ✉ University of Glasgow, University Avenue ☎ 0141 330 4221 ⊙ Mon.–Sat. 9:30–5 🍴 Café in university visitor center 💷 Free

Kelvingrove Art Gallery and Museum ✚ A4 ✉ Kelvingrove ☎ 0141 287 2699 ⊙ Mon.–Thu. and Sat. 10–5, Fri. and Sun. 11–5 (closed until June 2006) 🍴 Café 💷 Free

Museum of Transport ✚ A4 ✉ 1 Bunhouse Road ☎ 0141 287 2720 ⊙ Mon.–Thu. and Sat. 10–5, Fri. and Sun. 11–5 🍴 Café 💷 Free

Note: Admission fee for some temporary exhibitions.

PROVAND'S LORDSHIP

Opposite St. Mungo's Museum of Religious Life and Art stands the tall, sandstone Provand's Lordship. This is Glasgow's oldest dwelling, built in 1471 for a canon of the cathedral. It has served many functions in its long life, from a drinking den to a shop, and the displays within tell the story of some of them. The low ceilings and simple furnishings of the 16th century show the plain nature of a medieval cleric's life. Mary, Queen of Scots came to the house in 1566, allegedly, to meet her husband, Lord Darnley, who was sick with poison and shortly to be murdered mysteriously in Edinburgh.

✚ E2 ✉ 3 Castle Street ☎ 0141 552 8819 ⊙ Mon.–Thu. and Sat. 10–5, Fri. and Sun. 11–5 💷 Free ⓘ Guided tours (free)

A cleric's life is illustrated in Provand's Lordship

Scotland

Glasgow architect Charles Rennie Mackintosh   Willow Tea Rooms designed by Mackintosh

CHARLES RENNIE MACKINTOSH

Charles Rennie Mackintosh was born in 1868 in the Townhead area of Glasgow, not far from St. Mungo's Cathedral. This inner-city boy, one of 11 children, entered Glasgow Art School at the age of 16 and quickly became absorbed by the principles of art nouveau, with its stylized images from nature, flowing lines and subtle contrasting coloring. Mackintosh loved the outdoor colors of Scotland – green, purple and pink – and added to them a sense of form influenced by Japanese art, a big source of interest in Britain at that time. What he also realized was the artistic potential of a building designed as one harmonious whole – structure, furniture, glasswork, fixtures and fittings.

By 1896 Mackintosh was on his way as an independent, having won a competition to design the new Glasgow School of Art on Renfrew Street. Many commissions around Glasgow followed – notably the Willow Tea Rooms on Sauchiehall Street, where everything from the elegant long-handled spoons to the tall-backed chairs and highly colored glass windows was designed to give Glaswegians something to admire and talk about over the teacups, in a building itself long, elegant and light.

Another Mackintosh building that links various facets of his style is Queen's Cross Church on Garscube Road. This distinctive sandstone church – the only religious building that Mackintosh designed from beginning to end – is the headquarters of the Charles Rennie Mackintosh Society (☎ 0141 946 6600). Viewed from outside, the building seems to be tapering up to heaven. Inside all is dark and solemn, except where the light enters through cheerful pink and purple windows inlaid with Mackintosh's characteristic tall lilies and stylized hearts.

Toward the end of his life Mackintosh fell out with some of his colleagues and abandoned Scotland. He left behind a legacy of fascinating city buildings, including (in addition to the three mentioned above) the Daily Record Building on Renfield Lane; Martyr's School on Parson Street (where he was born); and The Hill House on Upper Colquhoun Street, which retains its original furnishings and decorations.

St. Mungo's Cathedral

St. Mungo's ought to have been destroyed, along with the other Roman Catholic cathedrals of mainland Scotland, during the religious upheavals of the 16th-century Reformation. But somehow this 13th-century Gothic masterpiece survived, thanks to the agreement of Glasgow's guilds to ensure Protestant worship in the church.

The cathedral is built on two levels, due to the slope of its site, and is divided into an upper and a lower church. The Lower Church, at the east end, is the crypt where the tomb of the original founder, St. Mungo, stands. Descending into the Lower Church, you find yourself among a thicket of columns rising to rib-vaulting around the saint's tomb. Mungo was a sixth-century ascetic, and his tomb became one of Britain's great medieval pilgrimage destinations. Even the iron-hard King Edward I, famed Hammer of the Scots, came here three times to pray.

The tall columns of St. Mungo's Cathedral

Located on the cathedral grounds is the unique St. Mungo Museum of Religious Life and Art, designed to bypass sectarian and religious bigotries and celebrate all of the world's religions. Particularly striking are a huge, many-armed statue of a dancing Shiva, exquisite Taoist porcelain, gloriously woven Islamic prayer rugs, richly glowing stained glass from medieval churches, and Salvador Dalí's 1951 bird's-eye-view painting of the Crucifixion.

🚩 E2 ✉ Cathedral Square ☎ 0141 552 6891 🕐 Mon.–Sat. 9:30–6, Sun. 1–5, Apr.–Sep.; Mon.–Sat. 9:30–4, Sun. 1–4, rest of year 💷 Free

St. Mungo Museum of Religious Life and Art
✉ 2 Castle Street ☎ 0141 553 2557 🕐 Mon.–Thu. and Sat. 10–5, Fri. and Sun. 11–5 🍽 Café 💷 Free
ℹ Guided tours (free)

The Tenement House

The National Trust for Scotland has painstakingly restored the extraordinary interior of this Victorian tenement (apartment) building. Here, between 1911 and 1965, lived shipping firm typist Miss Agnes Toward, a person who changed almost nothing in her house and threw away even less. It is thus a perfect time capsule, with every old-fashioned item in the parlor, kitchen and bedroom bespeaking a frugal, orderly, waste-not-want-not lifestyle that has long vanished in Britain.

🚩 A4 ✉ 145 Buccleuch Street, Garnethill ☎ 0141 333 0183 🕐 Daily 1–5, Mar.–Oct. 💷 $$

Time stands still in The Tenement House

Scotland

REGIONAL SIGHTS

Key to symbols

⊞ map coordinates refer to the Scotland map on pages 212–213; sights below are highlighted in yellow on the map.

⊠ address or location ☎ telephone number

⊙ opening times 🍴 restaurant on site or nearby

🖐 admission charge: $$$ more than £6, $$ £2–£6, $ less than £2 ℹ information

ABERDEEN AND ROYAL DEESIDE

Aberdeen, known as the "Granite City" because of the gray stone it is built with, is on Scotland's eastern coast. It is a town of two faces – dour and grimly impressive under clouds and rain, fresh-faced and sparkling in sunshine. It is a lively university city with plenty of restaurants, bars and nightlife.

Stroll along the large fishing harbor, especially when the early morning fish auction is in full swing, to the Maritime Museum on Shiprow near the harbor. The chief visitor attraction is the 16th-century Provost Skene's House on Guestrow, with rooms furnished and decorated in the styles of different centuries. The Satrosphere Science Centre is an excellent interactive science and technology exhibition. For a real Scottish experience you can learn to "curl" at the Aberdeen Beach Leisure Centre; curling involves players bowling a granite stone across an ice rink to reach a target.

Aberdeen stands at the mouth of the River Dee, whose scenic valley descends gradually from the Cairngorm mountains, 70 miles to the west. The valley is known as Royal Deeside because of its strong connections with the British royal family. They have been honorary Deesiders since 1852, when Queen Victoria and Prince Albert bought the huge Balmoral estate.

The Dee valley is home to a number of superb castles. Drum Castle is a 17th-century house added to a 13th-century stronghold; Crathes Castle, a 16th-century tower house, sprouts turrets like fungi. In its eerily named Green Lady's Room and Room of the Nine Nobles the ceilings are alive with macabre paintings.

The Dee rushes through Balmoral Forest

Balmoral Castle, near the pleasant town of Ballater, is the British monarch's Scottish holiday home in summer, a big, baronial-style castle built primarily for Queen Victoria. West of Balmoral is Braemar, where the Highland Gathering is held each September.

Aberdeen ⊞ D3

Tourist information ⊠ 23 Union Street ☎ 01224 288828; www.aberdeen-grampian.com

Provost Skene's House ⊠ Guestrow, Broad Street ☎ 01224 641086 ⊙ Mon.–Sat. 10–5, Sun. 1–4 🍴 Café 🖐 Free

Aberdeen Maritime Museum ⊠ Shiprow ☎ 01224 337700 ⊙ Mon.–Sat. 10–5, Sun. noon–3 🍴 Café 🖐 Free

Satrosphere ⊠ Aberdeen Beach Tramsheds, 179 Constitution Street ☎ 01224 640340 ⊙ Mon.–Sat. 10–5, Sun. 11:30–5 🖐 $$

Ballater ⊞ D3

Tourist information ⊠ The Old Royal Station, Station Square ☎ 013397 55306; www.aberdeen-grampian.com

Braemar ⊞ C3

Tourist information ⊠ The Mews, Mar Road ☎ 013397 41600; www.aberdeen-grampian.com

Drum Castle ⊞ D3

⊠ Off A93, 3 miles west of Peterculter ☎ 01330 811204 ⊙ Daily 10–5:30, Jun.–Aug.; 12:30–5:30, mid-Apr. through May 31 and in Sep. 🍴 Café 🖐 $$$

Crathes Castle ⊞ D3

⊠ On A93, 3 miles east of Banchory ☎ 01330 844525 ⊙ Daily 10:30–5:30, Apr.–Sep.; daily 10–4:30, in Oct.; Thu.–Sun. 10:30–4, rest of year 🍴 Restaurant 🖐 $$$

Balmoral Castle ⊞ C3

⊠ Balmoral ☎ 013397 425834 ⊙ Daily 10–5, late Mar.–early Aug. 🍴 Café 🖐 $$ ℹ Grounds are open for walks; some rooms are occasionally shown

Opposite: Balmoral Castle, Scottish home of monarchs

Grave of Burns' father at Alloway Old Kirk

AYRSHIRE AND ROBERT BURNS COUNTRY

The county of Ayrshire, southwest of Glasgow, is the native country of national poet Robert Burns (1759–96). Scots feel passionately about the "heaven taught ploughman" whose temperament during his short life summed up so many characteristics perceived to be typically Scottish – anti-authority, dryly humorous, by turns reckless and cautious, deeply

Statue of Robert Burns in Edinburgh

romantic, and fond of a dram or three.

Burns sites are numerous in Ayrshire. On B7024 in Alloway village, just south of the county town of Ayr, is the clay-walled cottage where he was born, now the Burns Cottage and Museum. The Grecian temple shape of the Burns Monument stands beside the village's Brig O'Doon, a medieval hump-backed bridge over which, in Burns' comic masterpiece *Tam O'Shanter*, the drunken Tam escapes from witches on his gray mare, Maggie. Tam had interrupted the witches at an orgy in Alloway Old Kirk, and this roofless old church also can be seen just by the bridge.

B744 and B730 intersect at Tarbolton, 5 miles northeast of Ayr, where the National Trust for Scotland administers a museum in the Bachelors' Club, a thatched house where Burns and his young friends enjoyed themselves. At Mauchline, about 4 miles east of Tarbolton, there are several Burns sites: Poosie Nansie's Tavern, where he drank; Burns House, where his mistress, Jean Armour (later his wife) entertained him; and Mauchline Church, where he did public penance for the sin of fornication.

Ayrshire is not all Burns, however. There are famous seaside golf courses at the towns of Troon and Prestwick and the village of Turnberry, and a grand clifftop castle at Culzean (pronounced "Cull-ain"), designed in 1777 by the architect Robert Adam. There also is a fine sandstone coast of empty, beautiful beaches.

Inland there is some invigorating high country such as the hills of Kyle Forest, where many rivers spring – among them the Coyle Water, or "Coila," as Burns styled her:

> *O, sweet are Coila's haughs an' woods,*
> *When lintwhites chant amang the buds,*
> *And jinkin hares, in amorous whids,*
> *Their loves enjoy,*
> *While through the braes the cushat croods*
> *Wi' wailfu' cry!*

Ayr ✚ B2

Tourist information ✉ 22 Sandgate ☎ 01292 290300; www.ayrshire-arran.com

Burns Cottage and Museum ✚ B1

✉ Burns National Heritage Park, Murdoch's Lone, Alloway ☎ Heritage Park 01292 443700; Cottage 01292 441215 🕐 Daily 9:30–5, Apr.–Oct.; 10–5, rest of year 🍴 Restaurant 🎧 $$

The ruins of Kelso Abbey

THE BORDERS

To rush through the Scottish Borders is to miss half of what Scotland is all about. The landscape between the border and the cities of Edinburgh and Glasgow, generally known as the Borders, is hilly country – not wild like the great mountains and glens of the northwest, but both intimate and grand. There are small towns such as Kelso, a trim little place where the rivers Tweed and Teviot meet; Melrose, with its tangle of narrow lanes and roadways and the Teddy Melrose Teddy Bear Museum on High Street; snug Victorian Peebles; and farther west the town of Moffat, surrounded by lovely countryside.

These towns have a well-earned reputation for quality knitwear and textiles ("tweed" means cloth), and the region is dotted with mills and shops selling woolen, cashmere and tweed goods. Many of the Border towns have "Common Riding" events every year, when riders on horseback follow the town's boundaries – a reminder of the days when the area's borders were continually under threat by English raids.

Tourist offices in Melrose and Selkirk, the latter open April through October only, can provide information about drives and walks through the hill and valley country of Teviotdale and Eskdale.

There are four 12th-century abbey ruins to visit hereabouts. The abbey in the town of Jedburgh has wonderfully carved, many-tiered Norman arches and a monastic garth (garden) behind the cloisters. To the north, the Tweed valley encloses the other three: Kelso's lofty north transept; the chapter house and extensive abbey church remains at Dryburgh (Sir Walter Scott is buried here); and farther upriver at Melrose, many rose-pink arches. Here lies buried the heart of that scourge of England and self-proclaimed King of Scotland, Robert the Bruce, who died in 1329.

Kelso ✚ D2

✉ Town House, The Square ☎ 08706 080404; www.visitscottishborders.com

Jedburgh Abbey ✚ D1

✉ Abbey Bridge End, Jedburgh ☎ 01835 863925
🕐 Daily 9:30–6:30, Apr.–Sep.; 9:30–4:30, rest of year
🖐 $$

Dryburgh Abbey ✚ D2

✉ Near St. Boswells ☎ 01835 822381 🕐 Daily
9:30–6:30, Apr.–Sep.; 9:30–4:30, rest of year 🖐 $$

Kelso Abbey ✚ D2

✉ Kelso ☎ 0131 668 8600 🕐 Open access
Mon.–Sat. all day, Sun. afternoons, Apr.–Dec. Apply
to key keeper for entry rest of year 🖐 Free

Melrose Abbey ✚ D2

✉ Abbey Street, Melrose ☎ 01896 822562 🕐 Daily
9:30–4:30 🖐 $$

The lonely lighthouse on Bass Rock, which is mainly inhabited by seabirds

DRIVE: EAST LOTHIAN COAST

Distance: 85 miles

The East Lothian coast, in southeastern Scotland, is a little-visited corner of the Scottish Borders. All the better, then, for anyone who enjoys exploring rugged sea cliffs, fishing villages and magnificent castle ruins along uncrowded roads.

Crumbling walls and towers at Dirleton Castle

Start at Berwick-upon-Tweed.
Make sure you walk a circuit of the famous walls around this tenacious little town, just across the border in England. Between 1147 and 1482, Berwick changed hands 13 times between England and Scotland.

From Berwick, proceed north on A1; after 5 miles turn right and wind steeply down to the tiny fishing hamlet of Burnmouth, typical of this craggy coast. Back on A1, turn right after another mile on A1107 to reach Eyemouth, another fishing village.
The excellent small museum at Eyemouth tells the story, partly through a locally woven commemorative tapestry, of the Great East Coast Fishing Disaster of October 14, 1881, when 189 fishermen drowned, 129 of the men coming from Eyemouth.

From A1107, side roads lead east to the cliffs.
Here are St. Abbs Head and its lighthouse, the jagged ruins of Fast Castle on a headland, and a million wheeling and shrieking seabirds. Footpaths along the clifftops offer memorable views of coast and sea.

Return to A1107 and drive for 11 miles before rejoining A1. After 5 miles, turn right on a side road leading to Barns Ness.
You will find a most unusual walking trail along the beach. Following it, you'll see many strange and beautiful fossils in the cliffs and shore rocks, known by such descriptive

Scotland

names as macaroni rock and devil's toenails.

**Beyond Dunbar, turn right on A198 and
head for North Berwick.**

North Berwick is a pleasant seaside and golfing
resort. Nearby are North Berwick Law, a 613-foot
volcanic plug worth climbing for the spectacular
view from the summit. Just offshore, Bass Rock
rears 350 feet out of the Firth of Forth, a nesting
place for thousands of gannets.

Nearby on the edge of the cliffs stands
grim Tantallon Castle, a stronghold of a
Scottish clan, Douglas. The castle was built in
1375 and never captured until General Monk,
commander of the Royalist army in Scotland,
besieged and battered it in 1651, the year that
Charles II was crowned at Scone. Looking at
the site and the walls of the castle dropping
down to vertical rock cliffs that in turn fall to
the sea, you can appreciate its invulnerability.

Just west of North Berwick is Dirleton
Castle, eye-catching 13th-century ruins on a
knoll. There are beautiful grounds and a
garden within the castle walls themselves.

Continue on A198 to Aberlady.

In Aberlady Bay there are vast numbers of
geese and other seabirds in winter, and much
to delight bird-watchers year-round.

**From Aberlady, follow A6137 southeast
to Haddington.**

Haddington is a pretty little town that has
carefully preserved its ancient houses and
church. You can stretch your legs here on a
stroll about town.

Take B6369 south to Gifford.

Gifford is neatly laid out in the shadow of the
Lammermuir Hills. One of the rebels who put
his signature to the American Declaration of
Independence in 1776, the Reverend John
Witherspoon, was born in Gifford in the
manse (minister's house) near the church.

The Lammermuir Hills are crossed by a
network of marked footpaths, several of
which begin at Gifford.

**Leave Gifford on B6355, which runs
across the shallow passes and through
the valleys of the Lammermuirs for
20 miles to Duns. Alternatively, take
the narrow hill road that leaves B6355
5 miles southeast of Gifford and snakes
through the remote heart of the hills
by way of Longformacus to Duns. It
is then a 15-mile journey eastward
from Duns on A6105 back to Berwick-
upon-Tweed.**

Berwick-upon-Tweed ✚ D2
Tourist information ✉ 106 Marygate
☎ 01289 330733; www.berwickonline.org.uk

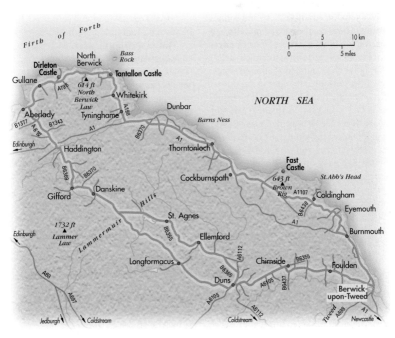

Scotland

Casks of whiskey maturing at the Glenfiddich Distillery at Dufftown

WHISKEY ON SPEYSIDE AND SPORT IN THE CAIRNGORMS

The River Spey, one of Scotland's most beautiful rivers, rushes northeast in a series of majestic curves on its journey into the Moray Firth in Spey Bay, halfway between Fraserburgh and Inverness. The Spey is a world-class salmon-fishing river, fast-flowing and relatively shallow, and you may see fly fishermen up to their wader-tops in the water almost anywhere along the river.

The many burns (mountain streams) that hurry their pure, peat-filtered water from the hills into the Spey make this classic malt whiskey country. (The drink is spelled "whisky" in Scotland.) The soft water of the burns is as much an essential ingredient of the liquid gold as are the carefully selected and malted barleys used by the string of whiskey distilleries along the valley of the Spey. These distilleries, many of them dating back 100 years, produce single malt whiskeys that are more expensive and exclusive – and, say the connoisseurs, a far subtler drink – than the more common blended whiskeys.

Well-known names along this beautiful river valley include Glenfiddich, Glen Grant, Glenlivet, Macallan and Glenfarclas, while smaller distilleries such as Knockando and Tamdhu are eagerly sought out by whiskey buffs.

There is a signposted Malt Whisky Trail, and a brochure guide is available from any local tourist office.

In its northward run to the Moray coast the River Spey shadows the western edge of the Cairngorms. These impressive mountains are a winter and summer playground for outdoor enthusiasts.

Walkers, climbers, skiers and snowboarders base themselves at Aviemore, in the valley of Strathspey to the northwest, or at Glenmore Lodge up in the mountains. There are ski lifts to the upper runs and marked walking trails; details are available at the Glenmore Visitor Centre.

Note: If you intend to walk in the Cairngorms, make sure you are properly equipped. Summer conditions can be unpredictable; winter conditions on the upper plateau and slopes can be sub-arctic, with 100 mph winds and whiteouts. These mountains are not tame, and never will be.

Aviemore ✚ C3

Tourist information ✉ Grampian Road ☎ 08452 255121; www.visithighlands.com

Glenmore Visitor Centre ✚ C3 ✉ Glenmore ☎ 01479 861220; www.forestry.gov.uk
🕐 Daily 9–5 🍴 Café ♿ Free

Scotland

Caerlaverock Castle, southeast of Dumfries, has an unusual triangular design

DUMFRIES AND GALLOWAY

In the southwestern corner of Scotland, the region of Dumfries and Galloway is another of those lowland areas that visitors tend to drive past rather than stop and explore. Yet here is a marvelous coast, a clutch of small towns, plenty of historic interest, and an interior of hills and forests.

The gateway to the area is Dumfries, a town built from the local red sandstone. Here you can take up the Robert Burns trail again (see page 236), for Burns spent his last few years as an excise officer in Dumfries. The Robert Burns Centre relates the story of his stay in town. Burns House, on Burns Street, is where he lived and died, and the Burns Mausoleum at St. Michael's Church is where he lies buried. At The Globe Inn, tradition says you must recite a verse of Burns poetry, or else treat everyone present to a drink.

J.M. Barrie, author of *Peter Pan*, went to school in Dumfries, and it was here that the ideas for his book originated while playing pirates with his friends. His math teacher is supposedly the character on whom he based the sinister Captain Hook. You can see some of Barrie's writings in Dumfries Museum.

The pretty town of Kirkcudbright (pronounced "Ker-*coo*-bree") consists of Georgian houses and fishermen's cottages in attractive disarray around the town center and harbor – perfect for the painters who

settled here in the early 20th century and established an "artistic colony." Some of their works, mostly of local scenes, are on display in Broughton House, on High Street.

Dumfries ✚ C1
Tourist information ✉ 64 Whitesands ☎ 01387 253862; www.visitdumfriesandgalloway.co.uk
Robert Burns Centre ✚ C1 ✉ Mill Road, Dumfries ☎ 01387 264808 🕐 Mon.–Sat. 10–8, Sun. 2–5, Apr.–Sep.; Tue.–Sat. 10–1 and 2–5, rest of year 🍴 Café 💷 Free ($ for audiovisual theater)
Kirkcudbright ✚ C1
Tourist information ✉ Harbour Square ☎ 01557 330494 🕐 Feb.–Nov.; www.visitdumfriesandgalloway.co.uk

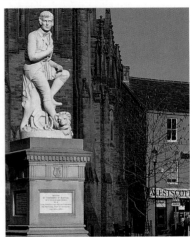

Statue of Robert Burns in Dumfries

Scotland

On a green at St. Andrews

Everything a golfer needs is supplied here

ST. ANDREWS, HOME OF GOLF

St. Andrews, a handsome and historic university town on the east coast of the county of Fife, is a mecca for golfers the world over. It was here on the flat, grassy dunes that the game developed in early medieval times. The Stuart kings of 15th-century Scotland banned it, lest young men should waste their leisure chasing the wee ball. But Mary, Queen of Scots gave golf a boost when she tried the fashionable game in 1567.

In 1754 the Society of St. Andrews Golfers was established to hold an annual competition, and golf received its ultimate stamp of respectability in 1834, when King William IV became patron of the society, which renamed itself the Royal and Ancient Golf Club.

Today it is every golfer's dream to play a round on the Old Course in front of the R&A's grand clubhouse – if not to be buried at St. Andrews Cathedral alongside the golfing greats interred there.

St. Andrews is not all golf, though. This is a civilized, historic university town with a fine castle and the notable 12th-century ruins of St. Andrews Cathedral. North Street is lined with the dignified buildings of St. Andrews University, while South Street boasts numerous fine Georgian houses and the delicate stone skeleton of the 16th-century Blackfriars Chapel.

✚ D2

Tourist information ✉ 70 Market Street ☎ 01334 472021; www.standrews.co.uk

British Golf Museum ✉ Bruce Embankment, St. Andrews ☎ 01334 460046 🕒 Mon.–Sat. 9:30–5, Sun. 10–5, Apr.–Oct.; daily 10–4 in Mar. and Nov.; daily 11–3, rest of year 🏷 $$

Where to Play

Golf is considered the "people's game" in Scotland, and there is little of the exclusivity associated with the game in England. There are more than 400 courses in Scotland, most of them comparatively inexpensive. At many public courses you can show up and play – advance tee times are not required. If you want to try your luck on a private championship course you will need to reserve a tee time in advance and bring your handicap certificate with you.

Turnberry ✚ B1 ✉ Turnberry, Ayrshire, 50 miles south of Glasgow ☎ 01655 331000

St. Andrews ✚ D2 ✉ St. Andrews ☎ 01334 466666

Carnoustie ✚ D3 ✉ Carnoustie, 10 miles east of Dundee ☎ 01241 853789

Gleneagles ✚ C2 ✉ Off A9 near Auchterarder, between Stirling and Perth ☎ 01764 662231

Royal Dornoch ✚ C4 ✉ Golf Road, Dornoch, 65 miles north of Inverness ☎ 01862 810219

Opposite: Down the fairway at St. Andrews

Inverness Castle beside the River Ness

INVERNESS AND THE NORTH

Once across the Great Glen, Inverness is the only sizable town in all of northern Scotland, a mini-capital that shoulders its historical weight with dignity. Beyond Inverness stretches the most northerly portion of mainland Britain, mountainous and wild in the west, rolling and bare in the east. Inverness is a handsome town, and compact enough to stroll around in an hour or two. The castle is a huge 19th-century edifice, still used for court sessions and the Cathedral of St. Andrew on the opposite bank of the River Ness dates back to the 1860s. The town's museum and art gallery, back to back with the tourist office on Castle Wynd, houses Highland memorabilia, including a collection of bagpipes and relics relating to the 1745 Jacobite rebellion.

North of Inverness via A9 lies the Black Isle, in fact a stubby peninsula separating the Moray and Cromarty firths. From here the A9 runs north to Dornoch Firth, then up the eastern seaboard through the fishing villages of Brora and Helmsdale.

Around Britain's northernmost town, the Norse-named Thurso, the fields lie low, crisscrossed with flagstone walls, and the wind blows constantly. Another 15 miles farther east, at John O' Groats, you can have your photograph taken against a signpost quoting the number of miles to your home town. Another mile east is Duncansby Head, the end of mainland Britain, a vista of dramatic cliffs plunging into wild water.

Inverness ✚ C4
Tourist information ✉ Castle Wynd ☎ 08452 255121; www.visithighlands.com
Inverness Museum and Art Gallery ✉ Castle Wynd ☎ 01463 237114 ⏲ Mon.–Sat. 9–5 🍴 Café 🎫 Free
Thurso ✚ C5
Tourist information ✉ Riverside ☎ 08452 255121; www.visithighlands.com ⏲ Apr.–Oct.

The "Last House in Scotland" at John O'Groats

Scotland

Memorial to the clansmen who were slaughtered

THE BATTLEFIELD OF CULLODEN

Prince Charles Edward Stuart, or "Bonnie Prince Charlie" as he came to be called, landed in Scotland in July 1745 from exile in France as the young and dashing claimant to the British throne. Charles' grandfather James Stewart, as King James II, had been deposed in 1688, and the Jacobites, supporters of the House of Stuart – both Scottish and English – longed to see their man crowned king.

The prince led his army as far south as Derby in a march on London. But then he retreated, losing men and morale all the way back to Scotland. It was on Drummossie Moor, 4 miles east of Inverness (well signposted from town) that the Bonnie Prince's dream came to a bloody and disastrous end on April 16, 1746. On the moorland battlefield the disciplined soldiers of the English Crown under the Duke of Cumberland overcame 5,000 wildly charging Highland clansmen with ease.

Terrible slaughter of fugitives and a scorched-earth policy followed quickly. The prince fled abroad to a long, sad decline in exile. The Gaelic-speaking clans were ruthlessly suppressed and their chiefs stripped of power. Within a century most of their lands had been sold, and the ordinary clan members scattered across the world by eviction and emigration. These infamous "highland clearances" brought a whole way of life to an end.

Today the battlefield is a national monument (very well explained in the excellent Visitor Centre), which you are free to wander at will.

Culloden ✚ C4
Culloden Moor ✉ On B9006, 5 miles east of Inverness ☎ 01463 790607 ⏰ Site: daily, all year. Visitor Centre: daily 9–6, Jun.–Aug.; 9–5:30, Easter–May 31 and Sep.–Oct.; 10–4, Mar. 1–day before Easter; 11–4 in Feb. and Nov.–Dec. 🍴 Restaurant 💷 Site free; Visitor Centre $$ ℹ Living-history displays in summer

The cairn on Culloden Moor commemorating the Highlanders

Castle Urquhart stands guard beside Loch Ness

DRIVE: THE WESTERN HIGHLANDS

Distance: 230 miles

This drive from Inverness through the wild and grand scenery of Wester Ross could be accomplished in the course of a day. But it would be far better to allow yourself a night's break around Dornie or Plockton in order to enjoy fully the splendor of the mountain scenery – not to mention giving yourself time to do some on-foot exploring.

From Inverness, it may seem strange to start a journey to the west by heading east, but if you are going to appreciate what underlies the silence and emptiness of the Highlands it is worth making the 4-mile *trip to Culloden Battlefield (see page 245).*

You can spend an hour or so discovering what life was like for the Highlanders before and after the 1745 Jacobite Rebellion. Their subsequent fate is reflected in the abandoned cultivation strips, tumbledown walls and empty glens of Wester Ross. This is a landscape missing its people, and all the more poignant in its sublime beauty because of that.

Returning to Inverness, head northwest on A835, crossing the mouth of Beauly Firth and then the neck of Cromarty Firth. Soon a right turn offers a little detour to Strathpeffer.

Strathpeffer is a neat Victorian spa town where you can still take the stinking sulphurous waters – should you wish.

Back on A835, continue west for 25 miles through countryside that soon becomes wild and hilly. Shortly before you reach

Braemore, turn left on A832 to wriggle north and west until Little Loch Broom opens an arm of the sea. Now the road winds through beautiful, harsh coastal scenery past Gruinard Bay and Gruinard Island, then Loch Ewe and the Isle of Ewe, before reaching the remarkable Inverewe Garden.

Here rhododendrons and azaleas bloom in mid-May, along with a host of other shrubs and flowers – testimony to the warmth of the Gulf Stream just offshore and the mildness of the climate in this far northern latitude.

Next come the villages of Poolewe and Gairloch, and a last look west at the island-scattered ocean. Continue on a long southeasterly descent along the south shore of beautiful Loch Maree as far as Achnasheen, then turn right on A890 and descend into majestic Glen Carron.

You'll traverse this wide, sweeping valley in company with the Skye and Dingwall Railway. At the top of Loch Carron there is an opportunity, if you would like to extend the drive, to follow A896 to Kishorn and then bear left at Tornapress on a narrow mountain road to the remote village of Applecross and on around the Torridon peninsula – a side trip of about 60 miles through beautiful scenery.

A890 proceeds through the village of Auchtertyre; turn left on A87 here.

You will see the fairy-tale castle of Eilean Donan, standing on a rock in Loch Duich.

A87 sweeps east along Glen Shiel between mountains and Loch Cluanie; then A887 continues through Glen Moriston and drops down into the Great Glen on the west bank of Loch Ness. Turn right here on A82 to Fort Augustus.

You will pass the gaunt gray Benedictine abbey and the head of the Caledonian Canal, where sailboats, trawlers and narrowboats (barges) wait their turn to pass.

B862 brings you back to Inverness up the quieter and more beautiful east bank of Loch Ness, with views across the loch to romantic-looking Castle Urquhart.

Every ripple in the peat-dark water of Loch Ness shapes itself into a monster to tease the overactive imagination. Have your camera ready, just in case...

Inverewe Garden ✚ B4 ✉ Off A832 near Poolewe ☎ 01445 781200 🕐 Daily 9:30–9 (or dusk if earlier), Easter–Oct. 31; 9:30–4, rest of year 🍴 Restaurant (Easter–Oct. 31 only) 💷 $$$ ❯ Guided walks (free) Mon.–Fri. at 1:30, mid-May to early Sep.

Eilean Donan Castle ✚ B4 ✉ Off A87 near Dornie ☎ 01599 555202 🕐 Daily 10–5:30, Apr.–Oct. 🍴 Café 💷 $$

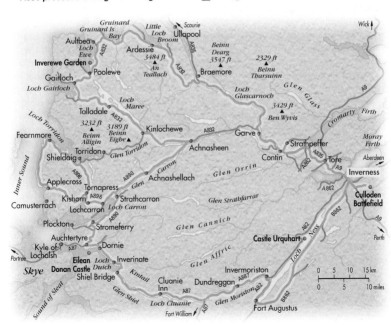

Beinn Edra and the Trotternish Ridge in the north of the Isle of Skye

ISLANDS OF SCOTLAND

There is nowhere in Britain where the harsh realities of life are quite so much at odds with a romanticized image as in the Scottish islands. Life is genuinely hard for the islanders, as many fugitives from the city discover when they buy up an old ruin and come to live the "good life" – only to back out after the first winter. Facing fierce Atlantic or North Sea storms, trying to make a living from fishing, farming, running a bed-and-breakfast or whatever else they can manage, islanders stare isolation and hardship in the face. All the more remarkable, then, is their unstinting generosity and hospitality, and courtesy that never seems ruffled. Scottish islanders, be they Inner or Outer Hebrideans, Orcadians or Shetlanders, are the most polite and genuine people you're likely to meet anywhere.

As for the wonderfully beautiful, impossibly romantic little "worlds in the water" that they inhabit – well, islanders know all about the magical effect on the visitor of that first sight of the Cuillin Hills of Skye, or the glory of a Western Isles sunset, or the ecstatic thrill of hearing a Shetland fiddler at full gallop. When you cross that gap of water and step onto an island, you step into a different frame of mind and a different rhythm to life, where time is not measured by the clock but by the job or the drink or the dance – how

long they last, and whether it is time to start a new one or not.

It is no good rushing through the Scottish islands – even if the vagaries of weather, transportation and timekeeping would allow you to. The only way to appreciate the islands properly is to arrive, take a deep breath, relax, and let it all come to you in its own good time – the landscape, the wildlife, the people.

Scotland's islands fall into three main groups: the Inner Hebrides, just off the west coast; the Outer Hebrides or Western Isles, lying parallel but 30 miles farther out into the Atlantic, and the twin archipelagos of Orkney and Shetland off the northern coast, collectively known as the Northern Isles. Each group of islands has its own distinctive character, and only experience will tell you which pleases the most. The ferry company Caledonian MacBrayne operates westward to the Inner and Outer Hebrides; Northlink Ferries sail north to Orkney and Shetland.

Before the Inner Hebrides, a handful of Clyde islands are sheltered between the mainland and the Kintyre peninsula – mountainous Arran; low-lying Bute and its holiday town, Rothesay; and little Great Cumbrae.

The Inner Hebrides lie off the west coast, with big, ragged-edged Skye the

The harbor at Tobermory on the Isle of Mull

chief island. Skye, although connected to the mainland at Kyle of Lochalsh by a road bridge, still has the romance lent to it by Bonnie Prince Charlie's flight "over the sea to Skye" with the help of local girl Flora Macdonald after the Battle of Culloden (see page 245). Features include the magnificent volcanic Cuillin Hills; the great basalt rock curtain of the Trotternish peninsula; and dramatic Dunvegan Castle, on the island's western side.

Mull, the other big Inner Hebridean island, resembles a basalt layer cake. Off its southwestern tip lies the tiny island of Iona, from which Celtic Christianity spread all over Britain during the Dark Ages.

Across the rough channel called The Minch is the 130-mile-long chain of the Outer Hebrides, or Western Isles, a stronghold of the Gaelic language. Here are incredibly beautiful beaches called *machair* – thick, flower-spangled turf that lies on top of shell sand. The islands' east coasts are spectacularly mountainous. The northern island of Lewis is a stronghold of the Free Church, a stern Presbyterian sect, while Barra, a southern island, is genially Catholic. Everyone, however, is extraordinarily hospitable.

The lush green Orkney islands shelter some of the world's most impressive prehistoric sites, from everyday dwellings to giant tombs thousands of years old. The Shetland archipelago, in contrast, has tremendous cliffs, seabirds by the million, and people at once tough and friendly, living in a dour, treeless landscape of windswept peat and heather.

Arran ✚ B2
Tourist information ✉ The Pier, Brodick
☎ 01770 303774 or 303776; www.ayrshire-arran.com
Bute ✚ B2
Tourist information ✉ Isle of Bute Discovery Centre, Victoria Street, Rothesay ☎ 08707 200619; www.visitscottishheartlands.com
Mull ✚ A3–B3
Tourist information ✉ The Pier, Craignure
☎ 08707 200630; www.visitscottishheartlands.com
Skye ✚ B4
Tourist information ✉ Bayfield House, Bayfield Road, Portree ☎ 01478 612137; www.visithighlands.com
Orkney ✚ Map inset E3
Tourist information ✉ 6 Broad Street, Kirkwall
☎ 01856 872856; www.visitorkney.com
Shetland ✚ Map inset E4–E5
Tourist information ✉ Market Cross, Lerwick
☎ 08701 999440; www.visitshetland.com
Ferry operators:
Caledonian MacBrayne ☎ 08705 650000
Northlink Ferries ☎ 08456 000449

Scotland

LOCH LOMOND AND THE TROSSACHS

An hour's drive north of Glasgow, Loch Lomond and the Trossach Hills are the city's country playground. Loch Lomond is famous wherever Scots gather to sing about its "bonnie, bonnie banks." A narrow, poorly maintained road runs most of the way up the east side of the loch to the Rowardennan Hotel, below Ben Lomond. The A82, also a narrow, winding road, runs up the west bank, giving views of the slopes and mountain waterfalls across the lake.

Northeast of Loch Lomond rise the Trossachs, offering the first real mountain scenery (although small in scale) that you encounter on your journey north. Much of the area is blanketed by the trees of Queen Elizabeth Forest Park; from the visitor center you can take the lovely Achray Forest Drive. North of here lies Loch Katrine, on which the steam cruiser SS *Sir Walter Scott* chugs about with visitors.

The Trossachs Trundler is a vintage bus that wends its way between Stirling and Port of Monteith where you can take a ferry to the island of Inchmahome.

Callander is another visitor-oriented town with plenty of tearooms, outdoor equipment stores and souvenir outlets. Local hero Rob Roy – a dashing Robin Hood to myth-maker Sir Walter Scott but a revengeful cattle thief to historians – is romanticized in the Rob Roy and Trossachs Visitor Centre here.

East of Aberfoyle is the calm Lake of Menteith, where you can take a boat to Inchmahome Island, site of the ruins of an abbey.

Aberfoyle ✛ C2

Tourist information ✉ Trossachs Discovery Centre, Main Street ☎ 08707 200604; www.visitscottishheartlands.com

Queen Elizabeth Forest Park ✉ Dukes Pass, Aberfoyle ☎ 01877 382258 🕐 Daily 10–6, Mar.–Oct.; 11–4, Nov.–Dec. 🍴 Café 💰 $ for parking

SS *Sir Walter Scott* ✉ Trossachs Pier Complex ☎ 01877 376316 🕐 Departs Thu.–Tue. at 11, 1:45 and 3:15, Wed. at 1:45 and 3:15, early Apr. to mid-Oct. 🍴 Café at pier 💰 $$$

Callander ✛ C2

Rob Roy and Trossachs Visitor Centre ✉ Ancaster Square, Callander ☎ 01877 330342; www.robroyvisitorcentre.com

Trossachs Trundler ☎ 01786 422707 🕐 Operates late May–early Oct. 💰 $$–$$$

Safety in the Hills

Scotland's mountains, glens and rolling Border hills offer the best walking in Britain. There is something here for every outdoor enthusiast, from gentle pastoral strolls to the toughest possible mountain hikes. Hiking tips:

1. Find out the local weather forecast.
2. Equip yourself properly, and know how to use your equipment.
3. Go with a party of four at least, so that if someone gets hurt one person can stay with the injured party, keeping him or her warm and dry, and two can go for help.
4. Be realistic about how fit and experienced you are, and be pragmatic about the weather. Discuss the route with a local expert – hiker, ranger or warden – if unsure. Be flexible enough not to set out if the weather is threatening or the route looks too tough.
5. Tell someone where you are going, and when and where you expect to finish. Stick to that route, and phone to report your safe arrival.
6. If bad weather or darkness threaten, find shelter quickly.
7. If there is an emergency, keep calm and optimistic. If you have observed Rule 5, the rescue services will soon find you.
8. Don't rely on a cell phone to get you out of trouble; it may not work when you want to use it. There is no substitute for these precautions.

Ben Nevis: Britain's highest mountain

Oban and the Southwest

Southwestern Scotland, from Fort William south to the Mull of Kintyre, is an enormous region of sea-battered coasts and wild hills cut by deep glens.

Oban, a small, attractive seaside town toward the island-spattered mouth of Loch Linnhe, has a busy and thriving fishing harbor, and – more importantly for the region's prosperity – is the chief ferry port for the Hebrides. It has a magnificent setting and plenty of facilities for visitors – stroll along the waterfront, shop for whiskey and tartan in the many gift shops, or enjoy freshly caught fish in one of the dockside cafés.

At the head of Loch Linnhe, nearly 50 miles north by road, Fort William is the gateway for those who want to explore the wonderfully wild and unfrequented peninsulas of the western coast. Just south of Fort William curves Glen Nevis, with the great bulk of Ben Nevis – at 4,406 feet, Britain's highest mountain – rising from its northern side. You can climb the mountain via a very well-marked path beginning at the Glen Nevis youth hostel. The trek is not difficult (although you must pay proper attention to the weather – see panel on opposite page).

Between Fort William and Oban the darkly dramatic valley of Glencoe cuts in eastward. Here can be seen the great hanging slopes up which survivors of the Massacre of Glencoe fled in the snow. This brutal act of ethnic cleansing took place on February 13, 1692, when 38 members of the local Macdonald clan – a thorn in the side of the authorities – were murdered by soldiers billeted in their houses.

From Oban A85 leads east. Just before reaching Dalmally, a right turn onto A819 will take you south to Inveraray, where a strikingly beautiful castle sits on Loch Fyne. A83 runs south from here via Lochgilphead for 100 miles, all the way to the southern tip of the Kintyre peninsula, the Mull of Kintyre. Paul McCartney bought a farm here to escape from the pressures of rock stardom, and you can appreciate his choice of location as you savor the peace and beauty of the area.

Oban ✚ B3

Tourist information ✉ Argyll Square ☎ 08707 200630; www.visitscottishheartlands.com

Fort William ✚ B3

Tourist information ✉ Cameron Square, High Street ☎ 08452 255121; www.visithighlands.com

Glen Nevis Visitor Centre ✉ Glen Nevis, Fort William ☎ 01397 705922 🕐 Daily 9–5, , Easter–Oct. 31 🎟 Free

Perth overlooks the River Tay

PERTH

Perth, "The Fair City," is handsomely set
on craggy hills above the River Tay, with
the Grampian mountains as a northern
backdrop. Sir Walter Scott's 1828 novel
Fair Maid of Perth is a good yarn to read
while you are here. On the meadows of
North Inch you can visualize the bloody
championship contest fought in 1396
between the clans of Chattan and Quhale,
as poetically described by Scott.

Northeast of Perth via A94 is the
enormous pink fantasy castle of Glamis
(pronounced "Glarms"). Shakespeare is
said to have used Duncan's Hall as the
setting for the murder of King Duncan by
Macbeth, and there is evidence that King
Malcolm II probably *was* murdered in or
near the castle.

Another splendid castle is at Blair, 35
miles north of Perth via A9. Turrets, gables
and memorabilia mark 700 years of castle
history. Its owner, the Duke of Atholl, still
maintains a private army and his own piper.
✚ C3

Tourist information ✉ Lower City Mills, West Mill
Street ☎ 01738 450600; www.perthshire.co.uk

Glamis Castle ✚ C3 ✉ Glamis ☎ 01307 840393
🕐 Daily 10–6, late Mar.–Oct. 31; noon–4, Nov.–Dec.
🍽 Restaurant 🖐 $$$; grounds only $$

Blair Castle ✚ C3 ✉ Blair Atholl ☎ 01796 481207
🕐 Daily 9:30–4:30, Apr.–Oct.; Tue. and Sat.
9:30–12:30, rest of year 🍽 Restaurant 🖐 $$$

Robert the Bruce looks out to the National Wallace Monument, just outside Stirling

STIRLING

Stirling sits at Scotland's narrow waist, forming the apex of a triangle with Glasgow and Edinburgh. Stirling Castle, spectacularly perched on a crag, was used by the Scottish Stewart monarchs as their Royal Court from the 1480s until James VI became King of England in 1603.

The castle houses the Regimental Museum of the Argyll and Sutherland Highlanders, a military regiment with plenty of dashing exploits to celebrate. The view from the battlements, 250 feet up, is superb.

The town's historic buildings include Argyll's Lodging, a 17th-century residence of the Dukes of Argyll; the grand but never completed Mar's Wark; the 15th-century Church of the Holy Rude (Holy Cross); and the Stirling Old Town Jail.

The National Wallace Monument celebrates William Wallace, who led Scottish resistance against the English in 1297. There is an audiovisual presentation, and for real-life views you can climb the 246 steps up the tower's spiral staircase.

 C2

Tourist information ✉ 41 Dumbarton Road ☎ 08707 200620; www.visitscottishheartlands.com

Stirling Castle ✉ Castle Wynd ☎ 01786 450000
🕐 Daily 9:30–6, Apr.–Sep.; 9:30–5, rest of year
🍴 Café 💷 $$$ 🎧 Audio guide

HOTELS AND RESTAURANTS

The hotels and restaurants in this book were selected by local specialists and include establishments in several price ranges. Since price is often the best indication of the level of facilities and quality of service, a three-tiered price guide appears at the beginning of the listings. Because variable rates will affect the amount of foreign currency that can be exchanged for dollars (and thus affect the cost of a room or a meal), price ranges are given in the local currency.

Although price ranges and operating times were accurate at press time, this information is always subject to change without notice. If you're interested in a particular establishment, it is always advisable to call ahead to book.

Facilities suitable for travelers with disabilities vary, and you are strongly advised to contact an establishment directly to determine whether it will be able to meet your needs. Older buildings may not be adequately designed or equipped for visitors with limited or impaired mobility.

Accommodations

Accommodations have been selected with two considerations in mind: a particularly attractive character or sense of local flavor, or a central location that is convenient for sightseeing. Remember that centrally located hotels fill up quickly, especially during busy summer vacation periods; make reservations well in advance. In-room bathrooms (sometimes referred to as "en-suite facilities") may not be available in smaller budget hotels.

Room rates normally include breakfast. In British hotels, this is likely to be a full meal of bacon, sausage, eggs, fried potatoes and toast that should leave you feeling well fed most of the day. Some hotels offer a price for overnight accommodations that includes an evening meal (known as "half-board" in Britain).

Eating Out

Listed restaurants range from upscale places suitable for an elegant evening out to small cafés where you can stop and take a leisurely break from a busy day of sightseeing. Other possibilities for getting a bite to eat are the cafeterias and restaurants on the premises of museums, galleries and other tourist attractions.

The British used to be mocked about their culinary prowess and considered unimaginative when it came to food – but no longer. Today, there is a real interest and excitement about eating out. Chefs are feted both in their kitchens and as media personalities. New restaurants are burgeoning, catering to all tastes and serving a variety of cuisine. Visitors will enjoy sharing this revival of British enthusiasm for good food.

Left: Doorman at Claridge's hotel, a byword for quality in London's exclusive Mayfair district

Southeast England

KEY TO SYMBOLS

- 🏨 hotel
- 🍴 restaurant
- ✉ address
- ☎ telephone number
- 🕐 days/times closed
- Ⓜ nearest metro/tube/subway station(s)
- AX American Express
- DC Diners Club
- MC MasterCard
- VI VISA

Hotels

Price guide: double room with breakfast for two people

- **$** less than £50
- **$$** £50–£100
- **$$$** more than £100

Restaurants

Price guide: dinner per person, excluding drinks

- **$** less than £15
- **$$** £15–£30
- **$$$** more than £30

INVITING AND FRIENDLY

Don't always believe that paying more will guarantee you a better standard of accommodation. Unless you demand the lap of luxury and the widest possible range of amenities, you will often find well-run bed-and-breakfast houses and country pubs just as clean and inviting as an upscale hotel, and probably a lot more friendly.

Southeast England

AMBERLEY

🏨 Amberley Castle $$$

Set in the South Downs, this 11th-century castle has a gatehouse, working portcullis, high walls, gardens and peacocks. It also is a hotel combining great charm and modern luxuries. The Queens Room restaurant offers several menus, including "Castle Cuisine," which is based on old English recipes.

✉ Amberley, West Sussex
☎ 01798 831992; fax 01798 831998
AX, DC, MC, VI

BOUGHTON LEES

🏨 Eastwell Manor $$$

This Jacobean-style manor in Kent sits on 3,000 acres of land. The menu features luxuries such as caviar and quails' eggs alongside hearty favorites such as loin of lamb and filet of Aberdeen Angus beef.

✉ Eastwell Park, Boughton Lees, Kent ☎ 01233 213000; fax 01233 635530 AX, DC, MC, VI

BRAY

🏨 Monkey Island $$$

Idyllically located on an island in the River Thames near Windsor, this accommodation is comfortable and smart. The island can be reached only by footbridge or boat.

✉ Old Mill Lane, Bray, Berkshire
☎ 01628 623400; fax 01628 784732
AX, DC, MC, VI

BRIGHTON

🏨 Imperial $$–$$$

Close to the seafront and occupying a row of Victorian-style town houses, the Imperial offers modern accommodations and a stylish restaurant.

✉ First Avenue, Hove, East Sussex
☎ 01273 777320; fax 01273 777310
AX, DC, MC, VI

🍴 One Paston Place $$$

This restaurant has a friendly atmosphere and serves some of the best food in Brighton. The imaginative menu includes excellent fish dishes.

✉ 1 Paston Place, Brighton, East Sussex ☎ 01273 606933 🕐 Closed Sun.–Mon., 2–3 weeks Jan.–Feb. and 2 weeks in Aug. AX, DC, MC, VI

CANTERBURY

🏨 Swallow Chaucer Hotel $$$

The Chaucer hotel, with 42 comfortable en-suite bedrooms, has retained its Regency appearance and stands opposite Canterbury's city walls, in a convenient location for all the city sights.

✉ 63 Ivy Lane, Canterbury, Kent
☎ 01227 464427 AX, DC, MC, VI

🏨 Ebury $$

The Ebury is a delightful family-run hotel surrounded by two acres of pretty gardens.

✉ 65–67 New Dover Road, Canterbury, Kent ☎ 01227 768433; fax 01227 459187 AX, DC, MC, VI

CHATHAM

🏨 Bridgewood Manor $$$

This hotel has extensive leisure facilities, including an indoor pool. There is a choice of dining in the informal Terrace Bistro or the more formal Squires restaurant.

✉ Bridgewood Roundabout, Walderslade Woods, Chatham, Kent
☎ 01634 201333; fax 01634 201330
AX, MC, VI

CHICHESTER

🍴 Comme Ça $$

This centrally located restaurant offers a selection of French-influenced recipes complemented by some delicious British specialties.

✉ 67 Broyle Road, Chichester, West Sussex ☎ 01243 788724
🕐 Closed Mon., Tue. lunch, Sun. dinner, 1 week at New Year's and 1 week at Christmas AX, DC, MC, VI

🏨 Millstream Hotel $$

Well-tended lawns surround this charming hotel, which has beautifully decorated bedrooms and public rooms. The restaurant has a daily changing menu.

✉ Bosham Lane, Bosham, near Chichester, West Sussex ☎ 01243 573234; fax 01243 573549 AX, DC

🏨 Suffolk House $$–$$$

The friendly proprietors offer a warm welcome to guests at this hotel, only a short stroll from the city center. The restaurant offers a good menu.

✉ 3 East Row, Chichester, West Sussex ☎ 01243 778899; fax 01243 787282 MC, VI

Southeast England

CHILGROVE

The White Horse $$–$$$
The White Horse is an inviting 18th-century village pub on the South Downs, convenient to Chichester and the Fishbourne Roman Palace. Stylish English cooking features local fish, crab, lobster and scallops.
✉ High Street, Chilgrove, near Chichester, West Sussex ☎ 01243 535219 AX, MC, VI

CRANBROOK

The George Hotel and Brasserie $$
Guests are given a warm welcome at this family owned and run hotel, housed in a landmark building which dates back to the 14th century. The dining room is superb.
✉ Stone Street, Cranbrook, Kent ☎ 01580 913348 MC, VI

DEAL

Dunkerleys $$
Fresh fish is the specialty at this seafront restaurant located opposite the pier, but there are some good meat dishes to try, too.
✉ 19 Beach Street, Deal, Kent ☎ 01304 375016 MC, VI

Royal $$–$$$
Set on the seafront overlooking the beach, the spacious Royal Hotel has a vibrant brasserie.
✉ Beach Street, Deal, Kent ☎ 01304 375555; fax 01304 372270 AX, DC, MC, VI

DOVER

Best Western Churchill $$
Located on Dover's waterfront, The Churchill has comfortable rooms complete with satellite television; some rooms have private balconies.
✉ Dover Waterfront, Dover, Kent ☎ 01304 203633; fax 01304 216320 AX, DC, MC, VI

Wallett's Court Country House Hotel and Spa $$$
Formerly a Jacobean farmhouse, with some original architectral features retained, Wallett's Court also has modern recreational facilities. The menu features excellent English country cooking.
✉ West Cliffe, St. Margarets-at-Cliffe, Dover, Kent ☎ 01304

852424 and 0800 035 1628 (toll-free); fax 01304 853430 AX, DC, MC, VI

EAST GRINSTEAD

Gravetye Manor $$$
A shining example of a country hotel, this Elizabethan stone manor house is set amid extensive grounds with a beautiful garden. Gravetye Manor is famous for excellent food, using ingredients from its own walled kitchen garden. It also is a convenient base for exploring the castles and great houses of Kent.
✉ East Grinstead, West Sussex ☎ 01342 810567; fax 01342 810080 MC, VI

FORDINGBRIDGE

The Three Lions $$–$$$
The Three Lions offers attractively furnished accommodations and is ideally located for exploring the New Forest.
✉ Stuckton, Fordingbridge, Hampshire ☎ 01425 652489; fax 01425 656144 Ⓒ Closed mid-Jan. to mid-Feb. AX, MC, VI

HASLEMERE

Lythe Hill $$$
This hotel is housed in a cluster of historic buildings, set amid 30 acres of grounds that include a bluebell wood and lakes. The Henry VIII Suite features a four-poster bed dating from 1614. The Auberge de France restaurant offers reliable cooking.
✉ Petworth Road, Haslemere, Surrey ☎ 01428 651251; fax 01428 644131 AX, DC, MC, VI

LONDON

The Beaufort $$$
This is a luxury hotel on a quiet, leafy square only 100 yards from Harrods department store.
✉ 33 Beaufort Gardens, Knightsbridge, SW3 1PP ☎ 020 7584 5252; fax 020 7589 2834 Ⓜ Knightsbridge AX, DC, MC, VI

Blue Door Bistro $$
Found in Bloomsbury at the Montague on the Gardens Hotel, Blue Door Bistro offers excellent value dining served by attentive yet unobtrusive staff in a friendly atmosphere.
✉ 15 Montague Street, WC1B 5BJ

☎ 020 7612 8416 Ⓜ Russell Square AX, MC, VI

Le Caprice $$–$$$
You can expect superb service at this London favorite—a magnet for celebrities, with its stark black-and-white decor. The menu features classic British and European dishes.
✉ Arlington House, Arlington Street, SW1A 1RT ☎ 020 7629 2239 Ⓒ Closed Jan. 1, dinner Dec. 24, Dec. 25–26 and Aug. bank holiday Ⓜ Green Park AX, DC, MC, VI

Fino $$
Located in central Fitzrovia, this Spanish tapas bar offers a mix of modern and traditional Spanish fare served by friendly and helpful staff. Décor is chic and minimalist with pale walls and careful lighting. Food portions are generous and the wine list is great.
✉ 33 Charlotte Street, W1T 1RR ☎ 020 7813 8010 Ⓜ Goodge Street AX, DC, MC, VI

The Gallery $$$
The Gallery Hotel is housed in two lovingly restored Georgian houses in South Kensington. There is a mahogany paneled lounge, and 24-hour room service is available.
✉ 8–10 Queensberry Place, SW7 2EA ☎ 020 7915 0000; fax 020 7915 4400 Ⓜ South Kensington AX, DC, MC, VI

Grange Blooms $$$
This stylish Georgian terrace house hotel in Bloomsbury, London's literary enclave, is just a step away from the British Museum.
✉ 7 Montague Street, WC1B 5BP ☎ 020 7323 1717; fax 020 7636 6498 Ⓜ Russell Square AX, DC, MC, VI

The Grapes $$
This Thames-side pub in London's East End was frequented by Charles Dickens. Today it specializes in very good fresh seafood.
✉ 76 Narrow Street, Limehouse, E14 8BP ☎ 020 7987 4396 Ⓜ Docklands Light Railway stations: Limehouse or West Ferry AX, DC, MC, VI

The Lanesborough $$$
Prestigiously located on Hyde Park Corner, this luxurious hotel offers the highest level of comfort, including

Southeast England

KEY TO SYMBOLS

🏨 hotel
🍴 restaurant
✉ address
☎ telephone number
🕐 days/times closed
Ⓜ nearest metro/tube/subway station(s)
AX American Express
DC Diners Club
MC MasterCard
VI VISA

Hotels

Price guide: double room with breakfast for two people
$ less than £50
$$ £50–£100
$$$ more than £100

Restaurants

Price guide: dinner per person, excluding drinks
$ less than £15
$$ £15–£30
$$$ more than £30

A CHOLESTEROL TREAT

Everywhere you stay in Britain you will be offered a "full English breakfast" of bacon, eggs, sausages and other trimmings to start your day. Few British households now eat like this at breakfast time; it is a treat reserved mainly for accommodation guests. If you don't want such a cholesterol blast first thing in the morning, just tell your hosts; most places will have a healthier Continental breakfast (rolls, toast, fruit, yogurt) up their sleeve.

lavish reception rooms and 24-hour service from a personal butler.
✉ Hyde Park Corner, SW1X 7TA ☎ 020 7259 5599; fax 020 7259 5606 Ⓜ Hyde Park Corner AX, DC, MC, VI

🏨 London Marriott Hotel County Hall $$$

All the relaxed style of the Marriott chain is here in the unique setting of London's refurbished former County Hall, right on the Thames. Guests can enjoy views of the Houses of Parliament and Big Ben.
✉ County Hall, Westminster Bridge Road SE1 7PB ☎ 020 7928 5200; fax 020 7928 5300 Ⓜ Waterloo AX, DC, MC, VI

🍴 Pied à Terre $$$

There is a stylish yet simple ambience and cutting-edge cuisine at Pied à Terre. Furthermore, the impressive wine list varies from reasonably priced favorites to some of France's great vintages.
✉ 34 Charlotte Street, W1P 1HJ ☎ 020 7636 1178 🕐 Closed Sat. and Mon. lunch and 2 weeks around Christmas and New Year
Ⓜ Goodge Street AX, DC, MC, VI

🍴 The River Café $$$

Simple, modern decor and a splendid interpretation of Italian country-style cooking prevail at this very popular, cozy riverside restaurant.
✉ Thames Wharf, Rainville Road, W6 9HA ☎ 020 7386 4200
Ⓜ Hammersmith 🕐 Closed dinner Dec. 22–Jan. 3, Easter and bank holidays AX, DC, MC, VI

🏨 The Stafford $$$

Quietly located in exclusive St. James's, this luxurious hotel contains individually designed bedrooms. The American Bar is famous for its celebrity paraphernalia; there also are several private dining rooms.
✉ 16–18 St. James's Place, SW1A 1NJ ☎ 020 7493 0111; fax 020 7493 7121 Ⓜ St. James's Park AX, DC, MC, VI

NEW MILTON

🏨 Chewton Glen $$$

A luxurious retreat within easy reach of the New Forest, Chewton Glen offers many thoughtful touches and excellent housekeeping. Superior cooking uses excellent ingredients,

and the wine list is impressive.
✉ Christchurch Road, New Milton, Hampshire ☎ 01425 275341; fax 01425 272310 AX, DC, MC, VI

PORTSMOUTH & SOUTHSEA

🏨 Queen's $$–$$$

This elegant Edwardian hotel, with magnificent views across the sea to the Isle of Wight, is only a mile from Portsmouth city center. Many of the rooms have sea views and balconies, and there is a heated outdoor swimming pool.
✉ Clarence Parade, Southsea, Hampshire ☎ 02392 822466; fax 02392 821901 AX, DC, MC, VI

🍴 The Wine Vaults

Wood-paneled walls, interesting paintings and artifacts all lend a relaxing atmosphere to this ale house. Evocatively named ales are served, including Greene King and Hopback Summer Lightning. The traditional English menu includes homemade soups and lamb stew.
✉ 43–47 Albert Road, Southsea, Hampshire ☎ 02392 864712 MC, VI

RYE

🍴 Mermaid Inn $$$

This medieval smugglers' inn is full of character, with walls draped in historical paintings and huge open fireplaces. The modern menu includes good fish dishes.
✉ Mermaid Street, Rye, East Sussex ☎ 01797 223065 AX, DC, MC, VI

🏨 The Old Vicarage Guesthouse $$–$$$

A pink house on the square next to the town church, this bed and breakfast offers a warm and friendly stay. Breakfast includes homemade jams and biscuits.
✉ 66 Church Square, Rye, East Sussex ☎ 01797 222119; fax 01797 227466 No credit cards

WINCHESTER

🏨 The Wessex $$$

This modern hotel is tucked away in the heart of the city and has magnificent views of the cathedral.
✉ Paternoster Row, Winchester, Hampshire ☎ 0870 400 8126; fax 01962 841503 AX, DC, MC, VI

Wykeham Arms $–$$

This famous old pub, right in the center of historic Winchester, has an innovative menu, an extensive wine list and a stylish atmosphere.
✉ 75 Kingsgate Street, Winchester, Hampshire ☎ 01962 853834
◎ Closed Sun. dinner AX, DC, MC, VI

WINDSOR

The Castle $$$

Rooms in the older part of this building, close to Windsor Castle, have been tastefully modernized and are traditionally furnished. The elegant restaurant offers a good seasonal menu. There also is a café for light meals and snacks.
✉ 18 High Street, Windsor, Berkshire ☎ 0870 400 8300; fax 01753 830244 AX, DC, MC, VI

Sir Christopher Wren's House Hotel and Spa $$$

Within easy walking distance of the castle, this hotel boasts views of the Thames; some rooms have private courtyards overlooking the river.
✉ Thames Street, Windsor, Berkshire ☎ 01753 861354; fax 01753 860172 AX, DC, MC, VI

The West Country

BATH

Bath Priory $$$

Intimate atmosphere in a Georgian building, which includes a recreation center with a Roman Baths theme. Bedrooms are furnished with antiques, while the restaurant serves stylish, modern cuisine.
✉ Weston Road, Bath, Somerset ☎ 01225 331922; fax 01225 448276 AX, DC, MC, VI

Cliffe $$$

Set at the crest of a wooded hill in a tranquil village 2 miles outside Bath, the Cliffe is a retreat from the bustle of the city. The gardens include an outdoor swimming pool.
✉ Cliffe Drive, Crowe Hill, Limpley Stoke, Bath, Somerset ☎ 01225 723226; fax 01225 723871 AX, DC, MC, VI

Dukes Hotel $$–$$$

This stylish hotel on a charming Georgian boulevard is near the beautiful Pulteney Bridge.
✉ Great Pulteney Street, Bath, Somerset ☎ 01225 787960; fax 01225 787961 DC, MC, VI

The Francis $$$

This traditional hotel, located on elegant Queen Square in the heart of Bath, offers a warm welcome.
✉ Queen Square, Bath, Somerset ☎ 0870 400 8223; fax 01225 319715 AX, DC, MC, VI

Lansdowne Grove $$

This Grade II listed building has high ceilings and delicate plasterwork and is surrounded by lovely gardens. The bedrooms have been refurbished and offer a high standard of comfort.
✉ Lansdowne Road, Bath, Somerset ☎ 01225 483888 AX, MC, VI

The Moody Goose $$$

Innovative seasonal cooking is served in this simple but elegant basement restaurant. Interesting combinations of flavors include veal with scallops and venison with pears.
✉ 7A Kingsmead Square, Bath, Somerset ☎ 01225 466688
◎ Closed Sun., 2 weeks in Jan. and bank holidays AX, DC, MC, VI

Queensberry $$$

Enjoy beautifully appointed bedrooms and the fresh cuisine of the Olive Tree Restaurant, located in a carefully restored Bath stone house a few minutes' walk from the town center.
✉ Russel Street, Bath, Somerset ☎ 01225 447928; fax 01225 446065 MC, VI

Redcar Hotel $$

This is a comfortable hotel within striking distance of the city center and offers a good value accommodation.
✉ 27–29 Henrietta Street, Bath, Somerset ☎ 01225 469151 AX, DC, MC, VI

The Royal Crescent $$$

Hospitality, service and fine cuisine are combined in this grand Bath setting – the curve of Georgian houses that is the Royal Crescent.
✉ 16 Royal Crescent, Bath, Somerset ☎ 01225 823333; fax 01225 339401 AX, DC, MC, VI

Tasburgh House $$$

There are sweeping views over the Avon valley from this charming Victorian hotel offering elegant accommodations and friendly service. The grounds slope down to the picturesque Kennet and Avon Canal, along whose towpath guests can walk right into the town center.
✉ Warminster Road, Bath, Somerset ☎ 01225 425096; fax 01225 463842 AX, DC, MC, VI

Woods $–$$

Located opposite the Assembly Rooms, Woods has a short, well-balanced menu and is known locally for delicious, good-value lunches.
✉ 9–13 Alfred Street, Bath, Somerset ☎ 01225 314812 ◎ Closed Sun. dinner, Jan. 1 and Dec. 26

BRADFORD-ON-AVON

Bradford Old Windmill $$–$$$

Rooms at the Old Windmill, in the heart of town, are individually decorated to match the character of this unique property. Breakfasts include vegetarian options as well as a conventional English one.
✉ 4 Masons Lane, Bradford-on-Avon, Wiltshire ☎ 01225 866842; fax 01225 866648 ☎ Closed Nov.–Feb. AX, DC, MC, VI

Georgian Lodge $$

This historic-looking building occupies an ideal spot in the center of town. All the accommodations are reached from the central courtyard. The split-level restaurant serves classic dishes with a few saucy touches of modernity.
✉ 25 Bridge Street, Bradford-on-Avon, Wiltshire ☎ 01225 862268; fax 01225 862218 AX, MC, VI

BRIDPORT

Bridport Arms $$

Located on the beach at West Bay, one mile south of Bridport, this popular thatched inn offers warm hospitality. Rooms are simply furnished, and meals are available in the restaurant and bar.
✉ West Bay, Bridport, Dorset ☎ 01308 422994; fax 01308 425141 MC, VI

BRISTOL

The Avon Gorge $$$

This hotel occupies a commanding position overlooking the Avon Gorge and famous suspension bridge in the heart of fashionable

Southeast England • The West Country

The West Country

KEY TO SYMBOLS

🏨 hotel
🍴 restaurant
✉ address
☎ telephone number
🕐 days/times closed
🚇 nearest metro/tube/subway station(s)
AX   American Express
DC   Diners Club
MC   MasterCard
VI   VISA

Hotels

Price guide: double room with breakfast for two people
$ less than £50
$$ £50–£100
$$$ more than £100

Restaurants

Price guide: dinner per person, excluding drinks
$ less than £15
$$ £15–£30
$$$ more than £30

TRADITIONAL CREAM TEA

One tradition you must observe when traveling in the West Country is the leisurely consumption of a cream tea. This stars a yellow biscuit (fruit-studded or plain), a thick layer of jam and an even thicker dollop of cream. Then another. Better eat breakfast early and dinner late if you know you will be embarking on a Cream Tea Day ...

Clifton. There is a choice of bars (one with a terrace above the gorge) and an attractive restaurant.
✉ Sion Hill, Clifton, Bristol
☎ 0117 973 8955; fax 0117 923 8125   AX, DC, MC, VI

🍴 riverstation $$

Contemporary decor and a Mediterranean-influenced menu prevail at this restaurant along Bristol's historic dockside.
✉ The Grove, Bristol   ☎ 0117 914 4434   🕐 Closed Jan.1 and Dec. 25   DC, MC, VI

CALNE

🏨 Fenwicks $

This small but delightful bed and breakfast property has views over open countryside and a location convenient for exploring the ancient stone circle at Avebury.
✉ Lower Goatacre, Calne, Wiltshire
☎ 01249 760645   AX

🍴 Lansdowne Arms $

With scenic views of the Avon valley, this Victorian coaching house offers an extensive menu and a good selection of beers.
✉ Derry Hill, Calne, Wiltshire
☎ 01249 812422   AX, MC, VI

CASTLE COMBE

🏨 Manor House $$$

Convenient for exploring Lacock and Avebury, this hotel is surrounded by 365 acres of gardens and parkland in the lovely village of Castle Combe. There are bedrooms in the main house and in a row of cottages on the grounds. Elegant cuisine is served in the restaurant.
✉ Castle Combe, Wiltshire
☎ 01249 782206; fax 01249 782159   AX, MC, VI

CHAGFORD

🏨 Gidleigh Park $$$

This mock-Tudor hotel, set on 45 acres within Dartmoor National Park, provides guests with a warm welcome. All rooms are of a high standard, and the grounds have streams, forests and a variety of recreational pursuits. The hotel restaurant offers outstanding dishes, many using local ingredients.
✉ Chagford, Devon   ☎ 01647 432367   AX, DC, MC, VI

CORFE CASTLE

🏨 Mortons House $$$

This charming hotel occupies a gorgeous Elizabethan manor house in the shadow of Corfe's dramatically ruined castle. Traditional features include an oak-paneled drawing room. Well-prepared cuisine also is available in the hotel restaurant.
✉ 49 East Street, Corfe Castle, Dorset   ☎ 01929 480988; fax 01929 480820   MC, VI

DORCHESTER

🏨 Casterbridge $$

This hotel is convenient to the town center. A bar, library, drawing room and conservatory are all options for relaxing during the day.
✉ 49 High East Street, Dorchester, Dorset   ☎ 01305 264043; fax 01305 260884   AX, DC, MC, VI

🏨 Yalbury Cottage $$

Located 2 miles east of Dorchester in the beautiful hamlet of Lower Bockhampton, the cottage was originally a shepherd's home. The oak-beamed restaurant has an inglenook fireplace, and the cuisine is award-winning.
✉ Lower Bockhampton, Dorchester, Dorset   ☎ 01305 262382; fax 01305 266412   MC, VI

DUNSTER

🏨 Dollons House $$

This historic property is in the medieval village of Dunster, within Exmoor National Park. Two bedrooms have views of the castle, and another overlooks lovely walled gardens.
✉ 10–12 Church Street, Dunster, Somerset   ☎ 01643 821880   MC, VI

EVERSHOT

🏨 Summer Lodge $$$

This country house hotel, with its charming walled gardens, is personally owned and run. Floral arrangements, log fires and watercolor paintings all add to the elegance. The hotel restaurant serves imaginative food.
✉ Evershot, Dorset   ☎ 01935 83424; fax 01935 83005   AX, DC, MC, VI

FALMOUTH

🏨 Royal Duchy $$$
Located in one of Cornwall's largest towns, the Royal Duchy is an elegant Victorian seafront hotel, with the benefit of such modern luxuries as a swimming pool, sauna, solarium and spa bath. Seafood features strongly on the restaurant menu.
✉ Cliff Road, Falmouth, Cornwall
☎ 01326 313042; fax 01326 319420 AX, DC, MC, VI

🍴 Royal Duchy Hotel $$
Originally a cheese and wine cellar, the Royal Duchy's restaurant has been tastefully decorated in art deco style. The menu features excellent seafood.
✉ Cliff Road, Falmouth, Cornwall
☎ 01326 313042 🕐 Closed lunch Mon.–Sat. AX, DC, MC, VI

GLASTONBURY

🏨 George and Pilgrims $
This 15th-century inn is steeped in history. It offers accommodations as well as a cozy bar and brasserie.
✉ 1 High Street, Glastonbury, Somerset ☎ 01458 831146; fax 01458 832252 MC, VI

🍴 Who'd A Thought It $
Unfussy, good food in a Georgian pub furnished with local artifacts and memorabilia.
✉ 17 Northload Street, Glastonbury, Somerset ☎ 01458 834460 MC, VI

LACOCK

🍴 The Red Lion $
Located in the timeless, photogenically preserved village of Lacock (where photography was invented), this refurbished inn offers good fare.
✉ 1 High Street, Lacock, near Corsham, Wiltshire ☎ 01249 730456 AX, MC, VI

🏨 The Sign of the Angel $$$
Even the beds have a history in this 15th-century former wool merchant's house: One was owned by celebrated engineer Isambard Kingdom Brunel. Excellent meals are served in the lovely beamed dining room.
✉ 6 Church Street, Lacock, near Corsham, Wiltshire ☎ 01249 730230; fax 01249 730527 AX, VI

LYNMOUTH

🏨 Rising Sun $$–$$$
This wood-beamed 14th-century inn on the waterfront at historic Lynmouth offers comfortable rooms. The kitchen specializes in local Exmoor game and excellent seafood, such as crab bisque.
✉ Harbourside, Lynmouth, Devon
☎ 01598 753223; fax 01598 753480 AX, DC, MC, VI

MOUSEHOLE

🏨 Old Coastguard $$
In the heart of the picturesque fishing village of Mousehole (pronounced "Mouzall"), this informal inn has a backdrop of subtropical gardens. The menu relies on locally caught fresh fish.
✉ The Parade, Mousehole, Cornwall ☎ 01736 731222; fax 01736 731720 AX, MC, VI

SALISBURY

🏨 Howard's House Hotel $$$
This welcoming hotel in a picturesque village 4 miles west of Salisbury has spacious, comfortably furnished rooms. In the restaurant, simple presentations allow the flavors to speak for themselves.
✉ Teffont Evias, Salisbury, Wiltshire ☎ 01722 716392; fax 01722 716820 AX, DC, MC, VI

🏨 Red Lion $$$
Located just off Market Square, the Red Lion is older than the town's magnificent cathedral and offers traditional standards of hospitality. Several rooms have four-poster beds. The restaurant serves English and French cuisine.
✉ Milford Street, Salisbury, Wiltshire ☎ 01722 323334; fax 01722 325756 AX, DC, MC, VI

SHEPTON MALLET

🏨 Charlton House $$$
This hotel occupies a 16th-century house on pretty grounds. Facilities include an indoor swimming pool, sauna and tennis courts.
✉ Charlton Road, Shepton Mallet, Somerset ☎ 01749 342008; fax 01749 346362 AX, DC, MC, VI

ST. IVES

🏨 Chy-An-Dour $$$
Delightful, family-owned hotel, with vistas over St. Ives, the harbor and the beach. Enjoy home-cooked meals for breakfast and dinner.
✉ Trelyon Avenue, St. Ives, Cornwall ☎ 01736 796436; fax 01736 795772 MC, VI

🍴 Pig 'n' Fish $$
Friendly French waiters serve marvelous local fish (in addition to other more meaty delights) in this light and airy upstairs restaurant.
✉ Norway Lane, St. Ives, Cornwall
☎ 01736 794204 AX, MC, VI

ST. KEYNE

🏨 Well House $$$
This charming small hotel offers personal hospitality and service, as well as afternoon tea with homemade biscuits on the terrace.
✉ St. Keyne, Liskeard, Cornwall
☎ 01579 342001; fax 01579 343891 MC, VI

STON EASTON

🏨 Ston Easton Park $$$
This sumptuous 18th-century Palladian mansion occupies extensive grounds. Bedrooms are luxuriously furnished with antique pieces. Aperitifs are served in the elegant salon, dinner in the dining room, and after-dinner drinks, coffee and petits fours in the smart library.
✉ Ston Easton, Somerset
☎ 01761 241631; fax 01761 241377 AX, DC, MC, VI

TOTNES

🍴 The Waterman's Arms $
Log fires, exposed beams and a riverside location make this a happily atmospheric place to stay. Pub meals are served in the bar.
✉ Bow Bridge, Ashprington, near Totnes, Devon ☎ 08703 3052034 MC, VI

WARMINSTER

🏨 Bishopstrow House $$$
This lovely Georgian house hotel (a convenient base for visiting Longleat House) is furnished with English antiques and 19th-century paintings.

The West Country

The West Country • Eastern England

KEY TO SYMBOLS

- ⊞ hotel
- 🍴 restaurant
- ✉ address
- ☎ telephone number
- 🕐 days/times closed
- Ⓜ nearest metro/tube/subway station(s)
- AX American Express
- DC Diners Club
- MC MasterCard
- VI VISA

Hotels

Price guide: double room with breakfast for two people

- **$**   less than £50
- **$$**   £50–£100
- **$$$**   more than £100

Restaurants

Price guide: dinner per person, excluding drinks

- **$**   less than £15
- **$$**   £15–£30
- **$$$**   more than £30

A TASTE OF EAST ANGLIA

Norfolk has a long tradition of fishing and shooting; dressed crabs, mussels and game feature strongly on many local pub and restaurant menus, while smoked kippers are a specialty at Cley-next-the-Sea village smokehouse. The seaside plant samphire (similar to asparagus) is another regional favorite, and the area is renowned for growing culinary herbs such as thyme and rosemary.

Several suites have whirlpool baths and four-poster beds. The Mulberry Restaurant and the Wilton Room offer traditional English fare.
✉ Warminster, Wiltshire ☎ 01985 212312; fax 01985 216769
AX, DC, MC, VI

WELLS

⊞ **Beryl $$**
This friendly, family-run hotel is in a small Victorian mansion set in 13 acres of parkland.
✉ Hawkers Lane, Wells, Somerset ☎ 01749 678738 MC, VI

WILLITON

⊞ **White House $$–$$$**
There is a wonderfully relaxed and easy going air at this hotel on the Somerset coast, where fresh fish and local game feature on the menu.
✉ Long Street, Williton, Somerset ☎ 01984 632306 and 632777
🕐 Closed late Oct. to mid-May AX, MC, VI

Eastern England

ALDEBURGH

🍴 **Regatta $–$$**
A bright and child-friendly bistro in the center of town, Regatta features local fish and delicious fries.
✉ 171 High Street, Aldeburgh, Suffolk ☎ 01728 452011 🕐 Closed Mon.–Tue. and Sun. dinner; restricted opening in winter AX, DC, MC, VI

⊞ **Wentworth $$–$$$**
This popular hotel, just a short walk from the seafront, is family-run and has a welcoming atmosphere.
✉ Wentworth Road, Aldeburgh, Suffolk ☎ 01728 452312; fax 01728 454343 🕐 Closed Dec. 28–Jan. 9 AX, DC, MC, VI

AYLESBURY

⊞ **Hartwell House Hotel, Restaurant and Spa $$$**
A grand country mansion with service to match. Rooms, some in a converted stable block, are full of character. The dining room offers an elegant atmosphere in which to appreciate an imaginative menu.
✉ Oxford Road, Aylesbury, Buckinghamshire ☎ 01296 747444; fax 01296 747450 AX, MC, VI

BURNHAM MARKET

⊞ **Hoste Arms $$$**
This combination pub, restaurant and hotel is upscale and stylish in appearance, yet down-to-earth and unpretentious in atmosphere.
✉ The Green, Burnham Market, Norfolk ☎ 01328 738777; fax 01328 730103 MC, VI

BURY ST. EDMUNDS

⊞ **Angel $$–$$$**
This is an elegant Georgian house, close to the cathedral. Bedrooms are tastefully decorated with period furniture and include such thoughtful extras as books and mineral water. There also is a bar and restaurant.
✉ 12 Angel Hill, Bury St. Edmunds, Suffolk ☎ 01284 714000; fax 01284 714001 AX, DC, MC, VI

⊞ **The Priory $$–$$$**
Convenient to town and popular with business guests, this hotel has a restaurant with an ambitious menu.
✉ Tollgate, Bury St. Edmunds, Suffolk ☎ 01284 766181; fax 01284 767604 AX, DC, MC, VI

CAMBRIDGE

⊞ **Arundel House $$–$$$**
Converted from a terrace of Victorian town houses, this hotel is located next to the River Cam and overlooks parkland.
✉ Chesterton Road, Cambridge, Cambridgeshire ☎ 01223 367701; fax 01223 367721 AX, DC, MC, VI

🍴 **22 Chesterton Road $$**
Chesterton Road emphasizes unfussy English cooking with touches of classic French cuisine, served in a relaxed atmosphere. Guinness bread is a specialty.
✉ 22 Chesterton Road, Cambridge, Cambridgeshire ☎ 01223 351880 🕐 Closed Sun.–Mon., daily lunch, Jan.1 and Dec. 25 AX, DC, MC, VI

COLCHESTER

⊞ **The Rose and Crown $$**
Located in the center of town, this lovely 14th-century house has smart accommodations and a restaurant with an extensive menu.
✉ East Street, Colchester, Essex ☎ 01206 866677; fax 01206 866616 AX, DC, MC, VI

Eastern England

DEDHAM

Maison Talbooth $$$
This stylish hotel has a lovely riverside setting.
✉ Stratford Road, Dedham, Essex ☎ 01206 322367; fax 01206 322752 AX, DC, MC, VI

Le Talbooth $$–$$$
Located half a mile west of Dedham and housed in a black-and-white timbered building, this restaurant has stunning river views. You can dine on the terrace in summer. The food is full of flavor and complemented by a good wine list.
✉ Stratford St. Mary, near Dedham, Essex ☎ 01206 323150 🕔 Closed Sun. dinner in winter AX, DC, MC, VI

ELY

The Old Fire Engine House $$
Excellent regional English cuisine is on the menu at this friendly 18th-century restaurant-cum-art gallery. Try the pigeon pie or the jugged hare.
✉ 25 St. Mary's Street, Ely, Cambridgeshire ☎ 01353 662582 🕔 Closed Sun. dinner AX, MC, VI

Springfields $$
Enthusiastic and friendly proprietors offer bed and breakfast accommodations in their beautifully maintained, ranch-style house.
✉ Ely Road, Little Thetford, Ely, Cambridgeshire ☎ 01353 663637; fax 01353 663130 🕔 Closed Dec. No credit cards

IPSWICH

Hintlesham Hall $$$
This fine country house hotel is much applauded for its atmosphere, elegance, stylish restaurant menu and excellent wine list.
✉ Hintlesham, near Ipswich, Suffolk ☎ 01473 652334; fax 01473 652463 AX, MC, VI

KING'S LYNN

The Tudor Rose $
The oldest part of this cozy, centrally located inn dates back to 1187 and was originally part of the winter palace of a Norfolk bishop. There are medieval-style tapestries on the walls. Dishes range from ham, egg and chips to Mexican chili, as well

as some tasty light snacks.
✉ St. Nicholas Street, King's Lynn, Norfolk ☎ 01553 762824; fax 01553 764894 MC, VI

LAVENHAM

Angel Hotel $–$$
This 15th-century coaching inn in the center of medieval Lavenham offers traditional pub fare.
✉ Market Place, Lavenham, Suffolk ☎ 01787 247388 🕔 Closed Dec. 25–26 AX, MC, VI

Lavenham Priory $$–$$$
This is a prize-winning bed and breakfast in a 13th-century priory, tastefully furnished and set amid large, beautiful gardens.
✉ Water Street, Lavenham, Suffolk ☎ 01787 247404; fax 01787 248472 MC, VI

LINCOLN

The White Hart $$–$$$
Located within the old city walls between Lincoln's magnificent cathedral and castle, this hotel is attractively decorated. Many rooms have lovely views over the city.
✉ Bailgate, Lincoln, Lincolnshire ☎ 0870 400 8117; fax 01522 531798 AX, DC, MC, VI

Wig and Mitre $–$$
This 14th-century hostelry, on a steep, cobbled medieval street close to the cathedral, offers a comprehensive menu of good English home cooking.
✉ 30–32 Steep Hill, Lincoln, Lincolnshire ☎ 01522 535190 AX, DC, MC, VI

NORWICH

Adam and Eve $
Norwich's oldest pub (originally a brewhouse for workmen building the cathedral) is built around a Saxon well. Today it serves good, hearty pub fare.
✉ 17 Bishopsgate, Norwich, Norfolk ☎ 01603 667423 MC, VI

Adlard's $$$
A charming restaurant on a character-filled old street, Adlard's specializes in modern versions of classic French cuisine.
✉ 79 Upper St. Giles Street, Norwich, Norfolk ☎ 01603 633522

🕔 Closed Sun., Mon. lunch and 1 week after Christmas AX, MC, VI

Beeches Hotel and Victorian Gardens $$–$$$
A peaceful retreat within walking distance of the city center, this hotel has a noteworthy sunken Victorian garden on the spacious grounds. Bedrooms are well maintained, and there is a restaurant as well as a bar that serves snacks all day.
✉ 2–6 Earlham Road, Norwich, Norfolk ☎ 01603 621167; fax 01603 620150 AX, MC, VI

Brummels $$–$$$
Brummels is an easygoing, ever-popular fish restaurant serving both local and international dishes.
✉ 7 Magdalen Street, Norwich, Norfolk ☎ 01603 625555 AX, DC, MC, VI

By Appointment $$
Sumptuous furnishings and bold colors give this restaurant a theatrical and romantic setting. Excellent seafood is the mainstay, including sea bream with champagne cream sauce.
✉ 27–29 St. George's Street, Norwich, Norfolk ☎ 01603 630730 🕔 Closed Sun.–Mon., daily lunch and Dec. 25 MC, VI

The Georgian House $$–$$$
An informal, friendly family hotel, The Georgian House is a short walk from the city center and includes a cozy bar and an elegant restaurant.
✉ 32–34 Unthank Road, Norwich, Norfolk ☎ 01603 615655; fax 01603 765689 AX, DC, MC, VI

Marriott Sprowston Manor Hotel and Country Club $$$
Housed in a 19th-century manor on 10 acres of parkland on the outskirts of Norwich, this hotel has family rooms and full suites. The leisure facilities are excellent, and there is an adjacent golf course. Modern European cooking is served in the manor restaurant.
✉ Sprowston Park, Wroxham Road, Sprowston, Norwich, Norfolk ☎ 01603 410871; fax 01603 423911 AX, DC, MC, VI

The Merchant House $$
This small restaurant is tucked away down a side street in the ancient city center. Specialties include Thai

Eastern England

KEY TO SYMBOLS

- 🏨 hotel
- 🍴 restaurant
- ✉ address
- ☎ telephone number
- 🕐 days/times closed
- Ⓜ nearest metro/tube/subway station(s)

AX   American Express
DC   Diners Club
MC   MasterCard
VI   VISA

Hotels
Price guide: double room with breakfast for two people
$ less than £50
$$ £50–£100
$$$ more than £100

Restaurants
Price guide: dinner per person, excluding drinks
$ less than £15
$$ £15–£30
$$$ more than £30

GUIDE TO BEER: PART 1

Ale, beer, bitter, best ... they all mean the same thing: what the British like to drink in a pint glass at a temperature slightly lower than that of the room they are drinking it in. It tastes best when pulled through a hand-pump, or poured into the glass straight from the barrel. Color, flavor and strength vary enormously from one district to the next – and from one day to the next, since beer is a living and ever-changing thing. Remember that the pint you order will be a British pint – 20 fluid ounces (instead of the U.S. 16 fluid ounces). If your thirst isn't up to a British pint, order a half (10 fluid ounces).

crab cakes, and rice pudding with blueberry jam and honey ice cream.
✉ 8–10 St. Andrews Hill, Norwich, Norfolk ☎ 01603 767321 🕐 Closed Sun.–Mon., Jan. 1, 2 weeks in summer, Dec. 25–26 and 2 weeks in winter AX, MC, VI

🏨 Park Farm $$$
Located on 200 acres of farmland 3 miles southwest of Norwich, this hotel combines Georgian features with modern comforts.
✉ Hethersett, Norwich, Norfolk ☎ 01603 810264; fax 01603 812104 AX, DC, MC, VI

🍴 Ribs of Beef $
This riverside pub incorporates part of an original 14th-century building destroyed in Norwich's Great Fire of 1507. Simple but pleasing bar food is served at lunchtime.
✉ 24 Wensum Street, Norwich, Norfolk ☎ 01603 619517 AX, DC, MC, VI

🍴 The Wildebeest Arms $$
The decor is African in style at this dining pub, but the food is Provençale-influenced. There are real ales on tap.
✉ 82–86 Norwich Road, Stoke Holy Cross, Norwich, Norfolk ☎ 01508 492497 🕐 Closed Dec. 25–26 AX, DC, MC, VI

SAFFRON WALDEN

🍴 The Cricketers' Arms $$
This inn 3 miles southwest of Saffron Walden consists of Elizabethan timber-framed cottages facing the village green. There also are comfortable accommodations in a modern extension. The restaurant offers mussels and good curries.
✉ Rickling Green, Saffron Walden, Essex ☎ 01799 543210 AX, DC, MC, VI

🏨 Rowley Hill Lodge $
This small country guest house offers a friendly retreat. Breakfast is served around the large wooden table in the dining room.
✉ Little Walden, Saffron Walden, Essex ☎ 01799 525975; fax 01799 516622 No credit cards

STAMFORD

🏨 Garden House $$–$$$
The comfortable rooms at Garden House are only a short walk from the

town center. Light meals are served in the bar and conservatory; there also is a good restaurant.
✉ High Street, St. Martin's, Stamford, Lincolnshire ☎ 01780 763359; fax 01780 763339 AX, MC, VI

🏨 The George of Stamford $$$
The George offers excellent accommodations and service. The restaurant is particularly enticing in the summer, when you can eat outside in the walled courtyard. An extensive wine list complements the restaurant's imaginative menu; light meals also are served in the bar.
✉ 71 St. Martins, Stamford, Lincolnshire ☎ 01780 750750 or 750700 (reservations) AX, DC, MC, VI

STOKE-BY-NAYLAND

🍴 The Angel Inn $$
This deservedly popular 16th-century inn is surrounded by lovely countryside in the River Stour valley. Exposed brickwork, beams and open fireplaces provide a relaxed setting for superb pub-style meals.
✉ Polstead Street, Stoke-by-Nayland, Suffolk ☎ 01206 263245 🕐 Closed Jan. 1 and Dec. 25–26 MC, VI

TAPLOW

🏨 Cliveden $$$
This is one of England's great country houses, located on a 375-acre estate. Visitors are treated as "house guests," and the staff perpetuates the country house tradition of service. There are lovely views across the formal gardens while eating in The Terrace restaurant; or try Waldo's for serious dining in discreet, well-upholstered luxury.
✉ Taplow, Buckinghamshire ☎ 01628 668561; fax 01628 661837 AX, DC, MC, VI

WARE

🏨 Marriott Hanbury Manor Hotel and Country Club $$$
The Marriott chain's British flagship, this Jacobean-style mansion occupies 200 acres of grounds and gardens. Original features include wood paneling, crystal chandeliers, antiques and open fireplaces. There also are outstanding leisure facilities.
✉ Ware, Hertfordshire ☎ 01920 487722 or 08704 007222 AX, MC, VI

Heart of England

BISHOP'S TACHBROOK

⊞ Mallory Court $$$
This lovely English country house on
10 acres of grounds is only a short
drive from Warwick Castle. Many
rooms have garden views, and some
have art deco bathrooms. The paneled
restaurant serves innovative cuisine.
⊠ Harbury Lane, Bishop's
Tachbrook, Royal Leamington Spa,
Warwickshire ☎ 01926 330214;
fax 01926 451714 AX, DC, MC, VI

BRIMFIELD

🍴 The Roebuck Inn $–$$
This 15th-century country inn near
Ludlow features a snug bar frequented
by locals and a beautiful dining room
serving very good pub food.
⊠ Brimfield, Ludlow, Herefordshire
☎ 01584 711230 ⊘ Closed Dec.
25–26 MC, VI

BUCKLAND

⊞ Buckland Manor $$$
Occupying extensive grounds near
the lovely Cotswold village of
Broadway, this imposing 15th-
century manor house has high-
quality accommodations and an
excellent restaurant.
⊠ Buckland, near Broadway,
Gloucestershire ☎ 01386 852626;
fax 01386 853557 AX, DC, MC, VI

BURFORD

🍴 The Lamb Inn $$
This vine-clad Cotswold inn, located
in the pretty village of Burford,
serves traditional, seasonal fare
with flair. Flagstone floors, antique
furnishings and open fireplaces all
add to the character.
Accommodations also are available.
⊠ Sheep Street, Burford, Oxfordshire
☎ 01993 823155 ⊘ Closed Sun.
dinner MC, VI

CHELTENHAM

🍴 Le Champignon Sauvage $$
Long-standing excellence in cooking,
decor and hospitality are maintained
at this very well-known and
respected city restaurant.
⊠ 24 Suffolk Road, Cheltenham,
Gloucestershire ☎ 01242 573449
⊘ Closed Sun.–Mon., 3 weeks in

Jun. and 10 days at Christmas AX,
DC, MC, VI

⊞ Hotel on the Park $$$
Polished, professional service
awaits visitors at this elegant
townhouse in the heart of
Cheltenham. Day rooms include a
bar, restaurant and drawing room, all
luxuriously furnished. The restaurant
serves excellent food.
⊠ 38 Evesham Road, Cheltenham,
Gloucestershire ☎ 01242 518898;
fax 01242 511526 AX, DC, MC, VI

CHIPPING CAMPDEN

⊞ Noel Arms $$$
Excellent food is served both in the
restaurant and bar of this 14th-
century inn in the heart of Chipping
Campden. Rooms are individually
furnished and have smart, modern
en suite facilities.
⊠ High Street, Chipping Campden,
Gloucestershire ☎ 01386 840317;
fax 01386 841136 AX, DC, MC, VI

GREAT MILTON

**⊞ Le Manoir Aux Quat' Saisons
$$$**
This 15th-century, mellow-stone
manor house, surrounded by
immaculate gardens, is 4 miles
southwest of Oxford. Beautifully
appointed bedrooms and suites offer
superb comfort, and some have their
own private terrace gardens. The
restaurant's cuisine, overseen by
chef Raymond Blanc, is outstanding.
⊠ Church Road, Great Milton,
Oxfordshire ☎ 01844 278881;
fax 01844 278847 AX, DC, MC, VI

HENLEY-ON-THAMES

⊞ Red Lion $$$
This attractively furnished hotel
is located on the riverside. Meals
are served in both the bar and
the restaurant.
⊠ Hart Street, Henley-on-Thames,
Oxfordshire ☎ 01491 572161;
fax 01491 410039 AX, MC, VI

HEREFORD

🍴 The Ancient Camp Inn $$
There are lovely views over the River
Wye from the terrace of this country
pub, built on the site of an Iron Age
fort 3 miles west of Hereford. The
food is very good.

⊠ Ruckhall, Hereford,
Herefordshire ☎ 01981 250449
⊘ Closed Mon., Sun. dinner and 3
weeks in Feb. MC, VI

⊞ The Green Dragon $$
This comfortable hotel, close to the
cathedral, also is renowned for
afternoon tea.
⊠ Broad Street, Hereford,
Herefordshire ☎ 0870 400 8113;
fax 01432 352139 AX, MC, VI

KINNERSLEY

⊞ Upper Newton Farmhouse $
Pearl and John Taylor run this
exceptionally friendly, well-organized
and first-class bed and breakfast.
⊠ Kinnersley, near Hay-on-Wye,
Herefordshire ☎ 01544 327727;
fax 01544 327727 No credit cards

LUDLOW

🍴 The Clive Restaurant $$–$$$
Beautifully presented, high-quality
English fare is served at this elegant
restaurant, just north of Ludlow.
Accommodations are available also.
⊠ Bromfield, near Ludlow,
Shropshire ☎ 01584 856565; fax
01584 856661 MC, VI

⊞ Feathers $$
Famous for its extraordinary carved
woodwork facade, this picturesque
hotel is one of Ludlow's best-known
landmarks. Rooms are furnished in
traditional style; English and French
cuisine is served in the restaurant.
⊠ The Bull Ring, Ludlow,
Shropshire ☎ 01584 875261; fax
01584 876030 AX, DC, MC, VI

OAKHAM

⊞ Hambleton Hall $$$
The epitome of an English country
house hotel, Hambleton Hall stands
in beautiful gardens against the lake
backdrop of Rutland Water. The
kitchen turns out top-quality dishes
using the best ingredients, and the
wine list is impressive.
⊠ Hambleton, Oakham, Rutland
☎ 01572 756991; fax 01572 724721
AX, DC, MC, VI

OUNDLE

🍴 The Mill at Oundle $
The River Nene flows right under the
bar at this converted water mill.

KEY TO SYMBOLS

🏨	hotel
🍴	restaurant
✉	address
☎	telephone number
🕐	days/times closed
Ⓜ	nearest metro/tube/subway station(s)
AX	American Express
DC	Diners Club
MC	MasterCard
VI	VISA

Hotels

Price guide: double room with breakfast for two people

$ less than £50
$$ £50–£100
$$$ more than £100

Restaurants

Price guide: dinner per person, excluding drinks

$ less than £15
$$ £15–£30
$$$ more than £30

GUIDE TO BEER: PART 2

If you really get the taste for beer, consider investing in a copy of the *Good Beer Guide*, published annually by the advocacy group Campaign for Real Ale (CAMRA). The campaigners have successfully resisted the big breweries' attempts to replace traditional beer – which is difficult to maintain in tip-top condition, but rewarding to drink – with fizzy pasteurized stuff that tastes blandly chemical but keeps for months. The *Good Beer Guide* lists thousands of pubs which serve beer the old-fashioned – and best – way.

Good pub food can be enjoyed as you watch the boats go by.
✉ Barnwell Mill, Oundle, Northamptonshire ☎ 01832 272621 AX, DC, MC, VI

🏨 Talbot $$

An atmosphere of Old World charm prevails at this coaching inn in the heart of Oundle.
✉ New Street, Oundle, Northamptonshire ☎ 01832 273621; fax 01832 274545 AX, MC, VI

OXFORD

🍴 Cherwell Boathouse $

Enjoy an afternoon by the river at this popular restaurant. The menu offers modern English food and there is an excellent set-price lunch.
✉ Bardwell Street, Oxford, Oxfordshire ☎ 01865 552746; fax 01865 553819 MC, VI

🏨 Eastgate $$$

Eastgate is a relaxing hotel with an informal atmosphere. It's close to Magdalen Bridge and has views of the famous Examination Schools.
✉ 73 High Street, Oxford, Oxfordshire ☎ 0870 400 8201; fax 01865 791681 AX, DC, MC, VI

🏨 Gables $$

A very comfortable and welcoming bed and breakfast on the western edge of the city, Gables has a conservatory and pleasant gardens.
✉ 6 Cumnor Hill, Oxford, Oxfordshire ☎ 01865 862153; fax 01865 864054 🕐 Closed Dec. 24–Jan. 1 MC, VI

🏨 Linton Lodge $$$

A peaceful hotel in a residential area north of the city center, Linton Lodge has a wood-paneled restaurant and a bar overlooking the croquet lawn.
✉ Linton Road, Oxford, Oxfordshire ☎ 01865 553461; fax 01865 553691 AX, MC, VI

🏨 Parklands Hotel $$

Parklands is a delightful hotel in a leafy residential area near to the town centre.
✉ 100 Banbury Road, Oxford, Oxfordshire ☎ 01865 515688 MC, VI

🍴 Le Petit Blanc Brasserie $$

This restaurant boasts a stylish interior, good service and a punchy, modern menu. The Mediterranean fish soup and the *moules marinière* (with *frites*, of course) are favorites.
✉ 71–72 Walton Street, Oxford, Oxfordshire ☎ 01865 510999 🕐 Closed Dec. 25 AX, DC, MC, VI

🏨 Pine Castle $$

A friendly welcome is guaranteed at this hotel, which occupies a late Victorian house convenient to the city center.
✉ 290–292 Iffley Road, Oxford, Oxfordshire ☎ 01865 241497; fax 01865 727230 MC, VI

🍴 Quod $$

Set in a former Geogian banking hall, Quod is a smart, buzzy restaurant serving Italian inspired, quality food.
✉ 92–94 High Street, Oxford, Oxfordshire ☎ 01865 202505 MC, VI

🏨 The Randolph $$$

This landmark Victorian hotel stands opposite the Ashmolean Museum. Renowned afternoon teas are served in the drawing room, and there is formal dining in Spires restaurant.
✉ Beaumont Street, Oxford, Oxfordshire ☎ 0870 400 8200; fax 01865 791678 AX, DC, MC, VI

🍴 The White House $

This pub, housed in an old tollhouse, serves well-cooked, delicious food and offers a range of beers.
✉ 2 Botley Road, Oxford, Oxfordshire ☎ 01865 242823 AX, DC, MC, VI

SHREWSBURY

🍴 Cromwells Hotel and Restaurant Bar $$

The oak-paneled restaurant offers internationally inspired dishes. Leave room for the delicious desserts.
✉ 11 Dogpole, Shrewsbury, Shropshire ☎ 01743 361440 MC, VI

STRATFORD-UPON-AVON

🍴 The Boathouse $$

Eat lunch or dinner enjoying the river views, then stroll along the River Avon to the Royal Shakespeare Company Theatre to see one of the Bard's plays. You also can rent a boat at the restaurant and cruise there.
✉ Swan's Nest Lane, Stratford-upon-Avon, Warwickshire ☎ 01789 297733 🕐 Closed Sun.–Tue. and Sat. lunch AX, MC, VI

🏠 Monk's Barn Farm $

A friendly bed and breakfast at a working farm, Monk's Barn is near the village of Clifford Chambers, a mile south of Stratford-upon-Avon.
✉ Shipston Road, Stratford-upon-Avon, Warwickshire ☎ 01789 293714; fax 01789 205886 MC, VI

TETBURY

🏠 The Close $$–$$$

This hotel has a warm country-house feel, with log fires in winter and a terrace in a walled garden for summer relaxation.
✉ 8 Long Street, Tetbury, Gloucestershire ☎ 01666 502272; fax 01666 504401 AX, MC, VI

WALLINGFORD

🏠 Beetle and Wedge $$$

Beautifully located on the edge of the River Thames, there are wonderful river views from many of this hotel's rooms and also from the dining rooms (brasserie-style or more formal).
✉ Ferry Lane, Moulsford, Wallingford, Oxfordshire ☎ 01491 651381 ⏱ Closed Sun. dinner and Mon. AX, MC, VI

WARWICK

🍴 Tudor House Inn $

This ornately timbered medieval inn at the gates of Warwick Castle has good hearty bar food that will revive visitors who are all castled out.
✉ 90–92 West Street, Warwick, Warwickshire ☎ 01926 495447 MC, VI

WOOTTON

🍴 Kings Head Inn $$$

A Tudor inn of Cotswold stone, located near Woodstock and Blenheim Palace, the Kings Head offers good imaginative cooking such as scallops with chili and lime.
✉ Chapel Hill, Wootton, Oxfordshire ☎ 01993 811340 MC, VI

Wales

ABERDYFI

🍴 Penhelig Arms Hotel $$

Fresh local fish is a specialty at this delightful Georgian inn, overlooking the broad Dyfi estuary on Cardigan Bay.

✉ Aberdyfi, Gwynedd ☎ 01654 767215 ⏱ Closed Dec. 25–26 MC, VI

ABERGAVENNY

🍴 Walnut Tree Inn $$–$$$

Much more than a pub, the Walnut Tree is famous for its daily specials with a Mediterranean flavor. It's convenient for those visiting the Black Mountains and the Brecon Beacons.
✉ Llandewi Skirrid, Abergavenny, Monmouthshire ☎ 01873 852797 ⏱ Closed Sun.–Mon. and bank holiday dinner MC, VI

ABERYSTWYTH

🏠 Conrah $$$

Beautifully located 3 miles south of Aberystwyth, the Conrah has spectacular views of the Cambrian Mountains. The hotel restaurant features local ingredients, including Black Welsh Mountain beef.
✉ Ffosrhydygaled, Chancery, Aberystwyth, Ceredigion ☎ 01970 617941; fax 01970 624546 ⏱ Closed Christmas week AX, DC, MC, VI

🏠 Queensbridge $$

This friendly hotel on the promenade is well-equipped, and many of the rooms have fine sea views.
✉ Promenade, Victoria Terrace, Aberystwyth, Ceredigion ☎ 01970 612343; fax 01970 617452 AX, DC, MC, VI

BETWS-Y-COED

🏠 Tan-y-Foel Country House $$

Many of the rooms here have lovely country views and thoughtful extras. An expert kitchen delivers both Welsh and international dishes in this well-maintained manor house in dramatically beautiful Snowdonia.
✉ Capel Garmon, Betws-y-Coed, Conwy ☎ 01690 710507; fax 01690 710681 MC, VI

BONTDDU

🏠 Borthwnog Hall $$

This 17th-century country house adjoins Garth Gell nature reserve on the Mawddach Estuary, in the south of Snowdonia National Park. Rooms are spacious, and one has its own separate sitting room. The Library Art Gallery contains original watercolors

and oils, and examples of pottery and sculpture can be purchased.
✉ Bontddu, Dolgellau, Gwynedd ☎ 01341 430271; fax 01341 430682 AX, MC, VI

CAPEL CURIG

🏠 Cobdens $

The mountaineering crowd frequents the bars at Cobdens, deep in the dramatic landscape of Snowdonia.
✉ Capel Curig, Conwy ☎ 01690 720243; fax 01690 720354 MC, VI

CARDIFF

🍴 Bistro 10 $$

This stylish eatery has a real buzz about it and attracts locals and tourists alike. Flavors are modern European with Italian influences.
✉ Unit 10, Mermaid Quay, Cardiff ☎ 029 2048 7070 MC, VI

🏠 Cardiff Marriott $$$

Ideally located in the city center, this large, modern hotel features smart new public areas and a good range of services. Eating options include the Chats café bar and the contemporary Mediterrano restaurant. Air-conditioned bedrooms are comfortable and furnished to a high standard. On-site parking.
✉ Mill Lane, Cardiff ☎ 029 2039 9944; fax 029 2039 5578 AX, DC, MC, VI

🏠 Copthorne Hotel Cardiff Caerdydd $$–$$$

Conveniently located for the city and the airport, this modern hotel and Raglans Restaurant overlook a lake. Leisure facilities include a swimming pool, sauna, gym and steam room.
✉ Copthorne Way, Culverhouse Cross, Cardiff ☎ 029 2059 9100; fax 029 2059 9080 AX, DC, MC, VI

🏠 Express by Holiday Inn Hotel and Conference Centre-Cardiff Bay $$

This smart, stylish hotel is on the new Cardiff Bay waterfront. The hotel has proved so popular that it recently doubled in size. It has excellent leisure facilities.
✉ Longueil Close, off Schooner Way, Atlantic Wharf, Cardiff ☎ 029 2044 9000; fax 029 2048 8922 AX, DC, MC, VI

Wales

KEY TO SYMBOLS

- ⊞ hotel
- ⊞ restaurant
- ✉ address
- ☎ telephone number
- ⊙ days/times closed
- Ⓜ nearest metro/tube/subway station(s)
- AX American Express
- DC Diners Club
- MC MasterCard
- VI VISA

Hotels

Price guide: double room with breakfast for two people
- **$** less than £50
- **$$** £50–£100
- **$$$** more than £100

Restaurants

Price guide: dinner per person, excluding drinks
- **$** less than £15
- **$$** £15–£30
- **$$$** more than £30

LOCAL RECOMMENDATIONS

Bed and breakfast (commonly known as B&B): Generally this means exactly what it says, a private house where you can find a bed for the night and a good breakfast the next morning. Very often these are the pleasantest places to stay in – not only because the host and hostess have their own personal pride and reputation on the line, but because they are only too happy to give you all the local gossip, along with their own worthwhile recommendations about what to see and where to eat.

⊞ Le Gallois-Y-Cymro $$$

Fish and meat are both beautifully cooked and complemented by a well-chosen wine list at one of Wales' brightest and best restaurants.
✉ 6-10 Romilly Crescent, Cardiff ☎ 029 2034 1264 ⊙ Closed Sun.–Mon., Jan 1, 1 week in Aug. and Dec. 25 AX, MC, VI

⊞ Gilby's $$

A lively place, Gilby's is popular for its seafood and local Welsh lamb.
✉ Old Port Road, Culverhouse Cross, Cardiff ☎ 029 2067 0800 ⊙ Closed Mon., Sun. dinner, 1 week in Jan., 2 weeks in Sep. and bank holidays AX, MC, VI

⊞ New House Hotel $$

A Georgian mansion in northern Cardiff, the New House has fantastic views across the city and Bristol Channel to the Somerset hills. The hotel restaurant offers an imaginative and ambitious menu.
✉ Thornhill, Cardiff ☎ 029 2052 0280 ⊙ Closed Jan. 1 and Dec. 26 AX, DC, MC, VI

⊞ St. David's Hotel and Spa $$$

Right on the Cardiff Bay waterfront, this very stylish new hotel has an impressive seven-story atrium and contemporary decor throughout. The bedrooms have their own balconies overlooking the bay, and leisure facilities are excellent.
✉ Havannah Street, Cardiff ☎ 029 2045 4045; fax 029 2048 7056 AX, DC, MC, VI

CHEPSTOW

⊞ Marriott St. Pierre Hotel and Country Club $$$

Hospitable leisure hotel with its own championship golf course. Rooms are either in the main house, at the lakeside or in the cottage suites.
✉ St. Pierre Park, Chepstow, Monmouthshire ☎ 01291 625261; fax 01291 629975 AX, DC, MC, VI

CRICKHOWELL

⊞ Bear $$–$$$

This 15th-century inn sits at the foot of the Black Mountains. The restaurant's good cooking takes advantage of local produce.
✉ Crickhowell, Powys ☎ 01873 810408; fax 01873 811696 AX, MC, VI

GELLILYDAN

⊞ Tyddyn-Du $$

This Tudor farmhouse, set amid spectacular scenery, is convenient to the nearby Ffestiniog railway. Delicious farmhouse food is created by the hostess.
✉ Gellilydan, near Porthmadog ☎ 01766 590281; fax 01766 590281 No credit cards

GREAT ORMES HEAD

⊞ The Lighthouse $$$

This former lighthouse is set on the northern edge of Great Orme, the spectacular headland northwest of Llandudno. One of the rooms is in the lighthouse's glazed dome. Each room is equipped with a pair of binoculars so guests can peruse the stunning views to the Irish Sea.
✉ Marine Drive, Great Orme's Head, Llandudno, Conwy ☎ 01492 876819; fax 01492 876668 MC, VI

HAY-ON-WYE

⊞ Old Black Lion Hotel $$

This fine old coaching inn was occupied by Oliver Cromwell during the English Civil War. The charming, cozy bar serves good pub food, and there also is a restaurant.
✉ 26 Lion Street, Hay-on-Wye, Powys ☎ 01497 820841 ⊙ Closed Dec. 25–26 MC, VI

⊞ The Swan-at-Hay $$–$$$

Accommodations at this hotel close to the town center are in former cottages. There also is a pleasant restaurant.
✉ Church Street, Hay-on-Wye, Powys ☎ 01497 821188; fax 01497 821424 AX, DC, MC, VI

LLANDUDNO

⊞ St. Tudno $$–$$$

This hotel has a popular restaurant, and reservations are advisable. The local seafood is particularly good.
✉ The Promenade, Llandudno, Conwy ☎ 01492 874411; fax 01492 860407 AX, DC, MC, VI

LLANGOLLEN

⊞ The Famous Britannia Inn $

At the foot of scenically stunning Horseshoe Pass, 1 mile from Llangollen, this old inn has beautiful gardens and serves enjoyable inn fare. Accommodations also are available.

✉ Horseshoe Pass, Llangollen, Denbighshire ☎ 01978 860144 AX, MC, VI

🏨 The Royal $$

This traditional hotel, where Queen Victoria once stayed, is located in the center of town overlooking the River Dee.

✉ Bridge Street, Llangollen, Denbighshire ☎ 01978 860202; fax 01978 861824 AX, DC, MC, VI

LLYSWEN

🏨 Llangoed Hall $$$

This imposing Edwardian country house is located amid Wye Valley parkland. Guests enjoy comfort and grandeur in the day rooms and library, and bedrooms are furnished with antiques. The menu has a Mediterranean and Provençal twist.

✉ Llyswen, Powys ☎ 01874 754525; fax 01874 754545 AX, DC, MC, VI

OLD RADNOR

🍴 Harp Inn $

This 15th-century pub, located beside a medieval church, has character and great views.

✉ Old Radnor, Presteigne, Powys ☎ 01544 350655 MC, VI

PARKMILL

🏨 Parc-le-Breos House $–$$

This 19th-century country house, the hub of a working farm, sits on 70 acres of grounds. Horseback riding is available.

✉ Parkmill, Gower Peninsula, Swansea ☎ 01792 371636; fax 01792 371287 No credit cards

PORTMEIRION

🏨 The Hotel Portmeirion $$$

Located in the heart of the make-believe village of Portmeirion, many rooms have balconies and private sitting rooms with spectacular views of the village and Traeth Bach Estuary. An art deco dining room offers modern Welsh cooking with a smattering of Mediterranean flavors.

✉ Portmeirion, Gwynedd ☎ 01766 770000; fax 01766 771331 AX, DC, MC, VI

ST. DAVID'S

🍴 Morgan's Brasserie $$

Simply decorated surroundings give center stage to the culinary arts at Morgan's. The menu is complemented by daily specials relying on fresh local ingredients.

✉ 20 Nun Street, St. David's, Pembrokeshire ☎ 01437 720508 AX, MC, VI

🏨 Warpool Court $$$

The main part of this Victorian hotel was originally the St. David's Cathedral's choir school. The lovely landscaped gardens have views of the sea, as do some of the rooms.

✉ St. David's, Pembrokeshire ☎ 01437 720300; fax 01437 720676 ⓘ Closed Jan. AX, DC, MC, VI

Northern England

AMBLESIDE

🍴 Drunken Duck Inn $$

This Tudor pub is located in the scenic heart of the Lake District.

✉ Barngates, Ambleside, Cumbria ☎ 015394 36347 ⓘ Closed Dec. 25 AX, MC, VI

BAKEWELL

🍴 Rutland Arms Hotel $$

Popular for both the Tavern Bar and the Four Seasons Restaurant, this Georgian inn on Bakewell's central square is said to be where Jane Austen wrote *Pride and Prejudice*.

✉ The Square, Bakewell, Derbyshire ☎ 01629 812812 AX, DC, MC, VI

BASLOW

🏨 Cavendish $$$

This is a country house among wooded hills on the edge of Chatsworth estate. Several of the works of art adorning the walls have been loaned by the Duke and Duchess of Devonshire (the estate's owners).

✉ Baslow, Derbyshire ☎ 01246 582311; fax 01246 582312 AX, DC, MC, VI

BEAMISH

🏨 Beamish Park $$

This hotel is near Beamish, The North of England Open Air Museum. International bistro food is served in the conservatory. There also is a classically styled dining room.

✉ Beamish Burn Road, Marley Hill, Beamish ☎ 01207 230666; fax 01207 281260 AX, DC, MC, VI

BLANCHLAND

🍴 Lord Crewe Arms Hotel $$

One of England's oldest inns, the Lord Crewe is full of ghosts and character. It's a convenient place to stop for lunch while exploring Hadrian's Wall.

✉ Blanchland, County Durham ☎ 01434 675251 AX, DC, MC, VI

BOLTON ABBEY

🏨 The Devonshire Arms Country House $$$

This very stylish country house hotel, owned by the Duke and Duchess of Devonshire, is situated at the foot of glorious Wharfedale, in the heart of the Yorkshire Dales.

✉ Bolton Abbey, Skipton, North Yorkshire ☎ 01756 710441; fax 01756 710564 AX, DC, MC, VI

CHESTER

🏨 The Chester Grosvenor and Grosvenor Spa $$$

Located adjacent to the Eastgate Clock and within the old city walls, the hotel serves elegant food. Guests can relax in the library bar to peruse the menu at their leisure.

✉ Eastgate, Chester, Cheshire ☎ 01244 324024; fax 01244 313246 AX, DC, MC, VI

DURHAM

🍴 Bistro 21 $$

A former farmhouse with stone-flagged floors and stone walls offers excellent value from a simple menu.

✉ Aykley Heads House, Aykley Heads, Durham, County Durham ☎ 0191 384 4354 ⓘ Closed Sun., Jan. 1, Dec. 25 and bank holidays AX, DC, MC, VI

🏨 Durham Marriott Hotel, Royal County $$$

This is a centally located, riverside hotel with extensive leisure facilities that include a swimming pool, sauna, gym, Jacuzzi and spa. Weekly live entertainment.

✉ Old Elvet, Durham, County Durham ☎ 0191 386 6821; fax 0191 386 0704 AX, DC, MC, VI

Northern England

KEY TO SYMBOLS

⊞ hotel
🍴 restaurant
✉ address
☎ telephone number
🕐 days/times closed
Ⓜ nearest metro/tube/subway
    station(s)
AX American Express
DC Diners Club
MC MasterCard
VI VISA

Hotels

Price guide: double room with
breakfast for two people
$ less than £50
$$ £50–£100
$$$ more than £100

Restaurants

Price guide: dinner per person,
excluding drinks
$ less than £15
$$ £15–£30
$$$ more than £30

MORE THAN A SANDWICH

In recent years there has been a
revolution in pub food. Not long
ago, very few pubs offered more
than a cheese sandwich;
nowadays the vast majority serve
decent food at reasonable prices.
Many have extensive menus with
dozens of items listed on a chalk
board. It's a relaxing way to eat,
enjoying wholesome food which
you can accompany with a pint of
the local brew.

GOATHLAND

⊞ Mallyan Spout $$–$$$

The famous Mallyan Spout waterfall
forms a backdrop for this ivy-clad
Victorian hotel in a scenic village in
North York Moors National Park.
Fresh fish from nearby Whitby is a
feature of the restaurant menu.
✉ The Common, Goathland, North
Yorkshire ☎ 01947 896486;
fax 01947 896327 MC, VI

HARROGATE

⊞ The Boar's Head $$$

The Boar's Head is an old inn
convenient to Harrogate, luxuriously
refurbished by Sir Thomas and Lady
Ingilby of nearby Ripley Castle.
✉ Ripley Castle Estate, Harrogate,
North Yorkshire ☎ 01423 771888;
fax 01423 771509 AX, DC, MC, VI

🍴 The Courtyard $$

Occupying an attractive corner of
Harrogate just west of Parliament
Street, this Mediterranean-style
restaurant offers relaxed service and
good-quality cuisine.
✉ 1 Montpellier Mews, Harrogate,
North Yorkshire ☎ 01423 530708
🕐 Closed Sun., Jan. 1 and Dec.
25–26 MC, VI

HAWORTH

🍴 Weavers $$

Set in a trio of weavers' cottages
close to the Brontë Parsonage
Museum, this restaurant offers both
modern and traditional British dishes
featuring seasonal local ingredients.
✉ 15 West Lane, Haworth, West
Yorkshire ☎ 01535 643822
🕐 Closed Mon., Tue. and Sat.
lunch, Sun. dinner, 1 week in Jun.
and 1 week at Christmas AX, DC,
MC, VI

HEXHAM

⊞ Beaumont $$$

Popular with business guests and
tourists, the Beaumont overlooks a
park in the town.
✉ Beaumont Street, Hexham,
Northumberland ☎ 01434 602331;
fax 01434 606184 AX, DC, MC, VI

HOPE

🍴 Cheshire Cheese Inn $

A 400-year-old inn in the heart of the
Peak District, the Cheshire Cheese
serves good food and local beers.
✉ Edale Road, Hope, Derbyshire
☎ 01433 620381 AX, MC, VI

LEEDS

⊞ Haley's $$$

The restaurant at this elegant hotel,
conveniently located north of the city
center, serves modern British cuisine.
✉ Shire Oak Road, Headingley, Leeds,
West Yorkshire ☎ 0113 278 4446;
fax 0113 275 3342 🕐 Closed Dec.
26–30 AX, MC, VI

🍴 Simply Heathcotes Leeds $$

This is a stylish, split-level
restaurant housed in an old granary
warehouse. Wooden floors and
linen-covered tables provide the
perfect backdrop for modern British
cooking.
✉ Canal Wharf, Water Lane, Leeds,
West Yorkshire ☎ 0113 244 6611
🕐 Closed Jan. 1–2, Dec. 25–26 and
Mon. bank holidays AX, DC, MC, VI

LIVERPOOL

🍴 Metro $$

This snappy, stylish restaurant
serves well-presented,
Mediterranean inspired dishes.
✉ 5–9 Fowlers Building, Victoria
Street, Liverpool, Merseyside
☎ 0151 236 2200; fax 0151 236
2266 MC, VI

⊞ Liverpool Marriott Hotel City
Centre $$$

This impressive modern hotel is
located in the newly developed
Queen Square area, close to St.
George's Hall. Accommodations are
elegant and spacious; there also is a
recreation center and a restaurant.
✉ 1 Queen Square, Liverpool,
Merseyside ☎ 0151 476 8000;
fax 0151 474 5000 AX, DC, MC, VI

MANCHESTER

⊞ Marriott Worsley Park Hotel
and Country Club $$$

This friendly, modern hotel is within
easy reach of the city center. The
leisure facilities include a golf course.
✉ Worsley Park, Worsley,
Manchester ☎ 0161 975 2000; fax
0161 799 6341 AX, DC, MC, VI

🍴 Le Bouchon $$

Classic French elegance awaits at

this intimate, yet affordable, friendly restaurant. Gallic prints line the walls and the tables are set with crisp white linen and sparkling crystal, creating a wonderful romantic ambience.

✉ 63 Budge Street, Manchester ☎ 0161 832 9393 MC, VI

MOLLINGTON

🍽 The Chester Crabwall Manor Hotel $$$

A turreted 17th-century manor house, Crabwall Manor offers traditional country house cuisine with subtle Mediterranean overtones.

✉ Parkgate Road, Mollington, near Chester, Cheshire ☎ 01244 851666 🕐 Closed Sat. lunch AX, DC, MC, VI

PICKERING

🏨 Forest and Vale $$–$$$

Several rooms in this pleasant hotel have four-poster beds; varied food is served in the bar and restaurant.

✉ Malton Road, Pickering, North Yorkshire ☎ 01751 472722; fax 01751 472972 AX, MC, VI

🍽 White Swan $$

Located in the marketplace between the church and the steam railroad station, this cozy paneled bar has a warm atmosphere.

✉ Market Place, Pickering, North Yorkshire ☎ 01751 472288 AX, MC, VI

RICHMOND

🍽 Charles Bathurst Inn $$

This inn, in remote and stunningly beautiful Arkengarthdale, features traditional open fireplaces, wooden floors and a relaxed atmosphere in which to enjoy freshly cooked seafood.

✉ Arkengarthdale, Richmond, North Yorkshire ☎ 01748 884567 MC, VI

SETTLE

🍽 Golden Lion $$

The Golden Lion is located in Settle's old marketplace. Diner's can choose between a hearty three-course meal in the restaurant or a light meal in the bar.

✉ Duke Street, Settle, North Yorkshire ☎ 01729 822203 MC, VI

🏨 Liverpool House $$

Close to the city center, this building was originally a gatehouse for an intended waterway link to the Leeds–Liverpool Canal. The bedrooms on the top floor have ceiling beams and are all comfortably furnished. A hearty breakfast is served in the dining room.

✉ Chapel Square, Settle, North Yorkshire ☎ 01729 822247 MC, VI

WASDALE HEAD

🍽 Wasdale Head Inn $$

Bulging with character, this inn boasts an incomparably beautiful and hauntingly lonely location in the Lake District. Rooms are available.

✉ Wasdale Head, Cumbria ☎ 019467 26229 AX, MC, VI

WINDERMERE

🏨 Holbeck Ghyll Country House $$$

The dramatic profiles of the Langdale Pikes are in view from this charming hotel, often with a beautiful sunset providing a fine backdrop as you enjoy dinner. Some rooms have private balconies.

✉ Holbeck Lane, Windermere, Cumbria ☎ 015394 32375; fax 015394 34743 AX, DC, MC, VI

YORK

🏨 Dean Court $$$

This city center hotel opposite York Minster provides quiet, comfortable rooms, in an ideal location for seeing the city sights.

✉ Duncombe Place, York, North Yorkshire ☎ 01904 625082; fax 01904 620305 AX, DC, MC, VI

🏨 Holgate Bridge $

This friendly, family-run hotel offers dinner as well as accommodations and is within easy walking distance of the medieval city center.

✉ 106–108 Holgate Road, York, North Yorkshire ☎ 01904 635971; fax 01904 670049 MC, VI

🏨 The Judges Lodging $$$

This is a renovated Georgian building in the city's pedestrianized area, a few minutes' walk from the Minster. All the bedrooms are comfortable and the serivce is excellent.

✉ 9 Lendal, York, North Yorkshire ☎ 01904 638733; fax 01904 679947 MC, VI

🏨 Knavesmire Manor $$

Friendly and full of character, Knavesmire Manor overlooks the York racecourse.

✉ 302 Tadcaster Road, York, North Yorkshire ☎ 01904 702941; fax 01904 709274 AX, DC, MC, VI

🍽 Melton's $$

This converted Victorian shop is decorated with prints by local artists. It is a fashionable and popular restaurant, renowned for its wine list.

✉ 7 Scarcroft Road, York, North Yorkshire ☎ 01904 634341 🕐 Closed Sun., Mon. lunch, 1 week in Aug. and 3 weeks at Christmas DC, MC, VI

🏨 Middlethorpe Hall Hotel, Resataurant and Spa $$$

This magnificent King William III country house is less than 2 miles from York city center. Guests can walk in the restored gardens, and the house contains fine paintings, furniture, and antiques.

✉ Bishopthorpe Road, Middlethorpe, York, North Yorkshire ☎ 01904 641241; fax 01904 620176 MC, VI

🏨 York Pavilion $$$

This comfortable hotel, set in lovely grounds, has an informal, brasserie-style restaurant with an inventive menu and knockout puddings.

✉ 45 Main Street, Fulford, York, North Yorkshire ☎ 01904 622099; fax 01904 626939 AX, DC, MC, VI

Scotland

ABERDEEN

🏨 Copthorne Hotel Aberdeen $$–$$$

Centrally located, the Copthorne Aberdeen has a restaurant specializing in emphatically Scottish dishes utilizing fresh local produce.

✉ 122 Huntly Street, Aberdeen ☎ 01224 630404; fax 01224 640573 AX, DC, MC, VI

🏨 Dunavon House $$

The bedrooms in this Victorian villa are attractive and well equipped, and the inviting lounge bar and restaurant offer an excellent range of dishes at both lunch and dinner.

✉ 60 Victoria Street, Dyce, Aberdeen ☎ 01224 722483; fax 01224 772721 AX, MC, VI

Scotland

KEY TO SYMBOLS

- 🏨 hotel
- 🍴 restaurant
- ✉ address
- ☎ telephone number
- 🕐 days/times closed
- Ⓜ nearest metro/tube/subway station(s)
- AX American Express
- DC Diners Club
- MC MasterCard
- VI VISA

Hotels

Price guide: double room with breakfast for two people
$ less than £50
$$ £50–£100
$$$ more than £100

Restaurants

Price guide: dinner per person, excluding drinks
$ less than £15
$$ £15–£30
$$$ more than £30

FRESH IDEAS IN CUISINE

The British have been self-conscious about their cooking for centuries, having been told by everyone else that it is stodgy and unimaginative. Don't believe it! A glance at the menu in a decent restaurant will show you what a long way British cooks have come in the last few years, operating kitchens that promise good fresh ingredients, especially local products such as fish near the coasts, mountain lamb in Wales, and organic home-grown vegetables.

ABERFELDY

🏨 Ailean Chraggan $$

Local game and salmon from the River Tay feature in the restaurant at this small hotel. Views take in the river and the hills beyond.
✉ Weem, Aberfeldy, Perth and Kinross ☎ 01887 820346 MC, VI

AUCHTERARDER

🏨 The Gleneagles $$$

This renowned Edwardian luxury hotel is surrounded by golf courses and extensive grounds. Afternoon tea and cocktails are served in the drawing room.
✉ Auchterarder, Perth and Kinross ☎ 01764 662231; fax 01764 662134 AX, DC, MC, VI

AVIEMORE

🏨 Ravenscraig $$

This comfortable, small guesthouse is in the center of Aviemore.
✉ Grampian Road, Aviemore, Highland ☎ 01479 810278; fax 01479 810210 MC, VI

AYR

🍴 Fouters Bistro $$

Located opposite the town hall, this long-established restaurant is in the vaults of a former bank.
✉ 2A Academy Street, Ayr, South Ayrshire ☎ 01292 261391 🕐 Closed Sun.–Mon. and Jan. 4–11 AX, DC, MC, VI

🏨 Savoy Park $$–$$$

The restaurant in this family-run hotel is reminiscent of a Highland shooting lodge, complete with wood-paneled walls and an open fire, offering a welcoming retreat on cold days.
✉ 16 Racecourse Road, Ayr, South Ayrshire ☎ 01292 266112; fax 01292 611488 AX, MC, VI

BALLATER

🏨 Balgonie Country House $$$

This Edwardian country house hotel is set in the midst of beautiful countryside on Royal Deeside.
✉ Braemar Place, Ballater, Aberdeenshire ☎ 013397 55482; fax 013397 55497 🕐 Closed Jan. 6–Feb. 28 AX, DC, MC, VI

🍴 Darroch Learg Hotel $$$

Perched on the "Hill of Oaks" above the scenic town of Ballater, there are river views and a restaurant that offers traditional Scottish dishes.
✉ Braemar Road, Ballater, Aberdeenshire ☎ 013397 55443 🕐 Closed Mon.–Sat. lunch, last 3 weeks in Jan. and Dec. 25 AX, DC, MC, VI

CALLANDER

🏨 Roman Camp Country House $$$

This hunting lodge was built in 1625 for the Dukes of Perth; wonderful entrées are complemented by vegetables from the hotel's own walled garden.
✉ Callander, Stirling ☎ 01877 330003; fax 01877 331533 AX, DC, MC, VI

CANISBAY

🏨 Bencorragh House $

With fantastic sea views across the Pentland Firth to the Orkney Isles, this working farm offers excellent value accommodation and is ideally positioned for the island ferries.
✉ Upper Gills, Canisbay, John O'Groats ☎ 01955 611449; fax 01955 611449 No credit cards

CULLODEN

🏨 Culloden House $$$

This historic mansion on 40 acres of wooded grounds and parkland is where Bonnie Prince Charlie left for the Battle of Culloden in 1746. It's now under American ownership and has been considerably renovated, although many traditional features remain.
✉ Culloden, Inverness, Highland ☎ 01463 790461; fax 01463 792181 AX, DC, MC, VI

EDINBURGH

🍴 Atrium $$

Atrium serves Mediterranean food with clearly defined flavors and has an extensive wine list. The surroundings are minimalist and very stylish.
✉ 10 Cambridge Street, Edinburgh ☎ 0131 228 8882 🕐 Closed Sun., Jan. 1–2 and Dec. 25–26 AX, DC, MC, VI

Scotland

🏨 Balmoral $$$

An elegant Edwardian luxury hotel that is conveniently located on Princes Street. Afternoon tea is served in the Palm Court, and there is a light and lively atmosphere in NB's bar. Diners can choose between the brasserie menu or more formal dining in the restaurant.
✉ 1 Princes Street, Edinburgh ☎ 0131 556 2414; fax 0131 622 8806 AX, DC, MC, VI

🍴 Best Western Bruntsfield Hotel $–$$

Try a taste of Scotland at the Cardoon restaurant overlooking the Bruntsfield golf course.
✉ 69–74 Bruntsfield Place, Edinburgh ☎ 0131 229 1393 ⊙ Closed daily lunch and Dec. 25 AX, MC, VI

🏨 The Bonham $$$

This award-winning hotel is an imaginatively designed conversion of a former university building, and it oozes with style. All bedrooms are spacious, with splendid bathrooms.
✉ 35 Drumsheugh Gardens, Edinburgh ☎ 0131 623 6050 and 0131 623 9116; fax 0131 226 6080 AX, DC, MC, VI

🍴 Channings $$

A light, bright conservatory is part of this restaurant, housed in five Edwardian terraced houses. Modern Scottish food with a Continental twist produces some adventurous, imaginative recipes.
✉ 15 South Learmonth Gardens, Edinburgh ☎ 0131 315 2225 ⊙ Closed Sun.–Mon. AX, DC, MC, VI

🏨 Dunstane House $$–$$$

The baronial-style Dunstane House offers bed and breakfast in a beautiful West End setting.
✉ 4 West Coates, Haymarket, Edinburgh ☎ 0131 337 6169; fax 0131 337 6060 AX, DC, MC, VI

🏨 George Inter-Continental $$$

A classical facade and marble foyer distinguishes this city hotel. It is home to a popular, clubby bar and a choice of eating options.
✉ 19–21 George Street, Edinburgh ☎ 0131 225 1251; fax 0131 226 5644 AX, DC, MC, VI

🏨 Malmaison $$$

Malmaison is a stylish conversion of a former seaman's mission located in the rejuvenated Leith harbor area. A French-style vegetarian buffet is served in the bar, and Mediterranean cuisine in the brasserie.
✉ 1 Tower Place, Edinburgh ☎ 0131 468 5000; fax 0131 468 5002 AX, DC, MC, VI

FORT WILLIAM

🏨 Inverlochy Castle $$$

The castle provides a grand setting for three elegant dining rooms with garden and loch views, serving very inventive dishes.
✉ Torlundy, Fort William, Highland ☎ 01397 702177; fax 01397 702953 ⊙ Closed Jan. 6–Feb. 12 AX, MC, VI

GAIRLOCH

🏨 Myrtle Bank $$

This hotel by Loch Gairloch has comfortably furnished bedrooms with views of the Isle of Skye.
✉ Low Road, Gairloch, Highland ☎ 01445 712004; fax 01445 712214 AX, MC, VI

🍴 The Old Inn $$

This friendly harborside inn has comfortable bedrooms. Hearty food is served in the bar and bistro.
✉ Gairloch, Highland ☎ 01445 712006 MC, VI

GLASGOW

🏨 Angus $$

This friendly guesthouse looks out over Kelvingrove Park, where many of the city's museums are located.
✉ 970 Sauchiehall Street, Glasgow ☎ 0141 357 5155; fax 0141 339 9469 AX, MC, VI

🍴 Gamba $$

This modern basement restaurant is decorated with a striking sea mural to match the menu, which specializes in Scottish seafood.
✉ 225a West George Street, Glasgow ☎ 0141 572 0899 ⊙ Closed Sun., Jan. 1–2, Dec. 25–26 and bank holidays AX, MC, VI

🏨 Glasgow Marriott $$–$$$

The Glasgow Marriott combines a convenient city location with high-quality facilities.

✉ 500 Argyle Street, Anderston, Glasgow ☎ 0870 400 7230; fax 0870 400 7330 AX, DC, MC, VI

🏨 Kelvin $–$$

The Kelvin occupies two Victorian houses near the Botanic Gardens.
✉ 15 Buckingham Terrace, Great Western Road, Glasgow ☎ 0141 339 7143; fax 0141 339 5215 AX, DC, MC, VI

🏨 Malmaison $$$

Malmaison is a contemporary hotel conversion with stylish rooms and an exceptionally friendly and helpful staff. Meals are served all day in the Café Mal.
✉ 278 West George Street, Glasgow ☎ 0141 572 1000; fax 0141 572 1002 ⊙ Closed Jan. 6–Feb. 12 AX, DC, MC, VI

🏨 One Devonshire Gardens $$$

This distinctive hotel is located in three adjoining terrace houses. Rooms are notable for the bold decor and luxurious bathrooms. In one house there is a stylish lounge and bar; in another an elegant cocktail lounge. Restaurant menus change daily.
✉ 1 Devonshire Gardens, Glasgow ☎ 0141 339 2001; fax 0141 337 1663 AX, DC, MC, VI

🍴 La Parmigiana $$$

Mediterranean flair and fresh Scottish produce are the winning combination of the excellent food served here. Italian specialties include a fabulous risotto with porcini mushrooms, and the desserts are equally as good.
✉ 447 Great Western Road, Glasgow ☎ 0141 334 8686; fax 0141 332 3533 ⊙ Closed Sun. MC, VI

🍴 Rab Ha's $$

Varied cuisine, including Scottish, Thai and Mexican dishes, is served in a traditional pub atmosphere.
✉ 53 Hutcheson Street, Glasgow ☎ 0141 572 0400 AX, DC, MC, VI

GLEN CLOY, ISLE OF ARRAN

🏨 Kilmichael Country House $$$

Located in what is thought to be the oldest house on the island, the Kilmichael Country House is a charming hotel with attractive grounds. Bedrooms in the converted

Scotland

KEY TO SYMBOLS

🏨 hotel
🍴 restaurant
✉ address
☎ telephone number
🕐 days/times closed
🚇 nearest metro/tube/subway
    station(s)
AX American Express
DC Diners Club
MC MasterCard
VI VISA

Hotels

Price guide: double room with
breakfast for two people
$ less than £50
$$ £50–£100
$$$ more than £100

Restaurants

Price guide: dinner per person,
excluding drinks
$ less than £15
$$ £15–£30
$$$ more than £30

HOMEY HOTELS

A familiar sight in remote
Scottish landscapes is a lonely
hotel, huge and baronial. In the
storms and snows of winter
these great dark ships of hotels
come into their own, as a cozy
"home away from home" for
locals, and as a welcoming
refuge for stormbound travelers
at any hour of the day or night.

barn are particularly stylish. The
dinner menu is simple but tasty.
✉ Glen Cloy, By Brodick, Isle of
Arran ☎ 01770 302219; fax 01770
302068 MC, VI

INVERNESS

🏨 Glenmoriston Town House $$$

Classic Italian cuisine and wine is
served at the Riviera restaurant in
this hotel, located on the River
Ness in the center of town
overlooking the cathedral and Eden
Court Theatre.
✉ 20 Ness Bank, Inverness, Highland
☎ 01463 223777; fax 01403 712378
AX, DC, MC, VI

🏨 The Palace Milton $$–$$$

Located beside the River Ness in
the heart of Inverness, with views
of the castle, the Palace Milton has
a range of health and leisure
facilities.
✉ 8 Ness Walk, Inverness, Highland
☎ 01463 223243; fax 01463 236865
AX, DC, MC, VI

KIRKCUDBRIGHT

🏨 Selkirk Arms $$

This 200-year-old inn offers
innovative Scottish cuisine. Local
beef and fresh fish are among the
choices in the elegant restaurant.
✉ High Street, Kirkcudbright,
Dumfries and Galloway ☎ 01557
330402; fax 01557 331639 AX, DC,
MC, VI

KIRKWALL, ORKNEY

🏨 Ayre $$–$$$

This family-run hotel stands on the
harbor in the town of Kirkwall, the
capital and administrative center of
the Orkney Islands. It's an ideal base
for visitors to the islands.
✉ Ayre Road, Kirkwall, Orkney
☎ 01856 873001; fax 01856 876289
AX, MC, VI

MELROSE

🏨 Burts $$

This welcoming 18th-century hotel
faces the attractive town square in
Melrose, one of the most appealing
small towns in the Scottish Borders.
✉ Market Square, Melrose,
Scottish Borders ☎ 01896 822285;
fax 01896 822870 AX, MC, VI

MOFFAT

🏨 Beechwood Country House $$

This delightful country house is
surrounded by an attractive garden.
✉ Harthope Place, Moffat, Dumfries
and Galloway ☎ 01683 220210;
fax 01683 220889 🕐 Closed Jan. 1
to mid-Feb. MC, VI

PORTREE, ISLE OF SKYE

🏨 Cuillin Hills $$$

This scenic Isle of Skye retreat has
views over Portree Bay to the Cuillin
Hills. The restaurant serves Highland
specialties and traditional favorites.
✉ Portree, Isle of Skye ☎ 01478
612003; fax 01478 613092 AX, MC, VI

ST. ANDREWS

🏨 The Old Course Hotel, Golf Resort and Spa $$$

This internationally renowned hotel
overlooks the world-famous golf
course; the conservatory and rooftop
restaurants have great views.
✉ St. Andrews, Fife ☎ 01334
474371; fax 01334 477668 AX, DC,
MC, VI

TURNBERRY

🏨 Westin Turnberry Resort $$$

This world-famous hotel sits on
800 acres of stunning countryside,
with views of the Firth of Clyde and
has a renowned golf course.
✉ Turnberry, South Ayrshire
☎ 01655 331000; fax 01655 331706
AX, DC, MC, VI

SALEN, ISLE OF MULL

🏨 Gruline Home Farm $$

A friendly bed and breakfast in the
midst of beautiful mountain
scenery. A country house party
atmosphere accompanies meals.
✉ Gruline, Salen, Isle of Mull
☎ 01680 300581; fax 01680 300573
MC

STIRLING

🏨 Stirling Highland $$$

This hotel was originally a high school.
Drinks are served in the old
headmaster's study and diners eat in
the Scholars Restaurant upstairs.
✉ 29 Spittal Street, Stirling
☎ 01786 272727; fax 01786 272829
AX, DC, MC, VI

ESSENTIAL
INFORMATION

"PLANNING advice and practical travel tips"

The information in this guide has been compiled for U.S. citizens traveling as tourists.

Travelers who are not U.S. citizens, or who are traveling on business, should check with their embassies and tourist offices for information on the countries they wish to visit.

Entry requirements are subject to change at short notice, and travelers are advised to check the current situation before they travel.

BEFORE YOU GO

PASSPORTS
The most important document you'll need to obtain before you travel is a passport. Passport application forms can be obtained by contacting any federal or state court or post office authorized to accept passport applications. U.S. passport agencies have offices in major cities; check the Yellow Pages (U.S. Government, State Department) for the one nearest you. You also can obtain passport information and request an application form by calling the National Passport Information Center at (877) 487–2778 (toll-free 24 hours). Comprehensive passport information and application forms are available on the U.S. State Department internet site at www.travel.state.gov – where travel warnings, consular information sheets, public announcements and publications information also can be accessed. Each person must have a passport; apply early, since processing can take around six weeks from the time of application. Rush service is available for an extra charge. Before departure, make sure your passport is valid for at least an additional six months after you are due to travel: Some European countries require this.

VISAS
In addition to a passport, some countries require a visa as an entry requirement. Travel visas are not necessary for American nationals traveling to Britain, but if you'll be traveling on to other nations, check entry requirements before you leave home.

TRAVEL INSURANCE
It is recommended that you are covered by insurance that will reimburse travel expenses if you need to cancel or cut short your trip due to unforeseen circumstances. You also should consider coverage for property loss or theft, emergency medical and dental treatment, and emergency evacuation if necessary. Before taking out additional insurance, check to see whether your current homeowners or medical coverage already covers you for travel abroad. If you make a claim, your insurance company will need proof of the incident or expenditure. Keep copies of any police report and related documents, or doctor or hospital bills or statements, to submit with your insurance claim.

ESSENTIAL FOR TRAVELERS

	● Required	● Recommended	● Not required
Passport			●
Visa			●
Travel, medical insurance			●
Round-trip or onward airline ticket			●
Local currency			●
Traveler's checks			●
Credit cards			●
First-aid kit and medicines			●
Health inoculations			●

ESSENTIAL FOR DRIVERS

	● Required	● Recommended	● Not required
Driver's license			●
International Driving Permit			●
Car insurance (for non-rental cars)			●
Car registration (for non-rental cars)			●

*see also DRIVING section

WHEN TO GO
The British Isles – infamous for damp weather – can actually have weeks of dry conditions in summer, although this is unpredictable. British winters are indeed rainy, although temperatures are rarely extremely cold. Snow is uncommon except in the higher elevations of northern England and Scotland. School vacations are another factor in planning when to schedule your trip. Schools in Britain are in session from early September until mid-July. This makes May and June good months to visit, both from a weather standpoint and the fact that there are likely to be fewer crowds at major attractions.

IMPORTANT ADDRESSES

VisitBritain
551 Fifth Avenue
Suite 701
New York, NY 10176-0799
☎ (212) 986-2200 or (800) 462-2748 (toll free)
Fax (212) 986-1188
www.visitbritain.com/usa

British and London Visitor Centre (walk-in only)
1 Regent Street, Piccadilly Circus
London SW1Y 4XT, U.K.
www.visitbritain.com
Open Mon. 9:30–6:30, Tue.–Fri. 9–6:30,
Sat.–Sun. 10–4 (Sat. 9–5, Jun.–Oct.)

American Embassy
24 Grosvenor Square
London W1A 1AE, U.K.
☎ 020 7499 9000
Fax 020 7495 5012
www.usembassy.org.uk

TIME ZONES

LONDON
12:00 noon

NEW YORK
5 hours behind Britain

CHICAGO
6 hours behind Britain

DENVER
7 hours behind Britain

SAN FRANCISCO
8 hours behind Britain

277

CUSTOMS

YES

Duty-free limits on goods brought in from non-European Union countries:
200 cigarettes or 100 cigarillos or 50 cigars or 250 g. tobacco ; 2 L. wine; 1 L. alcohol over 22% volume or 2 L. alcohol under 22% volume; 60 ml. perfume; 250 ml. toilet water; plus any other duty free goods (including gifts) to the value of £145. There are no restrictions on the amount of any currency you may bring into Britain.
On returning to the United States, you will be required to complete a customs declaration form. You are allowed $800 worth of personal goods or gifts (including items purchased in duty-free shops); keep sales slips and have them ready for inspection. The duty-free exemption can include 200 cigarettes and 100 cigars, as well as 1 L. of wine, beer or liquor if you are over 21.

NO

No unlicensed drugs, weapons, obscene material, counterfeit and copied goods, meat or poultry.

MONEY

Britain's currency is the pound sterling (£), which is divided into 100 pence (p). The denominations of pound bills are 5, 10, 20 and 50. There are coins of 1, 2, 5, 10, 20 and 50p and £1 and £2. You can exchange dollars or traveler's checks at banks, main post offices, exchange offices and some travel agencies. Buy traveler's checks in pounds sterling, so you do not lose money every time you change them. Credit cards are widely accepted throughout Britain, and ATMs ("cashpoints") are very common in shopping areas. When you are sightseeing, it is a good idea to carry a mix of large and small denominations.
Exchange rate at press time: $1 = £0.55

TIPS AND GRATUITIES

Restaurants (where service is not included)	10–15%
Cafés/bars	change
Taxis	10%
Porters	50p–75p per item
Hairdressers	£2
Chambermaids	change
Tour guides	£1–£2

COMMUNICATIONS

POST OFFICES

Buy stamps at post offices, gas stations, newsagents and grocery stores. Village post offices often close 1–2 p.m.

and Wednesday afternoon. Mailboxes (sometimes referred to as "pillar-boxes") are red. Pillar-boxes show who was monarch at the time of their installation (ER II, for instance, stands for Elizabeth Regina II).

TELEPHONES

Public telephones are widespread and easy to find. Use cash, a credit card or a phone card. Public telephones accept 10p, 20p, 50p, £1 or £2 coins. There is a minimum

charge of 30p which allows 15 minutes for a local or national call. If using a credit card there is a £1 connection charge.

Phoning in Britain
All British numbers in this book include an area code: dial the number listed.

To call the operator dial 100.

Phoning Britain from abroad
The country code for Britain is 44. Note that British numbers in this book do not include the country code; you will need to prefix it if you are phoning from another country. To phone Britain from the United States or Canada, omit the first zero from the British number and add the prefix 011 44. Example: 01122 334455 becomes 011 44 1122 334455.

Phoning from Britain
To phone the United States or Canada from Britain, prefix the area code and number with 00 1. Example: (111) 222-3333 becomes 00 1 111 222-3333. To call the international operator dial 155.

EMERGENCY NUMBERS

Police	999 or 112
Fire service	999 or 112
Ambulance	999 or 112

Emergency calls are free from phone booths.

Britain – Essential Information

HOURS OF OPERATION

- Stores Mon.–Sat.
- Museums/monuments
- Offices Mon.–Fri.
- Pharmacies Mon.–Sat.
- Banks Mon.–Fri.
- Post offices Mon.–Fri.

7 8 9 10 11 12 1 2 3 4 5 6 7

The times above are traditional hours of operation. Many malls and city center stores stay open longer hours and also on Sunday. Some grocery stores stay open until late in the evening.

Banks are open on Saturday and a few open on Sunday for limited hours. Post ofices open on Saturday 9–12:30. Some banks and post offices have shorter hours.

Museum opening times vary. Some major sights close on Monday and stay open later one evening a week; some minor sights of interest may close off season;check with the local tourist office.

Note that restaurants do not open for dinner until around 6 or 7 p.m.

NATIONAL HOLIDAYS

There are a number of national holidays in Britain (known as bank holidays), when banks, businesses, smaller stores and many museums close for the day. Almost all attractions, many restaurants, and some hotels close at Christmas, so it is always wise to check ahead.

Jan. 1	New Year's Day
Jan. 2	Bank Holiday (Scotland only)
Mar./Apr.	Good Friday
Mar./Apr.	Easter Monday
1st Mon. of May	May Day
Last Mon. of May	Spring Bank Holiday
First Mon. of Aug.	Summer Bank Holiday (Scotland only)
Last Mon. of Aug.	Summer Bank Holiday
Dec. 25	Christmas Day
Dec. 26	Boxing Day

RESTROOMS

 Public restrooms (toilets, lavatories, W.C.s or, colloquially, "loos") are generally easy to find and maintained to a high standard. Most are free, but a charge is made for those at major rail stations (about 20p). If you need to use the restroom in a café or bar, buy a drink first.

HEALTH ADVICE

 MEDICAL SERVICES
Private insurance is recommended. Visitors can receive treatment in emergency rooms but are charged if admitted to a hospital. You can seek advice from a doctor at a surgery or health center; you must make an appointment, and a charge will be made. Doctors are listed in the yellow pages, or ask at your hotel or a tourist office.

 DENTAL SERVICES
Dentists charge for consultations or treatment. Off-hours emergency treatment is available in towns and cities (see the yellow pages). Check if it is covered by your medical insurance.

 SUN ADVICE
During the summer months extended spells of sunshine are possible. Visiting historic sights can involve being outside for prolonged periods, so cover up, apply sunscreen and drink plenty of water. Remember that even on overcast days, sunburn is possible.

 DRUGS
Prescription and nonprescription medicines are available from pharmacies (chemists). Pharmacists can advise on medication for common ailments. Notices in all pharmacy windows give details of emergency facilities open outside regular hours.

SAFE WATER
Tap water is safe to drink, even in remote areas. Mineral water is widely available but can be expensive in restaurants.

PERSONAL SAFETY

 The cities, towns and villages of Britain are all generally safe places to be and are regularly patrolled by police. British police are usually helpful, friendly and approachable. Sensible safety precautions should prevail, however:
- Keep valuables hidden when you're on the move; a money belt is the safest option. Many hotels provide safe deposit boxes.
- Never leave bags unattended.
- Avoid walking alone in dimly lit areas at night.
- If you have belongings stolen, report the incident to the police immediately and get a written police report to provide to your insurance company as evidence for your claim.

NATIONAL TRANSPORTATION

AIR
There are airports in most major British cities and an extensive network of domestic flights, served by many international and regional carriers. Flights can be expensive, but are a good option for covering long distances (for example, London to Edinburgh), or for traveling to the Orkney or Shetland islands. Off-peak, stand-by and advance ticket discounts are generally available.

TRAIN
Rail services are generally efficient in Britain and serve most major towns. Most lines radiate from London, so "cross-country" services to some provincial towns may require a number of changes. There is a rail inquiry line to help you plan your journey (☎ 08457 484950), and it also is possible to reserve tickets in advance. There are a number of discount tickets available if you travel outside peak times. First class is comfortable but more expensive than standard class. If you plan to use trains frequently, rail cards, such as BritRail Passes, offer good discounts. You can purchase BritRail Passes prior to arriving in Britain: contact Rail Europe Group, Westchester One, 44 South Broadway, White Plains, NY 10604: ☎ (800) 361-7245. Once you are in Britain, Rail Rover passes are another option; ☎ 08457 484950. Eurostar provides regular daily train services to Europe through the Channel Tunnel. Services depart from London Waterloo and Ashford (Kent) to Calais, Lille, Paris and Brussels. It is advisable to reserve ahead to avoid disappointment.

BUS
Bus travel is less expensive than rail travel. The main operator for local (bus) and long-distance (coach) travel in England, and some parts of Wales and Scotland, is National Express. For details ☎ 08705 808080. For overseas (non-Briitsh) visitors the Brit Xplorer pass offers unlimited travel on National Express services for 7 days (£70), 14 days (£120) or 28 days (£190). The pass can be purchased in Britain from Brit Xplorer travel shops, from National Express agents or online at www.nationalexpress.com. In Scotland, Scottish Citylink (☎ 08705 505050) covers most of the country; Wales has a number of regional operators. In remote areas of Britain there are small Postbuses, run by the Royal Mail, carrying mail and passengers to destinations off the beaten track (☎ 08457 740740).

FERRY
Ferries serve the smaller British islands and Ireland, France, Spain, Belgium, The Netherlands, Germany, Denmark, Sweden and Norway. In Scotland, Caledonian MacBrayne (☎ 08705 650000) runs services to the main west coast islands, while Northlink Ferries (☎ 08456 000449) serve the Orkney and Shetland islands from Aberdeen and Scrabster.

PHOTOGRAPHY

Talking about the weather is a popular pastime for the British, and for good reason, because it's a fickle and unpredictable beast. With this in mind, you will need to consider a variety of film speeds. 200ASA works well, but if you're blessed with the sun then 100ASA would be better. However, if the clouds roll in and the sun skulks away for several days, you'll be glad you packed that 400ASA. If it's a gloomy day use your zoom to get in close, or switch the flash on to try and add color and contrast to the foreground. Look for the huge variety of architecture – castles, churches and houses – and the different landscapes, from mountains to dales, fens and shorelines. If you're taking a photograph inside a building, try to ask first. The same rule applies when taking someone's portrait. The British are known for their reserve, and some people may object to being caught by a camera. There are good facilities for buying film, developing and printing. In most towns you can find a specialist camera shop and processors. Pharmacies generally provide processing services, film and batteries. There is no need for concern about your camera and film going through airport scanners, as the equipment is safe for film rated up to 1600ASA.

MEDIA

National newspapers in Britain fall into three broad categories: the more sensationalist "tabloids" such as the *Sun*, the *Daily Mirror* and the *Star*, the mid-range tabloids such as the *Daily Mail* and the *Daily Express*, and the more serious dailies such as the *Daily Telegraph*, *The Times*, the *Guardian*, the *Independent* and the *Financial Times*. There also are local daily papers in most British cities, and weekly papers in towns. For listings, *Time Out* is a useful weekly guide to what's on in London. In larger cities, American newspapers (usually previous-day editions) and magazines are available; the most common are *USA Today*, the international edition of the *New York Herald Tribune*, and *Newsweek* and *Time* magazines. You can buy them at airports and central railroad stations as well as at newsstands. Britain has five television stations (BBC1, BBC2, ITV, Channel 4 and Five), but many hotels have satellite or cable television. In some regions of Scotland and Wales the BBC broadcasts a number of programs in Gaelic and Welsh, respectively, but programming is mainly in English.

ELECTRICITY

Britain has a 240-volt power supply. Electrical sockets take plugs with three square pins, so an adapter is needed for American appliances.
A transformer also is required for appliances operating on 110 or 120 volts.

Britain – Essential Information

Britain – Essential Information

DRIVING REGULATIONS

DRIVE ON THE LEFT
Drive on the left-hand side of the road and, at traffic circles (roundabouts), yield to traffic coming from your right.

SEAT BELTS
Must be worn in front seats at all times and in back seats where fitted.

MINIMUM AGE
The minimum age for driving a car is 17. However, some car rental firms will often stipulate a minimum age of 25.

BLOOD ALCOHOL
The legal blood alcohol limit is 0.08%. Random breath tests on drivers are carried out frequently, especially late at night, and the penalties for offenders are severe.

TOLLS
Limited-access highways are free (except the M6 toll motorway). Some bridges and tunnels levy a toll. In central London there is a weekday congestion charge (see page 24). Phone 0845 900 1234 for information.

ADDITIONAL INFORMATION

An International Driving Permit (IDP) is a document confirming that you hold a valid driver's license in your own country. It is a useful document to carry if you plan to drive in Britain and is available from AAA Travel Agencies. Some rental firms require this document, and it can speed up formalities if you are involved in an accident.

A Green Card (international motor insurance certificate) is recommended if you are driving a non-rental car. Car rental agencies will provide this with the vehicle; most companies include it in the rental price.

SPEED LIMITS

REGULATIONS
Speed limits are stringently enforced by police patrols and also by strategically positioned cameras that detect speeding motorists.

Limited-access highways (motorways); divided highways (dual-carriageways)
70 m.p.h.

Main roads
50 or 60 m.p.h.

Urban areas
30 or 40 m.p.h.

CAR RENTAL

The leading rental firms have offices at airports, train stations and ferry terminals. Hertz offers discounted rates for AAA members. For reservations:

	UNITED STATES	BRITAIN
Alamo	(800) 327-9633	08705 994000 (Europcar)
Avis	(800) 331-2112	08700 100287
Budget	(800) 527-0700	08701 565656
Hertz	(800) 654-3080	08708 448844

You will need a valid U.S. driver's license and preferably an IDP; you may be asked to show your passport, and possibly an additional credit card if you are renting a luxury car. European cars are generally smaller than those in the United States, and usually have manual transmissions. Find out exactly what insurance coverage is included, and check whether you need a collision damage waiver (CDW) – you may already be covered through your personal car insurance policy or credit card company. However, a CDW may not cover certain types of damage. Reciprocal arrangements with European motoring clubs may not apply if you are driving a rental car. Driving in British cities can be a daunting prospect if you're not used to the signs and driving habits. Rental companies should provide you with a chart of road signs and regulations and an area road map. AAA Travel Agencies can reserve a car for you before you leave or provide prepayment arrangements. Rates are lower if reservations are made in the United States prior to your departure, and guaranteed in U.S. dollars if you prepay.

FUEL

Gasoline (petrol) and diesel are priced in liters and are expensive. There are two grades of unleaded gas: super (98 octane) and premium (97 octane). Most gas stations are self-service, and 24-hour facilities are common in urban areas.

PARKING

If you are visiting a city by car, it is often possible to use "park and ride" facilities. You leave your car in a well-signed parking area just outside the city center and use public transportation to proceed downtown. Wherever you park, always check that there are no parking restrictions and that you pay for and display a parking sticker if necessary. There is no parking at any time on double yellow lines, and limited hours of parking on single yellow lines. In London, roads marked with red lines ("Red Routes") mean there is no stopping at any time. If you are parked illegally, a ticket may be left on the car windshield; the vehicle may also be wheel clamped or towed away.

Britain – Essential Information

AAA

 AAA AFFILIATED MOTORING CLUB
The Automobile Association (AA) Ltd.,
Fanum House, Basing View,
Basingstoke, Hampshire RG21 4EA
☎ 08705 448866, www.theAA.com (administration). For service while driving a privately owned car ☎ 0800 028 9018 (AA Breakdown Service). If in a rental car, contact the rental company's assistance partner. If you're staying for longer than 3 months ☎ 0800 587 7150 to obtain AA Breakdown Service. you can also purchase the service online.

BREAKDOWNS/ACCIDENTS

 There are emergency telephones at regular intervals on limited-access divided highways.
If you are involved in an accident ☎ 999 or 112 for police, fire and ambulance assistance. Most car rental firms provide their own free rescue service; if your car is rented, follow the instructions in the documentation. Use of a car repair service other than those authorized by your rental firm may violate your rental agreement.

ROAD SIGNS

Signs that give orders and prohibitions are usually circular. Red circles prohibit; blue circles give positive instruction. Triangular signs carry messages warning of hazards ahead. They should never be ignored and provide valuable information about what is just ahead or around the next corner.

Yield to traffic on major road

Crossroads

Other danger

Steep hill downwards

ROAD SIGNS (continued)

No through road

National speed limit applies

No passing

No entry for vehicular traffic

One-way traffic

Vehicles may pass either side to reach same destination

Ahead only

Keep left

Double bend, first to the left

Two-way traffic straight ahead

Britain – Essential Information

BRITISH AND AMERICAN ENGLISH

Although on the surface the same language, there are some quirky differences between American and British English. Britons have become familiar with Americanisms through imported American television shows and movies, and on the whole will understand American visitors when they request a "check" in a restaurant, instead of the English "bill." However, it is still possible to misunderstand when a British sales clerk directs you to the "first floor" of a shop (which is the American equivalent of the second floor). English words and phrases are in the left column, the American equivalent in the right column.

HOTELS

bath	bathtub
book	reserve
caretaker/porter	janitor
cot	crib
duvet	quilt
foyer	lobby
ground/	first/
first floor	second floor
lavatory/loo/toilet	restroom
lift	elevator
reception	front desk

EATING OUT

aubergine	eggplant
bacon rasher	slice of bacon
banger	sausage
bill	check
biscuit	cookie
broad bean	lima bean
chips	french fries
courgette	zucchini
crisps	potato chips
ice lolly	popsicle
jacket potato	baked potato
kipper	smoked herring
lager	light beer
mash	mashed potato
porridge	oatmeal
pudding	dessert
runner beans	string beans
scone	biscuit
sweets	candy
jelly	Jell-O

COMMUNICATIONS

phone box	telephone booth
post box	mailbox
post code	zip code
put through	connect
reverse charge	call collect
ring up	call

MONEY

bank note	bill
cashpoint	ATM
cheque	check
handbag	purse
quid (slang)	pound sterling
VAT	value added tax

SHOPPING

anorak	parka
bank holiday	public holiday
braces	suspenders
briefs	jockey shorts
carrier bag	shopping bag
chemist	drugstore/pharmacy
dinner jacket	tuxedo
ironmongers	hardware store
jumper	pullover
nappy	diaper
off licence	liquor store
pants	briefs (underwear)
plaster	bandage
queue	line of people
tights	pantyhose
trousers	pants/slacks
shop assistant	sales clerk

TRANSPORTATION

bike	bicycle
coach	long-distance bus
left-luggage office	baggage room
lost property	lost and found
return ticket	round-trip ticket
single ticket	one-way ticket
timetable	schedule
underground/tube	subway

DRIVING

boot	trunk (of a car)
bonnet	hood (of a car)
car park	parking lot
caravan	house trailer
diversion	detour
dual carriageway	divided highway
estate car	station wagon
filling station	gas station
flyover	overpass
gear lever	gear shift
layby	pull-off
manual	stick shift
motorway	freeway
pavement	sidewalk
petrol	gas
roundabout	traffic circle
zebra crossing	pedestrian crossing

WELSH WORDS AND PHRASES

English is spoken and understood almost everywhere in Wales, and in southern regions particularly there are many residents who don't speak or understand Welsh at all. However, the Welsh language is still very much alive in both its written and spoken form. In the north, visitors may hear it spoken among locals, and any visitor to Wales will certainly encounter it on bilingual road signs and maps. Understanding a few words can enrich a visitor's experience of the country and its culture. Here are just a few examples (see page 159 for a guide to pronunciation):

Meeting people

arfoll	*welcome*
boddhau	*please*
bore da	*good morning*
helô	*hello*
nos da	*good night*
prynhawn da	*good afternoon*

Place names

Caerdydd	*Cardiff*
Caernarfon	*Caernarvon*
Clawdd Offa	*Offa's Dyke*
Eryri	*Snowdonia*
Tyddewi	*St. David's*
Y Fenni	*Abergavenny*
Y Trallwng	*Welshpool*

Town and countryside

afon	*river*
ban, bannau	*peak*
betws/eglwys	*church*
caer	*fortress*
coed	*wood*
cwm/dyffryn	*valley*
dinas	*city, fortress*
fferm	*farm*
garth	*hill*
llyn	*lake*
myndd	*mountain*
porth	*harbor*
rhaeadr	*waterfall*
rhyd	*ford*
tre	*town*

REGIONAL ENGLISH

As you travel through England, you will encounter different accents and phrases. This is particularly noticeable in the way people (and maps) refer to the landscape, and it can be confusing for the uninitiated. Following are a few of the most commonly encountered:

dales	*valleys*
downs	*undulating open land*
fells	*high hills*
moors	*open, uncultivated area of high ground*
screes	*loose rock slopes*

SCOTTISH WORDS AND PHRASES

Three languages are spoken in Scotland: Gaelic, Scots and English. Gaelic is still spoken in the Outer Hebrides, but is most commonly heard in partially anglicized place names or geographical features, such as "loch" or "glen." Modern Scots (originating from the borders, or lowlands) is very much diluted by its near kinship with English. Essentially, English is spoken everywhere, and visitors may not even hear Gaelic or Scots spoken at all. However, you will likely encounter linguistic nuances or expressions and regional accents (the Glaswegian accent being famously tricky to comprehend). Below are just a few words in common, everyday usage (but don't use them yourself, or the Scots will perhaps think you are showing off):

Meeting people

aye	*yes*
bonnie	*pretty*
clan	*family group or tribe*
naw	*no*
ken	*to know*
do ye ken?	*do you know?*
ceilidh	*party or dance*
sassenach	*non-Scot*
wee	*little*

Eating and drinking

bridie	*a spicy meat pie*
champit tatties	*mashed potatoes*
clootie dumpling	*rich fruit cake*
dram	*measure of whiskey*
gigot or shank	*a leg of lamb or pork*
haggis	*mixture of offal and oatmeal, boiled in a sheep's stomach*
jeelie piece	*jam sandwich*
messages	*shopping for groceries*
neeps	*turnips*
piece	*sandwich*
stovies	*potato cooked with onion and meat*
tatties	*potatoes*

Weather

braw	*good*
dreich	*gray and dull*
droukit	*soaked*
glaur	*mud*
snell	*cold*

Geography

burn	*stream*
cairn	*pile of stones used as a marker on a hill*
clachan	*small Highland village*
croft	*small landholding*
firth	*large river estuary*
glen	*valley*
kirk	*church*
kyle	*inlet or strait*
loch	*lake*
sooth	*south*

Index

Index

Acknowledgments

Abbreviations for terms appearing below: (t) top; (b) bottom; (r) right; (c) center.
The Automobile Association wishes to thank the following photographers and libraries for their assistance in the preparation of this book.

BRUCE COLEMAN COLLECTION 203; EYE UBIQUITOUS 21; INTERNATIONAL PHOTOBANK 252; TOM MACKIE IMAGES 105; PICTURES COLOUR LIBRARY 100, 226; SPECTRUM COLOUR LIBRARY 64, 104, 114B; WORLD PICTURES 50, 52, 80.

The remaining photographs are held in the Association's own library (AA PHOTO LIBRARY) and were taken by Wyn Voysey with the exception of the following: Pat Aithie 171b; M Alexander 241t, 241b; M Alward-Coppin 169r; Adrian Baker 10/11, 107, 122/3, 195t, 195b, 242r, 243; Peter Baker 14/15, 18, 19, 56/57, 86, 178; Jeff Beazley 193, 196/7, 198/9, 234, 237; M Birkitt 24, 91, 94, 112, 113, 115, 117t, 118, 139, 145; Ian Burgum 156/7, 162, 163, 164, 165t, 165b, 166, 167b, 170; Michael Busselle 30/31, 53; Chris Coe 119; Douglas Corrance 219, 220, 224b; Peter Davies 99; Steve Day 2, 6, 75, 76, 79, 82, 89t, 90/91, 135t, 136, 137, 141, 142, 201, 202, 215, 251, 253; M A Delman 117b; Eric Ellington 210, 244b; Richard Elliot 225, 248/9; Derek Forss 23, 51, 54, 58, 62/63; Stephen Gibson 229, 230, 231b, 232l, 233t; Van Greaves 138, 150; Jim Henderson 244t, 245b; A J Hopkins 152, 194, 200, 206, 248; Jason Ingram 25; Caroline Jones 12/13, 124, 128/9, 159, 168, 172, 176, 177t; Paul Kenward 39t, 39b; Andrew Lawson 84t, 84b, 85b, 130, 132, 133t, 135b; T. Mackie 102; S&O Mathews 60b, 61, 62, 78, 140, 206/7, 208; Eric Meacher 77, 81, 92; Colin Molyneux 167c; C&A Molyneux 177b; John Morrison 205b; Robert Mort 47b, 49; Roger Moss 71; Mri Bankers Guide To Foreign Currency 277; Rich Newton 70, 83, 87, 89b, 93, 169b, 171c, 187t, 189, 190, 191, 204t, 204b, 232r; David Noble 17, 54/55, 56; Ken Paterson 217, 221t, 221b, 222, 223, 236t, 238t, 238b, 242l; Andrew Perkins 111b; Roy Rainford 144; Neil Ray 85t; Barrie Smith 36/37; Tony Souter 103, 110, 111t; Rick Strange 42/43, 43, 147t, 147t, 277t; Richard Surman 146; Michael Taylor 246; James Tims 46, 277b; Tom D Timms 171t, 173; Martin Trelawny 26, 278; Richard Turpin 41; Roy Victor 35, 38; Ronnie Weir 235, 240, 245t; Liz Wells 151t; A.S. Whitehorne 231t; Linda Whitwam 20, 98, 106, 108, 123, 185, 192; Harry Williams 88, 174; Tim Woodcock 45; Jon Wyand 147b, 148, 148/9.